D1548487

Donated to the students of
Southern Virginia College
by
Mr. & Mrs. Gary A. Terry

Hyrum Smith—Patriarch

Hyrum Smith, Patriarch

HYRUM
SMITH
Patriarch

PEARSON H. CORBETT

Deseret Book Company
Salt Lake City, Utah

To my wife Gladys
whose encouragement and help
made this biography possible.

"Again, verily I say unto you, let . . . my servant
Hyrum . . . take the office of Priesthood and Patriarch,
which was appointed unto him by his father,
by blessing and also by right."—D&C 124:91.

First printing in the Classics in Mormon Literature Series, May 1995

Library of Congress Catalog Card Number 94–80147

ISBN 0–87579–950–7

Printed in the United States of America

10 9 8 7 6 5 4 3 2 1

PUBLISHER'S PREFACE

On a September night in 1823, an obscure teenager named Joseph Smith, Jr., living in upstate New York, was visited by an angelic messenger sent from the presence of Deity. Among the sacred truths revealed to the young man on that momentous occasion was an unusual prophecy.

The angel told young Joseph that his "name should be had for good and evil among all nations, kindreds, and tongues, or that it should be both good and evil spoken of among all people." (Joseph Smith–History 1:33.) Sixteen years later, the Lord himself would reaffirm this prophecy by proclaiming to his servant, the now-mature Prophet Joseph Smith, "The ends of the earth shall inquire after thy name, and fools shall have thee in derision, and hell shall rage against thee." (D&C 122:1.)

The pages of history from those days to the present bear solemn witness of the fulfillment of those divine proclamations. Truly, the name of Joseph Smith is spoken with reverential respect by righteous men, women, and children throughout the earth, while the uninformed and the wicked disdain and deride him.

Yet, while the name of Joseph Smith is widely known throughout the earth, the name of one who stood loyally and almost inseparably by the Prophet's side throughout his ministry is virtually unknown.

Hyrum Smith, elder brother, mentor, protector, and loyal supporter of his prophet-brother, deserves to be better known by the Saints of God. He should be recognized for his significant contributions to the restoration of the church and kingdom of God.

In the annals of history there may be no individual who exceeds Hyrum Smith in *absolute* integrity of heart and in loyalty to God and his chosen servants. Hyrum was and is an unsung hero who sought neither position nor recognition. He was content to serve in the shadow of and in a supportive role to his younger brother.

In a world where men and women jealously compete for position and place, Hyrum Smith was a breath of fresh air. He did not suffer from the elder-brother syndrome of spitefulness and jealousy so classically evident in the sons of Jacob, who sold their younger brother Joseph into slavery, or in the elder brothers of Nephi, who so often complained about their younger brother's perceived favored status.

Indeed, as President Joseph Fielding Smith noted, "It seems almost, from the tender solicitude Hyrum displayed for Joseph that he felt in some way that there had been placed upon him a guardianship for his younger brother." (*Life of Joseph F. Smith* [Salt Lake City: Deseret Book Co., 1969], p. 39.) What a lesson in service and humility! What a lesson in sustaining and supporting those who are called to lead, regardless of one's relationship to them in a perceived pecking order of prominence, position, prior experience, or age!

Hyrum Smith was truly a model of character and faith whom all would do well to exemplify. President John Taylor, who was providentially spared from sharing the martyr's death that claimed Joseph and Hyrum Smith at Carthage, said of his fellow prisoner for Christ, "If ever there was an exemplary, honest and virtuous man, an embodiment of all that is noble in the human form, Hyrum Smith was its representative." (B. H. Roberts, *The Life of John Taylor* [Salt Lake City: Bookcraft, 1963], p. 142.)

Brigham Young was even more complimentary in his evaluation of this older brother of the Prophet Joseph: "Now Hyrum was as good a man as ever lived. . . . His integrity was of the highest order. . . . I used to think, and I think now, that [angels] dwelling in the presence of the Father and the Son possessed no more integrity in their hearts than did Hyrum Smith." (Address, October 8, 1866, Brigham Young Collection, Church Historical Department.)

It is therefore fitting that Pearson H. Corbett's pioneering volume, *Hyrum Smith—Patriarch,* be reissued as a classic in Mormon literature. When it was first published in 1963, The Church of Jesus Christ of Latter-day Saints had a membership of fewer than two million. Over three decades later, the Church has grown to a worldwide membership of more than nine million. Among those millions of members, relatively few know of Hyrum Smith's vital contributions to the kingdom of God.

Many would recognize his name as one of the Eight Witnesses to the Book of Mormon. Some might even know that he was one of the six original members of the Church. Most would know that he shared a martyr's death with his prophet-brother. Yet few would know the significance of his martyrdom.

Hyrum Smith *jointly* held the priesthood keys of the kingdom with the Prophet Joseph. He was not only Hyrum Smith, *Patriarch,* but he was also Hyrum Smith, *Prophet.* (D&C 124:94–95.) As pointed out by President Joseph Fielding Smith in the foreword to this book, "It was just as essential that Hyrum Smith lay down his life as the Second Witness as it was for the Prophet Joseph Smith." The deaths of these two testators placed their testimony in force. (See D&C 135:5.) Had the sealing of the testimony of two not been required, and had Hyrum survived the carnage at Carthage, he would have *remained* as the Prophet and President of the Church. (See Hoyt W. Brewster, Jr., *Prophets, Priesthood Keys, and Succession* [Salt Lake City: Deseret Book Co., 1991], pp. 45–47.)

In this respect, it is of interest to note that a portrait of Hyrum Smith hangs alongside that of Joseph Smith in the sacred council room used by the First Presidency and the Quorum of the Twelve Apostles on an upper floor of the Salt Lake Temple. The only other portraits to hang in this room are those of the men who have worn the mantle of the prophet from the time of Brigham Young to the living prophet of the present day. (There are also three paintings depicting the Savior's ministry hanging in this council room.)

Hyrum Smith's contributions to the kingdom of God on earth did not end with his death. Beyond his personal legacy of loyalty and integrity, Hyrum has bequeathed to the Church a posterity of loyal and faithful followers of Jesus Christ and his chosen servants. A marvelous promise was given to Hyrum shortly after the Church was organized in 1830. The Lord declared, "Thy calling is to exhortation, and to strengthen the church continually. Wherefore thy duty is unto the church forever, and this because of *thy family.*" (D&C 23:3; italics added.)

Among the more visible members of Hyrum Smith's family to have served the Church are two presidents—Joseph F. Smith and Joseph Fielding Smith. Additionally, Hyrum M. Smith and

M. Russell Ballard were called as apostles. Others of the Hyrum Smith family have served as Patriarchs to the Church and in other callings as general officers of the Church. Countless numbers of his posterity have served in priesthood and auxiliary callings at every level of Church government, while less visible but just as valued descendants have quietly and faithfully lived their religion and served wherever called as they have sought "to strengthen the church continually."

Yes, the legacy of Hyrum Smith's noble life continues! In a blessing pronounced upon his head by the Prophet Joseph Smith in 1833, Hyrum was promised that his posterity would "rise up and call him blessed." (As quoted in Joseph Fielding Smith, comp., *Teachings of the Prophet Joseph Smith* [Salt Lake City: Deseret Book Co., 1976], p. 41.) As one who is privileged to have descended in that blood line, I humbly add my small voice in fulfillment of that promise: I call the name and memory of Hyrum Smith "blessed."

Surely all who read this volume on the life of Hyrum Smith, and who seek to pattern their lives after the supernal example he set, will similarly "rise up and call him blessed."

Hoyt W. Brewster, Jr.
Great-great-grandson of Hyrum Smith

INTRODUCTION

When the Declaration of Independence was signed on July 4, 1776, a new nation was born. The colonial period was rapidly coming to an end, and a new era was beginning. The eyes of the world had for many years been focused on America, for the New World represented opportunity and freedom from the Old World traditions, customs, and tyrannies. Since Columbus's discovery of America, the entire economic and social outlook of the world had changed. Old concepts of world geography and old trade routes had to be revised, and a new concept of government was imminent. Knowledge of the new world fired the imagination of men, rousing in them a desire to migrate to this new land so rich in resources and opportunities.

Why had the Americas remained for so many centuries unidentified with the rest of the world? Perhaps there was a reason. Could there have been in the mind of the Great Creator a purpose for its obscurity? An old prophecy concerning America lends credence to such a supposition. It stated that the Lord God would raise up a mighty nation, and that this nation would become great; for it was decreed that it should remain a free nation, and those who possessed this land must either serve the God of the land, who was and is Jesus Christ, or be swept off the land. It was to be a land choice above all other lands, and was to be taken forth out of captivity and lifted up by the power of God above all other nations.[1]

The Constitution of the United States, as later devised, provided for life, liberty, and the pursuit of happiness, and determined that there should be no discrimination against color, race, or creed. It was a glorious standard, founded in the wisdom of God, a standard meant to be a heavenly banner to all people privileged to enjoy its protection. Indeed, this great Constitution

---

[1] Book of Mormon, 1 Nephi 22:7; 13:30; Ether 2:10-12; 1:42.

was like a tree under whose branches men from every clime might be shielded from the burning rays of the sun.[2]

God had preserved this vast continent of America as his peculiar treasure.[3] Here he intended to assemble the outcasts of Israel, thereby fulfilling his promise to Abraham: ". . . I will establish my covenant . . . for an an everlasting covenant, to be a God unto thee, and to thy seed after thee"[4] ". . . . and in thee shall all families of the earth be blessed."[5] America was destined to be blessed because of Abraham's descendants, and it was to play a role in the great spiritual drama of the last days.

After the Revolutionary War, political ties with the old world had been severed; and soon events would signal the opening of a new dispensation. Among the patriots of this infant nation were two, assigned to leading roles in the first apocalyptic scene. These two were the Smith brothers, Hyrum and Joseph, both citizens of New York State.

Subsequent happenings confirm the assumption that Hyrum and Joseph had been called in the pre-mortal world to do this special work. They were among those noble and great ones of whom the Lord had said: ". . . These I will make my rulers; . . ."[6]

The series of miraculous visions which came to Joseph Smith initiated a movement which was to astonish the world. In these visions, ancient religious concepts were revived and new ones revealed, with the result that the true concept of God and of his relationship to man was re-established. Once again communication was established between God and man, and this close relationship made it possible for him to share his authority and sovereignty with mankind.

The earth had been without the authority of the priesthood of God for many centuries. Because of the fallacious doctrines which subtly established themselves following Christ's crucifix-

---

[2]Joseph Smith, *History of the Church*, vol. III, p. 304.
[3]Psalm 135:4.
[4]Genesis 17:7.
[5]*Ibid.*, 12:3.
[6]Pearl of Great Price, Abraham 3:23.

ion, the priesthood was taken from the earth. Its loss had been preceded by a series of Christian persecutions which resulted in a loss of spiritual gifts and in an apostasy from the truth among the people. With the disappearance of the pristine church, which was complete by the end of the second century A.D., the ancient prophecy of Isaiah was fulfilled: "The earth also is defiled under the inhabitants thereof; because they have transgressed the laws, changed the ordinance, broken the everlasting covenant."[7]

It was necessary, therefore, for the gospel, and the Church to be restored, if God's promise to Israel was to be fulfilled. The fulfillment of the promise was revealed to the Apostle John on Patmos; for he "saw another angel fly in the midst of heaven, having the everlasting gospel to preach unto them that dwell on the earth, and to every nation, and kindred, and tongue, and people."[8] By the nineteenth century the time was ripe for God to restore the ancient Church with all its powers, gifts, and blessings. Sufficient preliminary preparation had been made for the first contact with man and the plan of Almighty God to save men's souls was restored to earth.

The role of Hyrum Smith in the restoration of the gospel subsequent to the organization of the Church was second only to that of his brother Joseph. The two brothers were as inseparable during many periods of trouble and crisis as they were in those less frequent times of peace and prosperity. Hyrum, the oldest living child of his father's family, early assumed the responsibility of overseer and counselor to his parents, brothers, and sisters. Seldom did the Prophet Joseph do anything of importance without first consulting Hyrum; always, when in trouble, he would seek out his older brother for help and advice.

When Joseph brought home the gold plates from which the Book of Mormon was translated, it was Hyrum who furnished the chest for their safe-keeping. At Kirtland, Ohio, Hyrum was made Counselor to Joseph in the First Presidency of the Church,

---

[7]Isaiah 24:5.
[8]Revelation 14:6.

and he carried his full share of important responsibilities. He was on the first building committee for the Kirtland Temple; and when Zion's Camp was organized, he recruited a number of men and joined the main camp along the way.

At Far West, Missouri, Hyrum was taken prisoner with Joseph and others and spent some six months in Liberty Jail. At the beginning of the Nauvoo period, Hyrum acted as President of the Church while Joseph went to Washington, D.C., to obtain redress for losses in Missouri. The Lord appointed Hyrum, as he had Joseph, to be a "prophet, and a seer, and a revelator" unto his Church and of him said: "Blessed is my servant Hyrum Smith; for I, the Lord, love him because of the integrity of his heart, and because he loveth that which is right before me, . . ."[9] Joseph's esteem for his brother was expressed in these words: "I could pray in my heart that all my brethren were like unto my beloved brother Hyrum, who possesses the mildness of a lamb and the integrity of a Job, and in short, the meekness and humility of Christ; and I love him with that love that is stronger than death, for I never had an occasion to rebuke him, nor he me." On another occasion Joseph said that if Hyrum could not make peace between two who were in disagreement, the angels themselves might not hope to accomplish the task. And when, about the twentieth of June, 1844, only seven days before the martyrdom, Joseph urged Hyrum to take his family to Cincinnati for safety, Hyrum answered simply, "Joseph, I cannot leave you. . . ."

Instead of going to Carthage where they had been summoned for trial on a fraudulent charge, Hyrum and Joseph crossed the Mississippi River so that they might escape to the Rocky Mountains. There, on the opposite bank of the river, they received certain messages, taunting them for deserting the flock. In a characteristic manner, Joseph turned to Hyrum and said, "Brother Hyrum, you are the oldest, what shall we do?" Hyrum said, "Let us go back and give ourselves up and see the thing out." After thinking for a few moments, Joseph said,

---

[9]D & C 124:15, 94.

"If you go back, I will go with you, but we shall be butchered." Hyrum said, "No, no; let us go back and put our trust in God and we shall be reconciled to our fate."[10]

Even during the last days in Carthage Jail, Hyrum's judgment was respected by his brother Joseph. A list of prospective witnesses for their defense was crossed out by Hyrum. When asked why he did this, he replied: "They don't know enough to answer a question properly"; and Joseph responded, "That is sufficient reason." When Hyrum fell, mortally wounded, Joseph exclaimed, "Oh, dear brother Hyrum!"[12]

The brothers died as they had lived, one in heart, one in spirit and soul. History has seldom if ever witnessed a parallel relationship of two men so willing to live and die for each other.

---

[10]Joseph Smith, *op. cit.*, vol. VI, pp. 549-550.
[11]*Ibid.*, vol. II, p. 609.
[12]*Ibid.*, vol. VI, p. 618.

FOREWORD

Hyrum Smith, Patriarch to the Church, and at the time of his martyrdom, Associate President of the Church, held the keys conjointly with his younger brother, the Prophet Joseph Smith. Hyrum was one of the greatest men of his time and his loyalty to the Prophet Joseph Smith was unsurpassed. From the time of Joseph's birth until their martyrdom Hyrum was never separated from his prophet brother for a period of more than a few months.

Hyrum Smith had a sympathetic and congenial nature and was always solicitous and filled with anxiety for the Prophet. Throughout Joseph's life, Hyrum guarded his younger and more favored brother as tenderly as if the Prophet had been his son instead of his younger brother. It was Hyrum who helped to nurse Joseph through a serious illness in his early youth and who remained stedfastly at his side throughout his life. Frequently, when a younger son is highly honored, the elder brothers in a family manifest a spirit of jealousy and envy, resulting in discontent and open opposition; but not so with Hyrum Smith. He accepted the great mission of his brother Joseph in the most sacred and loyal spirit of humility. On one of several occasions when William Smith, the Prophet's younger brother, abused Joseph with words of violence, Hyrum came to the defense of the Prophet. This action elicited the following expression of appreciation from Joseph:

> I could pray in my heart that all my brethren were like unto my beloved brother Hyrum, who possessed the meekness and humility of Christ; and I love him with that love that is stronger than death, for I never had occasion to rebuke him, nor he me, which he declared when he left me today.

On another occasion when the Prophet was recording the names of those who had been loyal to the Church and worthy of commendation for their faithfulness under the most trying and difficult circumstances, he wrote of Hyrum:

There was my brother who next took me by the hand—a natural brother. Thought I to myself, Brother Hyrum, what a faithful heart you have got! Oh, may Eternal Jehovah crown eternal blessings upon your head, and a reward for the care you have had for my soul! O how many are the sorrows we have shared together; and again we find ourselves shackled with the unrelenting hand of oppression. Hyrum, thy name shall be written in the book of the law of the Lord, for those who come after thee to look upon, that they may pattern after thy works.

It was the privilege of Hyrum Smith to be one of the eight witnesses who beheld and handled the plates whence came the Book of Mormon, likewise to be numbered among the six original members of the Church, at its organization, April 6, 1830. The greatest honor, however, that came to him, was to succeed Oliver Cowdery, who by transgression lost his place as the Second Elder of the Church. Oliver had been highly honored. To fulfil the eternal law of witnesses, it was necessary that two testators stand at the head of this dispensation, receiving the keys of authority and presidency. This great honor had previously been conferred upon Oliver Cowdery. Whenever the keys of authority and presidency had been revealed from the heavens, he had been present with the Prophet Joseph Smith to receive those keys under the hands of heavenly messengers. He had been the Associate President of the Church, and in this calling had stood preeminently distinguished ahead of Sidney Rigdon and Frederick G. Williams who were Counselors in the First Presidency. Commenting on this calling the Prophet said:

The office of Associate President is to assist in presiding over the whole Church, and to officiate in the absence of the President, according to his rank and appointment, Viz., President Cowdery, first; President Rigdon, second, and President Williams, third, as they were severally called. The office of this priesthood is also to act as spokesman, taking Aaron for an example. The virtue of the above priesthood is to hold the keys of the kingdom of heaven or the Church militant. (*MS Hist. of the Church* Book A. 1.)

The account of Oliver's ordination is given in this same record as follows:

After addressing the throne of mercy President Smith laid hands upon High Counselor Cowdery, and ordained him to the Presidency of the High Priesthood in the Church, saying: ("Brother in the name of Jesus Christ of Nazareth, who was crucified for the sins of the world, that we through the virtue of his blood might come to the Father, I lay my hands upon thy head, and ordain thee a President of the High and Holy Priesthood, to assist in presiding over the Church, and bearing the keys of this kingdom—which Priesthood is after the order of Melchizedek—which is after the order of the Son of God.")

But because of transgression all of Oliver's authority was transferred to the Patriarch Hyrum Smith, for the Lord by revelation said:

"And again, verily I say unto you, let my servant William (Law) be appointed, ordained, and anointed, as a counselor unto my servant Joseph, in the room of my servant Hyrum, that my servant Hyrum may take the office of Priesthood and Patriarch, which was appointed unto him by his father, by blessing and also by right;

"That from henceforth he shall hold the keys of the patriarchal blessings upon the heads of all my people,

"That whoever he blesses shall be blessed, and whoever he curses shall be cursed; that whatsoever he shall bind on earth shall be bound in heaven; and whatsoever he shall loose on earth shall be loosed in heaven.

"And from this time forth I appoint unto him that he may be a prophet, and a seer, and a revelator unto my church, as well as my servant Joseph;

"That he may act in concert also with my servant Joseph; who shall show unto him the keys whereby he may ask and receive, . . . and be crowned with the same blessing, and glory, and honor, and priesthood, and gifts of the priesthood, that once were put upon him that was my servant Oliver Cowdery;

"That my servant Hyrum may record of the things which I shall show unto him, that his name may be had in honorable remembrance from generation to generation, forever and ever." (D & C 124:91-96.)

From this time until the martyrdom, Hyrum Smith was the Second Witness, the Associate President of the Church, supplanting Oliver Cowdery who had lost that great honor. After his ordination and the conferring of keys of presidency, Hyrum Smith signed communications with Joseph Smith as a President of the Church. Had Hyrum Smith escaped martyrdom, he would have been the President of the Church and could have chosen two counselors to share the keys of that holy office with himself. However, it was just as essential that Hyrum Smith lay down his life as the Second Witness as it was for the Prophet Joseph Smith. But had Oliver Cowdery remained true, undoubtedly he, not Hyrum Smith, would have gone with the Prophet Joseph Smith to martyrdom.

This great truth does not seem to be universally known throughout the Church, but it is of utmost significance and in full accord with the divine law of witnesses.

Joseph Fielding Smith

PREFACE

Great events — political, scientific, or religious — depend for their success upon the work of great men, men who have the character, vision, and faith which denote both physical and mental ability. Hyrum Smith had these necessary qualities of greatness. His work, blended with that of others of similar ability, has helped to make America great. His role made him a leading figure in launching a religious movement that is destined to revolutionize the thinking of the world.

The purpose of this biography is to give due recognition to a man who did much to promote an organization that has perpetuated itself by developing the brotherhood of man—a brotherhood intended to bring salvation to all humankind. The religious society he helped to organize has built a great commonwealth in western America. It has established many cities, towns, and villages in the valleys of the mountains and has made the desert blossom as a rose. It has redeemed waste places and opened nature's treasure house of natural resources. It has extended its stakes into far-off lands and continents and sent thousands of missionaries to bring the restored gospel to the world, thereby strengthening the bond of understanding and friendship between nations and peoples.

Hyrum Smith's career ended with his martyrdom, in his forty-fourth year; but his life had been filled with intense activity. He had been a patriarch, a president, a counselor, and had stood close beside his younger brother, the Prophet Joseph Smith, in organizing and developing the Church. He had suffered repeated persecutions—mobbings, imprisonment, indictments, court trials, and threats upon his life. But his unwavering love for and loyalty to his brother had secured for him an honored place among his people.

In this volume it is the desire of the writer to give adequate and proper acknowledgment to the man who was second in command, to the man whose history paralleled that of his illustrious prophet brother. It has been a pleasure and a satisfaction for the writer to make available a history of Hyrum Smith's distinctive contribution in establishing so dynamic an organization, for it can truthfully be said that he and his descendants have supported the Church throughout the long struggle for establishment and during its subsequent growth.

Since no man can be studied apart from his times, the reader of this biography will become acquainted, in part at least, with the political, social, economic, and religious conditions in America during twenty-five or thirty years of the early nineteenth century. The writer has written this work within the framework of the LDS faith and theology; and the historical incidents have been accurately and fairly stated.

To obtain a more complete and accurate history, the writer has used national, state, and local liberaries and visited most of the places of historical significance in Vermont, New York, Ohio, Missouri, and Illinois. Visits were made to the nearest relatives of Hyrum Smith, in search of journals, diaries, documents, relics, pictures, newspaper articles, private collection of letters and documents. Among the more important sources were Hyrum Smith's diary and his journal, and his day-book or account book. Major sources of information were *The Documentary History of the Church* (seven volumes by Joseph Smith), *The Journal History; Life of Joseph Smith,* by his mother, Lucy Smith.

ACKNOWLEDGMENTS

Every available source of material related to this biography has been consulted. If there should be any related facts or important material overlooked, the author assumes full responsibility. Also, the author assumes responsibility for doctrinal interpretations. Where historical data was lacking, the writer, for the sake of continuity and interest, has supplied material of the highest probability.

The writer wishes to acknowledge the help and encouragement of the Latter-day Saint Historian's Office, especially that of Joseph Fielding Smith, Church Historian, and his assistants, A. William Lund, Preston Nibley, and members of the staff. The helpful co-operation of the library staff at Brigham Young University is sincerely appreciated. Patriarch Eldred G. Smith and Ralph Smith furnished original information which has enriched the history, as have other descendants of both Jerusha Barden Smith and Mary Fielding Smith. Emily Smith Stewart also furnished historical material from her collection of journals, papers, and documents. Acknowledgment is given to Mary R. Porter for genealogical data on Jerusha Barden Smith. Historian John Blackmore and President Israel A. Smith of the Reorganized Church of Jesus Christ of Latter Day Saints at Independence, Missouri, were most co-operative. To Dr. Russell R. Rich and Dr. Hyrum L. Andrus of Brigham Young University College of Religious Instruction for their critical reading of the manuscript and helpful suggestions, to Dorcus Hyde, James Ott, Beth Syphus, Walter Corbett and my wife, Gladys, for their careful reading and suggestions, and to Barbara Larkin and Cecelia Ann Corbett, typists, and others not mentioned here, the author is most grateful.

CONTENTS

ILLUSTRATIONS

Chapter I

HERITAGE

Before their second child was born, the family of Joseph Smith, Sr., had voiced their desires concerning the child. If it were a girl, the mother would have a helper in the home; if it were a boy, the parents would buy more land. When the midwife announced to the anxious father that the child was a boy, he praised God and shook hands with the neighbors who shared his vigil, declaring that their child's name was to be Hyrum; and the news of the birth spread through the village of Tunbridge, Vermont.[1]

Joseph Smith, Sr., and his wife, Lucy, had provided many comforts for the expected child, and it was well that they had, for February 9, 1800, was a bleak wintry day. Paths in the snow had been swept to the family woodpile, to the barn, and to the street. The large farm, which belonged to the family of Asael Smith, father of Joseph Smith, Sr.,[2] was among the best of the region and was the envy of many who were less fortunate in circumstance. The home, built of native lumber, was made comfortable by a cook stove and a large fireplace. The furnishings were of pioneer construction, sturdy and useful.

Not only did the Smiths have the security of a fine farm, but they had also a substantial sum of money at their disposal. Tucked away in Lucy's trunk was a thousand dollars, a wedding gift from her brother Stephen Mack and his business partner, John Mudget. Lucy and Joseph had acquired their home and furniture without the use of this gift.

At this time, Vermont, like other New England states, was a fairly well-settled region, with a population of about 154,000. But the land, having been intensively cultivated for nearly two

---

[1]Lucy Mack Smith, *History of Joseph Smith,* (Salt Lake City, Utah, 1945), p. 32.
[2]Mary Audentia Smith Anderson, *Ancestry and Posterity of Joseph Smith and Emma Hale,* (Independence, Missouri, 1929), p. 67.

centuries, was losing its fertility; and much of it was presently being used as grazing land for sheep and cattle. Hence the Smiths, like other farmers, had become adept at supporting themselves under pioneer conditions. Such homely tasks as spinning, weaving, killing animals and curing the meat were among their daily activities. Joseph Smith, Sr., was proud of the family farm. He had worked long hours with his father, Asael, and his brothers to clear the virgin land of timber and rocks, preparing it for the plow.[3]

The Smiths were an industrious family, always seeking to better themselves. Their history was one of pioneering. Much of the work of four generations, back to Robert Smith who had migrated from England in 1638, had been spent in clearing land for agricultural purposes. Robert Smith had lived in Toppesfield, County Essex, England, but on coming to America he first settled in Boston, Massachusetts. It is said that his was the third house to have a cellar in that city. From Boston, he moved to Rowley, Massachusetts; and from there to Boxford in the same county, where he purchased two hundred eighty acres of land. Later he became a resident of nearby Topsfield.[4]

The farm at Topsfield had become quite productive when the colonies rebelled against their mother country. Samuel, the son of Robert, had married well and occupied a fine home of his own. His family was prospering when his son Samuel, (Hyrum's great-grandfather) was called to fight with George Washington's army. Fortunately, at the end of the War for Independence, Samuel returned to Topsfield, a veteran, who had served his country honorably but was yet uninjured in the conflict. His having served in the army of General Washington gave him added prestige, and thereby more security for himself and family.

---

[3]Within a year after the birth of Joseph Smith, Sr. (July 12, 1771, at Topsfield, Massachusetts) the family moved to Windom, New Hampshire, where they remained for about five years. From Windom they moved to Derryfield (New Manchester) New Hampshire. In 1786 they left Derryfield and returned to their ancestral home in Topsfield. *Ibid.*, p. 66.

[4]*Ibid.*, pp. 51-53. An account of Robert Smith taken from the records of Ipswitch, Essex County, Mass., 1648.

Young Samuel's son, Asael, with his wife and nine of their eleven children, left the family home at Topsfield early in 1791. The two older children, Jesse and Priscilla, had married and were established in homes of their own. Another son, Joseph, Sr., was then twenty years old. He stood six foot two and like his father Asael was strong and well-built. In making the move, Joseph had helped to load the family wagons with household furnishings and supplies; and the work of organizing the family that they might assist in driving the livestock had been his chief concern.

The mother, Mary Duty Smith, rode in the wagon with her daughter, Mary, age fifteen, and Sarah, a baby nine months of age. Samuel, Silas, and John — thirteen, eleven, and nine respectively — walked most of the way, driving the animals. Susanna, seven, and Stephen, five, rode and walked periodically, taking care not to be in the way.[5]

The journey to Tunbridge seemed short. The strangeness of the country and the new people along the way broke the monotony of travel. As soon as they arrived and selected their land, they set to work. And by June several acres of land had been cleared and planted to grain and vegetables. The family built a home of native lumber large enough to accommodate all of them. They were happy to move from the cramped quarters they had rented in the village of Tunbridge, and life soon had settled into an orderly routine.

When Joseph, Sr. married Lucy Mack, he acquired his portion of the land and with the help of his neighbors "raised" a commodious house for himself. The walls were brought to the square, and the roof went on like magic. The home resembled the ancestral house at Topsfield, with the handmade shingles, the gable at each end, the steep, English roof, and the large chimney extending midway above the ridge. And there were small windows on each side of the door. (See cut.) The homestead, nestled in the low green hills of Vermont, was a thoroughly picturesque setting for the bride and groom.

---

[5]Joseph Fielding Smith, *Life of Joseph F. Smith*, (Salt Lake City, Utah, 1938), p. 9.

Joseph first met Lucy Mack in 1794 at the store owned by her brother Stephen. Over the years, the Smiths had been staunch friends of the Macks, who were noted for their hospitality. Joseph, Sr., had been a frequent visitor in the Mack home and had gone turkey hunting and sleigh riding with older members of the family.[6]

When the major's [Stephen Mack] eighteen-year-old sister, Lucy, arrived from her home in Gilsum, New Hampshire, she was the object of considerable interest. Unlike many of the local girls, (who were Amazons by comparison,) she was small and slender; and her neat and comely appearance, her gentle manners, and her serene poise were all evidence of comparative wealth and culture.

When Joseph met Lucy at the Major's store, their attraction was mutual. After the first house party, Joseph was seen with her about the village and often brought her to the family farm. Her hands were too white and soft, and her arms were too slim to be strong, said his parents; but cupid had already done his work. The older people little realized what latent capacities she possessed to endure the pioneer years ahead, for contrary to family predictions Lucy was to become her huband's greatest asset.

From the time they met until they were married, they were drawn to each other despite the objections of others. Their courtship lasted a little over a year, during which time Lucy went home for a brief period. She returned in the fall of 1795, and they were married January 24, 1796, by Seth Johnson, Justice of the Peace.[7]

Major Stephen Mack was more pleased than others with the marriage, even though Joseph was six years Lucy's senior. And shortly after their marriage, when they left for a visit to the bride's home in Gilsum, New Hampshire, the major and

---

[6]The mercantile establishment owned by Major (in the Continental Army) Stephen Mack had become a favorite gathering place for the young people, and several of the Smith boys had worked as apprentices in the Mack tin shop.

[7]Archibald Bennett, "Solomon Mack and His Family," The Improvement Era, vol. 59, From Tunbridge Town Record, BkA, p. 36.

his business partner gave Joseph and Lucy the thousand dollars mentioned above.

Time passed quickly for Joseph and Lucy, and they were blessed with a family. Alvin was born February 11, 1798[8] and in due course the second son, Hyrum, was welcomed. With two sons added to their number the father became aware of the need to improve his family's economic status. Lucy's brother was doing well in the mercantile business. Why couldn't he do the same? In Randolph, a frontier town, a few miles distant, there was no store, so Joseph, Sr., decided to rent his farm and venture into business. Lucy thought it a good idea, and the family ventured upon the new enterprise early in 1802.[9]

They could scarcely have foreseen the difficulties which lay ahead. This move was but the first of several which were to bring them reverses and severe trials. But the trials which began at Randolph and continued almost unabated thereafter found them strong and unafraid, able to bear whatever came their way.

After six months of struggle in establishing their business upon a firm footing, sickness struck the household. Mother Smith came down with a heavy cold which nothing seemed to relieve. The doctor diagnosed her symptoms and indicated that she had consumption. Lydia Gates Mack, Lucy's mother, came to help care for her daughter, but there was no apparent improvement. In later writing of these circumstances, Lucy said: "I continued to grow weaker and weaker until I could scarcely endure even a foot-fall upon the floor, except in stocking feet, and no one was allowed to speak in the room above a whisper."[10]

When the young mother continued to lose strength, the local Methodist minister was called. From his conversation she surmised that death was imminent. And after his departure, she seemed to see a light beyond the immediate darkness, and Joseph, her husband, came to her saying, "The doctors have given you up to die." The ensuing night for her was one of

---

[8]Their first child, a daughter, died unnamed. *Idem.*
[9]Lucy Smith, *op. cit.*, p. 32.
[10]*Ibid.*, p. 33.

contemplation about death; and she though of heavenly things, of her unreadiness to meet God, and of her husband and children.

It was then that she made a covenant with God, promising that if he would let her live she would endeavor to serve him to the best of her ability. Shortly afterward she heard a voice say: "Seek, and ye shall find; knock and it shall be opened unto you. Let your heart be comforted; ye believe in God, believe also in me."

In a few moments, Lucy's mother came in and joyously exclaimed, "Lucy, you are better!" Whereupon, she replied, "Yes, Mother, the Lord will let me live if I am faithful to the promise which I made to him, to be a comfort to my mother, my husband, and my children."[11]

From this moment, Lucy regained her strength. And, feeling the need to be instructed more in religious matters, she called on Deacon Davies. The deacon was so astonished at her recovery that he spent the whole of her visit asking how she was and trying to make her comfortable. She returned home disgusted and disappointed. However, her illness and healing made such an impression on her deeply religious nature that she continued to seek for information, and for some congenial spirit who would understand her feelings and help her to carry out her resolutions.

The next Sabbath she went to hear a Presbyterian minister, expecting to hear the word of life. Of this occasion she said: "When the minister commenced speaking, I fixed by mind with deep attention upon the spirit and matter of his discourse, but after hearing him through I returned home, convinced that he neither understood nor appreciated the subject upon which he spoke."[12]

Thereafter she became convinced that the true church was not upon the earth and determined to examine the Bible more carefully, taking Jesus and his disciples for her guide. This she did for a number of years and taught her children to do the same. But believing in the necessity of baptism, she asked

[11]*Ibid.*, p. 34.
[12]*Ibid.*, p. 35-36.

a preacher to baptize her without requiring that she join any of the denominations of the day; and after he granted her request, she continued to guide her life by reading the Bible.

Meanwhile, the family's mercantile enterprise at Randolph was proving to be very expensive. Soon after Lucy's recovery, another crisis developed, and more money was needed than the business was providing. Crystallized ginseng root was accepted as an effective remedy for an epidemic then raging in China. And for this reason Joseph, Sr., decided to concentrate all his means and efforts in collecting a large quantity of the herb. He refused the offer of three thousand dollars made to him by a merchant living at Royalton for his collection of the plant and went instead to New York harbor where he found a merchantman about to sail for the Orient. The captain of the vessel was contracted to sell Joseph's produce and to return the money to him. Meanwhile, the Royalton merchant, a Mr. Stevens, hearing of Mr. Smith's transaction, went to New York and made a similar agreement with the captain of the same vessel. It was also agreed that Stevens' son was to go along on the voyage to help with the business. In due time the ship returned, and Joseph was told that young Stevens had only a chest of tea as payment for the herb; there supposedly had been little market in China for ginseng.

This turn of events plunged the Smiths into debt. From his herb profits Joseph had intended to pay his Boston creditors eighteen hundred dollars he owed for merchandise. Lucy had warned him about giving so much credit on the goods he sold, and now too many bad debts forced him to sell the farm at Tunbridge — well worth fifteen hundred dollars — for only eight hundred.

Fortunately, Lucy had saved her wedding gift and with it they were able to raise the necessary eighteen hundred dollars to liquidate their Boston indebtedness. Meanwhile, Lucy's brother, Major Mack, discovered that young Stevens *had* sold the ginseng in China for a good price. But Stevens, fearing that Major Mack would tell Joseph, fled with the money to Canada, and Joseph was forced to abandon all hope of regaining his rightful share of the profits.

The trouble over the sale of the ginseng and the resulting loss of the farm made Lucy's approaching confinement doubly difficult. Consequently the Smiths decided to return to Tunbridge, where they remained until the birth of their daughter Sophronia, on May 16, 1803. Soon afterward they moved to Royalton, Vermont. The twelve years at Tunbridge and Randolph had held much happiness, even though misfortune seemed to stalk them; and their hearts were saddened at leaving their friends and the familiar surroundings even though they hoped that sometime they could return.

Royalton, a village not unlike that of Tunbridge, was situated in a hilly country, covered with lush vegetation. The farm they leased needed much improvement and the price was too high, so that the fall harvest was insufficient to pay the lease. After a council the family decided to rent a farm at Sharon, Windsor County, Vermont, a farm belonging to Lucy's father, Solomon Mack.[18] Since Sharon was situated only a short distance north of Royalton, the task of moving was not difficult.

The farm at Sharon was in good condition. Here it was possible for Joseph, Sr., to teach school in the winter as well as operate the farm. And they lived near enough to the families at Tunbridge and at Gilsum to make occasional short visits. The farm was located among rolling hills covered by a variety of trees, shrubs, and flowers; and abundance of rainfall assured good harvests; their home was comfortable; and it seemed that financial security was theirs.

It was here, two days before Christmas in 1805, that their fourth child was born, and they named him Joseph, after his father. This child was destined to exert an influence upon the world even greater than that of the ancient prophets of Israel. His mission would not only change the lives of his family and

---

[18]Solomon Mack fought as a soldier in the Revolutionary War. His children were Jason, Stephen, Daniel, Second Solomon, Louisa, Lovina, Lydia, and Lucy, in that order. Archibald Bennett, "Solomon Mack and His Family," The Improvement Era, vol. 59.

Hyrum and Joseph, The Prophet

Hyrum Smith, (by Mahonri Young), Statue on Temple Square, Salt Lake City, Utah.
(Used by permission of Church Historian's office.)

friends but would be of importance to the entire world. But all this was yet in the future.

Soon after the birth of Joseph, Jr., the home was again upset by talk of moving. But, by now, moving seemed to have become part of the regular routine of the family. The children had grown to expect a nomadic existence. Lucy Smith, in her memoirs, recorded with faithful detail the chronological events of these years of toil, moving and child-bearing. On leaving Sharon, the family gravitated to Tunbridge where employment was more abundant and education was available for the children. Being with old friends and relatives was a joy, but after a short period at Tunbridge they moved again, this time to Lebanon, New Hampshire.

During all this time, the Smiths did not subscribe to any particular religious denomination. The reason given by Mother Smith was that their belonging to a church "would offend their friends belonging to another denomination because they (the Smiths) would be considered in error, but by not belonging, the church people would say they were of the world."[14] Nevertheless, Joseph, Sr., was deeply religious and about this time had several impressive dreams. In one of these dreams, he was told that the ancient order as established by Christ and the apostles was not upon the earth.

During these years Hyrum was an active child, adjusting to an ever-increasing family. The boys added to the family circle were named Samuel Harrison, Ephraim, and William. It was not long before the necessity of education for the older children became acute. Since Lebanon offered little opportunity for education, the family decided that Hyrum should enroll in an academy at Hanover[15] and that the rest of the younger children were of sufficient age that they should attend the local school.

Hyrum had been at Hanover but a short time when an epidemic of typhus fever broke out and he returned home to

---

[14]Lucy Mack Smith, *op. cit.*, p. 31.
[15]Now Dartmouth University.

find several of the children ill, Sophronia was in a critical condition. But here again the prayers of the mother were answered and after eight days Sophronia's recovery was assured.

This crisis was no sooner passed·than another developed. Joseph, age seven, while recovering from the disease was stricken with a severe pain in his shoulder. The swelling which developed was relieved by lancing, but the severe pain thereafter settled in the bone of his leg. The boy suffered intensely and Mother Smith became ill due to the strain and work of caring for him. It was Hyrum who relieved her. Of this experience she wrote: "Hyrum, quite remarkable for his tenderness and sympathy, now desired that he might take my place. As he was a good, trusty boy, we let him do so. In order to make the task as easy for him as possible, we laid Joseph on a low bed and Hyrum sat beside him, almost day and night, for some considerable length of time, holding the affected part of Joseph's leg in his hands and pressing it between them, so that his afflicted brother might be enabled to endure the pain which was so excruciating that he was scarcely able to bear it."[16]

Hyrum's chances for an education were never again so good as they had seemed before the epidemic. However, the limited time he had spent in study awakened in him a keen desire for education, a desire which he later satisfied through observation and consistent home study.

His compassionate nature and his great concern for the welfare of the family matured the boy Hyrum beyond his years. Joseph's suffering on the above occasion elicited Hyrum's tenderest regard; and the experience they shared at this time cemented the brothers' mutual love and devotion. Hyrum's feelings found expression in his self-appointed but unassuming guardianship of his brother, which ended only when he fell mortally wounded by an assassin's bullet in Carthage Jail.

---

[16]Lucy Mack Smith, *op. cit.*, p. 55.

CHAPTER II

THE REVIVAL

Hyrum, a large boy for his thirteen years, met with the family in a council to decide what was to be done. The plague of fever had left Lebanon, New Hampshire, as suddenly as it had come; and with the crisis over the family felt that perhaps the best thing to do was to move again. The farm had not produced sufficiently, and a move at this time might give them a more favorable start toward improving their financial position.

The decision to move was unanimous, and the family chose Norwich, Vermont, as the site of the new home. The routine of moving was by now well established, and soon the familiar caravan of wagons and livestock was in motion. On arriving at their destination they located a farm, the property of Esquire Moredock. The rent was reasonable, and the family once again settled to the task of wresting a living from the soil.

They arrived in plenty of time to seed the available land to grain. But the crop, after promising a start, was a failure. However, several acres of fruit trees bore in abundance. Hyrum with the others, picked the best of the fruit and sold it in the village; the windfalls and culls were stored for their own winter use. The winter that followed was severe, with deep snows. Hyrum's hopes of returning to school at Hanover were abandoned. The family needed money, and Hyrum, even at his tender age, considered his personal desires to be secondary to the needs of his family. That winter the family felt fortunate to obtain the bare necessities, and Hyrum accepted any available opportunity for work.

The second year's crop was also a failure, and again the family had to improvise a means of livelihood. "Another year's try," thought the hopeful Joseph, Sr., after a council with his boys, "might prove a success." They were determined to persist. But as the third crop of grain neared maturity, an untimely frost destroyed it, and with that frost came famine. It seemed that bad luck dogged their very footsteps. On March 15, 1816 the household had been enlarged once more by the arrival of a ninth child — a baby boy whom they named Don Carlos. With the year's crop failure and the new birth, the situation of the family became desperate. Another move was in the offing.

Reports of abundant wheat crops in the state of New York were causing many Vermont farmers to migrate to the West.[1] On the other hand, the thought of returning to Royalton, scene of past failure, was unendurable. The name of Palmyra, New York, came to Joseph, Sr.'s, attention again and again, but he decided to scout the New York area for a suitable location before making a final decision. Before the end of the summer he accepted an invitation to accompany a Mr. Howard to Palmyra; and soon afterward the family received word that he had made arrangements to buy a farm, and that they should begin preparations for the move.

Mother Smith took charge. Hyrum and Alvin worked early and late making ready for the arrival of the team and wagon. Their father had arranged to hire transportation and dispose of his livestock in order to pay their debts. The family was just taking what small comfort they could from the thought that all their bills were paid when several of their creditors demanded settlement.

This sudden turn made it almost impossible to leave. Two gentlemen, a Mr. Flagg and a Mr. Howard, knowing the circumstances, urged Mother Smith either to take the claims to court or to have their friends contribute to their aid. But since she was an independent person, she refused both suggestions and somehow raised the required hundred and fifty dollars to settle the claims. Then with her family and aged mother, Lydia Gates Mack, she left for Palmyra.

On their way they stopped at Royalton. Here they left grandmother Lydia with her son Daniel Mack where she made

---

[1]Whitney R. Cross, *The Burned-Over District*, Cornell University Press, (Ithaca, New York, 1950), pp. 5-6.

her home until her death. Mother and daughter wept at parting. Grandmother Mack had been with the family since they had moved from Vermont. But now her aged condition and the distance to Palmyra made it unlikely that they would see each other again.

As the little caravan reached a point twenty miles west of Utica, New York, their teamster, Mr. Howard, removed the load of household goods and attempted to abscond with the team and wagon. Mother Smith, when told by Alvin of this attempt, called the teamster into the inn and there, before several other guests, said: "Gentlemen and ladies, please give your attention for a moment. Now, as sure as there is a God in heaven, that team, as well as the goods, belong to my husband, and this man intends to take them from me, or at least the team, leaving me with eight children, and without the means of proceeding on my journey." Then turning to Mr. Howard she said, "You can go about your business; I have no use for you. I shall take charge of the team myself."[2]

Mother Smith was not sorry to part with Howard's services. He had been overbearing with the children, forcing them to walk beyond their endurance. This had been particularly hard on young Joseph who was still lame. For Hyrum and Alvin, ever obedient to the wishes of their mother, to help drive the remainder of the distance to Palmyra was infinitely pleasant.

The village of Palmyra looked good to the newcomers. Its population of 2500 was rather scattered; but there was a heavily rutted main street lined with trees and board sidewalks, and several stores were doing a good business. Up the street and off to the right was a typical church, and just beyond were two similar buildings. The Presbyterians, the Baptists, and the Methodists had all become established, as the town had been settled twenty years before.[3]

---

[2]Lucy Smith, *op. cit.*, p. 63.
[3]Palmyra is a small town in western New York with a population of about 3,000. It is located on Highway 31, just twenty-three miles southeast of Rochester. On the main street in Palmyra is an intersection known as "four corners" where there are churches of different denominations on each corner of the street, typifying, even today, the different conflicting creeds which existed at the time of young Joseph's First Vision.

Father Smith, who had been anxiously waiting for several days, was greatly relieved when at last he saw his family plodding wearily up the main road into town. When his wife explained the cause of their long delay and the trouble encountered on the way, he almost wept.

The journey over the Adirondack Mountain Range had been a long and tiresome trek, and some of their goods had had to be sold to buy food. All that was left to them was the team, the wagon, a few boxes of personal objects, and two cents in cash. Little wonder that the town looked good to the family. Here there was a school for the children, and a friendly atmosphere prevailed.

The small frame building that Father Smith had rented east of town, on the corner of Johnson and Vienna Streets, was a welcome sight. Lucy was grateful for the roof over her head as winter soon set in. The inconveniences of the crowded home seemed trivial when they remembered that the family was together again. Lucy's was a buoyant spirit! In such a family any trouble could only be temporary, even when the autumn of 1816 proved to be but a repetition of bygone years. Once again a family council was required to devise some plan to overcome the familiar difficulties.

The older boys had little trouble finding work. Hyrum and Joseph helped their father on contract projects from which they learned the Cooper's trade (how to make barrels, split-wood chairs, baskets, birch brooms) and masonry (the digging of wells and curbing them), as well as brick-lining (cisterns, fireplaces, and stone walls). The boys marveled at their father's proficiency, and at the end of the first hard year the family was able to count a gain. It had been a year of work, of long hours spent on the rented land and, for Hyrum and Alvin, of "hiring out" to earn much needed cash after the summer and fall farm work was finished.[4] But they had prospered in their work.

Alvin had displayed such aptitude for the carpenter's trade that he was soon in demand as a carpenter's helper on house-

---

[4]Lucy Smith, *op. cit.*, p. 65.

construction crews. Even Mother Lucy and the oldest daughter, Sophronia, went to work. They established a business, and money from Lucy's painted oilcloths aided in the purchase of their new home. A "cake and beer" business which they operated on Saturdays and holidays provided additional income.

Education on the frontier placed a poor second to agriculture. Time spent for education was time lost from the clearing of new land, the erecting of houses, the building of roads, and from food production and manufacturing, all of which were necessary to survival. The luxury of formal education could not have been enjoyed by the Smith children for more than a few months of the year. It is probable, however, that they did attend sometime during the year, for there was a log schoolhouse on nearby Durfee road. One may safely conclude that here the younger members of the Smith family learned at least the rudiments of reading, writing, and arithmetic.

The Smiths recouped their fortune during their first two years at Palmyra, and they adjusted easily to the social pattern of this frontier community, where their neighbors were the "old" settlers. There was Martin Harris, the son of Nathan Harris who was one of the original owners of this choice land. His six-hundred-acre tract just north of the village had been purchased by his father for only two shillings an acre. Near the town was Wintergreen Hill from whose summit could be seen the homes and farms and the settlers felling trees below. There were landmarks, too, such as the blockhouse which had been erected as protection against the Indians, now remaining a mute testimony of earlier struggles.

Father Smith, with the help of Hyrum and the other boys, soon began looking for a larger tract of land, one not too expensive and fairly close to town. The savings of almost two and one-half years would be sufficient to make a down payment on at least a hundred acres of unimproved land. By the fall of 1818 such a tract had been selected. It was located two or three miles south of Palmyra on the north border of Manchester Township, Ontario County, and was almost completely covered

by the heaviest stand of timber the boys had ever seen. Among
the various trees, there were about fifteen hundred sugar maples,
which proved a good source of sugar molasses.

It did not take long for the Smith family to prepare for
this move. A house had to be erected, but the hundred-acre
tract was itself an excellent source of materials for its construction. A temporary, one-story, two-roomed log structure with
two attic bedrooms was soon completed. Later, another bedroom
of sawed slabs was added. By the following year (1819) thirty
acres had been cleared for the plow, and another thirty acres
were soon added.

William Smith, a brother of Hyrum, later said, "Relative
to the life of the family while on the Manchester farm: We had
a good place. We cleared sixty acres of the heaviest timber
I ever saw. . . . We worked hard to clear our place, and the
neighbors were a little jealous."[5]

Hyrum was happy that the family finances were improved.
And it was pleasant to have a part in community life. For the
first time the Smiths could really hope with some security to
build a larger and more commodious home. The children were
growing up, and their increasing demands made greater economic independence a necessity.

New people came regularly to take up land, and, since the
Smith boys had established a good reputation for being hard
workers who could be depended upon to give satisfaction, they
were much in demand. Hyrum and Alvin, twenty and twenty-
two respectively, were near the same size by the beginning of
1820. Not only did their physical aspects correspond, but also
their personalities. Both were of a kindly disposition, helpful
to the younger children and considerate of their parents. Seldom,
if ever, did one hear quarrelling or scolding among the members
of the family. As they attained a degree of security, family affairs
settled into a steady routine. Time only was needed to achieve

---

[5]Pomeroy Tucker, in his book, *Origin, Rise and Progress of Mormonism* states that the
Smith family were shiftless and lazy, were regarded as an illiterate, whiskey drinking, ir-
religious race of people. Mr. Tucker, a citizen of Palmyra, when the Smiths moved to
town, supports William's appraisal of the townfolks as being a little jealous of their
accomplishments.

their objectives. Although their new-found prosperity was but the prelude to an impending storm, the two and one-half years of prosperity were long enough for them to put down strong roots and enable them to survive the events to come.

The snows melted very fast in the spring of 1820; but the season, except for its precipitance, seemed much like any other. Nature burst forth in abundance. There had been little sickness during the winter, and several of the children were able to finish a term of school. They hurriedly planted the seeds for an early garden; and as the length of the workday increased, less time was left to read the Bible. The family had always enjoyed listening first to Father Joseph then to Mother Lucy read or tell favorite Bible stories.

Many times as Hyrum and his brothers were sent to the village store for supplies, they would listen to the usual gossip and gather bits of news. The store, like others of its kind, had long been a favorite meeting place for neighbors and friends. Here religion, politics, marriage, deaths and newcomers were discussed at great length and in minute detail. On the subject of religion there were great differences of opinion, for the second, third, and even the fourth generation of early immigrants had, like their ancestors, cast off formal religion like a threadbare coat.

When America had won her freedom, the way was paved for abolishment of compulsory taxes to support the church and to the elimination of inquisitions or heresy trials. In this new land man could choose his religion. The colonies had differed in their opinion over the principle of separation of the church and state. Roger Williams, Anne Hutchinson, and others had been persecuted and banished for their views. But the Old World idea of state religion was finally abandoned. Why then should free Americans find it necessary to subscribe to any tenet or sect?

The rebellion against religion by the first settlers had had its influence upon their children. Many frontiersmen were believers in God and the Bible but not in any sect. Only about five percent of the people were enrolled on church records; and because of this lack of interest in formal religion, the religious leaders of the prominent Protestant groups were extremely anxious to prevent the souls of frontiersmen from going to hell.

The early colonies had seen several religious "awakenings." They still remembered the wave of revivalism sparked by Charles A. Finney, Jonathan Edwards, and George Whitefield, in which thousands of the "unchurched" had been saved.[6] Early in the nineteenth century particularly another wave of religious fervor developed. Renewed emphasis was placed upon the importance of religion and the necessity of revival meetings.

The Smith family had heard through friends who were members of the several congregations then established in Palmyra that there would soon be an outdoor religious revival. But not until Hyrum returned one evening from shopping at the store did they learn that the expected revival was actually to be held. This news had its effect on the Smiths. Were they in need of religion? None of them had been "saved." Of course they read and believed the Bible and were not in the category of the sinful. They were sober, honest, industrious people who believed in an all-wise Creator. Yet they felt the necessity of investigation. If a church had the power to save, they desired membership in it.

Hyrum had brought word that there would be a revival which was to have its beginning in the several church buildings of Palmyra. Whenever their work permitted, members of the Smith family and their friends attended.

The Reverend Jesse Townsend, a young Yale graduate recently assigned to the Palmyra Presbyterian pastorship, had been the first to catch the religious fervor, and it was he who had started the present revival. He had been joined by his colleague, another Presbyterian minister of East Palmyra, and they soon were joined by the local Baptist minister and two Methodist ministers of the same place. The initial crowds were large; the farmers had not yet started their spring plowing

---

[6]William Warren Sweet, *The Story of Religion in America,* Harper and Brothers (N.Y. 1930), pp. 250-251.

because of the late spring. The meetings began the latter part of April and ran well into May. Businessman closed shop to attend, many of them becoming self-appointed missionaries who urged others to do likewise. The thought uppermost in the minds of many people was, "What shall I do to be saved?" Therefore, the success of the revival was more than the ministers had hoped for. By the beginning of the second week in May, when many had to leave the revival to plant their crops, there had been two hundred conversions among those who had attended from Palmyra, Macedon, Manchester, Ontario, and Lyons; and by the end of that week over four hundred had confessed. Both old and young were among the "saved."

During these early years of the nineteenth century, camp meetings played an important part in western revivals. While those of the northern region were not as violent as the revivals of the south, there was manifest at Palmyra considerable agitation and emotional fervor. The magnetism of the speakers swayed the audience with their alternating loud to plaintive voices picturing heaven and hell with varying degrees of intensity exploiting the fears of a burning hell for the unrepentant sinner. The atmosphere became tense with shouting and ill-will, foreign to the true spirit of Christ, particularly when the supposed candidates left the preacher to go in an opposite direction. The manifest confusion, uncertainty, and anger all contributed to defeat the essential purpose of the revival meetings. Because of such religious hysteria, many who came to listen returned to their homes unconvinced and unsaved.

Such was the situation at the Palmyra revival when the meetings began to break up and the people separated to their respective churches. The amity, peace, and goodwill among the group turned to rivalry and contention. Hyrum, who had joined the Presbyterians, wondered why his minister was so jealous of his colleagues. All had seemed tranquil until each leader counted his disciples; and then such imprecations and shouting as followed were certainly unbecoming to the several ministers involved.

It had been very important to Hyrum that he be baptized, as had his mother, his sister Sophronia, and his brother, Samuel Harrison. He felt at the moment that others of the family exhibited far too little concern for their souls. Even Joseph, who had favored the Methodists, hestitated to declare himself.

The leaders of the Presbyterians, Methodists, and Baptists had attempted to disprove each other in doctrine and Bible interpretations. The Methodist minister, while admonishing his listeners to pray about which church to join, quoted James 1:5: "If any of you lack wisdom, let him ask of God, that giveth to all men liberally, and upbraideth not; and it shall be given him." To Hyrum this passage of scripture seemed logical; but he, like many others, felt that he had found the truth. He did not know that his brother, Joseph, had been pondering this passage from the moment he first heard the Methodist minister quote it: nor did he know that this passage had made a strong impression on his fourteen-year-old brother.[7]

When the excitement of the revivals had died down, Hyrum was happy to have it over and to get on with his daily tasks. He had believed the convincing arguments of his minister and was content to adjust his religion to the popular concepts of the day without critical analysis or logic as to its authenticity. Sooner than he realized, however, he was to be rudely and effectively disillusioned and to have any and all settled ideas of religion rooted out.

---

[7]Lucy Mack Smith, *op. cit.*, pp. 46-58.

CHAPTER III

PALMYRA AND A NEW RELIGION

The unsettled condition of the Smith family from the time they left Tunbridge, Vermont, until they settled in Palmyra, New York, had matured Hyrum Smith, now in his twentieth year. Perhaps the hardships, suffering, and disappointments of this period were for a good purpose; for that which lay ahead, the past had been a period of preparation. The common problems of self-preservation against hunger, sickness, and poverty, had helped to weld the family in love and loyalty. Fortunately such family devotion under many trying circumstances had proved to be a guarantee for their survival as a family.

The writer is indebted to Hyrum's mother, Luck Mack Smith, for glimpses of his early life as recorded in her book on the life of Joseph Smith. Hyrum in this book is held in worthy esteem as an older son to be relied upon — always faithful, dependable, and kind. These qualities she tenderly describes in his role in nursing Joseph during the surgical operation. Hyrum's steady nerve and patience made him equal to meet a crisis to which the mother felt unequal.

Hyrum was a product of the frontier — serious, unpolished in speech and manners; healthy, with a body of hardened muscles and a responsive reservoir of energy, with a litheness of movement in a gangling sort of way. He had suddenly grown up, tall and spindly, and the process of aging would not perceptibly make him otherwise in appearance. He would always be on the thin side, lean and tall. He was what a farmer would call a man with an appearance for hard work and dependable demeanor. His labor was always in demand. Early in life he exhibited a singleness of purpose. The long and difficult task of clearing the heavy timber from their large farm and preparing the soil for the seed reveals strength of character. Soon there would come into Hyrum's life a new type of challenge. It would be something quite different from clearing deep-rooted trees and underbrush from the stubborn soil, but an activity requiring much more will power and tenacity to succeed — the eradication of age-old traditions, superstitions carried down in men's minds from generations of the past.

Hyrum was quite unconscious at the moment of certain events which were destined to change the course of his life. As a citizen in an agrarian culture on the American frontier, there was an air of serenity, contentment, peace, and security prevailing which beckoned the Smiths. If there were any movement or undercurrent to change the status quo it could not be detected. The sameness of plowing, planting, harvesting, and clearing virgin land occupied the major portion of a hard-working people.

The tranquil existence of Hyrum, the Smiths, and the local citizens was soon to be rudely upset. Conditions over which he had no control were developing close by. Very soon after the revival another family council was announced. This one, however, was somewhat different from others pertaining to family policy and procedures. A certain member of the family, a non-conformist, had been up to something behind Hyrum's back. Hyrum had not been consulted nor had any other member of the family, but now the time had come to bring the problem out into the open because it concerned every member of the family, especially Hyrum. The atmosphere seemed to be super-charged as the hour had arrived and time for each to take his favorite place around the family living room.

With Alvin on his right, Hyrum seated himself comfortably near the large fireplace. He wanted to catch every word and facial expression of his brother, Joseph. The light from the fire cast shadows, as did the oil lamp, and Hyrum leaned closer. They little dreamed that what they were about to hear was the beginning of the most unusual story in modern times.

"This morning," Joseph began, "I felt a strong desire to ask God which of all the churches was right. I couldn't feel right about you, Hyrum, and Mother, Sophronia, and Samuel joining the Presbyterians. Even my friend, the Methodist minister, seemed confused. During the revival I felt a spirit of uneasiness and depression. No one was able to speak with authority. Even on so important a doctrine as baptism there was no agreement. Some preached immersion, some sprinkling, and others none at all, because they said, ordinances were unimportant; man was saved only by the grace of God."

Hyrum shifted uneasily in his seat as he listened, for he remembered his minister's explanation about God saving men's souls only when they were destined to be saved.

"The scripture of James," Joseph continued, "preyed on my mind, If any one lacked wisdom, let him call upon God. It seemed that I could not rest until I asked God. You remember the place where we've been cutting down trees to enlarge our corn patch? It was just beyond there, to the west, in the thickest part of the trees where I went to pray. I hope you will understand me. It was about ten o'clock; the sun was bright, but the ground was shady. At first it was hard for me to pray because I had never talked out loud to God, but I was determined to try.

As I began to pray I was pounced upon by some unseen power. It choked me so that I could not make a sound. I began to lose my senses; great gloom and darkness pressed in upon me. I became panicky and prayerinwardly for relief from this overwhelming power. Just as I was giving up to face destruction something most unusual happened.

A soothing light descended from directly over my head. As the light came nearer I gazed transfixed at it; not knowing what to expect.

As I looked upward into this light, there appeared two personages standing a little above me in the air. The light immediately around them was so bright it blinded me at first. But all alarm and excitement left when I heard a soft, intimate thrilling voice saying, (Joseph,) and he pointed to the person on his right, "This is my beloved Son; hear him!"

As I looked at the Son, I saw an expression on his face of love and kindly inquiry, as if he were saying, "What is it that you want?" I opened my mouth and began to speak and said; "Which of all the sects is right, and which shall I join?" He answered, "Joseph, you must join none of them, for they are all wrong; their creeds are an abomination in my sight. Their leaders are corrupt; they draw near to me with their lips, but their hearts are far from me; they teach for doctrine the commandments of men, having a form of Godliness, but they deny the power thereof."

He reminded me again that I should join none of them. He told me many other things of great importance, which I cannot tell you now. At the end of the visit the personages departed as they had come; the heavenly light faded away, and I was left alone, looking about. I was lying on my back looking up at the blue skies through the trees. It was difficult to move for I had no strength. As I lay there pondering on all I had seen and heard, my stength gradually returned; but it was some time before I could stand on my feet.[1]

When Joseph finished his story, there was a moment's silence. Hyrum's face was sober and thoughtful. He and Alvin, together with others of the family, sat transfixed. So intent on the story had they been that each had seemed to experience vicariously all that Joseph told them. Not one person in the room doubted the truth of a single detail. They felt as surely as if they themselves had participated in these events, that they were true.

This was a memorable evening for Hyrum. His heart was attuned to that of his younger brother Joseph. Almost at once he became aware of the significance of many peculiar happenings that had preceded this occasion. He realized that it had been the dark powers of evil which had stalked the family, settling finally on the young Joseph. "I must," thought Hyrum, "assume a share of my brother's responsibility; he will need my help for the great work ahead. " From that night on Hyrum's resolve to be always mindful of and helpful to Joseph was in effect.

The next day the Smith family awakened to the realization that they were something more than a family engaged in agricultural and business pursuits. The very air seemed charged with apprehension. A revelation from God had been given. The ancient concept of God was reestablished. Visions had not been done away with. Prayers could be literally answered, and the biblical pronouncement of the reality and power of the evil one was reaffirmed. All the sects and creeds presently upon the earth were mere machinations of men's minds. They bore no official sanction from Jesus Christ, the author of salvation.

---

[1]See Luck Mack Smith, *op. cit.*, pp. 71-72; Pearl of Great Price, Joseph Smith, 2:15-20.

The implications of the revelation were overwhelming. From the status of common frontiersmen, the Smiths were now thrust by a strange chain of events and a curious public into a new and strange role. A younger member of the family had unwittingly triggered the powers of heaven and unleashed a blast of knowledge and power strong enough ultimately to change the entire world.

To the tall, serious-minded Hyrum, the turn of events was both startling and exhilarating. So overwhelmed was he by his brother's story that his mind at first failed to grasp the full import of such an experience. But as the days passed, the true significance of it was borne in upon his understanding. He remembered how seriously Joseph had listened to the revivalists and how his meditations exceeded even his study of the Bible. Joseph's refusal to join any of the various sects had given offense to some, one person in particular; for someone had tried to kill him. But the bullet had missed him and lodged in the neck of a cow. Hyrum wondered what new perils would come to Joseph with the announcement of his story.

To all outward appearances the Smith family was the same — the crops were planted, more land cleared of timber, and the daily routine went on as usual through the summer and fall. But inwardly, though their actions seemed calm and natural, expectation ruled their thoughts. Gossip at the store and among church members was focused on the fourteen-year-old Joseph. Hyrum and the other members of the family became alarmed at the changing attitude of former neighbors and friends. During the evening family hour, the children told how people had stared at them and had pointed their fingers and ridiculed them with biting words which were spoken loudly enough for them to hear.

Even the friendly Methodist minister turned against Joseph. He told Joseph not to circulate his story because visions had ceased with the holy apostles, and Joseph should repudiate what he had said. Hyrum was pleased to hear Joseph say of this encounter with the minister that he had borne his testimony to the truthfulness of his experience, and that to deny such an experience would be to offend God; for he knew that he had had a vision, and he dared not deny it.

During the slack period on the farm, the older boys had usually secured jobs in the village. But now, as news of the vision became common knowledge, work became harder to get. To hire or befriend any member of the Smith family was to condone their belief in the vision. This rather sudden alienation made it necessary for the father and his sons to find some new means of supplementing their farm income. They erected a small cooper shop where they could make barrels, splitwood chairs, baskets, sap bowls, and bee guns. They also cut cordwood and made maple syrup and birch brooms to increase their saleable offering. While the men did this, the mother and girls, on public days, resumed their cake and beer business in the village.[2] And toward fall there was demand for farm products such as vegetables, maple sugar, and molasses.

The persistent and continuous industry of the family so won the admiration of the community that antagonism began to waver. A tenth child, daughter Lucy, was born at this time; and with her advent a larger home was needed. By November of 1822, the frame of the new home was raised. The materials were put together by the help of many friendly hands. Alvin was heard to remark, "I am going to have a nice, pleasant room for father and mother to sit in and everything arranged for their comfort, and they shall not work any more as they have done."[3] His hopes were realized more quickly than he had expected; for by the summer of the next year, the family moved in; and by contrast with the log house, the new frame structure was

---

[2]Pomeroy Tucker, *Origin, Rise, and Progress of Mormonism*, (Palmyra, New York, 1867), p. 15. Note—The animosity toward the Smiths was expressed in these words by Mr. Tucker: "At this period in the life and career of Joseph Smith, Jr., or Joe Smith, as he was universally named . . . the chief subject of this biography being unanimously voted the laziest and most worthless of the generation. From the age of twelve to twenty he is distinctly remembered as dull eyed, flaxen haired, prevaricating boy-noted only for his indolent and vagabondish character and his habits of exaggeration and untruthfulness," etc.
[3]Lucy Mack Smith, *op. cit.*, p. 85.

a mansion. The old log house was put to good use as a comfortable barn for their livestock.[4]

There was still much work to be done on the new house when the family moved in. Wallboards had to be raised; a stairway had to be finished to the upper bedrooms; cupboards had to be built in and additional furniture purchased or built. By fall of 1823, the Smiths were quite comfortable. The boys seemed suddenly to grow up. The village prejudice, excepting for the clergymen who believed them doomed to hell, had temporarily subsided. The routine of the family had settled into a pattern of co-operative activity.

But this state of affairs was not to continue for long. The next act in the great drama of the gospel restoration was imminent. It was now nearing the end of September 1823; several frosty nights had opened nature's paint pot on the maple, oak, and birchwood trees, and had readied the crops for harvesting. The squash had to be gathered and the corn cut. The virgin soil had yielded its strength and the laborers must claim their reward. Thus, when the sun rose on the morning of September 22, it found the Smiths with much work to do. At an early hour father and sons had adjourned to the corn patch close by the house. But Joseph was to do little harvesting that day. The Lord had other plans for him.

It was an anxious day for Hyrum; he sensed the unusual happenings, and desired to know more about them. That evening the parents asked the children to finish their chores early, for there was to be a family council. As each of the family was taking his accustomed place around the open hearth, Joseph was heard to say, "No one must speak outside this family circle of the things you hear tonight."

The parents, sitting opposite Joseph and Hyrum in their easy chairs, motioned for the children to get settled. Hyrum moved his position to the opposite side of the rock fireplace, where he could better watch Joseph's face in the light of the

---

[4]Tucker, *op. cit.*, pp. 34-35. The author, very prejudiced, was part owner of the Wayne *Sentinel*.

fire. Hyrum studied the scene, and so mature beyond his years and so inspired did his young brother seem that Hyrum's heart ached for all that Joseph had suffered.

Standing in the light of the sputtering oil lamp and the flickering fire, Joseph began:

It seems just yesterday when I told you about seeing the Father and the Son. We as a family have been singled out as being different from other people. I feel that we are going to have trouble and that more changes are coming into our lives. Last night, I went to bed quite early, for it had been a hard day harvesting the crops. I felt the need to pray. I had a troubled conscience because of some foolish things I had said and done. I wanted to know where I stood with God.

It was while I was praying that I became aware that the room was filling with light. The light increased until the room was brighter than noonday, but I was not as afraid as I was when I saw the light in the grove. To my surprise I saw the figure of a man, a person glorious to look upon; for he, like the other vision, was enveloped in a soft heavenly light, the light being most intense close to his body. His bare feet did not touch the floor; and he was dressed in a robe of exquisite whiteness, opened at the neck and extending to a little above the ankles. His head and arms were bare, as were his neck and bosom. The opening in his robe below his neck made it appear that the robe was his only covering. His face was handsome and full of intelligence.

At first I was somewhat afraid; but then he said, "Joseph, I have been sent from the presence of God; my name is Moroni. I am to tell you that God has a work for you to do and that your name shall be spoken for both good and evil among all nations, kindreds, and tongues."

Hyrum glanced at his mother and father in order to catch, if possible, their reaction to these words. It was evident to Hyrum that Joseph's story was being accepted by the rest of the family.

Joseph continued:

The angel said, "There is a book deposited, written upon gold plates, about a people who once lived upon this American continent many centuries ago. This book contains the fullness of the ever-lasting gospel as preached by the Savior. There are with the plates two stones set in silver bows. These stones are fastened to a breast plate, and are called the Urim and Thummim. God prepared these stones for the purpose of translating the book, and they were used in ancient times."

The angel then quoted and explained a number of Old Testament prophecies. From Malachi he quoted the last passages about turning the hearts of the children to the fathers. He also spoke of the days to come when the earth should burn as an oven and all the wicked would be destroyed. He quoted Isaiah 11 and Job from 2:28 to the last. From the New Testament he quoted Acts 3:22-23.

Then he told me that in time I would obtain the hidden plates and the Urim and Thummin, but that they are not be shown to anyone; if I disobey, I shall be destroyed. While he was telling me about the plates, I saw in vision where they are deposited.

The hour had grown late, and the room was chilly. Hyrum suggested that Samuel replenish the fire. There were some questions that he wanted to ask Joseph, but to do so would disturb the spirit and quiet, for there was more to be told; so Hyrum remained silent.

"This morning," Joseph continued, "I was so tired that I felt like staying in bed, but I knew that I had my share of the work to do. Fearful of disbelief I decided to tell no one. When I picked up the corn cutter, I was too exhausted to use it. Father noticed that something was wrong with me and told me to go home. On my way home, as I climbed through the fence, I fainted. When I came to my senses, I heard again the voice of Moroni who stood before me surrounded by light as before. He repeated again all that he had told me the night before. And then he told me to go and tell father what I had seen and heard."

Joseph related how relieved he had been to share so great a responsibility with someone else and how happy he had been to have his father understand.

He then told them of going to the place on the hill where the plates were buried. The three mile walk alone over the winding dirt road had given him time to control his feelings, and renewed excitement had made him forget his fatigue.

He said, looking at Hyrum,

As I neared the hill I knew right where to go. Do you remember where we used to go hunting, there where we could get a good view of the surrounding farms? We couldn't see our house because of the heavy trees and undergrowth but we could see others. I approached the barren top of the hill from the heavily wooded area at its base. And I went to a spot on the west side of the hill near the top, close by several sugar maples. The stone lid of the box was actually visible where the center protruded through the soil. I removed the dirt and using a pole for a lever pried up the heavy covering. I looked in and beheld some glorious golden plates, with the Urim and Thummim and the breast plate. The box was made of stone slabs cemented together. In the bottom were two narrow stones, laid cross-wise to keep the plates from touching the bottom of the box.

I attempted to remove the plates from the box; but the angel appeared and forbade me to touch them, telling me to return to the spot in one year at which time he would again meet me. He told me that I was to come to this place once each year for four years, and that at the end of that time, if I was worthy, I would obtain the plates.[5]

In the Smith living room the hour was now very late. Hyrum noted the fatigue lines in Joseph's face, the experience of the former night and day had taken a heavy toll of his brother's energies. But though the firelight had grown dim and the flame of the oil wick sputtered at its base, the famly did not stir.

It was Alvin who finally suggested that Joseph, being weary, should get his rest. "Now, brother," he said, "let us go to bed, and rise early in the morning in order to finish our day's work at an early hour before sunset; then, if mother will get our supper early, we will have a fine long evening, and we will all sit down for the purpose of listening to you while you tell us the great things which God has revealed to you."[6]

The following evening the young Prophet continued his story. Again he warned them not to mention outside the family circle the things he was telling them; for wickedness in the world was so prevalent that if knowledge of these things was spread abroad their very lives might be in constant danger. Then if he were permitted to obtain the plates and to tell his story to the world at a future time, it would be rejected. Their very name would be thought evil by all people.

The parents continued to call the family together evening

[5]Joseph Smith, *History of the Church*, vol. 1, pp. 14-16.
[6]Lucy Smith, *op. cit.*, p. 81.

after evening to hear more of the revelations. The mother, writing of these evenings, said: "I presume our family presented an aspect as singular as any that ever lived upon the face of the earth — all seated in a circle, father, mother, sons and daughters, and giving the most profound attention to a boy, eighteen years of age, who had never read the Bible through in his life. He seemed much less inclined to the perusal of books than any of the rest of our children, but far more given to meditation and deep study."[7]

As the cold of the winter approached, the new home, although not finished, was snug and comfortable, and doubly warmed by the love of a family that had faced a great responsibility with unity and harmony.

The secret of the visions was well kept for a time until a friend of the family, Martin Harris, became a confidant. Hyrum, Joseph, and the other boys had worked for Mr. Harris on his farm and had been well paid. During the summer of 1824, while Father Smith, Joseph, and Hyrum were walling up a basement and digging a well for Mr. Harris, he asked to be told more about the vision in the grove which now was common knowledge. Because of Mr. Harris's evident sincerity and interest, the father confided to him the secret of the visit of Moroni. Whereupon, Martin Harris told his wife.

Hyrum was apprehensive over this breach of confidence, especially when he learned that town gossip had again begun to spin its web about his younger brother Joseph. It was told that young Joe Smith had a curious stone whereby he could detect hidden treasures of great value — gold and silver. Joseph, so said the stories, had dug for buried treasure on the hill near his home. But "just at the moment the treasure chest was near the seer's grasp it vanished away."[8]

Toward the middle of November, 1823, the family suffered a tragedy. Alvin, almost twenty-six, took sick with bilious colic. At two o'clock on the afternoon of November 15, he came to

[7]*Ibid.*, p. 82.
[8]Tucker, *op. cit.*

the house ill and asked his mother to call a doctor. The family physican not being available, she called a Dr. Greenwood, who gave Alvin a heavy dose of calomel. At first the medicine was refused, but after much persuasion he took it. It was a disastrous mistake. Three days later Dr. McIntyre, the family doctor, and four others were called for a consultation in a final effort to save Alvin's life.

Alvin, however, had a premonition that nothing would help and he called Hyrum to his side, saying to him "Hyrum, I must die. Now I want to say a few things which I wish you to remember. I have done all I could to make our dear parents comfortable. I want you to finish the house and take care of them in their old age, and do not any more let them work so hard as they are now in old age."[9]

He then called Sophronia to his bedside and gave her similar instruction regarding his parents. Joseph was also called and urged to live righteously that he might be worthy of obtaining the record. Alvin called each of his brothers and sisters to his bedside in turn and admonished them. The baby Lucy, of whom he was especially fond, put her arms around his neck and kissed him repeatedly. At last he said: "Farewell! I can now breathe out my life as calmly as a clock." Alvin died November 19, 1823.[10]

His mother, speaking of Alvin said: "He was a youth of singular goodness of disposition — kind and amiable, so that lamentations and mourning filled the whole neighborhood in which he resided."

With Alvin's death, Hyrum assumed more of the responsibilities of the family. Because of his desire to bolster the family fortune and secure for his folks the comforts of life, Hyrum deferred the additional responsibility of a home of his own. However, he continued to keep company with an eligible young

---

[9]Lucy Mack Smith, op. cit., pp. 86-87. The present home south of Palmyra was where Alvin died. Much work was needed to finish it. There is good reason to believe that the room on the southeast corner upstairs was where the Angel Moroni visited Joseph.
[10]Date taken from Mother Smith's History of Joseph Smith, pp. 331-332, is taken as correct. His death as recorded in Church History was November 19, 1824 and November 19, 1825. Vol. I, p. 16.

woman of Palmyra, who had already met with the approval of his family. Jerusha Barden[11] was known for her singular beauty and fine character, and it was she whom Hyrum courted.

All during his courtship, Hyrum was burdened with family responsibility. At this time the family received letters from Joseph, Jr., who was working for Josiah Stoal, a friend of the family at Harmony, Pennsylvania, about 150 miles south of Palmyra. Mr. Stoal had visited the Smiths in 1825 to ask for some help in mucking out an abandoned silver mine. He had also heard about some gold plates found by Joseph and supposed Joseph had a discerning eye for treasures. The Smiths' curiosity was aroused by Joseph's repeated mention in his letters of a girl named Emma Hale, the daughter of one Isaac Hale at whose home be was boarding.

Hyrum and Jerusha talked of marriage, but it was difficult for Hyrum to set a date. Alvin's death was a great loss to the family. With help scarce and Joseph away, the work load was much increased for Hyrum. And this, coupled with the social ostracism caused by gossip of visions and the family's refusal to affiliate with local church congregations, made him almost despair of ever being able to marry.

But with the consent of Mother Smith, the date of their marriage was finally set for November 2, 1826, and Hyrum made plans to secure a house for his bride. After the home wedding, Mother Smith wrote, "My oldest son formed a matrimonial rela-

---

[11]Jerusha Barden was born February 15, 1805, at Norfolk, Litchfield County, Connecticut. Her parents were Seth and Sarah Barden (Sarah's maiden name unknown), grandparents — Seth Barden and Ruth (last name unknown). Seth and Ruth moved from Stafford, Lolland County, Conn., into Norfolk when it was first settled. There Seth, Jerusha's father was born. They left Norfolk shortly after the birth of Jerusha. It is uncertain as to where they lived prior to moving to New York. One writer states he came from Canada to New York. They settled in the Newark Valley in 1840, and her father died March 16, 1844 at Barton, New York. Buried beside her father is a wife, Huldah. He probably married her after Sarah's death.

Seth Barden, Jerusha's father, was born September 4, 1769, at Norfolk, Connecticut. Her grandfather, Seth Barden Sen., was born September 22, 1737, at Stafford, Connecticut, his father, Abraham Barden, born December 11, 1698 at Scituate, Massachusetts, was married to Priscilla Alden and later to Esther Sampson. His father was Abraham Barden, born May 14, 1647 at Barnstable, Massachusetts. His father was William Barden, born (circa) 1642 in England, his wife was Deborah Barker. The date of his migration to America is unknown. . . . Mary R. Porter, a wife of a descendant of Jerusha and Hyrum Smith.

tion with one of the most excellent of women, with whom I saw much enjoyment."[12]

Shortly after Hyrum's marriage, Joseph, Jr., arrived home from Harmony. He had persuaded Mr. Stoal to give up the search for silver. He told his parents that he was lonesome and that he wished to marry Emma Hale. To his proposed marriage they gave their hearty approval and invited Joseph to bring his new bride home with him.

Since the Smiths had obtained their farm, others had moved to the section to take up land. There was a new real estate broker sent into the locality to handle a certain section called the Everson land of which the Smiths' tract had originally been a part. Only one payment remained to secure it. In order to pay this, the Smiths, having grown a great deal of wheat, signed a contract to sell their crop in the form of flour to Josiah Stoal and Joseph Knight. The money from this crop, Joseph, Sr., thought, would be ample to take care of the last payment on the place. Father Smith sent Hyrum to Canandaigua to inform the new agent that the final payment on their farm would be paid no later than December 5, 1826.

The arrangement for finally securing ownership of the farm gave the family a feeling of security and well being, but not for long. Father Smith accompanied Joseph back to Pennsylvania, leaving his wife and Hyrum to look after things. This was one of those rare periods of happiness and peace in the household.

A few days later there came three men to visit the Smiths. One of the men was a Mr. Stoddard, a carpenter who had helped build their house. Mother Smith became upset when they began to ask impertinent questions concerning the last payment on the place, and whether or not the Smiths would consider selling the place, and where Mr. Smith and Joseph had gone. She replied that arrangements had been made to make the final payment without any idea of sale. Without further words the men left the house and talked to Hyrum who was then coming

---

[12]Lucy Smith, *op. cit.*, p. 94.

up the walk. His replies reinforced those of his mother.

Whereupon the men said, "We now forbid your touching anything on this farm, and we also warn you to leave forthwith and give possession to the lawful owners."

Hearing what they said, Mother Smith fainted. However, she quickly revived and she and Hyrum talked to the men for some time, trying to dissuade them from their wicked course. Their only reply was: "Well, we've got the place, and d--n you, help yourself if you can."

Hyrum hurried to an old friend, Dr. Robinson, and related to him the whole story. That elderly gentlemen immediately sat down and wrote at considerable length concerning the character of the family, of their industry and faithful exertions to secure their home, the things he knew of the Smiths which might restore confidence in them with respect to business transactions. When he had finished writing, Dr. Robinson took the paper and went through the village. In an hour he had procured sixty subscribers. He then gave the paper to Hyrum to carry to the land agent who lived in Canandaigua.

On receiving the signed writing the agent was highly enraged. He said that the men had told him that Mr. Smith and his son Joseph had run away and that Hyrum was cutting down the sugar orchard, hauling off the rails, burning them, and doing all manner of mischief to the farm. He had believed their false accusations and had been induced to sell the place, for which he had given a deed and received the money.

Hyrum told him the circumstances under which his father and brother had left home and discussed the probability of their being detained on the road home to attend to some business. The agent directed Hyrum to address a number of letters to Mr. Smith and have them sent and deposited in public houses on the road which he would be traveling in order that one of them might reach him and bring him home more speedily than he would otherwise come. The agent then dispatched a messenger to the men who now held the deed to the Smith farm in hopes that he might compromise with them; but they flatly refused to co-operate. The agent then sent another message to them, stating that if they did not make their appearance forthwith, he would fetch them with a warrant. To this they gave heed and came without delay.

The agent tried to convince them of the disgraceful and dishonest course which they were pursuing and did his best to persuade them to relinquish their claim and let the land revert to Mr. Smith.

For sometime they said but little, except in a sneering and taunting way to the effect that they had the land and the deed, and just "let Smith help himself. Oh, no matter about Smith, he has gold plates, gold Bibles, he is rich — he don't want anything."[13] But finally they agreed that if Hyrum could raise one thousand dollars by Saturday at ten o'clock in the evening, they would give up the deed.

It was then Thursday noon and Hyrum was at Canandaigua, which was nine miles from his home. He returned home with a heavy heart. There he found his father, who had come in a short time ahead of him. One of Hyrum's letters had reached him at a point fifty miles from home and he had hurried home with all possible haste.

The following day Mother Smith, at the request of her husband, went to see an old Quaker gentleman with whom they had been quite intimate since first acquiring their farm, a man who had always seemed to admire the farm's neat management. They hoped that he would be both willing and able to purchase the place so that they might at least have the benefit of the crops then maturing. But she was disappointed, not in his will or intention, but in his ability. He had just paid out to the land agent all the money he could spare to redeem a piece of land belonging to a friend in his immediate neighborhood. Had she arrived at his house thirty minutes earlier she would have found him with fifteen hundred dollars in his pocket.

As soon as she left, the old gentleman set out in search of someone who could afford to assist the Smiths, and hearing

---

[13]*Ibid.*, p. 97.

that night of a Mr. Durfee who might be able to assist them, he directed the Smiths to go and see what he could do for them.

Father Smith started without delay for Mr. Durfee's and arrived at his house before daylight the next morning. Mr. Durfee sent him three miles farther on to one of his sons who was high sheriff, instructing him to say to the young man that his father wished to see him as soon as possible. Mr. Durfee, the younger, was obedient to the call. Immediately after he arrived at his father's home the three set out for the Smith farm, arriving about ten o'clock in the morning. The visitors looked at the farm, and they rode on to see the agent and the unscrupulous men who held the deeds to the place.

Father Smith and the Durfees arrived in Canandaigua at half past nine o'clock in the evening. The agent sent immediately for Stoddard and his friends, and they came without delay; but in order to make things more difficult, they contended that the agreement was broken, that it was after ten o'clock. However, since this was not true, they were forced to turn over the deed to Mr. Durfee, the high sheriff, who now became possessor of the farm.

At the conclusion of this unhappy experience, the farm seemed even more dear to the family. After the trouble Joseph Sr., left with his son Joseph to resume his business activities and to see Mr. Knight and Mr. Stoal. It was now the forepart of January, 1827, and Joseph proceeded on to Harmony, Pennsylvania, to claim his bride. He and Emma Hale were married on January 18, 1827.[14]

By this time Hyrum had established a home of his own not far from his parents. It is quite likely that the marriage of Hyrum was the culmination of an acquaintance which had lasted several years: The romance and the wedding had been heartily approved by friends and neighbors, and it was a good marriage. The material and moral support of the Bardens was evidenced by their constant interest and concern, Jerusha's sisters being

---

[14]B. H. Roberts, *Comprehensive History of the Church,* vol. I, p. 82; Joseph Smith, *History of the Church,* vol. I, p. 86.

frequent visitors. Jerusha herself proved to be a devoted wife and mother.

Hyrum, head of his own household, took his place in the community and became a substantial citizen. He was a Presbyterian and was eligible to hold civic positions of responsibility. His plans were to live and die in this locality so rich in opportunity and natural resources: The settling of Kentucky, Ohio, Illinois, and the regions farther west held no attraction for him. His roots were firmly established, and his foremost desire was to carve a niche for himself and his family from the land in western New York.

CHAPTER IV

THE STORM BREAKS

The birth of Lovina was the beginning of Hyrum and Jerusha Smith's posterity. While Jerusha was still confined, friends and neighbors called to congratulate the happy parents, and when the baby was about a week old the Barden sisters — Clarissa, Lucinda and Sarah[1] came and were invited to stay for dinner.

While Hyrum was seated at the table enjoying this festive occasion, the visitors were alarmed by his sudden action. His young brother, Don Carlos, had run suddenly into the room just as Hyrum was raising a cup to his lips. As he saw his brother, Hyrum dropped his cup, ran through the open door into his wife's bedroom, seized a small wooden chest, turned it up-side-down scattering its contents on the floor, hoisted it upon his shoulder, and raced out of the house toward the Smith home. Jerusha calmed her astonished sisters who were exclaiming, "He must be crazy!" Laughing heartily, his wife replied, "Oh, certainly not in the least; he has just thought of something which he has neglected; and it is just like him to fly off on a tangent when he thinks of something that way."[2]

Hyrum had agreed to deliver the chest[3] to Joseph as soon as the plates were brought home from their hiding place in the old birch log at the foot of the hill, perhaps not realizing how soon it would be needed. The added work and concern over the new baby made him forget. Since Lovina's birth on

---

[1]Jerusha's older sisters and brothers were: Clarissa, born March 7, 1792; Lucinda, March, 1794; Seth, December 17, 1795; Sarah, July 18, 1799; Ahira, October 28, 180 and Amasa, birth date unknown.
[2]Lucy Mack Smith, *op. cit.*, p. 109.
[3]This chest, the first such repository for the gold plates and the Urim and Thummim, is in the possession of Hyrum's descendants. Its inside measurements are $16\frac{1}{4}"$x$14\frac{1}{2}"$. It has a sloping lid, attached by metal hinge to a four-inch wide strip across the back of the top side. A keyhole is located in the outside center of the lid through the wood to the metal lock. On the right of the lock craved in the inch board is the word "Alvin." Joints are dove tail construction, and the floor of the chest is one piece of inch lumber.

September 16, 1827, Hyrum had not been fully aware of what was going on at his parents' home. He soon learned that Joseph had kept his appointment with the Angel Moroni at the hill and had received possession of the records. Mother Lucy told him how Joseph and Emma had gone at night to the designated place and had returned the next morning with them.

The four years since Moroni's first visit to Joseph had been a period of development for Hyrum as well as for his brother. Hyrum had matured religiously, for he had sat in the family gatherings to hear Joseph tell the story of his many meetings with Moroni and other angels. The experience had been something like a four-year academic course, under the tutelage of a heavenly teacher who was endowed with the Holy Spirit. In some ways the gold plates were a diploma, signifying the success of the pupil. Hyrum in turn had been Joseph's pupil, and an apt one, for he gave his utmost attention and readily learned the basic concepts of God and the gospel.

Joseph had told the family how on his first visit at the hiding place, Moroni had instructed him concerning the safety of the plates. Joseph had been shown the forces of evil mustered against him. The angel had warned him again concerning his responsibility for the safekeeping of the plates. If he, through his carelessness, should let them fall into evil hands he would be destroyed.

Sometime during the following December, 1827, Joseph came to say goodbye to Hyrum and Jerusha. It was difficult for Hyrum to see his brother go as far away as Harmony, Pennsylvania, over snow-covered country roads. Alva Hale, Emma's brother, had come at Joseph's request to help them move. For the Smith family, the past several months had been full of apprehension and excitement. They had been beset by curiosity seekers. The gold plates had had several close calls by the enemy, once when hidden behind a stone in the fireplace, and once when they were hidden in the old cooper shop across the way. Warrants had been presented permitting search for stolen

Hyrum Smith's birthplace, Tunbridge, Vermont. Photograph taken by Elders W. D. Brinkerhoff and Alma S. Clark, July 30, 1914. (Published—Liahona, Elders Journal. Independence, Missouri, September 15, 1914. Vol. 12 - No. 12.)

Smith ancestral home—Topsfield, Massachusetts

A portion of Hyrum Smith's diary with his signature. (Courtesy of Ralph Smith.)

goods, as a pretext to find the plates. A company of armed men had surrounded the house, and Joseph and the family had used the stratagem of his grandfather Mack to disperse them. Joseph banged open the door and rushed out, shouting commands and instructions in every direction, as if he had a legion at hand; the mob sneaked away in confusion.

Because of such constant molestation there had been no time to translate the record; hence, Joseph and Emma planned to move to the more friendly community where Emma's folks lived, in hope of some quiet and seclusion in which to work.

The Smith family had wondered where Joseph could get enough money to make the trip and were happy to hear that Martin Harris, a well-to-do farmer, had given Joseph fifty dollars with which to do the Lord's work.[4]

When the heavily loaded sleigh pulled away early on December 27th, they little realized the danger to the gold plates, for no sooner did the sleigh with its fast-trotting team get beyond the village than a sheriff's posse stopped them under the pretext of searching for stolen goods. But the "posse" failed to search at the bottom of a barrel of beans and thus failed to secure the plates.

For the next three months the household of Hyrum Smith was one of peace and tranquility. The source of excitement had been removed from Palmyra, New York to Harmony, Pennsylvania. Several letters had been received from Joseph and from these it was learned that he had purchased a small house and a few acres of land from his father-in-law. He and Emma had also accepted the hospitality of her family until they could move. Meantime Joseph's friend and benefactor, Martin Harris, went to act as scribe for Joseph.

It was gratifying to know that at last Joseph was beginning to reveal the hidden meaning locked in the curiously engraved characters which appeared on the plates. It had taken much study and effort on the part of the young seer to obtain the

---

[4]Lucy Mack Smith, op. cit., pp. 117-118.

English equivalents even with the aid of the Urim and Thummim.

The work of translating the record from the gold plates became the most important concern of the Smith family. While Joseph was exerting every effort to fulfil his heavenly assignment, Hyrum at the head of his household and aiding his parents and his brothers and sisters in the task of providing the necessary physical comforts of life, stood by to aid Joseph if or when the necessity occurred.

It is quite probable that Hyrum shared the worry and anxiety of Joseph's trouble with Martin Harris who had become Joseph's first scribe. Mr. Harris had been sent to New York City with a copy of the characters from the sacred record for verification of their authenticity. He had failed to obtain a certificate from Professor Anthon but his visit succeeded in convincing him that the characters were authentic. Soon afterward, to pacify his wife, who had opposed his support of Joseph Smith, he asked the prophet to allow him to take 116 pages of translated manuscript home to show to his wife and others.

The manuscript was not returned to Joseph because Mr. Harris failed to keep his word and permitted certain unauthorized persons to see the manuscript. Thus in attempting to avoid trouble more trouble was created. Joseph, not hearing from Harris, decided to journey to Palmyra to make an investigation. On June 15, 1828, a few days prior to his departure his wife, Emma, gave birth to their first child, a son, who died the day he was born. The death of his child and the concern over the manuscript made the trip one of great travail. He rode a stage most of the way; the last few miles were on foot through a forest. A stranger with whom he had become acquainted accompanied him to his home. They arrived early in the morning, the stranger after breakfast left without divulging his identity. Hyrum was shocked to see Joseph in such a state of despondency and gloom which was in contrast to his natural sunny and cheerful disposition.

Word was sent for Mr. Harris to come to the Smith home.

After several hours' delay the dejected man arrived. Having waited breakfast until noon to have their guest eat with them, they immediately sat down to the table. Mr. Harris sat motionless, drew the attention of Hyrum who exclaimed, "Martin, why do you not eat, are you sick?" At these words Mr. Harris pressed his hand to his temples, and cried out in a tone of deep anguish, "Oh, I have lost my soul!"

Joseph sprang from his chair exclaiming, "Martin, have you lost the manuscript?"

"Yes, it is gone," replied Martin, "And I know not where."[5]

Mr. Harris then related in detail his effort to recover the lost pages. The household was enveloped in gloom as Joseph walked the floor crying and sobbing, not knowing what would befall him. The entire family was in a state of grief. His mother attempted to comfort him, but she felt her work was ineffectual. The next morning he set out for his home with a heavy heart. It seemed that all that the family had so fondly anticipated, all that had been the source of so much secret satisfaction, had in a moment fled forever.[6]

Joseph's departure was one of sadness and deep humiliation. Nor was his journey home free from forebodings. Hyrum, anxious to share Joseph's trouble, wanted to accompany his brother. But his place was at home since in July the farm required constant attention and labor.

Joseph, then in his twenty-second year, was being educated for a greater role, and his lesson was a hard one. He had to learn to become as clay in the hands of the Great Sculptor. But he was an apt student, quick to learn from each problem and crisis as it developed.

It is not known just when Moroni, the heavenly messenger, came for the Urim and Thummim and the record[7] except that soon after Joseph arrived in Harmony, sometime in July, 1828.

---

[5]*Ibid.*, p. 123-129.

[6]It has since been conjectured that the vengeful Mrs. Harris hid the manuscript in hope of altering the wording to make any retranslation look spurious, and thus in one moment, destroy its authenticity and show Joseph a false prophet. D & C 10:11-18.

[7]Lucy Mack Smith mentions only the Urim and Thummim being taken, but the Prophet Joseph said the plates were taken also. See *Church History*, vol. I, pp. 21-22.

The angel came as Joseph was pouring out his soul in supplication to God for forgiveness and mercy. He declared that Joseph had sinned in delivering the manuscript into the hands of a wicked man and that he would have to suffer the consequences of his indiscretion. Moroni then told Joseph to return the Urim and Thummim into his (Moroni's) hands.

As Joseph handed them to the angel, he was told that if he remained humble and penitent he might have them returned to him again on the twenty-second of the following September.[8]

On September 22, the seer stones were restored to Joseph by the angel, who told Joseph that the Lord would send him a scribe. He was told that he must pray always in order to be successful in his work, for Satan had tried and would continue to try to destroy him.

When the Smiths arrived from Palmyra to visit Joseph, some time in February, 1829, the household of their son Joseph was in a happy state of routine activities. Progress on the record had been slow but steady. Until a new scribe could be secured, Emma had been writing for Joseph, but the work was often interrupted because of her household duties.

The Smiths became acquainted with Emma's father, Isaac Hale, and his wife Elizabeth, and their sons Jesse, David Alva, Isaac Ward, and Reuben, and daughters Phoebe and Elizabeth. As Mother Smith later wrote: "They were an intelligent and highly respectable family, pleasantly situated, and living in good style in the town of Harmony on the Susquehannah River, within a short distance of the place Joseph resided. The time of our visit with them we passed very agreeably, and returned home relieved of a burden which was almost insupportable, and our present joy far over-balanced all our former grief."[9]

The trip had been beneficial both to Joseph and to his parents, but trouble awaited them at home. Upon their arrival, Hyrum met them at the door with the news that both Sophronia

---

[8]Lucy Mack Smith, *op. cit.*, pp. 133-135.
[9]*Ibid.*, pp. 135-137.

and Samuel were very ill and that he (Hyrum) had quit his business to spend his full time taking care of affairs.

The life of Hyrum Smith during the early New York period was closely interwoven with that of his father's family; the decisions and activities of the family reveal much about his character and personality. It is quite probable at this time there was a period of expectancy and waiting by the Smiths for any eventuality. In the meantime there was work to be done on the farm and a living to be made. This was Hyrum's responsibility, otherwise he would have been with Joseph at Harmony. However, this first separation was only temporary, for within a few months his interest and presence would be associated with certain events at Harmony, Pennsylvania.

CHAPTER V

THE TRANSLATION

Hyrum Smith, with the other members of the school board of Palmyra, was in meeting to discuss the availability of a suitable schoolteacher for their locality when a knock came at the door. It was Lyman Cowdery who had conferred with Hyrum the day before about the teaching job. After he was asked several questions he was hired, but the next day he notified Hyrum that he would be unable to accept the position. That evening the trustees were again summoned to a meeting, and they chose Lyman's brother Oliver to take his place.

The new teacher, who came to board at the Smiths, soon heard about the golden plates. The story seemed to him fantastic, and yet it intrigued and fascinated him. Being a stranger, he was not completely trusted at first, and he had difficulty piecing together the facts of the narrative. But he won the confidence of Joseph Smith, Sr., who then told him Joseph's story.

Oliver Cowdery was deeply impressed by what he heard. To Mr. Smith, he said: "Since hearing about the plates I have been in deep study upon the subject all day, and it has been impressed upon my mind that I should yet have the privilege of writing for Joseph. Furthermore, I am determined to make him a visit at the close of school."[1]

When Oliver learned from the family that Samuel was leaving for Harmony, he questioned whether or not Samuel, who was recovering from a recent illness, was sufficiently strong to make the journey alone and to endure through the spring with Joseph. He then requested permission to go with Samuel to Joseph's home. It had been impossible for Oliver to get the subject off his mind: "It is working," he remarked to the family, "in my very bones." He made the journey a matter of prayer

---

[1] See Lucy Smith, *History of Joseph Smith*, (Salt Lake City, Utah, 1945), p. 139.

and became convinced that it was the will of the Lord that he should go. So absorbed was he in the subject of the record, that he could scarcely talk about anything else.[2]

It was sometime in March, 1829, that litigation involving the Smith property was finally resolved, and the family was forced to move. The details leading up to this event are missing, but we know that with the loss of their home the family moved in with Hyrum and Jerusha until another house could be obtained. Oliver Cowdery was advised that he should look for another place to board and room, but he begged Mother Smith, "Let me stay with you, for I can stay in any log hut where you and Father live, but I cannot leave you, so do not mention it."[3]

It was something of a relief to Hyrum to have Oliver Cowdery and Samuel leave for Harmony. The winter had been long, their house overcrowded; and there had been the usual sickness during the cold weather.

By the latter part of May, Samuel returned feeling much improved in health, and overjoyed at the progress made by Joseph. While with Joseph, Samuel had obtained a testimony of the truth of Joseph's work and had been baptized.

Hyrum listened carefully to all that Samuel had to say of his journey. The road had been miserably muddy and rough, in places almost impassable. Joseph had been delighted at their arrival, having again had a premonition of their coming. Joseph and Oliver had gone right to work for it was urgent that the translation of the plates be completed. Therefore, on April 7, 1829, the second day[4] after Oliver's and Samuel's arrival the important work got underway again.[5]

The story of Samuel's conversion and baptism left no question in Hyrum's mind about the importance of baptism; but when Samuel told about the visit of John the Baptist, who had appeared in his resurrected state to confer the keys of the Aaronic Priesthood, Hyrum wondered. However, he thought,

---

[2]See *ibid.*, p. 139.
[3]*Ibid.*, p. 141.
[4]B. H. Roberts, *op. cit.*, vol. I, p. 120.
[5]According to the Prophet Joseph's account Samuel did not come to Harmony until the latter part of May.

such an occurrence was quite reasonable. If the divine authority of the gospel had been taken from the earth, then at some time God would surely restore it.

Samuel explained the details of the restoration of the Aaronic Priesthood.[6]

Samuel's story so greatly impressed Hyrum that plans were made immediately for Hyrum to depart for Harmony. Samuel agreed to take Hyrum's place in looking after things at home. Hyrum's journey to see Joseph was one of great anticipation. He needed to have a serious visit with his prophet brother, for there were several questions to be answered; and he felt a great concern over what his own work was to be.

The roads had dried out, the countryside had donned its spring attire, and the air was warm and balmy. The change from the confining routine work of the winter was exhilarating, and Hyrum's mount seemed to sense his carefree mood, for the miles to Harmony were covered in record time.

When he arrived, the brothers exchanged warm handclasps and hugged each other affectionately; it had been months since they last had seen each other. And then they talked and talked.

They agreed that certain ordinances were necessary for one's salvation. They discussed baptism. Had not the Savior told Nicodemus, "Except a man be born of water and of the Spirit, he cannot enter into the kingdom of God"? (John 3:5.) They talked about authority. Hyrum knew that Joseph had not acted of his own volition but had been called as had Moses and Aaron. And John the Baptist had been sent under the direction of Peter, James, and John, who in turn had been ordained by Jesus Christ. Thus Joseph's authority could be traced directly to the Savior himself.

Hyrum's one remaining question concerned his place in the great work of restoration, and the answer to that question came from the Lord through the Urim and Thummim:

Behold thou art Hyrum, my son; seek the kingdom of God, and all things shall be added according to that which is just.

---

[6]Joseph Smith, *op. cit.*, vol. VII, p. 216.

Build upon my rock, which is my gospel;

Deny not the spirit of revelation; nor the spirit of prophecy, for woe unto him that denieth these things;

Therefore treasure up in your heart until the time which is in my wisdom that you shall go forth. . . .

Behold I am Jesus Christ, the Son of God. I am the light and life of the world.

I am the same who came unto my own and my own received me not;

But verily I say unto you, that as many as receive me, to them will I give power to become the sons of God, even to them who believe on my name.[7]

The Lord advised Hyrum to seek not for riches but for wisdom; telling him that the mysteries of God should be unfolded unto him, and that he should be made rich inasmuch as he that has eternal life is rich.

He was to say nothing of this revelation but was to declare repentance unto this generation, and keep the commandments, and he would be blessed.

Hyrum was not to declare God's word until he sought to obtain that word; then his tongue would be loosed, and he would receive the power of God to the convincing of men. He was to study the word of God, both the word that had gone abroad and the words which were being translated, until he had obtained all which God would grant unto the children of men in this generation.[8]

There was now no doubt left in Hyrum's mind as to the truth of God's work. He pondered over and over the things the Lord had told him. He was to seek the kingdom of God, to deny not the spirit of revelation, and to thrust in his sickle (do missionary work). He had been introduced to Jesus Christ the Son of God, and told what Christ's relationship was to the world and how he had been rejected by his own.

Hyrum returned home imbued with enthusiasm for Joseph's work. Like his brother Samuel, he was fully convinced of the

[7]D & C 11.
[8]See entire section 11.

truth of all that Joseph had told him. But no sooner had he returned, than reports of trouble began to pour in upon him. Joseph had told him how the people of Harmony were beginning to oppose his work and that much of this opposition was led by ministers of the various Protestant groups. And for Hyrum there was added to the trouble in Harmony that in Palmyra. Mrs. Martin Harris had been busy. She had succeeded in getting signed affidavits proclaiming Joseph Smith to be dishonest and had then gone before a magistrate of Lyons, New York, and arranged for court proceedings.[9]

Mrs. Harris sent Lyman Cowdery, who may have been a county official, to Pennsylvania to have Joseph imprisoned. When the time came for the trial and the witnesses for the defense had left Harmony for Palmyra, Hyrum was asked by Mother Smith what could be done.

"Why, Mother," he replied, "we can do nothing except to look to the Lord: in Him is all help and strength; He can deliver from every trouble."[10]

At his words Mother Smith's face brightened. She had never neglected her prayers, and now she decided to petition God to help them during this critical hour."

That evening the court convened and after several witnesses had taken the stand, Martin Harris was called to testify. "I can swear," he said in his testimony, "that Joseph Smith never got one dollar from me by persuasion, since God made me. . . . This I can pointedly prove; and I can tell you, furthermore, that I have never seen in Joseph Smith a disposition to take any man's money, without giving him reasonable compensation for the same in return. And as for the plates which he professes to have, Gentlemen, if you do not believe it, but continue to resist the truth, it will one day be the means of damning your souls."[11]

The magistrate told the court that there would be no more witnesses. He took the written testimonies that had been

---

[9]Lucy Mack Smith, op. cit., pp. 143-146.
[10]Ibid., p. 144.
[11]Ibid., p. 146.

given and tore them to pieces, telling the witnesses to go about their business and trouble him no more with such ridiculous folly.[12]

In Harmony, the forces of evil continued to crowd in upon Joseph and Oliver as they labored to finished the translation of the plates. The clergy of the community spread rumors that young Joe Smith was a deceiver and was mentally unbalanced, that he was perpetrating a great fraud upon society, and that something should be done to stop him. And added to these unfair accusations was the gnawing anxiety over a dwindling food supply. Their labors left them no time to work for their daily bread.

Fortunately, about this time, an old friend of the family, one Joseph Knight of Colesville, New York, had heard of Joseph's work of translating the records at Harmony, and he felt impressed to take some supplies to help the young man out. As a youth, Joseph had worked for Mr. Knight on his farm. This kindly old friend, in his anxiety over the young Prophet, inquired about their circumstances and, discovering their need, soon returned with more supplies. Thus the work of translating was able to continue.[13]

The revelation from the Lord to Hyrum had been a call to the ministry, but the time was not yet ripe. The Book of Mormon was yet to be published and the Church to be organized. Until that time he must be content to remain at home and prepare himself to answer the call when it came.

He kept himself informed on the progress of the translation. The news of Joseph's and Oliver's move from Harmony, Pennsylvania, to Fayette, New York, greatly concerned him. Enemy pressure had caused a second delay, and precious time had been spent in moving and finding a suitable place to live. The Peter Whitmer family had been most kind in offering room and board. This family had been friendly ever since they had heard of Joseph and his work from Father and Mother Smith who had stayed

---

[12]*Idem.*
[13]Joseph Smith, *op. cit.*, vol. I, p. 47.

with them overnight while on their trip to Harmony.[14]   David Whitmer, a son of Peter, had met Oliver Cowdery and Samuel Smith when they were on their way to see Joseph.[15]   This chance encounter had prompted Oliver to write a letter to David, and that letter proved providential.   David responded to Oliver's request, and thus relief was afforded in a difficult situation.   A Whitmer family council decided that David should take his team and wagon and bring Oliver, Joseph, and family to Fayette.

It was the latter part of June, 1829, that the work of translation began in Fayette.   Long uninterrupted hours were spent, and the work progressed rapidly.   Soon Hyrum received word that Joseph was coming to Palmyra for an important occasion. Joseph explained that there were to be witnesses to the truth of the coming forth of the Book of Mormon.   Hyrum was overjoyed to learn that he was to be one of the eight witnesses to be called with his father and Samuel.

The day before Joseph and several others arrived at Palmyra, the three witnesses (as prescribed in Ether 5:2-4) had been chosen, and Oliver Cowdery, Martin Harris, and David Whitmer had seen the plates at the hands of the Angel Moroni and had heard the voice of the Lord commanding them to testify to the reality of the record and of the power by which it was brought forth.

According to a revelation it was necessary also that eight witnesses see and handle the plates.   From the Whitmers and the Smiths the following were chosen: Christian Whitmer, Jacob Whitmer, Peter Whitmer Jr., John Whitmer, (all sons of Peter Whitmer), Hyrum Page (Peter Whitmer's son-in-law), and Hyrum, Samuel H., and Joseph Smith, Sr.

The twenty miles from Fayette to Palmyra had been covered in record time and the business at hand was not delayed.   In a secluded place where the Smith family were in the habit of offering up their secret devotions to God, eight men were shown

[14]Lucy Mack Smith, op. cit., p. 149.
[15]B. H. Roberts, op. cit., vol. I, p. 120.   Oliver met David Whitmer in Palmyra.

the plates at the hands of Joseph the Prophet.[16] The solemnity and spirit of the occasion made Hyrum feel like weeping. That the plates were real they knew, for they lifted them as they turned the leaves which were about six by eight inches in size and fastened together with three metal rings.

The plates looked ancient and strange. The fine hieroglyphic figures were symmetrical and beautifully engraved. To Hyrum it was a never-to-be forgotten occasion; before the eight witnesses stood Joseph, his brother, so young; and yet it was with the power and authority of a seer that he spoke. As Hyrum listened, a spirit of peace and joy came over him and it seemed that he was experiencing a foretaste of heaven.

Following this significant occasion, the group rejoiced. It was a time of triumph and success in the midst of evil and opposition. Hyrum noticed how happy Joseph was and heard him remark that now others had seen the plates and knew for themselves that he did not go about deceiving mankind.[17] The burden had been almost too much for Joseph to bear alone, and now there were others to share his responsibility.

The translation of the Book of Mormon was soon completed and a copyright obtained. After Joseph and the others had conferred with several publishers, E. B. Grandin, owner and manager of the Wayne *Sentinel*, agreed to print the book, although his binding equipment was inadequate for such a job. A contract was signed August 25, 1829, for an edition of five thousand copies.[18]

When all arrangements were made for printing the book, Joseph returned to his home in Harmony, Pennsylvania. Oliver had been instructed to write a duplicate copy as a precautionary measure, before the printing began.

Oliver acted as companion and bodyguard to Hyrum in delivering to the printer a daily supply of copy. Peter Whitmer, Jr., was stationed on guard at Hyrum's home to protect the

[16]*Ibid.*, vol. I, p. 147.
[17]Lucy Mack Smith, *op. cit.*, p. 152.
[18]Joseph Smith, *op. cit.*, vol. I, p. 71.

manuscript. The work of printing continued from August 1829, until March 30, 1830.

Mr. John H. Gilbert, Esquire, adviser to E.B. Grandin in printing the Book of Mormon, remembered Hyrum Smith, Martin Harris, Oliver Cowdery, and the Prophet Joseph Smith coming to the place of Mr. Grandin. Part of his description is as follows:

When the printer was ready to commence work, Harris (Martin) was notified, and Hyrum Smith brought the first installment of manuscript, of 24 pages, closely written on common foolscap paper — he had it under his vest, and vest and coat closely buttoned over it. At night Smith came and got the manuscript, and with the same precaution carried it away. The next morning with the same watchfulness, he brought it again, and at night took it away. This was kept up several days. The title page was first set up, and after the proof was read and corrected, several copies were printed for Harris and his friends. On the second day Harris and Smith(Hyrum) being in the office — I called their attention to a grammatical error, and asked whether I should correct it. Harris consulted with Smith a short time, and turned to me and said: "The Old Testament is ungrammatical, set it as it is written. . . ."

After working a few days, I said to Smith on his handing me the manuscript in the morning: "Mr. Smith, if you would leave this manuscript with me, I would take it home with me at night and read and punctuate it." His reply was, "We are commanded not to leave it." A few mornings after this, when Smith handed me the manuscript, he said to me: —"If you will give your word that this manuscript shall be returned to us when you get through with it, I will leave it with you." I assured Smith that it should be returned all right when I got through with it. For two or three nights I took it home with me and read it, and punctuated it with a lead pencil. This will account for the punctuation marks in pencil, which is referred to in the Mormon Report, an extract from which will be found below.

Martin Harris, Hyrum Smith, and Oliver Cowdery were very frequent visitors to the office during the printing of the Mormon Bible. The manuscript was supposed to be in the handwriting of Cowdery. Every Chapter, if I remember correctly, was one solid paragraph, without a punctuation mark, from beginning to end. . . .

Cowdery held and looked over the manuscript when most of the proofs were read. Martin Harris once or twice, and Hyrum Smith once, Grandin supposing these men could read their own writing as well, if not better, than any one else; and if there are any discrepancies between the Palmyra edition and the manuscript these men should be held responsible.

Joseph Smith, Jr., had nothing to do whatever with the printing or furnishing copy for the printers, being but once in the office during the printing of the Bible, and then not over 15 or 20 minutes.

Hyrum Smith was a common laborer, and worked for any one as he was called on.

Cowdery taught school winters — so it was said — but what he done summers, I do not know.[19]

During the long months of printing, serious threats were made by the enemy who wanted to stop the work. One Sunday, Hyrum felt uneasy and persuaded Oliver to accompany him to the printer's. There they discovered a Mr. Cole busily inserting perverted portions of the Book of Mormon into his weekly paper called *Dogberry Paper on Winter Hill*. When he was accused of illegal use of copyright material, he wrathfully defended himself; and it was necessary to send for Joseph before he could be made to desist.

Another attempt was made to stop the press. The enemy circulated a rumor that Martin Harris, who had underwritten the cost of printing, was unable to raise the money. Further rumor stated that when the book was published no one would buy it.

Mr. Grandin stopped the press, and it was all Joseph could do to persuade him to continue.

Deacon Beckwith, with members of a committee who aimed to steal the manuscript of the Book of Mormon and destroy it, called at Hyrum's house. When Mother Smith received them, the deacon as spokesman began:

"Mrs. Smith, we hear you have a Gold Bible; we have come to see if you will be so kind as to show it to us?"

"No, Gentlemen," she replied, "we have no Gold Bible, but we have a translation of some gold plates, which have been brought forth for the purpose of making known to the world the plainness of the gospel, and also to give a history of the people which formerly inhabited this continent."[20]

---

[19]Wilford Wood, *Joseph Smith Begins His Work*, (Copyright 1958), Wilford Wood, Publisher in the United States of America. From unnumbered pages in the front of the book from memoranda made by John H. Gilbert, Esquire, Sept. 8, 1829 at Palmyra, N.Y.
[20]Lucy Mack Smith, *op. cit.*, p. 160.

She explained in part what the Book of Mormon contained, dwelling particularly upon some of the principles of religion and pointing out the similarity between these principles and those taught by Jesus Christ in the New Testament.

"Notwithstanding all this," she said, "the denominations are very much opposed to us. The Universalists are alarmed lest their religion should suffer loss, the Presbyterians tremble for their salaries, the Methodists also come, and they rage, for they worship a God without body or parts, and they know that our faith comes in conflict with this principle."[21]

After hearing her through, the gentlemen said, "Can we see the manuscript then?"

"No, sir," she answered, "you cannot see it. I have told you what it contains and that must suffice."

He made no reply to this, but said instead, "Mrs. Smith, you and most of your children have belonged to our church for some length of time, and we respect you very highly. You say a good deal about the Book of Mormon which your son has found, and you believe much of what he tells you, and they do wish — I wish — that if you do believe those things, you would not say anything more upon the subject. I do wish you would not."

"Deacon Beckwith," she replied, "if you should stick my flesh full of faggots, and even burn me at the stake, I would declare, as long as God should give me breath, that Joseph has got that record, and that I know it to be true."

Turning to his companions the deacon said, "You see it is of no use to say anything more to her, for we cannot change her mind." Then turning back to Mother Smith, he continued, "Mrs. Smith, I see that it is not possible to persuade you out of your belief; therefore I deem it unnecessary to say anything more upon the subject."

"No, sir," she said, "it is not worth your while."

Bidding Mrs. Smith goodbye, they left the house and meeting Hyrum, Deacon Beckwith said:

---

[21]*Ibid.*, p. 161.

"Mr. Smith, do you not think that you may be deceived about that Record which your brother pretends to have found?"

"No, sir," Hyrum answered firmly, "I do not."

Beckwith: "Well, now, Mr. Smith, if you find that you are deceived, and that he has not got the Record, will you confess the fact to me?"

Hyrum: "Will you, Deacon Beckwith, take one of the books when they are printed and read it, asking God to give you an evidence that you may know whether it is true?"

Beckwith: "I think it beneath me to take so much trouble; however, if you will promise that you will confess to me that Joseph never had the plates, I will ask for a witness whether the book is true."[22]   And without further ceremony the three gentlemen left.

In June of 1829 Hyrum's household had been blessed by the addition of a second baby girl whom they named Mary. These June days were days of comparative peace and calm while Hyrum waited for his call to assist Joseph in the work of the ministry. He was not yet ready to declare God's word, for according to the revelation the Lord had advised him to get wisdom and not to deny revelation from heaven.   There should be no doubt about the objective of his mission which was to build up God's kingdom here upon the earth.   Hyrum's twenty-ninth year was a period of new and significant experiences.   The potential of his intellect and emotional powers were being exploited to their maximum capacity.   The ground work for Hyrum's place beside Joseph had been well laid.

Perhaps, among the many qualities of character favoring Hyrum were his humility and teachableness, coupled with a deep sense of family loyalty, love, and devotion.   He had been an apt pupil of Joseph in theological matters.   There were no disagreements between them relative to the priesthood, its powers and method of restoration.   In regard to the reality of God's revelation it was not necessary for him to accept only a metaphysical explanation or proof thereof, for he had actually beheld with his

[22] Ibid., pp. 162-163.

eyes and felt with his hands the gold plates which had been written and preserved by the power of God. Every means had been used to give him the certainty and assurance of the absolute truth that this was God's work.

A precedent was being established when Joseph put Hyrum in charge of seeing the Book of Mormon through the press, for this was the beginning of shifting a major responsibility from the shoulders of the younger brother to those of the older, and is an indication of the confidence and complete trust Joseph had in the judgment and trustworthiness of Hyrum. The pressure of evil influences had weighed heavy on the Prophet during the exacting period of translation. There is no doubt that to have a person of Hyrum's caliber assume the responsibility of completing final work of publication was a great relief to Joseph.

Fortunately, Hyrum, Oliver Cowdery, and Peter Whitmer, Jr., were successful in their assignment which took more than six months to complete, notwithstanding the stratagem of their enemies, particularly Squire Cole and Deacon Beckwith, to destroy the project. How Hyrum was regarded by the citizenry of Palmyra was revealed when Esquire Gilbert spoke of him as "a common laborer, and worked for any one he was called on." This appraisal was partly true at the moment, but it could not portend the future for Hyrum Smith.

CHAPTER VI

CHRIST'S CHURCH RESTORED

When Hyrum Smith read of the publication of the Book of Mormon in the Wayne *Sentinel* for Friday, March 26, 1830, he was greatly relieved. The notice was headed the BOOK OF MORMON and read:

"The above work, containing about 600 pages, large duodecimo, is now for sale, wholesale and retail at the Palmyra Bookstore by E. B. Grandin."

Hyrum remembered a preview of the book published by the same firm on Friday June 29, 1829 — almost a year before. It had read in part: "It is generally known and spoken of as the 'Golden Bible.' Most people entertain an idea that the whole matter is a result of gross imposition, and a grosser superstition...."

The announcement of the new volume of scripture was the signal for renewed opposition and persecution. Nearby newspapers joined in the denunciation. On April 2, 1830, the Rochester *Telegraph* said:

The Book of Mormon has been placed in our hands. A viler imposition was never practiced. It is an evidence of fraud, blasphemy and credulity, shocking both to Christians and moralists. The author and proprietor is Joseph Smith Jun., a fellow who by some hocus pocus acquired such influence over a wealthy farmer of Wayne County that the latter mortgaged his farm for $3,000.00 which he paid for the printing and binding of 5,000 copies of the blasphemous work. The volume consists of about 600 pages and is divided into the books of Nephi, of Jacob, of Mosiah, of Alma, of Mormon, of Ether, of Helaman. Copyright secured.

The style of the work may be conjectured from the preface, and testimonials, which we subjoin.

After nearly three months the sentiment against the Book of Mormon was unabated. The Palmyra *Reflector*, on June 20, 1830, said:

The age of miracles has again arrived, and if the least reliance can be placed upon the assertions daily made by the "Gold Bible" apostles (which is somewhat doubtful), no prophet, since the destruction of Jerusalem by Titus, has performed half so many wonders as have been attributed to that spindle-shanked ignoramus: Joe Smith. This fellow appears to possess the quintessence of impudence, while his fellow laborers are not far behind in a greater or lesser degree,—denouncing dire damnation on such as may withhold their approbation from one of the most ridiculous impostures ever promulgated.

To Hyrum, Joseph, Oliver Cowdery, and friends, the vituperations of the press, clergy, and citizens against the new movement only confirmed what Moroni had told the Prophet seven years before — that Joseph Smith's name would be know for good and evil throughout the world. Prophecy was being fulfilled. The negative publicity, although hard to bear, acted like a double-edged sword: Some people sensed the exaggerations and the prejudice underlying the fantastic statements of the enemy and were led to investigate. There were those among the frontier people of New York and Pennsylvania who listened, read, and discovered the truth. The book never lacked for friends and supporters; and like a smoldering forest fire, the everlasting gospel which it contained would yet burst into a flame of good, never again to be smothered.

With the coming forth of the book, the work of the Lord gained a foothold in the earth, and the prelude scenes were finished: the keys of the priesthood had been restored, the Book of Mormon (the ancient record as scripture) had been translated and printed, and strong men of character had been converted to supply the personnel. The time for the organization of Christ's Church had arrived.

This event would be most significant for it would signal the beginning of missionary work and provide an opportunity for all mankind to partake of the blessings which would lead to eternal life. That the powers of evil did not underestimate the gravity of this new development, God's servants were well aware. They recognized the persecution and the unfavorable publicity for what they were, attempts by the evil one to thwart God's purposes.

Until this time, the Prophet Joseph Smith, Oliver Cowdery, Hyrum Smith, and others had formed an undeclared organization based on a natural and spiritual relationship. But in order to gain legal recognition and thus be able to own property, license missionaries, and buy and sell property for the Church, it was expedient that a formal organization be made. Civil law demanded the presence of a minimum of six persons to initiate a religious organization. And in order to fulfil this requirement Joseph called a meeting of the brethren for April 6, 1830, at the home of Peter Whitmer, Sr., in Fayette, New York. Hyrum was one of those requested to be present.

This journey from Palmyra to Fayette, was for Hyrum one of joy and anticipation. He remembered the thrilling, never-to-be forgotten experience of the year before when he had seen the plates containing the ancient record. And as he rode along it seemed to him that the setting was perfect for the restoration of the true Church.

It was balmy spring weather, and spring for Hyrum symbolized the truth and light which the world was expectantly awaiting. Nature was emerging from a winter's sleep, and the swelling buds and fragrant blossoms denoted for Hyrum a time of beginning, a time of reawakening.

The ten years of preparation for the organization had matured Hyrum. He had witnessed the gradual change in the social status of his father's family. Joseph's visions had reoriented his religious thinking. His experience as a witness to the Book of Mormon and his participation in its publication gave him a deep conviction of the truth of the work. But he had been admonished to curb his impatience and wait awhile before he set out to do missionary work.

When the meeting was at last called to order, a modern reporter might have described it as the meeting of a group about to organize a young men's club. The oldest, Hyrum Smith, had just turned 30; David Whitmer was 25; Joseph Smith, 24½;

Oliver Cowdery, 23½; Samuel H. Smith, 22; Peter Whitmer Jr., 20. Their average age was 24. Others were present — the elder Whitmers, Hyrum's parents, and perhaps Martin Harris, all of whom were farmers except for Oliver Cowdery, who was a teacher.[1]

After a solemn prayer the Prophet Joseph asked the brethren present if they would accept him and Oliver Cowdery as their teachers in the things of the kingdom of God. If the brethren were willing to do this they could proceed to organize the Church according to the commandments of the Lord. The brethren unanimously consented. Joseph then ordained Oliver an elder in The Church of Jesus Christ:[2] and Oliver, in turn, ordained Joseph. The Sacrament was then administered to those who had previously been baptized and had hands laid on their heads for the reception of the Holy Ghost. Some of those present enjoyed the gift of prophecy, and all rejoiced exceedingly. Of the six charter members, Oliver Cowdery and Joseph Smith Jr. had baptized each other in the Susquehanna River on May 15, 1829, and Samuel H. Smith, May 25. They had baptized Hyrum Smith, David Whitmer, and Peter Whitmer Jr. June 29, 1829, in Seneca Lake. (Hyrum and David by the Prophet and Peter by Oliver Cowdery.)

During the day of the organization meeting (April 6, 1830) all were baptized into the Church, as were Hyrum's parents, Martin Harris, and Orrin Porter Rockwell.[3] When Father Smith came up out of the water, Joseph, standing on the shore, took him by the hand and exclaimed with tears of joy, "Praise to my God, that I live to see my own father baptized into the true Church of Jesus Christ."[4]

The period of time between the adoption of the Federal Constitution and 1830 is usually called the Era of Nationalism;

---

[1]John Henry Evans, *Joseph Smith, The American Prophet,* (1934, Macmillan, Co. N.Y.), p. 52.
[2]"Latter-day Saints," by revelation was added in 1838. In the Prophet's story he gives the full name.
[3]Joseph Smith, *op. cit.,* vol. I, p. 79. Joseph Fielding Smith, *Essentials of Church History* Deseret Book Co. (Salt Lake City, Utah, 1922), p. 92.
[4]Lucy Mack Smith, *op. cit.,* p. 168.

and with equal appropriateness, the period from 1830 to the opening of the Civil War may be termed the Era of Sectionalism. This division held true in both politics and religion.

The first period was characterized by a spirit of Nationalism fanned by an intense insistence of individual freedom. Old Royalist traditions, religious dogma, and the idea of the divine right of kings were discarded. The Industrial Revolution, shortly to come, would create a new order, raising individual man to new heights of personal dignity. With the rise of sectionalism — the North versus the South, slavery versus freedom, High Church versus Low Church — the old religious orders were breaking up.[5]

A young nation, on the threshold of world power, was pushing westward where a virgin land waited settlement. Here industries would flourish; here natural resources, undreamed of, waited discovery.

Into the maelstrom was swept a new religion, destined to play an important role in the westward movement in America. From Fayette, Seneca County, New York, this obscure movement would roll westward, influencing the lives of millions not only religiously, but also socially, politically, and economically.

Foundation stones of the Church were being laid. A new body of holy writ had come into existence, and others were to come. A democratic lay organization had been formed which would fit into the new scheme of political life guaranteed by the national Constitution. The principles of the new Church emphasized the importance of the human personality — man was God's greatest creation, a veritable son of God. All those who made contact with these new ideas were elevated from the role of the innately depraved, suffering, and forgotten individual to an eminence second only to that of Deity. For if man is the literal offspring of God, then reasonably he may in time become like his Heavenly Sire. This new doctrine of eternal progression lodged in the hearts of many, but others clung tenaciously to their traditional religious concepts.

---

[5]Warren Sweet, *The Story of Religion in America*, Harper Brothers, (N.Y., 1939), pp. 373-411.

The revolutionary doctrines of the restored Church seemed to marshal the forces of truth and to set themselves against the powers of darkness and error. The odds were, at that moment, against this infant organization; and it seemed for a time that it could never survive. However, its success, even during the lifetime of Hyrum and Joseph Smith, was phenomenal.

The continued success of this brave new organization depended much upon the kind of leadership it would be able to draw to its ranks. Fortunately, the right leaders emerged at the right time and at the right place to give the movement the forward thrust it needed. Our narrative, centering around Hyrum Smith, must consider the contribution of others associated with him to make it complete.

From a humble beginning the church organization was soon strengthened. It was revealed that Joseph Smith was to be called a seer, a translator, a prophet, an apostle of Jesus Christ, and an elder of the church, walking in all holiness, in patience, and faith. The keys of authority had been given to direct the affairs of the Church. To one man, God would give revelation for the guidance of the Church and to that man would go the power to officiate. From him to all male members who were worthy would go the priesthood, from the deacon to the apostle.[6]

On April 11, 1830, the Sunday following the organization of the Church Hyrum and his family traveled to Fayette to attend its first Sabbath meeting. A unique pattern of worship was begun. The presiding elder called the meeting to order and announced the hymn to be sung. Following the congregational singing an extemporaneous prayer was reverently offered, followed by another song. The bread and the wine were blessed and passed to all baptized members. The prayer on the Sacrament had been revealed to the Prophet Joseph and was repeated in exact form. Oliver Cowdery arose and with inspiration and power preached the first sermon. A closing hymn was sung, and following the benediction a baptismal service was held. Six converts were made members by Oliver Cowdery.

---

[6]D & C 107.

This simple and humble meeting of hardworking frontier farmers, dressed in their homespun, established a precedent in worship. The religious devotion was manifest by a lay (non-professional) participation much like the congregational church polity indigenous with America. The collection plates were conspicuously absent. There was no ministerial peculiarity of dress to set the clergy apart. The membership of the Church was subject to be called upon to render voluntary service without pay. From this humble beginning men and women from a wide range of occupations would be called upon to teach, lead, and proselyte.

This new Church was destined to be like the one established by Jesus and spoken of in the New Testament. It was to be primarily a missionary church. The presence of the Book of Mormon, the inspiration of the Holy Spirit, and a desire to share the glad tidings became a powerful motivation to spread the word.

Hyrum Smith was among the members of the Church who met in conference for the first time on Sunday, June 9, 1830, at the home of Peter Whitmer, Sr. It was a happy occasion. The meeting was opened with singing and prayer, and the Sacrament was administered. Those who had been recently baptized were confirmed members of the Church, and others were ordained to the priesthood.

The sanctity of the occasion was intensified by the realization that they were following the pattern set by the holy apostles of old. The solemnity of these proceedings, the powers of the priesthood, the gifts and blessings of the Holy Ghost, and the goodness and condescension of a merciful God, all combined to create within them a sensation of rapturous gratitude and to fill them with fresh zeal and energy in the cause of truth.[7]

At this conference Samuel H. Smith was ordained an elder by Oliver Cowdery, and Joseph Smith Sr., and Hyrum Smith were each ordained to the office of priest. They were seated in the conference according to the order of licenses — Hyrum with the priests.

---

[7]Joseph Smith, op. cit., vol. I, pp. 84-86.

The entire Smith family from Hyrum to the youngest became active in the Church. All the male members, even Don Carlos, who was then only fourteen years of age, were ordained to the ministry, and Samuel was called to be the church's first missionary. Taking several copies of the Book of Mormon, he went to nearby Livonia to preach, and if possible, to sell the books.

The press of mounting church business made it very difficult for Hyrum to make a living. Evenings and week ends found him traveling to Fayette where the Prophet and Oliver now were, to aid in teaching, counseling, and answering questions of investigators. The new volume of scripture (the Book of Mormon) roused the people, either to a defense or a condemnation of Joseph, Hyrum and the Church.

The time would soon arrive for Hyrum to be called as a missionary. In the meantime Samuel, who was better situated to leave home, had taken advantage of the opportunity to be the first one to spread the gospel message, and when he returned from his mission Hyrum was depressed in spirit by the news that the mission had been a near failure. He scarcely realized how difficult it would be to plant the gospel seed in such stubborn soil.

The spirit of missionary work was ever present in Hyrum's home. Members of his household, including not only Samuel but also Father and Mother Smith, were missionaries. Samuel had left a Book of Mormon with one Reverend John P. Greene which eventually converted the reverend and his kinsmen.

Father Smith and Mother Lucy paid a visit to Father Smith's brothers and sisters. They found Jesse Smith, the oldest brother, extremely bitter against the new religion. John and Silas, however, had been favorably impressed. Father Asael said he had felt that some manifestation would come which would make known the true gospel.[8] Joseph and Lucy left copies of the Book of Mormon with all the members of the family, except Jesse

---

[8]Asael died October 31, 1830.

who refused to read the book or listen to anything concerning the gospel, and then returned home to Palmyra, to find crises developing at both Palmyra and Colesville.

While Hyrum Smith maintained a home at Palmyra for his parents and brothers and sisters, the Prophet Joseph, with his wife Emma, Oliver Cowdery, and John and David Whitmer went to visit Mr. Joseph Knight at Colesville. The friendliness of the place had instilled in them the hope of building up the membership of the Church. For a time this hope was justified, but success was soon succeeded by bitter persecution, just as it had been in Palmyra and Harmony and as it would be in other places yet to come.

During the weeks that followed the organization of the Church the enemy had openly attacked it. Several charges which required a court action were made against Joseph Smith. But with the help of his family and friends he was acquitted and left for his home in Harmony, Pennsylvania.

Conditions at Palmyra rapidly became unbearable for Hyrum and his family. He planned to move his family to a more friendly community. Also Father Smith decided to move to Waterloo, not far from Colesville, and there prepare a place for his family.

*   *   *

It was about this time that Parley Parker Pratt, a Campbellite preacher from Ohio and a descendant of the 1639 settlers of Hartford, Connecticut, knocked one day at the door of the Smith family and inquired for the Prophet Joseph Smith. He had heard of the Book of Mormon at Newark, New York, while on his way to the city of New York and had lost no time in making his way to the Smith home.

Concerning this incident Parley P. Pratt, later had this to say:

I overtook a man who was driving some cows and inquired of him for Mr. Joseph Smith, the translator of the Book of Mormon. He informed me that he resided in Pennsylvania, some one hundred miles distance. I inquired for his father, or for any of the family. He told me his father had gone on a journey; but that his residence was a small house just before me; and, said he, "I am his brother." It was Hyrum Smith. I informed him of the interest I felt in the book, and of my desire to learn more about it. He welcomed me to his house and we spent the night together for neither of us felt disposed to sleep. We conversed most of the night, during which I unfolded to him much of my experience in my search for truth.

Hyrum presented Mr. Pratt with a copy of the Book of Mormon. After traveling thirty miles to keep an appointment, he returned to Hyrum's place demanding baptism and remained overnight. Next day Hyrum accompanied him twenty-five miles to Mr. Whitmer in Seneca County arriving in the evening. He was baptized by Oliver Cowdery in Seneca Lake, September 1, 1830.[9]

On his return he stopped in Columbia County, New York, to visit with his brother Orson. So strong was his testimony and so great was the Spirit of the Lord in him that he succeeded in baptizing his nineteen-year old brother. They then planned to return to the conference to be held at Fayette, September 26, 1830,[10] a conference called for the purpose of consolidating the position of the Saints against their enemies.

The two youthful Pratt brothers, caught in the gospel net, were destined to play a major role as stalwart exponents and defenders of the restored Church.

The difference between mediocrity and superiority is often determined by the ability a person has to follow the direction of his convictions, particularly when the principal basis for his security is threatened. The greater the treasure the greater the desire to cherish and protect it against all hazards. From all indications Hyrum was balancing himself on a perpetual edge of disaster, for he had neither economic, social, nor political security. When he, with his family, moved from Palmyra, once again the old pattern of "moving" was resumed, thus flaunting material gain as a sanctuary of rest. It was now a move toward an uncertain future with only the hope of direct intervention of God's power which was based on hope and faith. Apparently these qualities were not lacking in Hyrum, for there is no evidence of discouragement during this crucial move. He had put his hand to the plow never to look back.

Chapter VII

THE SMITHS MOVE WEST

In the early fall of 1830, Hyrum Smith settled his business in Manchester in order to be at liberty to do the Lord's work. His brother, Joseph, arrived from Harmony, Pennsylvania, to confer with Hyrum and decide on plans to cope with the enemy. Threats had been made to take the lives of Hyrum and his father. At Hyrum's request Joseph inquired of the Lord for a revelation on the matter. The answer given was for Hyrum to take his family and move to Colesville; his father with his family was to move to Waterloo.

The next day, Hyrum and Joseph took affectionate leave of each other, Joseph going to Macedon and Hyrum to Colesville. Jerusha and the baby Mary, and Lovina, accompanied Hyrum, leaving Father and Mother Smith and Lucy alone at home.

When Hyrum and his family had departed for Colesville about 10:00 a.m., the neighbors took notice and decided to make trouble. They began to call, one after another, inquiring very particularly for Hyrum. The parents knew that these people had no business with Hyrum. Knowing that there could be no valid reason for these visits, they were thrown into a state of tense anxiety. That night Father Smith became ill under the pressure of extended worry, and when morning came he was unable to eat breakfast. About ten o'clock, Mother Smith prepared him some porridge, but before she could serve it a Quaker gentleman called, asking to see Mr. Smith.

The Quaker had purchased a twelve-dollar note owed by Father Smith and had come that morning to collect the money. He threatened to force Mr. Smith's arrest on failure of immediate payment. Joseph, Sr., offered him six dollars cash and the payment of the balance in produce at a later date, but the Quaker refused the offer and running toward the fireplace made violent gestures toward the fire, crying: "If thou wilt burn up those Books of Mormon I will forgive thee the whole debt."

"That I shall not do," answered Joseph, Sr.

"Then thou shalt go to jail."

Mother Smith interrupted, offering in payment her gold beads. Again the Quaker refused the offer: "Unless the money is paid," he replied, "thy husband shall go straightway to jail."

To which she replied: "You have come here to distress me by taking my husband to jail, and you think by this that you will compel us to deny the work of God and destroy a book which was translated by the gift and power of God, but, sir, we shall not burn the Book of Mormon, nor deny the inspiration of the Almighty."

The Quaker then stepped to the door and called a waiting constable. The constable came forward and laying his hands on Father Smith's shoulder said, "You are my prisoner."[1]

The officer refused both Mother Smith's plea that she be allowed to get someone for her husband's security and that Joseph, Sr., be permitted to eat the porridge prepared for him. He was forced to sit in the burning sun, faint and sick, with the Quaker standing guard over him, while the unprincipled officer returned to the house and ate the food Mother Smith had prepared for her husband.

Of this Mother Smith later wrote: "Any human heart can imagine how I felt. But verily, verily, those men shall have their reward."[2]

The next morning she walked several miles to secure the assistance of Abner Lackey, who went without delay to the magistrate's office and had papers prepared to insure Joseph, Sr.'s, release from his jail cell. However, he was still confined to the jail yard.

Soon after Mrs. Smith returned home, a young man came

---

[1] At this time, in the state of New York, people could be imprisoned for debt. Lucy Mack Smith, *History of Joseph Smith,* p. 180.
There was a New York State Law forbidding imprisonment for debt less than $25.00.
[2] Lucy Smith, *op. cit.,* p. 181.

to the house inquiring for Hyrum. When told he had gone to Colesville, the visitor said that Hyrum owed Dr. McIntyre a small bill, and since the doctor was away, he had been ordered to collect the bill for him. Mother Smith told him the bill was to be paid in corn and beans and that she would send it over the next day.

The following day a man was hired to deliver the produce to the doctor's house. When the man returned, he informed Mother Smith that the clerk had agreed to erase the account. This business prevented Mother Smith from doing anything to relieve her husband who was still in jail. She decided therefore, to wait until the next day, hoping that in the meantime some of her family would return.

As night came on, Mother Smith was lonely; the darkness oppressed her; even the familiar objects in the room were scarcely discernible as she sat contemplating her condition and that of her family: Her loving husband was in a debtor's cell, and where were her children? Alvin, dead because of a quack physician, was at peace; Hyrum had been forced from his home by a combination of plots against him; Joseph had only recently escaped from his tormentors; Samuel had gone without purse or scrip to preach the gospel and was in return as much despised and hated as had been the ancient disciples. With William away, Mother Smith found herself quite alone. Unlike Naomi, she had not even a daughter-in-law to comfort her heart in her affliction.

While she was thus meditating, there came a heavy rap on the door which brought her to her feet. A stranger, at her invitation, entered and asked in a hurried manner, "Where is Hyrum?" She gave the usual reply. Just then a second person came in and was told by the first, "Mrs. Smith says her son is not at home." The second stranger replied that while he had been at a neighbor's home he had seen Hyrum arrive. This Mother Smith denied. But the stranger insisted, adding: "We have a search warrant, and if you won't give him up we'll take what belongs to him!" Finding some corn stored in the chamber above the room where Hyrum had lived, they declared their intention to take it, but Mother Smith forbade their touching it.

At this instant a third stranger entered, then a fourth. The last one, looking about, gave the excuse that he had come to light his candle. In response to this Mother Smith complained that she didn't know what to think but had been given little reason to consider herself safe day or night. She asked them what their business was, and for what cause they were seizing her property.

One replied that it was for the debt Hyrum owed Dr. McIntyre. When told that the debt had been paid that very day, he disputed her word and ordered the men to take the corn. As they climbed the stairs, Mother Smith glanced out the window and caught a glimpse of the approaching lights of two candles and a pair of carriage lamps. The forms of men appeared from every direction, some on foot, some on horseback, and still more in wagons.

No longer cherishing any illusion of fair play, Mother Smith determined that no troop of ribald blacklegs would seize so much as a particle of her household goods while she sat unresistingly by. She knelt before the Lord and begged that he would not let her children fall into these evil hands, and that these men might be satisfied by material plunder without taking life.

As she prayed, William bounded into the house. "Mother," he cried, "in the name of God, what is this host of men doing here? Are they robbing or stealing? What are they about?" She told him that they had taken his father to prison and had come after Hyrum, but that not finding him, they were plundering the house. Hearing this, the outraged William seized a handspike, sprang up the stairs, and in one instant cleared the scoundrels out of the chamber. They scampered downstairs where he flew at them. Bounding into the midst of the crowd, he brandished his handspike exclaiming, "Away from here, you cutthroats! Instantly! or I will be the death of every one of you!"

The lights were immediately extinguished, yet he continued to harangue them vigorously until he discovered that his audience had slipped away. The mob, taking him at his word, had fled in every direction.[3]

Between twelve and one o'clock Calvin Stoddard and his wife Sophronia joined the Smiths. They stated that they had been impressed to come. Within an hour Samuel also came, tired and ill. But after a little nursing and a good meal he felt better, and in the morning went to Canandaigua where his father was being held in jail. Because it was Sunday the jailer refused to liberate Father Smith. Samuel found his father confined in a dungeon with a man who had been committed for murder.

I shuddered when I first heard these heavy doors creaking upon their hinges, but then I thought to myself, I was not the first man who had been imprisoned for the truth's sake, and when I should meet Paul in the Paradise of God, I could tell him I too, had been in the bonds for the Gospel which he had preached. And this had been my only consolation.

After four days in the damp, crowded room, without food except for a pint basin of weak broth, he was allowed to work out his indebtedness at a copper shop in the jail yard. And during his thirty day's imprisonment, through his Sunday preaching, he converted and baptized two persons.[4]

During Hyrum's visit to Colesville, he decided after careful consideration not to settle there, but to move with his parents to Waterloo. There was available for rent a commodious house which would accommodate meetings. When the day arrived for them to leave Manchester, the Smiths were happy to go.

Having endured the fatigue and the accompanying inconveniences of travel, they found great promise in the warmth of new neighbors. They moved into a house belonging to a Mr. Kellogg and had scarcely unloaded their goods when one of their neighbors, a Mr. Osgood, came to invite them to drive their stock and team to his barnyard. He insisted that they could be fed from his barn free of charge until further arrange-

3*Ibid.*, pp. 183-186.
4*Ibid.*, pp. 185-187.

ments could be made. Many of the neighbors came to welcome the Smiths to Waterloo, among them a Mr. Hooper, a tavern keeper, whose wife came along, bringing delicacies for the Smith table.

The commodious quarters made it possible for Hyrum to have his father's family live with him. The new home also permitted a church group of twelve to twenty members to meet regularly for singing and prayer. Shortly after his arrival, Hyrum became the leader of this branch of the Church.

There was much to be done to encourage and instruct the new members in the gospel. When time permitted, Hyrum would visit Colesville and Fayette to hold meetings and perform ordinances of baptism and confirmation.

The six months since the organization of the Church had gone rapidly and new members had been added. The Smiths journeyed early to Fayette, New York, for the conference to be held on Sunday, Monday, and Tuesday, September 26, 27, 28, 1830. When the meeting opened there were thirty members in attendance. Thirty-two members had joined the Church since June 9.

As the conference convened, the Sacrament of the Lord's Supper was administered; then the presiding officers confirmed and ordained those who were ready. The power of God was manifest among them; peace, faith, charity, and hope filled their hearts. With such harmony prevailing, the business of the Church was settled satisfactorily, and the members felt keenly the spirit of their mission to go forth and labor with all their powers in promulgating the truth of the gospel. Many new members were baptized during the conference.

The future role of Hyrum Smith in the Church was determined very largely by what happened at this conference. Certain developments drew the attention of the Saints to the west. In the Book of Mormon, Ether 13:8, is a prophecy concerning the establishment of a holy city: "Wherefore, the remnant of the house of Joseph shall be built upon this land; and it shall be a land of their inheritance; and they shall build up a holy city unto the Lord, like unto the Jerusalem of old; and they shall no more be confounded, until the end come, when the earth shall pass away." This city of "Zion" was first discussed at the September conference.[5]

Prior to the conference a revelation had been made public. This revelation called for men to go on missions. Oliver Cowdery was instructed to fill a mission to the Lamanites (Indians) and to preach the gospel to them. This was a direct fulfilment of a prophecy found in the Book of Mormon; for on the flyleaf of that book is a passage clearly stating that the Book of Mormon, containing a fulness of the gospel, was first to be taken to the Lamanites, who were a remnant of the house of Israel.

Hyrum held a meeting October 14 at the home of Hezekiah Peck, an uncle of Newel Knight's. Of this meeting Brother Peck later wrote: "Brother Hyrum had great liberty of speech and the spirit of the Lord was poured out upon us in a miraculous manner. . . ." After the meeting Hyrum stayed with Newel's uncle. During the night, Newel, by request of Mr. Peck, healed Mrs. Peck by casting out the evil one. In closing his account of the incident, he wrote: ". . . She believed and stretched forth her hand and cried unto me, and Satan departed from her."[6]

As the news of the Church and of the Book of Mormon spread, persons impressed with the new teachings made their way to inquire further of the growing movement. On November 4, Orson Pratt, the brother of Parley, arrived at the Prophet's home after a journey of two hundred miles. He had received a testimony of the Prophet's mission and requested Joseph to ask the Lord what he should do. In Peter Whitmer's house, in the room where the Church had been organized, Orson Pratt was favored by a revelation. John Whitmer acted as scribe.

The lad was told to repent because the second coming of the Lord was near and to raise his voice in warning to the people to repent. If he would do this, he was promised that he could prophesy and enjoy the power of the Holy Ghost.[7]

---

[5]Joseph Smith, *op. cit.*, vol. I, pp. 115-118.
[6]*Journal History, op. cit.*, October, 1830. From Newel Knight's *Journal*.
[7]D & C 34.

Then on Wednesday, December 1, 1830, Orson Pratt was sent on a mission to Colesville, New York. Here he met Hyrum and with him and the members of the Colesville Branch, he received his first experience preaching the gospel. Toward the end of the month he returned to Fayette with Hyrum.

As the presiding officer over the Fayette and Colesville branches, Hyrum assisted the Prophet Joseph in the selection and direction of new volunteers to preach the gospel and do missionary work. Soon the effects of the western mission were felt. In December, Sidney Rigdon and Edward Partridge from Kirtland, Ohio, came back to visit the church founders. The Smith brothers were thrilled to hear from these potential leaders the story of their conversion by Parley P. Pratt and his companions. Pratt, a former colleague of Rigdon, had presented him with a Book of Mormon. This Campbellite preacher and his wife, convinced of the truth of this unusual history, were baptized November 4, 1830.

Sidney Rigdon and Edward Partridge, both of whom were eight years Hyrum's senior, had come to Fayette to obtain a testimony and to further confirm their faith in Mormonism. In this search they were not disappointed. The new Church attracted strong leaders, men of character and ability. Rigdon was to become the Prophet Joseph's counselor, and Partridge the first bishop of the Church.

Like Hyrum, who had asked the Prophet to inquire of the Lord what he was to do, others did the same. In each case the Lord promised them great blessings. To Sidney Rigdon he said in part: ". . . Behold thou wast sent forth even as John, to prepare the way before me. . . ." To Edward Partridge: ". . . Preach the gospel as with a trump; cry repentance to this untoward generation. . . ."

At the close of 1830, Hyrum Smith's name was listed with those called as missionaries: Joseph Smith, Jr., Oliver Cowdery, John Whitmer, Samuel H. Smith, Joseph Smith Sr., Don Carlos Smith, Parley P. Pratt, Newel Knight, Richard Ziba Peterson,

Peter Whitmer, Jr., Sidney Rigdon, Frederick G. Williams, John Murdock, and Orson Pratt, were listed.[8]

During the last nine months of 1830, 100 members were baptized in New York state and 150 in Ohio. Branches at Kirtland, Geauga County, Ohio, and Warrensville, Cayohoga County, Ohio, had been organized and were presided over by Sidney Rigdon and John Murdock respectively.

It had been a busy year for Hyrum and there was always much to do. Soon he would have to bid farewell to Joseph, for already a letter had come from Ohio. It was known that Joseph had received a revelation to move to Kirtland, Ohio. Joseph had been warned of the evil intentions of the enemy to take his life and that this move would be for his own sake and for the sake of his friends. This meant that the Prophet would have to cease the revision of the Bible and move his family.

The weather was bitter cold when the little flock met in the last conference (January 2, 1831) prior to Joseph's departure. At this meeting a new revelation was given. The Lord spoke of the city of Enoch and of the wickedness of the world, of Christ's coming to reign as king, of true riches that consisted of eternal life — rich and poor alike belonged to him. The Lord told the Saints that the covenant they had made would entitle them to possess the land as their inheritance and that they were to look after the poor and the needy. The minutes contain no exact record of the happenings of this conference.

With the conference over, Joseph departed for Ohio the last week in January, accompanied by his wife, Emma, Sidney Rigdon, and Edward Partridge. The snow lay deep as they bade Hyrum and the others good-bye, and the team pulled the sleigh with difficulty.

As he watched the company out of sight, Hyrum wondered how long he would have to remain behind. But sooner than he had dared hope he received a letter from Joseph which told

---

[8]*Journal History, op. cit.,* December 1830. Hyrum Smith labored as a missionary with Newel Knight and Orson Pratt in the fall of 1830.

him to prepare the Saints of the Colesville Branch to move west and to bring with them Joseph, Sr., and his family.

There was much to be done before they could all leave. Property had to be disposed of — either sold, rented or traded, and means of travel had to be provided. The news of Joseph's departure increased the desire of the Saints to be on their way. Hyrum's folk at Waterloo planned to be among the Waterloo Saints when they moved.

Until spring came Hyrum continued to do missionary work and to look after the branches under his charge. Jared Carter came to Colesville to learn more about Mormonism. John Peck had told the astonished Carter about the Book of Mormon. Carter, after reading parts of it and praying earnestly, was convinced that it was a revelation from the Lord. At first his wife opposed him but finally gave her consent for him to visit the Saints in Colesville. Experiences with enemies of the Church, who intended to steer him from the young Prophet's following, only convinced him that such people, if not themselves wicked, were wickedly deluded. After each meeting, he visited with the Saints and soon determined to apply for baptism. It was a thrilling experience to have Hyrum Smith baptize him, even in the freezing waters of February. Of his baptism he wrote:

> As I was being immersed I felt the influence of the spirit of God upon me, for as I stepped out of the water I was enraptured in the Spirit of God, both spirit and body, so that the chill of the water was taken entirely from me and I walked a half a mile and felt no more cold than if I had not been in the water at all. This I knew to be a new world. The next day Brother Hyrum Smith told me many things of a prophetic nature.[9]

When Jared Carter returned home, he began immediately to bear his testimony of the restored gospel. His family and friends opposed him. Thinking he suffered from a delusion, Mrs. Carter turned against him. The miraculous healing of their sick child, however, made her reevaluate her husband's new faith. The next day Hyrum Smith visited the family and bore

---

[9]Jared Carter, *Private Journal*, J. H., February, 1831.

a strong and powerful testimony to the truth of Mormonism. These things softened the heart of Mrs. Carter, yet she could not make up her mind to go West with the Colesville Branch. But Brother Carter, who had overcome many influences, made up his mind to take his family and his wife and go with the Saints.[10]

Meanwhile, the Prophet Joseph was anxious that his brother Hyrum should wind up his affairs in New York and hasten to Ohio. Joseph had, since arriving in Ohio, missed the companionship and counsel of his older brother. There were problems in Kirtland that demanded Hyrum's personal help. Therefore, a little over a week after his arrival, Joseph wrote Martin Harris, Palmyra, Wayne County, N. Y. "I send you this to inform you to come here as soon as you can, in order to choose a place to settle on which may be best adapted to the circumstances of yourself and brethren in the East. You may choose a place that may suit yourself anywhere in this part of the country so as to be as compact as possible; and as you will be better able to make choice than we, it is better for you to come before the rest of the brethren so that when they come they may have places to go. You will also bring, or cause to be brought, all books (meaning, undoubtedly the Book of Mormon), as the work here is breaking forth on the East, West, North, and South.

You will also inform the elders who are there in New York State that all of them who can be spared should come here without delay, if possible, and this by the commandment of the Lord, as he has a great work for them all in this our inheritance. We have received the "Laws of the Kingdom"[11] since we came here and the disciples in these parts have received them gladly.

You will see that Father Smith's family are taken care of and sent on. You will send to Colesville and have either Hyrum Smith or Newel Knight come immediately or both of them if they can be spared. You will not sell the Books (the Book of Mormon) for less than ten shillings.

Signed—

Joseph Smith[12]

---

[10]*Idem.*

[11]D & C, 42. Many basic instructions — Joseph's work, ten commandments, sickness, church trials, and death, remuneration for bishops, etc.

[12]Joseph Smith, *Letter* J. H., February, 1831 (Original document on file).

But it was not possible for Hyrum to leave as Joseph had suggested, and when over a week elapsed without his having heard anything, Joseph wrote directly to Hyrum:

Kirtland, Geauga Co. Ohio
March 31, 1831

Bro. Hyrum,

Safe arrival—busy regulating the church here. Disciples numerous—devil has made attempts to overcome. Serious job but the Lord is with us; have overcome and all things regular.

Work breaking forth on right and left — good call for Elders here. (Here the Prophet copies a letter from Oliver Cowdery inserted under its proper date and continues by addressing Hyrum as follows:)

My dearly beloved brother Hyrum, I have had much concern about you, but I always remember you in prayers, calling upon God to keep you safe in spite of men or devils. I think you better come to this country immediately, for the Lord has commanded that we call the Elders together in this place as soon as possible.

Mar. 4, this morning, after being called out of bed in the night to go a small distance, I went and had an awful struggle with Satan, but being armed with the power of God, he was cast out, and the woman is clothed in her right mind. The Lord worketh wonders in this land. I want to see you all.

May the grace of God be and abide with you all, even so, amen.

Your brother forever, Joseph Smith, Jr.

P. S. If you want to write to Oliver, direct letter to Independence, Jackson County, Missouri. Samuel Harrison Smith and Orson Pratt arrived here Feb. 27. They left our folks well. David Jackway had threatened to take father with a subpoena writ.

You had better go to Fayette and take father along with you. Come in a one horse wagon if you can. Do not come through Buffalo, for they will lie in wait for you. God protect you.

I am, Joseph.[13]

The letter from Joseph signaled another move for Hyrum. His first thought was that here was a chance to escape the mounting pressure of the enemy. But this impulse was soon overshadowed by the urge to do the Lord's will. During the sixteen years since leaving Vermont the roots of the Smiths had sunk deep into the soil of New York. But the good life Hyrum hoped

---

[13]The above letter was addressed to Hyrum Smith, Harpersville, Broome County, New York. (Original on file.)

to achieve was immediately abandoned in favor of being near his brother Joseph.

Hyrum lost no time in making arrangements to take his wife and family to Kirtland, Ohio. Prior to his own departure, he laid plans for a company of Saints at Colesville, New York, to move West. During the latter part of February 1831, the branch met and decided to go by boat on the Erie Canal to Buffalo and thence to Kirtland on the south shore of Lake Erie.

Thus it was that, ragged and worn under the mounting persecution, Hyrum and the other Saints turned hopefully to the West. The New York period was rapidly closing. Pressure from the enemy neutralized the nostalgia which might have possessed Hyrum's family at their leaving. This was their home — the land where they had grown up and shared the tribulations of a pioneer life.

The journey of Hyrum and his father to Ohio was uneventful. Taking Joseph's advice, they avoided Buffalo and arrived without notable incident. No doubt the depression felt at leaving friends and neighbors was eased by knowing that many of them would soon follow. Hyrum worried about his mother and brother William who remained behind at Colesville to come later.

To Hyrum, Kirtland was much like the country of western New York.[14] There were rolling hills interspersed with gulches, and deep water courses lined with native trees and shrubs. He felt that it was a goodly land. The friendly people of the village warmly welcomed them, and this seemed a good omen. However, the scarcity of houses to rent created an immediate problem, for in a few days others would be arriving.

The latter part of March, the Colesville Branch arrived at Fairport on Lake Erie. The company, numbering sixty to eighty souls, had been detained on the way at Buffalo, New York. Their

---

[14]A small town in the rolling hills of western Ohio which had a population of 6,018 in 1830. . . . It was comparable to the nearby towns of Painesville, Hiram, and Warren. The people of the community were nearly all farmers. . . . The area had been settled by westward movement along the shore or on the newly opened Erie Canal, by people from Connecticut, then later from New England, New York, and Pennsylvania. Willis Thornson, "Gentile and Saints at Kirtland," *The Ohio State Archaeological and Historical Quarterly*, January, 1954, vol. I, p.8.

canal boat became blocked by ice. Mother Lucy Smith, who was in charge of the company, was hard pressed to maintain the morale of the passengers. When the gloom was at its height, prayers were offered, and the ice broke with a terrifying crash, parting just enough to allow the vessel to pass through the harbor before the bewildered and frightened company was astounded to see the gap in the ice close behind the boat.[15]

The safe arrival of the Colesville Branch was to Hyrum and Joseph an act of divine providence. Mother Smith delineated the trials and hardships they had encountered. Many had come with insufficient food and clothing, expecting to be taken care of by those who had plenty. There were periods of seasickness and complaints about their safety. Mother Smith had had to scold the young women for flirting with strange men when the boat made periodic stops along the canal and to warn certain of the young men not to leave the boat and run the risk of being left behind.

It had been a comfort to know that the boat's captain was a friend of Lucy's brother, Major Mack. This friendship had made the captain most helpful and co-operative. When the boat departed from Buffalo, the onlookers feared that because of so many passengers aboard the vessel would sink. The stern was so low in the water that the local paper, assuming that the people would be drowned, published an account of the boat's loss. Later the Saints read the account of their own deaths.

While Hyrum was preparing a place for his family, Samuel and Joseph went to greet their mother at the wharf. Samuel had been told in a dream to meet the company and had feared that some disaster had befallen them. They were all happy to learn

---

[15]An account of the miraculous passage of the river boat out of the harbor at Buffalo, N.Y., was printed in the *Niles Register*, a weekly newspaper, dated July 16, 1831. Reflecting the general attitude, it read: Certain knaves started a new religion; 1000 souls joined — recruited from among the lazy and worthless class of society. They say that a miracle was worked in their behalf by clearing a passage through the ice at Buffalo. Some of them affect a power even to raise the dead and perchance (such is the weakness of human nature) really believe they can do it. The chiefs of these people appear to exempt themselves from labor and herein is, probably the grand object for which they have established their new religion.

that their mother was well despite the heavy burden of responsibility which had been hers on the journey.

It seemed good to Hyrum to be united with his family once again, and for them to resume once more the old custom of regular family councils to discuss such problems as adequate housing and farm acreage for a comfortable living.

The quiet town of Kirtland came suddenly to life with the arrival of the Saints. There was an urgency to get things done: to get acquainted with the new members who had been converted from the Disciples Church by Parley P. Pratt and his missionary companions, and to establish the Church. The prayers of Joseph in Hyrum's behalf had been answered. It gave Joseph a feeling of assurance and satisfaction to have his older brother again nearby.

When the Smiths arrived in Kirtland, Ohio, a new era for church growth began. Pressure from their enemies was lessened which allowed time to lay the foundation of the Church. The urgency and magnitude of the work evidenced in the Prophet's urgent appeal for Hyrum to come to Kirtland at the earliest possible moment presaged a role Hyrum was to occupy in the councils and the ministry of the Ohio period. In temperament and spirit he was prepared. His effectiveness as a leader of influence was declared by the new members of the Church, Hezekiah Peck and Jared Carter: "Hyrum had great liberty of speech and the spirit of the gospel was poured out upon us in a miraculous manner." Not only did he have great liberty of speech but liberty of action and thought uninhibited.[16] No doubt he realized the importance of his position and work in the ministry.

---

[16]*Supra.*

CHAPTER VIII

THE SETTLEMENT IN OHIO AND MISSOURI

For Hyrum Smith and his family, the spring of 1831 was a time of getting settled and adjusted in a new locality. The knowledge of the successful arrival of Mother Lucy Smith and the Colesville Branch filled all of them with a spirit of well-being and happiness, and Hyrum assumed the responsibility of locating a house for his parents and brothers and sisters. The Colesville members settled sixteen miles northeast of Kirtland at a place called Thompson.

Hyrum himself became a member of a co-operative plan, in which he and those of the Colesville Saints who joined agreed to have all property in common and to place all surplus in a fund for needy families and missionaries. This co-operative organization was called Consecration and Stewardship.

Through a revelation (D & C 51) to the Prophet Joseph in May 1831, the Lord appointed Edward Partridge to organize the Saints into the Society of Consecration and Stewardship and gave instructions for regulating the relationships of its members. This organization, thriving and active in its initial stage, was doomed to failure when the branch moved to Missouri.

A few weeks after Hyrum was settled in Kirtland, he realized the full meaning of Joseph's statement about the "work of the Lord breaking forth on every hand." On June 3, 1831, he planned to attend a general conference of the Church to be held at Kirtland. Parley P. Pratt had brought astonishing news from Western Missouri. His effort to take the gospel to the Indians had failed, but his observations of that goodly land had succeeded in attracting Joseph, Hyrum, and the Saints. Perhaps the Lord was preparing his people for the future westward migration.

When the conference convened Friday morning, facilities were inadequate to seat the two thousand members and investigators in attendance. Hyrum, who sat near the speaker's stand, observed the congregation. He saw the missionaries who had been called in from the field for the conference, among whom were his brothers Samuel and William, and Parley Pratt, Newel Knight, John Whitmer, David Whitmer, Jared Carter, Edward Partridge, Sidney Gilbert, Newel K. Whitney, and Sidney Rigdon. Their presence gave an additional spirit of urgency to the important business of the conference. The increased frequency of new revelations coming to Joseph Smith made it mandatory that he make them known to the people.

In addition to the members and the returned missionaries, many nonmembers were present. The sudden influx of Mormons into that part of Ohio had aroused the curiosity of many citizens; and such a meeting, being the first of its kind in Ohio, provided an opportunity for the people to see the leaders of this new religion. When Joseph called the meeting to order all eyes were upon him. The skeptical and radical element tried to discover the secret of his influence over his followers and were astonished by the gentlemanly bearing of this youthful man with the prominent eyebrows, heavy light brown hair, and meticulous grooming. Their curiosity was partially satisfied, for Joseph looked like a man of influence. He was large in stature and had a natural dignity and poise which marked him as a leader.

As Hyrum and each of the other leaders were called upon to participate, a similar critical appraisal was made. Onlookers noticed that Hyrum was much like Joseph, a large man (six foot two) of light complexion and lowered sideburns whose thin face had as its most notable feature a rather prominent nose. A cordial, relaxed air radiated from his friendly countenance.

During the course of the conference, the Prophet preached a powerful sermon. He was moved upon by the Holy Ghost to prophesy concerning the last days, the gathering of Israel, the second coming of Christ, and the fate of the wicked. He declared that many would suffer martyrdom for the sake of the religion of Jesus Christ.[1]

---

[1] John Whitmer, *History of the Church*. Francis Kirkham, *Source Material concerning the Book of Mormon.*

Other speakers, moved by inspiration from the Lord, propounded words of tremendous power. Some of the missionaries were then ordained elders in the Melchizedek Priesthood. Lyman Wight, after being ordained, prophesied concerning the coming of Christ and God's great work in the last days.[2]

The day following the conference Joseph received a revelation to send twenty-eight elders by twos into the western country to preach along the way until they reached Missouri, a land consecrated to the remnants of Jacob and all other heirs, according to the covenant.[3]

The Colesville Saints had arrived in Ohio during the first week of May 1831, and by June were preparing to continue their emigration to Missouri. Their departure was hastened by the bad faith of one Leman Copley, a Shaking Quaker, who had previously joined the Church and agreed to sell a large tract of land to the Colesville Branch at a fraction of its worth. Later he apostatized and broke his agreement, bringing considerable confusion and disappointment to the Saints who had counted on the land for homes. Edward Partridge, the bishop in charge of the United Order, appealed to the Prophet for advice. The Prophet inquired of the Lord and was told in revelation that the New York group should proceed at once to Missouri, lest their enemies come upon them.[4]

Under the leadership of Newel Knight, the group set out for Missouri. The twelve-hundred-mile journey to Independence took them through rough, partially settled country. Frontier towns and villages lined the rivers and waterways, which were used for traffic and transportation. The roads, little more than muddy pioneer trails, gave scant aid to the travelers. Streams had to be forded or ferried. Traveling was tedious, laborious, and time consuming. But they finally ended their journey at a point twelve miles west of Independence, Jackson County, Missouri, on the edge of the prairie in Kaw Township (now a part of Kansas City), where they established a settlement.

[2]Joseph Smith, *op. cit.*, vol. 1, p. 176.
[3]*Ibid.*, pp. 186-188.
[4]*Idem.*

Such difficulties as distance and rough terrain had little adverse effect upon Hyrum Smith and his companions — John Murdock, Lyman Wight, and John Corrill—as they left Kirtland for the west. To be a missionary, thought Hyrum, was the most acceptable way to please the Lord. When he took affectionate leave of his family on June 14, 1831, he realized that his ambition to be a missionary was about to be fulfilled. This was the beginning of a church service for Hyrum which would continue for an extended period of time.

When Mother Lucy Smith learned that Hyrum's missionary itinerary included Detroit, Michigan, she decided to take her niece Alvira Mack and accompany the missionaries there to visit her brother, General Stephen Mack[5] and his family. The overnight trip over Lake Ontario on the steamer *William Penn* was a pleasant one.

Since the hour was late when they arrived at Detroit, Hyrum suggested going to a tavern for the night rather than to the home of their relatives. The next morning the missionaries were anxious to be about their business, but Mother Smith insisted that they call on Aunt Lovisa Cooper—Alvira's sister—whom they found sick in bed. Alvira asked her sister if Aunt Lucy, who waited in the front room, could come to her bedside. Grudgingly, Mother Smith was permitted to enter the room.

After the usual greetings, Mother Smith said, "Lovisa, I have with me four of my brethren, one of whom is your cousin Hyrum; if I stay, my son and his companions must be invited also."

"Oh, no, no, I never can consent to it!" she exclaimed. "Why aunt, I am so nervous I am scarcely able to see any company."

"Now, Lovisa," Mother Smith replied, "do you know what ails you? I can tell you exactly what it is. There is a good spirit and an evil one operating upon you, and the bad spirit has almost got possession of you. When the good spirit is least agitated, the evil one strives for the entire mastery and sets the good spirit to fluttering because it has so slight a foothold. But you have

[5]Archibald Bennett, *The Improvement Era* "Solomon Mack and His Family," vol. 58, 59. General Mack was one of the first merchants at Detroit, also at Pontiac, Michigan; when he died he left his family an estate of fifty thousand dollars

been so for a long time, and you may yet live many years. These men who are with me are clothed with the authority of the Priesthood, and through their administration you might receive a blessing. Even though you may not be healed, do you not wish to know something about your Savior before you meet him? Furthermore, if you refuse to receive my brethren into your house, I will leave it myself."[6]

The missionaries were invited in and given a sumptuous dinner. They spent most of the day there and in the name of the Lord and by the laying on of hands administered to the sick woman. In the afternoon they left for Pontiac; and when Lovisa learned that they wouldn't be back, she was greatly distressed because she had not urged them to stay and preach.

John Corill and Lyman Wight did not stop at Pontiac but continued on, taking the northern route to Missouri. Hyrum and his companion tried during the day to secure a place to hold a meeting in Pontiac. But failing to do so they wiped the dust of that city from their feet and left for Chicago by way of Pigeon Prairie, Michigan, and on to Peking, where they arrived on June 16. Here they preached six times.

In accordance with instructions from Joseph that they preach the gospel at every opportunity, Hyrum and John remained in the vicinity of Peking for six days. On the last day, a Methodist minister challenged them to prove from the Bible that baptism by immersion was required, and before an assembled group they proceeded to do so. During the debate, the minister became very angry and tramped out of the house in a rage.

Leaving their friends the next day (Thursday) they traveled in three days a distance of seventy-six miles. They preached on Sunday, and on Monday walked thirty-six miles, wading across several large streams of water. They continued to preach as they journeyed through White Pigeon Prairie in St. Joseph County, Michigan, southwest of Detroit. On the following Friday they lodged with some Pottawatamie Indians, taking supper and

---

[6]Lucy Mack Smith, *op. cit.*, pp. 213-214.

breakfast with them. For their kindness, the Indians were given some articles which the missionaries had brought with them.

On July 3, Hyrum and his companion arrived at New London which appeared to be a wide-open, very wild place. Here John Murdock came down with a cold, and they took lodging in a tavern. To protect themselves against marauders, Hyrum slept on the outside of the bed, holding his hand over their clothes which hung on a chair. During the night someone seized his wrist. Hyrum cried out, "Who is there?" at the same time wrenching his wrist free and waking Elder Murdock. They later heard the bedstead in the next room squeak, which was an indication to them that their unwelcome visitor had gone back to bed.[7]

Continuing their journey the next day they reached Salt River where they remained for seven days. Elder Murdock again was ill so they hired William Ivie to take them to Chariton, seventy miles away. For the ride Elder Murdock gave his watch as payment. At Chariton the two missionaries remained a week. During this week their flagging spirits were revived by a meeting with the Prophet Joseph, Sidney Rigdon, David Whitmer, and Harvey Whitback, who were returning from a visit to the Saints at Independence. While they were all together they decided that their group should contribute enough money to purchase a pony for Elder Murdock to ride, and this enabled him and Hyrum to proceed on their way. The ailing Elder Murdock rode the pony fifty miles to Lexington, located on the Missouri River. At Lexington, Hyrum and Elder Murdock slept in an unfinished building where only half the floor was laid. During the night Elder Murdock, suffering from a high fever, attempted to get to an open window on the opposite side of the room. In doing so he stepped off the floor and fell across the uncovered joints. Hyrum, hearing the crash and the groans which followed, sprang from his bed and assisted his companion back to the floor and into bed.[8]

Despite their trials as they pressed westward, Hyrum and his companion followed the command of the Lord to preach the gos-

---

[7]John Murdock *Journal* J. H.: Church Historian's Office, Salt Lake City, Utah.
[8]*Idem.*

pel at every opportunity. In the villages, towns, cities, and frontier homes they found a heterogeneous people: some righteous, some believers, some cultured, and some exactly opposite to all of these. The missionaries often were depressed in spirits over the conditions of wickedness, ignorance, and priestcraft they met on all sides. However, they continued to sow their seed and found that some of it fell on fertile soil. There were people who listened, investigated, and received a conviction of the truth.

When at last they reached Independence, Missouri, these two now-seasoned missionaries met the Saints who had preceded them with a great feeling of rejoicing, which manifested itself in tears of joy.

Little progress had been made by the missionaries who had been sent the previous winter to this frontier region. Oliver Cowdery in a letter to Joseph Smith dated May 7, 1831, stated among other things: ... "I have nothing to write concerning the Lamanites. ... Brother Ziba Peterson and myself went into the east country forty miles ... we called on the people to repent. ... I pray they may find the precious treasure, for it seems to be wholly fallen in the streets."

Independence, Missouri, was a typical frontier village, an outfitting post for western fur traders. On the town square were a five-year-old log courthouse, "two or three stores, and fifteen or twenty houses, mostly of logs." The census for Jackson County in 1830 was 2,823 people, a scattered population living mostly on farms. The town designated as the central place of Zion was located among rolling hills, which alternated with prairie and woodland, about three or four miles south of the Missouri River in the northern part of Jackson County. It lay between two small rivers which flowed northward into the Missouri. The river on the west was called the Big Blue and the one on the east Little Blue.[9]

The rolling, verdant country of Jackson County was unlike the green of New York and Vermont. In this part of the Great

---

[9]Brigham H. Roberts, *Comprehensive History of the Church of Jesus Christ of Latter-day Saints*, (Salt Lake City, Utah, 1921), vol. I, p. 320.

Mississippi Basin there were no extensive forests, only the strips of trees one-half to three miles in width which lined the water courses. A hospitable and friendly folk inhabited the shores of the tree-lined waterway and offered food and lodging, in welcome, to occasional travelers.

On August 9, the Prophet, after holding a conference and dedicating the temple site, accompanied by ten elders, returned to Kirtland. Before Hyrum and his companion returned to Kirtland another conference was held in Jackson County, Missouri. Hyrum discoursed on Zion and the gathering of the Saints there and read part of Psalm 102.[10] There remained no doubt that God would redeem Zion. This sudden realization overwhelmed Hyrum.

Upon his departure for the return trip to Kirtland, Hyrum found it difficult to leave his friends. He assured them that he would return at the first opportunity. The thought of leaving so few Saints, surrounded by primitive nature and a hostile human element, melted his heart. A thousand miles or more would separate them. Only God, he felt, could oversee things for their best good. He realized, to some degree, the problems of settling such a country, and that the keys for the successful building of Zion were obedience, co-operation, and brotherhood. He wondered if the hearts and minds of the members were mature and experienced enough in the gospel to surmount growing obstacles. The implication of such a project was tremendous! Zion in all her glory was to be established — the ancient prophecies of Isaiah concerning the New Jerusalem were about to be fulfilled. Hyrum was sobered and humbled as he pondered the greatness of the project. He was now able to appraise objectively the work that must be done and his responsibility to help guarantee its success.

---

[10]*Far West Record No. 6*, Church Historians Office, Salt Lake City, Utah.

CHAPTER IX

HYRUM THE MISSIONARY

It was late in September when Hyrum Smith arrived home in Kirtland from his long and arduous journey to western Missouri. His family rejoiced and gave thanks to the Lord for his safe return. Harvest time seemed a favorite time for the Smith family to meet together. At their gathering, Hyrum narrated his experiences as ample proof of the Lord's blessings, and those who remained at home briefed him on the town news and on the employment of the family members. Mother Smith had even taken in boarders.

Hyrum was often seen with his brothers — in groups of two, three, or four — walking down Kirtland's main thoroughfare, with the townspeople crowded around them. The admiring Saints eagerly anticipated hearing the experiences, advice, and counsel of the kindly Hyrum.

With the announcement that Zion was to be established, many began to formulate plans for the trek west. Each week brought an increasing number of strangers into Kirtland, investigators bent on determining for themselves the truth of the gospel message. Hyrum made himself available to explain the doctrines of the new church and to supply information about the gathering to the land of Zion.

Several problems had to be met during the fall and winter of 1831: first, the settling of Jackson County, Missouri; second, the establishing of facilities at Kirtland for the headquarters of the Church; and third, the developing a canon of scripture by making certain revisions and corrections of the Bible and making available new scripture. The new scripture included revelations pertaining to such local problems as investigators coming to Kirtland expecting a sign or a miracle to confirm their faith. The status of such people and the iniquitous implications thereof were given in a revelation known as section 63 of the Doctrine and Covenants. The miraculous events leading to the establishment of the Church such as the visions and the bringing forth of the gold plates were not to be considered in the same category as a person seeking a sign from heaven.

In the records Hyrum's name is listed with others who attended a conference at John Johnson's home October 11th, for the purpose of instructing the elders of the Church in the proper procedure of conducting a meeting, and to decide on a policy of which leaders of the Church should be reimbursed. Among those who were giving full time to the Church were as follows: Joseph and Hyrum Smith; Peter, Christian, and Jacob Whitmer; Samuel, and Don Carlos Smith, and Joseph's scribe, Sidney Rigdon.[1]

Two weeks later another conference was held at Orange which included twelve high priests, seventeen elders, four priests, three teachers, and four deacons, together with a large congregation. During the two days, Tuesday and Wednesday, October 24, 25, 1831, part of the business transacted was the enlargement of the finance committee on which Hyrum was called to serve with Simeon Carter, Orson Hyde, and Emer Harris.

Many of the brethren expressed themselves as willing to consecrate their all to the cause. The following expression may well apply to Hyrum when he heard his brother Joseph say, "I have nothing to consecrate to the Lord of the things of the earth, yet I feel to consecrate myself and family, and am thankful that God has given me a place among his Saints, and I am willing to labor for their good." Joseph speaking of those who should receive material aid from the Church said: "The Lord held the Church bound to provide for the families of the absent Elders while they were proclaiming the Gospel."[2]

Later — November 1, 1831 — another conference was held in order that important business might be transacted. The need for new scripture was acute, especially for the missionaries. It was announced that the revelations were to be published in book form.

---

[1]Joseph Smith, *op. cit.*, vol. I, 236.
[2]*Ibid.*, p. 220.

This would help correct many false ideas on religion. The Lord had revealed the preface for the proposed book which was to be titled The Book of Commandments. Three thousand copies were to be printed at Independence, Missouri.

The great press of business necessitated another conference at Hiram, Ohio, November 12th. Among the several problems to be considered was a report from Hyrum on the work of the finance committee. He spoke of being anxious that missionaries be called to work where they were most needed. Aside from business, such meetings provided an opportunity to develop the spirit of brotherhood and acted as a school to teach the gospel. The leaders felt that there was need of such occasions for learning, contemplation, and spiritual uplift. Each conference also marked giant steps in the development of the church organization.

Beginning in November, Hyrum resolved to keep a journal. He was aware of the advice and instruction to all missionaries to keep a daily journal. Accordingly, he obtained a notebook from which he cut about sixty blue-lined sheets 3½ x 4½ inches in size and fitted them into a black oilcloth cover decorated on the outside with red and yellow hand-painted flowers. With a needle threaded with flax string, he sewed the pages along the crease to the oilcloth back.[3]

The brief jottings of Hyrum reveal the strength of his faith and his determination as a missionary. The fading ink obscures some of the words, but the first entry reads:

On November the 18th, 1831, George S. Gaimes ordained an Elder of the Church of Christ under the hand of Elder Hyrum Smith.

David Eliot was ordained Priest the 20th of November in the year of our Lord 1831 under the hand of Joseph Smith, Senior.

I, Hyrum Smith and Reynolds Cahoon the disciples of Jesus Christ being called and chosen of God in these the last days to preach the Gospel, which is to be proclaimed to all nations before the end shall come. I, Hyrum, having traveled through the various parts of the continent which is the Continent of America — even up to Zion and through the mercy of God have

[3]See cut.

returned to my place of residence whence I started from and often resting for a short time and traveling and proclaiming in these regions, I Hyrum and Reynolds on the 13th of December in the year 1831, the second year of the rise of the Church of Christ — started to journey eastward — the first day of our journeyings called for an opportunity to proclaim in the town Concord but no admittance; traveled till night in the town of lavory (sic).

Stopped and labored with a sectarian Priest but his heart was hard and unpenetrable and mocked the truths of God but we bore testimony against him to his own destruction if he did not repent.

From thence to the town of (Thompson) and labored with the members of the church at (Thompson) the best part of two days and found but little or no success. Labored with David and the son-in-law of P. Copley. They expressed their desire to remain in the church after exhorting them to faithfulness left them and journeyed eastward to the town of Rome. Held meeting at the house of James Balwin (sic) on the Sabbath day — on Monday visited the house of Joseph Scott and labored with them in the Gospel. Consenting to their request and held a meeting on Monday evening — after baptized Hannah Shover — On Tuesday visited the house of a brother and labored with them and blessed their children — Wednesday, labored with a Baptist priest and bore testimony against him with power and (indistinct).

Started from thence to go to the town of Bloomfield. Stayed all night labored with the family. They were formerly from Connecticut. They spurned at offered Mercy — On the morning of the 24th started on our journey. Passed through the town of Farmington and labored with Brother Bee and from thence to the town of Hiram and the 25th and 26th went to Savanah and heard the exposition upon Booth's letters[4] delivered by Brother Sidney. From thence to Hiram and from thence to Weatherfield. Labored and bore testimony unto them of the works of God in these the last days and from thence to Kirtland to our own homes to rest from our laboring for a little season.[5]

Prior to Hyrum's assignment with Brother Cahoon he had been ordained a high priest and had accompanied Elder Orson Hyde on a mission to Elyria, Loraine County; and Florence, Erie County, Ohio. They were privileged to convert and baptize many and to organize these new members into three branches of the Church. Several sick persons were brought to them and were healed by the power of faith and the priesthood. On their return

[4]Joseph Smith, *op. cit.*, vol. I, pp. 215-216. Ezra Booth, the first apostate, published material against the Church.
[5]*Hyrum Smith's Diary*, in possession of his descendants. Manuscript appears as in the original except for minor corrections in spelling.

Elder Hyde wrote in his journal: "I found Hyrum a pleasant and agreeable companion, a wise counsellor, a father, and a guide."[6]

In spite of the cold winter weather, Hyrum was constantly on the move as a missionary and as an officer in the Church. His earnest application made it possible for the Prophet and Sidney Rigdon at Hiram, Ohio, to continue their work on the scriptures without interruption.

It is quite likely that Hyrum spent Christmas and the New Year holiday with his wife, Jerusha, and their two little girls, Lovina and Mary. During this season they visited with friends and cared for his parents who were occupying a part of his home. After catching up on his business affairs, he continued his missionary labors, recording his activities:

Saturday the 14th of January (1832) after resting a few days from my labors started again for the visit [to] the churches in the regions westward stopped at the house of a disciple in the town of Uclet in order to labor with the people—a congregation was called but the wicked raged in such a manner that we could not keep order and were obliged to dismiss the meeting. We adjourned to Cleveland and from thence three miles south of Cleveland and labored with some old acquaintances but little or no success—from thence to Flourance passing through Amherst, held a meeting at Brother Moses Dayly's on the 19th of January — having the good pleasure through the mercy of God of meeting a goodly number of our Brothers and Sisters from New London — the 19th visited Brother Blackman he being sick he called upon myself and Elder Hyde to pray for and lay our hands upon him—accordingly we did—and he began to recover from that time forth. We left the house of Brother Blackman on the morning of the 20th. Visited a neighbor two miles south-east and held a meeting in the evening on the 22nd being on the Sabbath day. Held a meeting in the forks of the Vermillion river and in the evening of the same day at the house of Brother John Dayly's and from thence to Brother Armean Carters in Amherst. On the evening of the 24th arrived at Brother Gideon Carters—on the 25th attended conference—on the 26th-27th returned home to Kirtland—28th commenced at home in temporal concerns for a little season.

February the 2nd in the year of our Lord 1832 — it being the 2nd month—

Labored in a conference meeting with Calvin — (indistinct) which was called in consequence of his open rebellion against the laws of God. At-

6*Idem.*

tended meeting in the evening of the same day and ordained Brother (Asa Dada) to the High Priesthood of the holy order of God.

February the 7th 1832

Attended meeting in the evening and baptized Harriet by the laying on of the hands.

On the evening of the 10th of February held council with the bishops and brother Cahoon in Kirtland, to counsel concerning the hiring the Mourley farm and also concerning idlers and diverse things.

Was ordained an assistant for the Bishop and also was Reynolds Cahoon.

On the Evening of the 11th held a council with brother Roberts concerning the Tavern stand—February 21st called for to lay hands upon Sister Huggard she being sick—Other elders were called Elders Fredric Williams, Reynolds Cahoon, Lincoln Hoskins was baptized by Brother Cahoon and confirmed by my own hand on the same day—the 21st of Feb. 1832.

On Monday on the 2nd month on the 27th day of the month Reynolds and myself were called to brother Dick Bless to lay our hands on a sick child accordingly we went but to no avail. On Wednesday of the same month myself called to preach a funeral sermon. . .who both departed this life a few days before. Held a council on the first day of the third which is called March, with the bishop and then Joseph, Sidney, Reynold's father and go myself.

March 10th 1832, brother Titus Billings ordained an Elder under the hands of brother Thomas Marsh. And also . . . to take the lead of the Kirtland Church while traveling to the land of Zion. March 13th held a meeting at Kirtland for the purpose of covenanting all to God. On the evening of the same day the Saints of God that are going to Zion covenanted to consecrate their properties to the bishop of Zion after their arrival.

March 23, labored for to find a place Biglow, Let Sister Marsh have two of potatoes 4/50 March 21st—shoed sister Marshes oxen—$1. April of the 3rd and 4th went to Hiram and returned with a brother Reynolds Cahoon for a wise purpose in God.

Monday 9th sold 12 books to brothers Gideon Carter and Sylvester Smith, elders in the Church of Christ.

Sister Marsh, Dr to 1-bu potatoes 2/25 April 10 do two bushel.

April 11 4/50 Sister Marsh Dr. plowing 75.

April 22, myself and Reynolds went to Mayfield and labored with the church. 23rd held a conference and tried the case of brother Thayer and B-rbigs. . (indistinct) both became penitent.

April 25 received of Ansonclions (?) 1.00 for the Evening and Morning Star.[7]

---

[7]Hyrum Smith, *op. cit.*

His diary reveals an intimate, day-by-day account of his ministry. Periodically be returned home to look after his temporal affairs. He was versatile in applying himself to many different situations. He could shoe an ox, plow, sell books, trade potatoes, preach a funeral sermon, try a case, administer to the sick, ordain, rebuke the wicked, give counsel, aid the poor, perform ordinances, and preach the gospel.

He considered himself called and chosen of God, a disciple of Jesus Christ, to perform an important work in the last days. He and his missionary companion were ordained assistants to the bishop. His mission field was to be in various parts of the continent of America. His first mission was to Zion, and he acknowledged the mercy of God on his safe arrival home from the mission field. He did not consider the Missouri Mission by itself a complete fulfillment of his call. He spoke of his home as a place "from whence I started from, often resting for a short time and traveling and proclaiming in these regions."

There was to be no set time for Hyrum to complete his mission. It was to be a continuous one with various companions. Before the year ended he had taken Reynolds Cahoon with him into the eastern region.

Nothing was recorded about what his stipend might be from the Church nor that of the others who were eligible for such consideration. His diary reveals a kind and altruistic nature, particularly in helping the poor and the widows and in counseling his friends and neighbors. Great courage was demonstrated in debating with ministers and preachers and bearing witness of the truth and divinity of Jesus Christ. The years of 1830 and 1831 was a period of spiritual and mental growth for Hyrum Smith. He had, like Paul of old, been set on fire with the spirit of his new calling, for the inspiration of his words were impressive to those who listened to him. He spoke in the vernacular of the times with power and authority and was developing into a person with a missionary zeal, an individual in his own right endowed with transcendant qualities of character.

CHAPTER X

A SHEPHERD OF THE FLOCK

When the year 1832 dawned, it was apparent to Hyrum
Smith that he was to be a shepherd of the flock at Kirtland, Ohio.
The second year in the life of the Church revealed the need of
someone who could personally administer the affairs of the
organization. More important work such as receiving and recording new revelations, revising the Bible, planning and holding conferences, and directing the missionary work, occupied most of the
Prophet Joseph's time. During the spring and summer months
he planned another visit to Jackson County, Missouri. Hyrum
agreed to take care of affairs at home.

The intensification of the missionary program was creating
new problems. Hyrum and Joseph spent many hours together
conversing on them. Often the Smiths as a family would meet
together. Their united spirit gave the infant Church strength
and stability.

The task of setting up a new Church and teaching new doctrines in the presence of prevailing organizations with their set
works was a considerable one. The initial success of the new
Church offended the members of other churches. Proselyting
among such an "enlightened" Christian folk was to place the
converted in the "unsaved," "heathen," category. However,
many of those who were disgruntled and dissatisfied in traditional churches were converted to The Church of Jesus Christ of
Latter-day Saints.

The church leaders were well aware of such reaction among
contemporary religious groups. The influence of Hyrum Smith
with his kindness and understanding was felt by the investigators,
for often it was the expression of love and sincerity more than
logic of the scriptures and reason that brought about conversion.
The diversity of personalities drawn as by a magnet into an orbit
of new and strange beliefs created a perplexing problem. Many

were like children who came to be taught a new way of life. Others had deep-seated beliefs or philosophies based on old creeds which must be erased before they could accept new ideas. This was most difficult for some, a few of whom refused to make a clean break with the past. The new theological beliefs were radically different from those of human depravity and predestination — they were different from salvation through the sacraments or sudden regeneration. The idea of a personal God, a Father of our spirits who could communicate his will to man was hard to accept. New revelation impugned the Bible. Some reasoned that if the Bible contained all of God's word what need was there for new scripture? But the power of reason supported the missionaries. If God is the same yesterday, today, and forever, why would he favor generations past with knowledge and cease giving needed knowledge to those since Bible times?

The task of amalgamating a wide diversity of personalities into a new society required a strong and confident leadership. There had to be a meeting of minds on vital issues. When situations arose needing immediate attention, the Prophet would seek counsel. His brother, Hyrum, was among the first to whom he would turn. There was no precedent to follow.

The Church, as revealed to Joseph Smith, was radically different from all existing churches. Its doctrines were fascinating to contemplate and satisfying to the soul.

* * *

Hyrum Smith had been a missionary long enough to realize the great importance of scripture. People of the frontier believed in their Bible. The dearth of literature and an abundance of time had favored the good book as a source of intellectual stimulation. Therefore, it became necessary that the scriptures in as pure a form as possible be made accessible to the missionaries.

The church looked toward Hiram, Ohio,[1] for more new scripture. Already the word of the Lord in pamphlet form was distributed among the missionaries. The Book of Doctrine and Covenants was being created but not yet under that name; and its

---

[1]Hiram, Ohio, was located about 35 miles southeast of Kirtland, Ohio.

revelations were being written in the vernacular and adapted to the times. The book contained principles of the gospel which were as ancient as Adam, but the language expressing them was new.

In the seclusion of the Johnson home at Hiram, the young seer, Joseph Smith, and his scribe, Sidney Rigdon, had made much progress in the work on the scriptures. Hyrum had taken the role of leader at Kirtland to shield his younger brother from the press of daily church affairs; but the privacy at Hiram was only temporary, for with the breaking up of winter and the drying of the roads, the leaders would soon be on the move again. Plans for increased activity were laid well in advance for the year 1832.

Near the end of March, rumors were heard of enemy action against Joseph. Such information, via the grapevine, was discounted until more tangible evidence appeared. On his last visit to the village of Hiram, Hyrum had mentioned the rumor to Joseph. There were several enemies who had made threatening remarks. A few enemies were later identified as Olmsted, Eli, Edward, and John Jr., sons of John Johnson. In addition, there were apostates Ezra Booth and Simonds Ryder, former ministers of the Methodist and Campbellite churches. Ryder, who had been an elder, turned against the Prophet when he discovered his name misspelled by Joseph in a letter. Instead of "Ryder" it was "Rider." Ryder claimed that if God's prophet failed to spell correctly, he could not be a true prophet.[2]

Joseph returned to Kirtland from a trip to Missouri and made his report. The success of the recent trip to Zion was evidenced in the reports of Joseph, Sidney Rigdon, and Newel K. Whitney. The Lord had given more light on the importance of righteous living and on the seriousness of failing to live up to the commandments. Where much is given, he told the Saints, much was expected. Every man was told to improve his talents, and to be equal in claim on the management of the stewardship according to his wants and needs, as long as his wants were just.

Soon after Joseph's return from Missouri, Hyrum and Jeru-

---

[2]Joseph Smith, op. cit., vol. I, p. 261.

sha suffered the loss of their little Mary, born June 29, 1829, at Palmyra, New York; but their oldest daughter, Lovina, almost five, helped to assuage their sorrow, and they were further comforted by the birth on September 22, of a baby boy whom they named John. This boy was destined to succeed his father as patriarch to the Church.

Hyrum expressed his feelings of sorrow and anguish in his journal:

> I, Hyrum, on the 28th day of January after returning home from conference went to work with mine hands for the support of my family. I and also in Churches whenever an opportunity permitted not suffering much tribulation until the 29th day of May, then I was called to view a scene which brought sorrow and mourning. Mary was called from time to eternity on the 29th day of May. She expired in my arms — such a day I never before experienced, and oh may God grant that we may meet her again on the great day of redemption to part no more.[3]

During the summer of 1832, Hyrum continued to keep his journal, recording sundry transactions. Money was scarce and much of the trading was done in kind. It will be noted how the Book of Mormon was used as an object of barter.

Continuing in his diary Hyrum recorded:

> June 7, 1832, Elder Thayer Dr. (debtor) took four Books of Mormon. June 7 went to Parkem with Brother Parley Pratt and baptized three and confirmed them, from thence to the town of Hiram.
> Pheeleresill (Indistinct) and bought nineteen sheet of Brother Follet and paid eight books which is ten dollars and paid ten dollars toward cows I bought of Slina.
> June 7, carried Joseph's calf skin to the tanners to be tanned. June 11th carried my calf skin to the tanners the 18th one more skin to the tanners the 30th one for Joseph to be tanned.
> June 30, 1832, received of brother Dibble $3 for the assistance of the poor and also of Reynolds Cahoon 1 bus. corn for the poor.
> Pd to the poor 1 bus. corn for /.50 ditto 16 lbs veal - 3 cents per lb. 48 cents June 27—sold 2 books to Joel Johnson July 4, received of Joel Johnson 3 dollars. Joel Johnson, Dr. (debtor) *Book of Mormon* July 12, 1832 Gilbert

---

[3]Hyrum Smith, *Journal.*

and Company Dr. 2 days and 2/3 of a day 20—$2.50 July 10, 1832 Reynolds Cahoon Dr. to 4 *Books of Mormon* $5—to $1 cash July 16, 1832 to Reynolds Cahoon—cow $12.

Diana Blanchard took away from here July 8, 1832—kept Sister Blanchard 2 w'ks and 4 children—July 1832, July 8th took Sister Blanchard to keep. July 27, 1832 bought of Zebedee Coltrin one horse saddle and bridle $28. Paid to Zebedee one watch $18 and 16 *Books of Mormon* which books he left in my charge. The said books he is to receive himself on order.

/s/ Hyrum Smith

July 22 visited the Mayfield Church held a meeting and preached to them. July 27th a conference of High Priest were called for the purpose of ordaining Zebedee Coltrin to the High Priest to the Holy Order of God. He was ordained by my hands this by the voice of the conference

President
Newel K. Whitney
/s/Reynolds Cahoon
H. Smith

July 27, 1832 - Brother Sherman Dr. 8 Books of Mormon received of brother Sherman $4 in advance for the books.

July 28, 1832 brother Sydney was ordained to the high Priesthood for the second time.

July 30, bought (Indistinct) one horse saddle and bridle—Paid for it 52 dollars and 75 cents. Paid 10 dollars in cash and 35 of the *Books of Mormon*.

Aug. 6th, 1832, pd Zebedee Coltrin 6 *Books of Mormon* out of the 16 I was to pay for the horse I bought of him.

August 21, 1832 baptized Fannie Simmons.

August 21, 1832 Thomas and Simmons Dr. to 1 *Book of Mormon* $1.25.

August 26, 1832—went to Painsville with horses and wagon to Sister Vienny and Sister Gray . . mger. Grovenner and group went on the 29th and brought the remainder of her goods. September 9, 1832 sat in conference of High Priests and ordained Joseph Wood and David Patten High Priests by my own hand. Their place of residence Michigan.

Joseph Smith Dr. to me September 1832 to one horse $55 2 cows $25. 1 heifer $7 18 sheep $55 1 plow $7 16 pigs $8 2 hogs $13 due me on settlement.

September 1, 1832 James Angel was baptized into the church of Christ by the hand of Zebedee Coltrin 24 September and was confirmed by the hand of Hyrum Smith 25 September.

John Smith was born September 22, 1832 and was confirmed or blessed the 8th day in the evening by the hand of his grandfather, Joseph.

Hyrum Smith's home at Kirtland, Ohio. (Photo taken in 1954 by P. H. Corbett.)

Jerusha Barden Smith, wife of Hyrum Smith. (Courtesy of Patriarch Eldred G. Smith.)

September 7, 1832 I baptized David Clough into the Church of Christ and was confirmed by the hand of Joseph Coe.

William Cowdery Dr. October 14, 1832 to ½ Bu. Corn 25 cents—to one peck of potatoes ½ bu. corn in the ear 2/25 to ½ bu corn shelled 2/25 to one *Book of Mormon* one dollar.

I Hyrum on the tenth month of the year of our Lord one thousand eight hundred thirty two, baptized Lucy Hodges in the name of the Lord Jesus unto the Church of the living God.

William Cowdery, December 29, 1832 11 lbs. pork @ 6 cents a lb.

Here Hyrum discontinued his entries. He kept no journal until the following spring. He failed to mention any of Joseph's difficulties at Hiram or the trouble with Sidney Rigdon, except to say that Rigdon had been ordained a high priest for the second time. Perhaps the Prophet had dropped him from the priesthood for disciplinary measures and had later reinstated him.

The miscellaneous activities of Hyrum recorded in his diary afford a glimpse into his private affairs. Because of the shortage of circulation medium (money) accounts of various transactions had to be carefully kept of various commodities, whether labor, produce, books, or items such as watches, saddles, etc.

While attending to his temporal affairs, he did not neglect the work of the ministry. He visited at various places, called meetings, and "preached to them." In order to attend to official duties he called a conference for the purpose of ordaining a man to the office of high priest. He wrote, "He was ordained by my hands this by the voice of the conference." He baptized and confirmed members, "in the name of the Lord Jesus unto the Church of the living God."

He took a mother and her four children into his home for two weeks, and then helped her on her way; and another person as a charity case, for he wrote, "took Sister . . . to keep." On another occasion he went to "Painesville with horse and wagon to Sister . . . and . . . and brought the remainder of her goods."

Hyrum's altruism was demonstrated when he took a calfskin and one for Joseph to be tanned Also, his account with Joseph indicated he owed him for itemized list of livestock, including one horse, two cows, one heifer, 18 sheep, 16 pigs (small) and two hogs; he listed also one plow, a total of appraised value of $174 "due me on account." He carefully discriminated between business and charity in his transactions where property was exchanged and monetary value was recorded, even with his brother, Joseph.

During July Hyrum received the first issue of the *Evening and Morning Star* which contained a number of revelations and topics of spiritual truth to gratify and enlighten the humble inquiries of the Saints and investigators. The brethren at Kirtland were delighted with the work and that so small a band of Saints had grown so strong in so short a time as to be able to issue a paper of their own.

Toward fall the missionaries began returning from their missions. From their various fields of labor they reported their successes and failures, giving an account of their stewardship where property of the Church was in their hands. Many new members had been baptized and many new branches organized, all of which caused Hyrum to rejoice.

The missionary work in the east was making satisfactory progress. On September 8, 1832, in the *Niles Register*, appeared the following: "Two preachers visited Boston and baptized fifteen converts. Certain of these converts gave considerable sums of money into stock and were to depart for the promised land in Jackson County, Missouri — the precious spot having been lately discovered."[4]

The favorable reports were offset by worry and anxiety over the progress of the Church in Missouri. Because of unrighteousness among the new members then converging on Zion, all was not going well. All were not joining the United Order, others who had joined the Church were apostatizing.

On November 6, the day after Joseph had returned from a six-week mission to New York and Boston, Joseph's household, like that of Hyrum's, was blessed with the birth of a baby boy whom they named Joseph Smith, III.

While Hyrum and Joseph were rejoicing over their new sons,

---

[4]*Niles Register, op. cit.,* September 8, 1832.

a horse and wagon pulled up in front of Father Smith's home with three serious-faced gentlemen from New York. One was Joseph Young, a former Methodist preacher; one was his younger brother, Brigham, age thirty, also a former Methodist; and the third was their friend, Heber C. Kimball, who was driving his own outfit and was an ex-Baptist of Irish descent, also just thirty years old. They had arrived in Kirtland a few hours earlier and had spent a few minutes visiting with the John P. Greene family who had moved into Kirtland a few days before. The Greenes had first introduced Brigham Young to the Book of Mormon, an act which had resulted in his conversion.

One of the three knocked at the door and inquired for Joseph. Upon being told that Joseph, with Hyrum and his brothers, was cutting wood nearby, the men lost no time in finding the Smith brothers who were getting in their winter's fuel supply. Of this occasion Brigham Young later wrote: "Here my joy was full at the privilege of shaking the hand of the Prophet of God and receiving the sure testimony by the spirit of prophecy that he was all that any man could believe him to be a true prophet."[5]

The conversion of Brigham Young and Heber C. Kimball to the Church added great strength to the governing body. Their talents, skills, and versatility were immediately in demand. They became apt pupils of Joseph, Hyrum Smith, and others in the work of the ministry, and in time filled their particular niche and performed a work beyond the province and possibility of the present leaders.

During December the indefatigable Hyrum took a Miss Tyler two miles on an ox sled to Lake Erie, cut a hole through the ice, and baptized and confirmed her. The ordinance could have been performed earlier in the year had it not been opposed by her father.[6]

At the close of the year 1832, Hyrum Smith was greatly worried over conditions among the Saints in Missouri. He met often in council meetings giving suggestions on the course of ac-

---

[5]Joseph Smith, *op. cit.*, vol. I, p. 297.
[6]*Scraps of Biography*, Tenth Book Faith Promoting Section, Juvenile Instructor Office, (Salt Lake City, Utah, 1883).

tion. His little family was his main concern, and he feared for their material comfort and for the welfare of the widows and orphans, to whom he gave what aid he could. Out of the kindness of his heart, he took people into his own family,[7] at the same time realizing his own inability to support them. The financial help voted by the council was insufficient to meet the needs of his growing family, for he wrote in his journal, "I worked with mine hands for the support of my family."[8]

But there developed no rancor or malice in the man, even though he had to toil for his necessities. This new society was to be built on a foundation of love, faith, and service, not on the basis of economic advantage.

The building of Kirtland revealed the character of Hyrum Smith. He had set himself like flint against adversity, and he exhibited a complete dedication of purpose. He had a mission to fill.

---

[7]Hannah Grinnels, Margaret Bryon, Jane Wilson, and George Miles were a few that made their home with Hyrum.
[8]*Supra,* (footnote 6 has these words.

CHAPTER XI

A CITIZEN OF KIRTLAND

The year 1833 was an important one for Hyrum Smith. He was thrust into several roles which increased his stature as a leader in the community of Kirtland, Ohio. Because of the demands upon his time and his responsibility to his growing family, there were several things which had to be done that weighed heavily on his mind.

One of the problems from the beginning of his sojourn at Kirtland, Ohio, was adequate housing. The converging of the Mormons on this western village created an acute need for places to live. The Smiths had had to share one home when they first arrived from New York State, but as the building of new houses got underway the situation was relieved. It may be supposed that Hyrum at this time acquired a home. The records are silent as to whether he built or purchased it ready for occupancy. The home he and his family occupied is still in an excellent state of preservation. It was constructed from native timber, two stories high, with an architectural appearance typical of those times. [1] (See cut.)

No doubt the home gave Hyrum added security and enabled him to conduct his business and fulfil his social obligations. There was need for extra accommodations for overnight guests and charity cases he frequently took into his home. If his capacity was limited to take care of a worthy person he made every effort to find aid and support among the membership of the Church.

---

[1]The home is located on Joseph's street in Kirtland, Ohio, Route 2, Willowby Street (present address). The house was purchased by the Reorganized Church of Jesus Christ of Latter Day Saints from Mrs. Dora McFarlane, a neighbor. The author visited the home in 1954. The former owner pointed out a medium-sized room located in the center of the ground floor with a door in the center of each of the four walls. The doors were convenient for escape if the occupants were suddenly attacked. It was in this room that Joseph Smith spent much of his time on the revision of the Bible.

Hyrum's blessings were constantly acknowledged as he addressed the Saints, in his prayers, both public, private, and in the family circle. In his journal appears a diversity of accounts of certain people who may have been in his personal employment. The thoughts he expresses about Joseph, his brother, his place of birth and the acknowledgment of his blessings, indicate the things uppermost in his mind, and no doubt these sentiments were often expressed and referred to among the people with whom he associated.

The journal, after a lapse of time, is continued:

April 18, 1833, Harvey Stanley Foreman on account labor by the month — for eight months to the 14th of November. H. Stanley Dr. (debtor) to met pair of shoes, calf skin topping boots 50 cents, to two by six pense cash.

The remainder of his journal records his business transactions and journal notes.

Accounts:
        Ezra Thayer
        Sidney Rigdon
        Silas Smith
        F. G. Williams
        Joseph Smith, Senior
        William Smith

H. Smith was born in Tunbridge, Orange County, State of Vermont.

I, Hyrum Smith received a blessing under the hands of my father Joseph Smith, Senior,[2] President Rigdon, my brother Joseph Junior, the Prophet of the Living God who was raised up in the last days: I was blessed with the privilege of obtaining the desires of my heart in all things.

Sold to Simeon Carter 2 books, 2 to Brother Sherman, May 31, 1832.

Jenkins Salisbury, Dr. to me one book 10 lines $1.25 May 31, 1832.

July 30, 1832, Sister Blanshard to me one *Book of Mormon.*

Jenkins Salisbury another *Book of Mormon.* Took Sister Marsha's cow to keep March 21, 1832. Pasturage on the cow.

Note: The dates on entries in the diary are not chronological, they may have been added as an afterthought, among the 1833 entries.

---

[2]See text of blessing chapter 12.

March 3, 1832, Sold to a peddler 6 Books of Mormon and received pay as follows:

6 yards calico
13 yards cotton cloth
4 yards calico
4 tin pans
Sieve tin
One cheese weighing 6 lbs. 5 ounces
1 paper of tins (pins)
January 31, 1832
Presented to William McKlevin 8 copies of Book of Mormon $10
To Samuel H. Smith, Dr. 8 copies of Book of Mormon $10
Ezra Thayer (to) two Books of Mormon $2.50[3]

Hyrum's journal also reveals how he obtained some of his household necessities and the price of the Book of Mormon.

It is probably at this time that with a steady increase in population and new homes and buildings being erected that the Smith family was beginning to feel more secure. Most of the church leaders had homes of their own and it was time now to build the Lord's house. The Prophet Joseph had received a revelation concerning the building of a temple or a house of the Lord at Kirtland but had as yet failed to take action. Perhaps the unstable condition of the Mormons in Missouri indirectly contributed to the delay.

The construction of such an edifice would require hard work and sacrifice. When the meeting was held to plan methods of erecting the proposed structure, there was no one as well situated and endowed as Hyrum to work as chairman of the building committee. On June 1, 1833, the committee which included Reynolds Cahoon and Jared Carter drew up a circular to stress the necessity of such a building and to remind the membership of the need of their faith, prayers, labor, and money, for this building was to be a meetinghouse, a temple, and a school all in one. Despite the prompt action of the building committee, the Saints were slow in getting started on the building; and so urgent was

---

[3]End of entries in diary until 1835.

the need for a temple that their tardiness brought a rebuke from the Lord:

> For ye have sinned against me a very grievous sin, in that ye have not considered . . . in all things, that I have given unto you concerning the building of mine house; . . . it is my will that you should build a house.[4]

This rebuke stirred immediate action. Hyrum and his committee met in a meeting called by the Prophet and listened attentively to a discussion of the architectural plans for the building. The size and the dimensions had been revealed by the Lord. They agreed with Joseph that a house of the Lord should not be built out of lumber or logs as was suggested, and a careful outline was made as to what should be done. At the close of the meeting a site was selected for the building. They chose the northwest corner of a wheat field which was part of the farm where the family of Joseph Smith, Sr., was then living. It had been sown by Hyrum and his brothers the previous fall.

The fence was removed and the standing grain was leveled to prepare a place for the building. Hyrum, with Reynolds Cahoon, broke the ground. With their own hands they commenced digging a trench for the wall on June 5, 1833, and completed it that same day, Hyrum having declared that he would strike the first blow on the house. On the following Monday, the brethren went to work on the house with great ambition; and though only thirty families of Saints now remained in Kirtland, they did not permit the work to stop until the building was completed.

With building stone available at a quarry near Kirtland, Lorenzo D. Young hitched up his team and took Hyrum, Joseph, Brigham Young, and Reynolds Cahoon to see whether or not the right quality of stone could be obtained there and if the amount would be sufficient. They decided that the stone would do, and after putting part of a load on the wagon they returned to town where the rock was put on the temple site.[5]

---

[4]D&C 95: 3, 11.
[5]Lorenzo D. Young, *Journal*, J. H. June, 1833.

The days that followed were busy ones for Hyrum. On July 23rd, he with five elders laid the cornerstone of the temple[6] amidst an atmosphere of solemnity which made the occasion memorable. Hyrum's enthusiasm was similar to that of the others present, and unitedly they felt the urgency of constructing the temple at once. This building project was a forerunner for the building of other temples in this the Dispensation of the Fulness of Times, a period when God would restore all important principles and ordinances for the benefit of mankind.

No doubt Hyrum felt keenly his responsibility as chairman of the building committee. He was aware that he must solicit the co-operation of everyone. He, therefore, urged the Saints to make the temple their first consideration, telling them that labor on the farms had to be shared with that on the house of the Lord. His plea brought a gratifying response, and fortunately, under his leadership there developed a spirit of unity and sacrifice sufficient to soon make their dreams a reality.

With the arrival of Uncle John Smith and his family from Potsdam, New York, more willing hands were added to the work. Uncle John's fifteen year-old son, George Albert, who was destined to play an important part in the growth of the Church, went immediately to work. Since Uncle John was the first of Hyrum's paternal relatives to join the Church, there was double cause for rejoicing at their arrival at this time. Of this occasion George A. Smith wrote:

Arrived at Kirtland, Ohio, May 25, 1833. We were greeted with a hearty welcome from my cousin, Joseph. He conducted us to his father, who lived in a large log house, spending the summer quarrying and hauling rock for the temple. It was built of bluish sandstone, and the basement story, corner, window-caps and sills, were of neatly cut stone, and afterwards cemented and finished off to match the basement. The first two loads of rock taken to the Temple grounds were hauled June 5th from the standard quarry by Harvey Stanley and myself.[7]

---

[6]*Journal History*, July, 1833. Also Joseph Smith, *History of the Church*.
[7]*Memoirs of George A. Smith*, President's Office, Salt Lake City, Utah, p. 10.

On September 22-23, 1832, Hyrum sat in conference with the brethren. During the conference period, a special meeting of the twelve high priests was called to consider a letter from Brother Sidney Gilbert, W. W. Phelps, and John Corrill of Jackson County, Missouri. Grave problems had arisen among the Saints in Zion, problems such as too many poor people; not enough saintliness due to pride, jealously, and a lack of co-operation; and the well-to-do who hesitated to consecrate their property into the new social order known as the "United Order."

When the letter was read, it was observed that the Missouri brethren expressed hope that there (Missouri), the church headquarters soon would be established. The letter stated that the little branch needed the presence of Joseph, Hyrum, and the other brethren. At the moment this was not possible because the proximity of Kirtland to the larger centers of population to the east and north provided better opportunity for missionary work. For the time being, contact with Missouri could be maintained only by frequent letters and visits.

Two months later came another letter from Sidney Gilbert, this one a gloomy message dated December 10, and followed on December 15 by one from W. W. Phelps which contained — as the leaders expressed it — "low, dark, and blind insinuations which were not received from the fountain of light," (Sidney Gilbert,) and "which betrayed a lightness of spirit that ill becomes a man (W. W. Phelps) placed in the important and responsible station he is placed in."[8]

A reply had to be written to meet the growing crisis. The council agreed that Hyrum Smith was the man to write it and appointed Orson Hyde to assist him. On January 14, 1833, Hyrum sat down and wrote the following: "Kirtland Mills,[9] Geauga Co., Ohio, From a conference of Twelve High Priests, to the Bishop, his Council and the Inhabitants of Zion." The epistle contained several passages from revelations to show the importance of humility and obedience to the commandments of the Lord. It admonished the Missouri Saints to read the revela-

---

8Joseph Smith, op. cit., vol. I, p. 319.

tions and the Book of Mormon and to abide by their teachings, telling them that unless they repented the judgments of God would fall upon them. It also stated that Brother Joseph did not seek monarchial power and authority but was striving to magnify the high office and calling which were his by the command of God and the united voice of the Church. If the people of Zion did not repent, the Lord would seek another place and another people. Continuing, Hyrum said, "We have the best of feelings and feelings of the greatest anxiety for the welfare of Zion: We feel more like weeping over Zion than we do like rejoicing over her, for we know that the judgments of God hang over her, and will fall upon her except she repent. . . . We now say to Zion, this once in the name of the Lord, Repent! Repent! Awake! Awake! put on thy beautiful garments. . . ."[9]

At the close Hyrum mentioned the opening of the School of the Prophets — "If the Lord will, in two or three days, — that all were in good health, the cause of God was advancing rapidly in the eastern country; the gifts are beginning to break forth so as to astonish the world."

Hyrum Smith met regularly with the brethren as one of the twelve high priests.[10] A conference of the high priests was called on January 22, 1833. The services were conducted with the gift of tongues, and all present bore testimonies and greatly rejoiced at the outpouring of the gifts of the Spirit.

In March, the Prophet was given Sidney Rigdon and Frederick G. Williams as his Counselors to hold and share equally in the keys of the high priesthood, and more missionaries were called to the eastern country. Plans were made to establish a stake of Zion[11] at Kirtland. Also seven high priests (Oliver Cowdery, W. W. Phelps, John Whitmer, Sidney Gilbert, Bishop Partridge, and his two Counselors) were sent from Kirtland and

---

[9]*Ibid.*, pp. 317-321. Named as such because of grist and sawmills along the Chagrin River running through Kirtland.
[10]These were: Joseph Smith, Jr., Sidney Rigdon, Frederick G. Williams, Newel K. Whitney, Zebedee Coltrin, Joseph Smith, Sr., Samuel H. Smith, John Murdock, Lyman E. Johnson, Orson Hyde, and Ezra Thayer.
[11]An ecclesiastical division. Term "stake" symbolic to supporting a tent (church) with cords. See Isaiah 54:2.

were appointed to stand at the head of the Church in Zion (Missouri). These officers were to be submissive to the constituted authority and to engage actively in bringing the people together from the ends of the earth to the place the Lord had appointed.

A conference of about eighty officials was held April 6, 1833, at the ferry on Big Blue River near the western limits of Jackson County in the land of Zion. Soon after this conference a mob of about three hundred old settlers met at Independence, Missouri, to devise a plan for the removal or immediate destruction of the Church in Jackson County. A few of the elders met and prayed that the designs of the mob would be frustrated. The mob, after a day of fruitless effort to unite on a scheme for "removing the Mormons out of their diggings," became a little worse for their liquor and broke up in a regular Missouri "row."[12]

The letter Hyrum wrote in January, 1833, to the Missouri Saints, had had little effect in stemming the pressure that had been building up among them. Like the July heat the flames of mobocracy broke out in Missouri. While Hyrum, Joseph, and others were laying the foundation of the temple, reports from August until December grew progressively worse.

The dark days of Missouri mobocracy were increasing in intensity. At this time the future of the western church was obscure. The details of the Mormon expulsion from Jackson County is well known. The critical reverses in this frontier country helped to shape the destiny of Hyrum Smith and also the other leaders of this new movement. Quite probably the older brother of the Prophet Joseph had in mind alternatives of action to help meet the crisis. He no doubt thought of armed intervention under the protection of the Federal Government, particularly when citizens were forcibly dispossessed of their property. The atrocities committed by the mob-element of Jackson County weighed heavy on Hyrum's mind. He had given his consent and support to the plan that had placed the Mormons in such unfavorable circumstances. When he heard the particulars of what happened he wept.

---

[12]Joseph Smith, *op. cit.,* vol. I, pp. 341-342.

The failure of the Church in Jackson County, Missouri, placed a great strain on Hyrum Smith and his associates in the ministry. The responsibility to organize the resources of the little band of Mormons at Kirtland to begin construction of the temple was heavy and no doubt at times, frustrating. The enthusiasm for the building up of Kirtland was blunted by the suffering in Missouri. Nevertheless, they knew the new edifice must be built; not to do so would bring the displeasure of the Lord.

How did Hyrum react during intermittent crises? He did not resign his position nor move away. Rather, he exhibited great faith in the Church and remained steadfast as it successfully met the challenge of adversities. In his journal he expressed his faith in the divine calling of his brother Joseph, and a spirit of gratitude: "I was blessed with the privilege of obtaining the desires of my heart in all things." He cherished his patriarchal blessing from his father. His attitude was the same as was his mother's at the time Joseph was charged with dishonesty by Mrs. Martin Harris: "We can do nothing except look to the Lord." He was willing to pay the price no matter the cost — whether it was in the privation of personal comforts to himself and family, or the enduring of threats, slander, and the loss of time and money. His success in overcoming each obstacle bode well and there awaited him greater ones in the not-too-distant future.

CHAPTER XII

A SHAFT IN THE HANDS OF GOD

The mobbings and persecutions in Missouri cast a deep gloom over the membership of the Church and particularly the leaders. The foreboding of Hyrum Smith concerning the Jackson County Saints since his visit there was being confirmed.

The missionaries observed that the "precious treasure," meaning the gospel, seemed to be wholly fallen in the street.[1] Perhaps this was due to what the Prophet Joseph wrote: ". . . there were present here representatives of all the families of the earth: Shem, Ham, Japheth, a number of respectable negroes . . . and the balance made up of citizens representing themselves as pioneers of the west."

Hyrum Smith did not underestimate the seriousness of the trouble in Missouri nor was he able at the present to understand the implications or the true purposes of such extreme tribulation. There was danger of the green twig, the beginning of the growth of a mighty oak tree (the Church) being permanently singed by the white heat of persecution. The recuperative power of this infant organization was soon to be put to the test. The pattern of Satan in fighting the Church was becoming well established. While severe losses occurred of homes, land, and liberty, the valiant Saints were becoming inured and strong in their determination and faith. The events which occurred demonstrated the indominable spirit of the brethren. There was no time to mourn over their losses, immediate action must be taken; they gathered up the broken pieces and moved ahead. God had not forsaken them, even though the Saints in Missouri, like ancient Israel, had been driven from their holy land — he would still forgive and bless them.

---

[1] B. H. Roberts, *Comprehensive History of the Church of Jesus Christ of Latter-day Saints* (Salt Lake City, Utah, 1921,) vol. 1, pp. 321-322.

It was during this distressing time that Joseph met with Hyrum and a number of elders in the office of the printing press in Kirtland to dedicate the printing press to the Lord.[2]

This occasion was a significant one. The first patriarchal blessings given in this dispensation were given by Joseph the Prophet, December 18, 1833.[3] In addition to Hyrum he blessed his father and mother, his two younger brothers, Samuel Harrison and William, also, Oliver Cowdery. Not only did he give blessings, he also ordained his father Joseph Smith, Sr., the first presiding patriarch of the Church.[4]

The heart of Hyrum melted as he heard the voice of his prophet brother pronouncing blessings on him and on others at this time. A spirit of peace soothed the troubled feelings of the brethren.

If the distress of persecutions in Jackson County, Missouri, had begun to wane, it was just beginning in Kirtland. The citizens of Kirtland had grown more and more to resent the work on the temple and the things for which it stood. Scarcely had the year 1834 begun when, on the night of January 8, Hyrum and his family, along with the rest of the Kirtland Saints, were awakened by the booming of a cannon. The enemy had converged on a hill about a half mile northwest of Kirtland and fired thirteen rounds of shot, not to destroy but to terrorize the already worried Saints. The threats of the mob against building the temple increased, making it necessary, all through the fall and winter, for the brethren to be on constant guard. Day laborers on the temple were kept busy at night also, protecting the walls they had laid during the day. For weeks the workmen were not permitted to take off their clothes and were forced to sleep with guns in their arms.[5]

---

[2]The first sheets of the reprint *Evening and Morning Star* were struck off since it was decided to continue the periodical in Kirtland until the press could be restored in Independence.
[3]Oliver Cowdery, holding jointly the keys of the priesthood with Joseph, gave a number of patriarchal blessings.
[4]Joseph Fielding Smith, *Essentials of Church History*, (Salt Lake City, Deseret Book Co., 1935), p. 168-169.
[5]Joseph Smith. *op. cit.*, vol. II, pp. 1-3.

The Church, in its poverty and distress, seemed destined to failure. The wisdom necessary for the solution to these problems, like that for those which had come and gone before and like that for those yet to come, was sought through the medium of united prayer. The brethren went before the Lord in fervent prayer on the evening of January 11th. In the several petitions was the expressed hope that the Lord would deliver Zion and gather in his scattered people to possess it in peace . . . that they perish not from hunger or cold.[6]

Governor Daniel Dunklin of Missouri had told the Mormons that if they could organize themselves he would raise volunteers to assist in their being restored to their homes in Jackson County, and also, that the firearms taken from them would be restored.

On February the twenty-fourth, the Lord gave a plan to the brethren through a revelation which promised the restoration of Zion and which read in part: "Behold, I say unto you, the redemption of Zion must needs come by power; . . .

"But I say unto you: Mine angels shall go up before you, and also my presence, and in time yet shall possess the goodly land."[7]

Just how this was to be done the Lord further explained: "It is my will that my servant Parley P. Pratt and my servant Lyman Wight should not return to the land of their brethren until they have obtained companies to go up unto the land of Zion, by tens, or by twenties, or by fifties, or by an hundred, until they have obtained the number of five hundred of the strength of my house."[8]

Immediately after receiving this revelation, Joseph called the brethren for a consultation. Hyrum agreed that Joseph the Prophet should be the commander-in-chief of the expedition, and prepared to leave his family for another extended absence. When he told his faithful wife that he had been chosen to go with Frederick G. Williams on a volunteer-and-contribution-raising mission for the Missouri journey, she supported her husband as was her customary response.

---

[6]*Idem.*
[7]*D & C* 103:15, 20.
[8]P. 38.

In a few days Parley P. Pratt and Lyman Wight arrived from Liberty, Clay County, Missouri, to make a report of the true situation in Zion. Hyrum and Joseph met with them and the high council (organized for the first time in Kirtland, February 17, 1834) in the Prophet's home on February 24th to hear the report. Hyrum took the place of John Smith, a member of the council, who was absent. It was gratifying to the Prophet and to Hyrum to hear the visiting brethren report the friendliness of the people in Clay County — how they had taken the exiled Saints into their communities and supplied them with food, clothing, and employment, and had endeavored to make them comfortable in every way.

After much discussion, Joseph arose and said, "I am going to Zion to assist in redeeming it." A vote was called which unanimously affirmed his going, and forty volunteered to accompany him.

In company with Lyman Wight, Hyrum Smith went East to contact the branches of the church for the support of this expedition to Zion which was to be known as "Zion's Camp." The Prophet, with Parley P. Pratt, went into other branches, recruiting aid. After two months of intensive travel and countless appearances, over a hundred volunteers gathered at Kirtland to begin the westward trek. With the addition of new recruits at intervals during the journey, the little army was finally doubled.

With the loss of skilled workmen gone on the expedition to Zion, the problem of building the temple at Kirtland was intensified. Many of the volunteers had to depend upon their wives and children to run their farms and operate their businesses. The money required for clothing, food, ammunition, wagon, and teams for the expedition was a serious burden to the struggling Saints. This call, added to threats and persecution, required a sacrifice which proved the stability and faith of the members of the new organization.

Soon after Hyrum's return he bade a final goodbye to his wife Jerusha and parents before leaving to accompany Lyman

Wight on another trek, this time to Michigan to recruit volunteers for Zion's Camp. It was a trial for Hyrum to leave his wife, still in childbed after the birth of their second son - young "Hyrum." Hyrum had spent most of his time at home since the April birth. Lovina, seven years old, was a great help, and three-year old John, the pride of his parents, saved many steps by running errands. The leavetaking, always difficult, was eased and made beautiful by the genuine affection and prayers of the family.

By Monday, May 5, 1834, Hyrum and Brother Wight had been organizing a company of fourteen, mostly from Pontiac, Oakland County, Michigan, and the little group started their journey to Missouri. By coincidence they departed the same day the Prophet Joseph left Kirtland with the main body of militia men.

The brethren had agreed that Hyrum's company would meet the main group at Salt River, Missouri, where a branch of the Church was located.[9] Orders had been issued that the company arriving first was to wait for the others.[10]

A quarrel was started in the camp when some of the brethren insinuated that one couple had not done their full share of the work. This seemingly insignificant incident, stimulated by travel-weary bodies and frayed nerves, grew to alarming proportions, until Hyrum Smith called them together for advice and counsel. The company readily acknowledged the error, felt humble, confessed their faults before each other and to God with uplifted hands, and covenanted to forgive and forget all that had passed and find fault with each other no more. They were then three miles into Indiana Territory.

On Sunday, May 25, they stopped at Pleasant Grove Branch, presided over by Brother Rich. Hosea Stout who lived near the mouth of crow creek (exact location unknown) wrote as follows:

---

[9]Journal History, op. cit., June 8, 1834, (Elijah Fordham's Journal). There were eleven women (wives) and seven children in Zion's Camp. History of the Church, vol. II, p. 185.
[10]Joseph Smith, vol. II, pp. 87-88, 185.

Hyrum Smith, Lyman Wight, and others passed by here on their way up to Jackson County and staid several days during which time they preached several times here.

The effect of their preaching was powerful on me and when I considered that they were going up to Zion to fight for their lost inheritance under the special direction of God it was all that I could do to refrain from going. James and I let them have one yoke of oxen. Elder Charles C. Rich went with them.[11]

The travelers joined the congenial congregation in morning and evening worship service. The next day the sisters washed their clothing. Brother Wight held a meeting in a nearby village and purchased a large wagon and a yoke of cattle. On Thursday they took leave of the brethren and traveled to Pekin, Lazewell County, Illinois, on the Illinois River. A wheel on the large wagon broke and was repaired by a man at Pekin.

Then the company of Michigan Saints under Hyrum Smith and Lyman Wight continued their journey toward Quincy (Illinois), now over good road, and camped at the junction of the Mormon and Quincy Roads. They traveled through Quincy, a settlement with about seventy houses, two inns, nine stores, and an open square in the center. Here they purchased some lead for six cents a pound and also, for the first time, saw the Mississippi River which was about a mile wide, full of islands, with a strong current of roily water. As they were ferried over they noted that Quincy, also, had a saw and grist mill. Camp was made that night in Missouri.

Heber C. Kimball wrote:

At Salt River we were joined by Hyrum Smith and Lyman Wight with another company. The camp now numbered two hundred and five men, all armed and equipped. It was a delight to see the company, for they were all young men with one or two exceptions, and all in good spirits.[12]

---

[11]*Hosea Stout, Utah Pioneer Statesman,* Wayne Stout, pp. 79-80.
[12]Orson F. Whitney, *Life of Heber C. Kimball,* (Salt Lake City, Utah, 1888), pp. 79-80.

On Monday the sisters washed the clothes, after which they moved to the general camp and pitched their tents.[13]

It was Thursday, June 12, when the combined camp moved again toward western Missouri. During the four days rest, the company of two hundred five men organized themselves into squads of twelve, with a captain over each squad. The Prophet Joseph was named commander-in-chief; a bodyguard of twenty men with Hyrum Smith as captain was set near him, and George A. Smith was named arms bearer. Lyman Wight was elected as a general of the camp. After a half-day's strenuous drill led by General Wight, some had aching muscles. Their firelocks were inspected, and they fired them by platoons at targets.

George A. Smith, the son of Uncle John Smith, then a lad of fifteen, had been elected by the Prophet to make this journey. His father had outfitted him with a musket, a pair of pantaloons made of bed-ticking, two cotton shirts, a straw hat, cloth coat and vest, a blanket, a pair of new boots, an extra shirt, and a pair of pantaloons which his mother packed in a knapsack. He was large for his age and had weak, inflamed eyes. The first day out he blistered his feet in walking twenty-seven miles. Joseph gave him a pair of his boots, and he continued the trek with ease. He served at first in the quartermaster corps, helping with the rations; then he was made an arms' bearer.

Young George, when on the march through towns and villages, would be assigned to walk a few paces behind the company, where curious citizens would try to inveigle information from him, thinking he was a straggler, with his crumpled straw hat, his baggy pantaloons worn to shreds between the legs, and his sore eyes and simple look. He would give humorously evasive answers because the real purpose of their mission could not be divulged.

When asked where they were going he would answer, "To the West." In answer to "Where did you come from?" "From the East." "Who's your leader?" First one and then another," etc.

George Albert later recalled that on May 30, when they were

---

[13]Joseph Smith, op. cit., (Elijah Fordham's Journal.)

camped about three miles from Springfield on Spring Creek, a brother came to see them with the news that George's cousin, Hyrum, had passed westward the day before, about thirty miles north of them. The man said, "He has a fine company and they all looked mighty pert." On Saturday, May 31, after an hour on the road, the brother who had given them the news of Hyrum Smith's company the day before rode into camp and gave Joseph $100 and said he was sorry he couldn't give more.

While this well-organized army was nearing its objective, the Saints at Clay County were negotiating with Governor Daniel Dunklin of Missouri to return the fifty-two guns and one pistol taken from them some time previously under false pretenses.

Hyrum Smith organized his guard to protect the Prophet night and day, and kept himself near at all times. For security reasons Joseph was called "Squire Cook," and Father Parker gave him a large watch dog.[14] The next two weeks would see their mission completed with events crowding in to make history. Hyrum was happy to hear reports that the people of Salt River had great respect for the company as evidenced by the large number accompanying them for several miles.

Thanks are due Elijah Fordham, the camp historian, for his detailed description of Hyrum's company. The success of the project reflects the kind of leadership found in the persons of Hyrum Smith, Lyman Wight, and Samuel Bent. The personnel of the company manifested a high degree of faith and loyalty. They were willing to submerge their personal feelings for the good of the group. Without complaining they endured stormy weather, frequently slept cold at night because of insufficient bedding, and when their food ran low they were content to do without or to eat a very simple menu. They made friends along the way and seemed always able to obtain food. Evening and morning prayers were part of the rigid organizational schedule, and when a visitor came and talked too long the prayer period was deleted, rather than causing any offense or discourtesy. During the Sabbath no opportunity was lost to preach to the local citizenry.

---

[14]George A. Smith, *Memoirs*, President's Office, Salt Lake City, Utah.

There prevailed a spirit of co-operation and gratitude, and each campsite, much like ancient Israel traveling through the wilderness, they gave a name having a particular meaning which described a blessing, e.g., they named this place "Ezengeber" because here they were blest of the Lord with much instruction and with the Holy Spirit. When sickness occurred everything was done to bring relief, even through faith and prayer and the laying on of hands.

The five week journey from the Huran Branch in Michigan to the Allred settlement on Salt Creek in Monroe County, Missouri, covered approximately seven hundred miles. When they arrived the day after the main camp, Charles C. Rich had been added to their company which totaled seventeen.

Already Hyrum could point to fulfilment of several parts of his patriarchal blessing. His name had proved a blessing to his little company of recruits as the difficult trek through a strange and primitive section of the country had been highly successful. And he was emerging as a shaft in the hands of his God to execute judgment upon his enemies. The blessings of ancient Israel were upon Zion's Camp, and the patriarchal blessings were being fulfilled.

Chapter XIII

AN EXPERIMENT

It was quite natural for Joseph Smith to have his brother, Hyrum, in charge of his bodyguard. Not only would it be possible for Joseph to have full confidence of maximum security, but he would have the companionship of his older brother, whose counsel and advice would be available at any time. It was no doubt a great comfort and satisfaction to Joseph to have Hyrum once again with him, for there was great need for such relationship because all was not well with Zion's Camp. Joseph had on an occasion called the company together and warned them about dissention, faultfinding, and evil speaking, and that unless it ceased a terrible sickness would come upon them.

When the company ferried across the Mississippi River, they were in enemy territory. Rumors of their coming had preceded them and the people of Jackson County, Missouri, were alerted and mobilizing for war. Zion's Camp was placed on a twenty-four hour alert, and every precaution was taken against a surprise attack. There could be no trifling with the rules and regulations of this military expedition; even though it was small in number it was mighty in power, for the Lord has said, "Mine angels shall go up before you, and also my presence, and in time ye shall possess the goodly land."[1] It was very important that nothing stand in the way to thwart their efforts in redeeming Zion.

The mob militia of Jackson County, realizing that the Mormons were marching upon them, hastened to place guards at ferries, roads, and waterways. At this time many of the houses formerly owned by the Mormons, in which the mob were then living, were burned to the ground. Some blamed the Mormons, thereby exciting the wrath of their neighbors. John Corrill and A. S. Gilbert had replied to their legal counsel that the Saints would never sell their property in Jackson County to promote

---

[1]D & C 103:20.

peace because they (the Mormons) were American citizens under the Constitution, having the right to own propery without molestation.

On June 3, 1834, Orson Hyde and Parley P. Pratt returned from Jefferson City, Missouri, with a message from Governor Dunklin that he would not reinstate the exiles on their land in Jackson County. Governor Dunklin had written to the Saints earlier that he would call out the state militia to reinstate them on their land if they (the Mormons) would return, but he had changed his mind on the grounds of impracticability.

This information was a severe blow to the hopes of Zion's Camp and to the Saints scattered in Clay County. While the camp journeyed toward Northern Missouri, Judge Ryland called an important meeting which was held at Liberty, Clay County, Missouri.

There were eight hundred to a thousand souls present, including the Mormon leaders, and a deputation from Jackson County which presented a proposition. The principal terms of the proposal were that a committee of arbitrators would appraise the Mormon lands, would then add 100 percent to the appraised value and pay the Mormons within thirty days. The same proposition would also apply if the Mormons desired to purchase the old citizens' property.

The offer was obviously insincerely made because it would be impossible in thirty days to raise sufficient money to make the deal either way.

Following the reading of the proposed agreement, Samuel Owen's spokesman from Jackson County made a flaming war speech and General Doniphan, an officer at Far West who later defended Joseph, Hyrum, and others, replied on the side of peace. A Rev. Mr. Riley, Baptist Priest, spoke hotly against the Mormons. He said: "The Mormons have lived long enough in Clay County and they must either clear out or be cleared out!"

Mr. Turnham, the moderator of the meeting, answered in a masterly manner saying, "Let us be republicans; let us honor our country and not disgrace it like Jackson County. For God's sake don't disfranchise or drive away the Mormons. They are better citizens than many of the old inhabitants."

General Doniphan exclaimed, "That's a fact, and as the Mormons have armed themselves, if they don't fight they are cowards. I love to hear they have brethren coming to their assistance. Greater love can no man show than he who lays down his life for his brethren."[2]

Following the meeting, the Mormons answered the proposition by saying that they were not authorized to say whether their brethren would agree, and asked that they be given until the next Saturday or Monday to reply. Their great desire was to bring about a permanent peace as freeborn citizens of these United States. They pledged themselves to have no designs on the hospitable people of Clay County as a people or to commence hostilities against the aforesaid citizens of Jackson County or any other people. As a postscript they would use their influence to prevent any of the Mormons then moving to Jackson County from going there until they received an answer to the proposition.

Zion's Camp was depressed by the primitive condition of this new country with its virgin forests, streams, and rolling plains, all accentuated by the primitive urges of man's nature to hate, destroy, and kill his fellow man. Rumors began to come in more regularly about the enemy preparing to attack them. They crossed the Wakenda and looked for a place to camp. Ahead lay twenty-three miles of prairie without timber or palatable water to drink.

The camp was informed that a party of men was gathered together on the Missouri to attack them at night. Some of the men wanted to make camp near a strip of timber and were about to pitch their tents when Joseph decided that they should carry water and timber to a campsite on the prairie. Lyman Wight and Sylvester Smith opposed the Prophet by persuading about twenty men to remain with them for the night. Hyrum Smith said, in the name of the Lord, that he knew that it was best to go on to the prairie. His brother Joseph concurred with him by

---

[2]Joseph Smith, *op. cit.*, vol. II, pp. 97-98.

saying: ". . . and as he was my elder brother, I thought best to heed his counsel." The main company moved on eight miles and camped. They had little food, and the water carried in an empty powder keg was unfit to drink. At eleven o'clock the next day, Lyman Wight, with his company, arrived. The Prophet called them together and reproved them for their contrary actions. He told Lyman Wight never to act thus again. Whereupon, Lyman promised to stand by Joseph forever and never forsake him again.

That morning they traveled seventeen miles without breakfast. The Prophet was so sick he had to ride, leaving the affairs with Lyman Wight. They crossed a slough a half a mile wide through which most of the brethren waded waist deep in mud and water. General Lyman Wight, who had traveled from Kirtland without stockings on his feet, carried Brother Joseph Young through on his back. Their breakfast consisted of corn meal mush or hasty pudding.

Wednesday, June 18, they camped on a small prairie surrounded by a thicket of hazel brush, having passed within one mile of Richmond, Ray County. The Prophet bringing up the rear saw the danger of the mob attacking them from the thickets and went aside to pray. He was assured that Zion's Camp would be safe for the night. Early the next morning they marched about nine miles and stopped for breakfast. While passing through Richmond, they were warned by a black woman that a company of men were lying in wait there to kill them.

The camp halted on an eminence near a farmhouse for breakfast. The farmer gave them enough milk to add relish to their bacon and corn dodger which their commissary had obtained that morning. The farmer refused to take money for the milk saying, "If I had known you had been coming, I would have let you have more." The farmer reminded them that they had many enemies about here and said that it was a shame that every man couldn't enjoy his religion without being molested. Near noon, when they finished their breakfast, they moved on, determined to go on to Clay County. After going a short distance a wagon broke down and the wheels rolled from off others. It seemed impossible to speed their way. That night they pitched camp on an elevated piece of land between the Little Fishing and Big Fishing Rivers.

As they were making camp, five armed men with guns rode into camp and told them that they would "see hell before morning," a remark which was accompanied with oaths indicative of the malice of demons. They were told that sixty men were coming from Richmond, Ray County, and seventy more from Clay County to join the Jackson County mob who had sworn their utter destruction. During the day about two hundred of Zion's Camp made arrangements to cross the Missouri River to be ready to meet the Richmond mob near Fishing River Ford.

While the five men were in their camp, swearing vengeance, the wind, thunder, and rising clouds indicated an approaching storm, and a short time after they left the rain and hail began to fall.

"The storm was tremendous," wrote the Prophet. Wind and rain, hail and thunder met them in great wrath and soon softened the mobsters' determination and frustrated all their designs to "kill Joe Smith and his army." Instead of continuing a cannonading which they commenced when the sun was about an hour high, they crawled under wagons, into hollow trees, and filled an old shanty till the storm was over; then their ammunition was soaked.

Very little fell in our camp, but from a half mile to a mile around the stones or lumps of ice cut down the crops of corn and vegetation generally, even cutting limbs from trees while the trees themselves resembled witches as they were twisted by the wind. The lightning flashed incessantly which caused it to be so light in our camp throughout the night we could discern the most minute objects. The roaring of the thunder was tremendous. The earth trembled and quaked; the rain fell in torrents and united. It seemed as if the mandate of vengeance had gone forth from the God of battles to protect His servants from the destruction of their enemies, for the hail fell on them and not on us and we suffered no harm . . . while our enemies had holes made in their hats . . . even the breaking of their rifle stocks and the fleeing of their horses through fear and pain.

Many of my little band were sheltered in an old meetinghouse through the night. In the morning the water in Big Fishing River was about forty feet deep where the previous evening it was no more than to our ankles. Our enemies swore that the water rose thirty feet in thirty minutes in the Little Fishing River. They reported that one of their men was killed by lightning and that another had his hand tore [sic] off by his horse drawing his hand between the logs of a corn crib while he was holding him on the inside. They declared that if that was the way God fought for the Mormons, they might as well go about their business.[3]

The next morning, Friday, June 20, Zion's Camp drove five miles on to the prairie where they prepared food for themselves and their horses. While camped here, Saturday June 21, Colonel Sconce with two others from Ray County, came to see them, desiring to know what their intentions were, "For," said he, "I see that there is an almighty power that protects this people, for I started from Richmond with a company of armed men, having a fixed determination to destroy you, but was kept back by the storm and was not able to reach you."

"When he entered our camp," wrote Joseph later, "he was seized with such a trembling that he was obliged to sit down to compose himself, and when he had made known the object of their visit, I arose and addressed them, gave a relation of the sufferings of the Saints in Jackson County, and also our persecutions generally, and what we had suffered by our enemies for our religion; that we had come one thousand miles to assist our brethren, to bring them clothing, etc., and to re-instate them upon their own lands; that we had no intention of molesting or injuring any people, but only to administer to the wants of our afflicted; that the evil reports circulated about us were false and got up by our enemies to procure our destruction. When I had closed a lengthy speech, the spirit of which melted them into compassion, they arose and offered me their hands and said they would use their influence to allay the excitement which everywhere prevailed against us. They wept when they heard of our afflictions and persecutions and learned that our intentions were good."[4]

The sheriff of Clay County, Cornelius Gillum, came to see Joseph Smith. The company of brethren were marched to a

[3]Joseph Smith, *op. cit.*, vol. II, pp. 103-105.
[4]*Ibid.*, p. 106.

grove and placed in a circle to hear the sheriff. Upon his desiring first to know which one was their leader, Joseph arose, this being the first time he had made himself known to his enemies since leaving Kirtland, and said, "I am the man." The sheriff then gave them instructions concerning the manners, customs, and disposition of the people, and what course they ought to pursue to secure their favor and protection.

The attitude of Governor Dunklin of Missouri was revealed in a letter to Colonel J. Thornton, City of Jefferson, dated June 6, 1834. He said he had refrained from entering the trouble to help compromise the issues because he felt that his intervention would do no good. He recognized the right of free citizens to own property and to arm themselves to defend it, but said: "I am fully persuaded that the eccentricity of the religious opinions and practices of the Mormons is at the bottom of the outrage committed against them."

The Governor counseled a course to avoid trouble by having the Mormons sell their property and leave or set aside a certain section and live within those bounds. He gave the law concerning other counties marching troops to the aid of Jackson County to drive the Mormons out, saying that the citizens of the county might organize and arm themselves for mutual protection.

In closing he said: "The character of the state has been injured in consequence of this unfortunate affair and I sincerely hope it may not be disgraced by it in the end."[5]

The march of Zion's Camp to Missouri aroused both excitement and comment. On June 7, 1834, the *Niles Register* contained the following: "It is said that these poor fanatics, the Mormonites, have armed themselves to conquer their 'Holy Land,' in Missouri. They count 500 men and seem mad enough 'for the trial of battle.' "[6] The *Fayette Monitor* wrote under title of "Mormons in Missouri" that "the people may look for the worst." *The Missouri Enquirer,* printed at Liberty, Missouri, June 18, 1834, said: "No compromise, the affair to involve the whole upper country in civil war and bloodshed. The citizens

---

[5]*Idem.*
[6]*Niles Register, op. cit.*

of Jackson County it appears, though inferior in number to the
Mormons, are resolved to dispute every inch of ground, burn
every blade of grass, and suffer their bones to bleach on their hills
rather than let the Mormons return to Jackson County."

False rumors were circulated. On July 26, the *Niles Register* declared:

> The report of battle with the "Mormons," in Jackson County, Missouri,
> was not true, but these people to the number of 800 to 1000 well-armed
> advanced, assured by their Prophet Smith that he would raise all that
> would be killed in fighting the battles of the Lord! The people of
> Jackson County had also armed themselves and a bloody fight must have
> ensued, had the parties come into contact. But they had not at the
> latest advices and a hope is expressed that some negotiations may be entered
> into to quiet the controversy.[7]

The people of Jackson County were informed through the
press under date of July 12, 1834, about the situation of the
Mormons and about apprehension of war breaking out between
the Mormons and citizens of Jackson County:

> It appears that war is inevitable. Even though the Mormons have
> greater numbers than the people of Jackson County. . . .[8]

The frenzy of excitement among the people gave rise to
blaming the Mormons for every crime. At this time a report was
circulated blaming the Mormons for the sinking of a ferryboat
at Everett's Ferry following a committee meeting. Eight members
of the Missouri Committee were on board. It sank from being
flooded from the bottom. Five men were lost.[9]

*   *   *

The journey of Zion's Camp continued toward Liberty, Clay
County. When they were within five or six miles of Liberty they
were met by General Atchison and other gentlemen who warned
them not to go to Liberty because of the intense hostility and
hatred of the people against them. Taking this advice, the camp

---

[7]*Idem.*
[8]*Idem.*
[9]*Idem.*

wheeled to the left, crossing the prairie and woodland, came to Brother Algernon Sidney Gilbert's residence and camped on the bank of Rush Creek.

The citizens of Clay County were assured by a statement signed by the Prophet and others that the purpose of Zion's Camp was to come to the aid of their brethren and was of a peaceful nature.[10] The warning given the camp that sickness would break out if certain ones did not humble themselves and repent of their evil ways was not heeded. This warning was recalled when cholera struck and several of the brethren were overcome. Thomas Hayes was the first to die, June 21, 1834.

On the night of June 24, the air was rent with cries, moanings, and lamentations which attested to the sudden attack of the disease. Some fell to the ground when they were on guard. Joseph and Hyrum attempted to administer to the sick and rebuke the disease, but they were also seized with cramps. To use Hyrum's description, "It seized us like the talons of a hawk.[11] Joseph said, "If my work is done, you would have to put me in the ground without a coffin."

After the epidemic passed, fourteen had died. Hyrum Smith escaped death and thus was permitted to administer to the sick and lay away the bodies. Great love was shown for one another, and many tears were shed. Later, at Lyman Wight's near Liberty, the Prophet told the brethren that if they humbled themselves before the Lord and covenanted to keep his commandments and obey his counsel, the plague would be stayed from that hour and there should not be another case of cholera among them. This they agreed to do with uplifted hands, and the plague was stayed.

The last week in June witnessed the demobilization of Zion's Camp amid scenes of sickness and distress. The object of the expedition was not achieved. The Lord, in a revelation to the Prophet at Fishing River on June 22, said in part: "Verily I say unto you who have assembled yourselves together that you may learn my will concerning the redemption of mine afflicted people

---

[10]Joseph Smith, *op. cit.*, vol. II, pp. 118-120.
[11]*Idem.*

... were it not for the transgressions of my people, speaking concerning the church and not individually, they might have been redeemed even now... they have not learned to be obedient to the things which I require at their hands, but are full of all manner of evil and do not impart of their substance as becometh Saints, to the poor and afflicted among them."[12]

After organizing the stake and high council, the Prophet instructed Lyman Wight to discharge every man of the camp who had proved himself faithful.

Incidents relative to Zion's Camp were told by many of the brethren. Joseph Holbrook wrote that they all walked carrying their muskets and knapsacks with only the sick and crippled riding the heavily loaded baggage wagons. They had to help lift the wagons out of the swamp lands of Ohio. It took them forty-seven days to reach Clay County, Missouri, with thirty-seven traveling days. Because of the unfamiliar terrain the distance was increased by a circuitous route.[13]

George A. Smith, in describing the hardship of the Camp said: "Joseph walked most of the time, never complaining of sore toes, scanty provisions, poor bread, bad corn dodger, 'frousy' butter, strong honey, maggoty bacon and cheese. When the dog would bark they would complain to Joseph. If they camped with bad water it would cause a rebellion, yet we were the Camp of Zion. Many of us were careless, heedless, foolish or devilish, yet we did not know it. Joseph had to bear with us like children. There were many, however, in the camp who never murmured and who were always willing and ready to do the will of our leaders."

The contribution of Hyrum Smith for the partial success of Zion's Camp was considerable. He supported his brother, Joseph, by sound counsel and advice, and by acting as his personal bodyguard, and companion. And, as before on similar occasions, the mutual sharing of sorrow incident to the cholera scourge and the refusal of Missouri's governor to come to their aid pointed up the importance of Hyrum in the life of Joseph the Prophet.

---

[12]Ibid., vol. II, p. 108.
[13]Joseph Holbrook, The Life of (Diary) Brigham Young University, Provo, Utah.

Hyrum Smith's home at Nauvoo, Illinois. (Courtesy of Church Historian's office.)

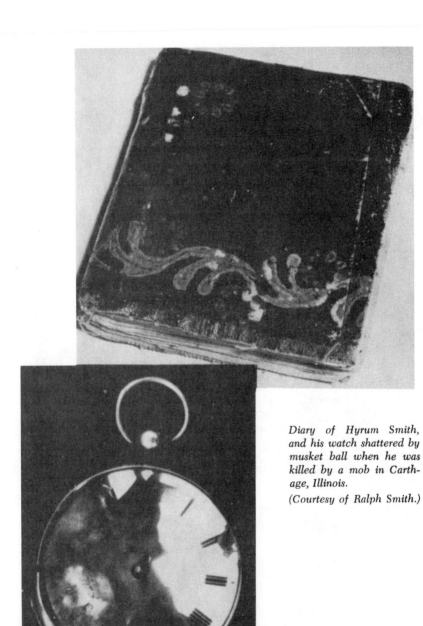

Diary of Hyrum Smith, and his watch shattered by musket ball when he was killed by a mob in Carthage, Illinois.

(Courtesy of Ralph Smith.)

CHAPTER XIV

HYRUM THE PEACEMAKER

Hyrum Smith took affectionate leave of his brethren at their camp just outside Liberty, Missouri. He felt that the trials along the way, the suffering, the sickness and the many casualties from cholera had strengthened their love and affection for each other. He shed a few tears that Monday morning, July 9, 1834, as he watched General Lyman Wight muster out the remaining militiamen of the original two hundred five men. He knew that a few of these men, with no families to return to, would remain in Missouri to make their homes. The others in small groups would travel in leisurely fashion to their families in Ohio.

As they loaded Hyrum's personal effects into one of the two-horse wagons, he felt that the mission was complete. There was satisfaction in having been obedient to the call to assist the unfortunate brethren. Thus thoughtfully, he turned and climbed to the buggy seat with his brother Joseph. Brothers Frederick G. Williams and Sidney Rigdon were riding in one of the baggage wagons, on which they were to take turns.

As they rode out, Hyrum thought of the new stake that had been organized in Missouri, with David Whitmer as president, W. W. Phelps and John Whitmer as counselors. This new ecclesiastical organization assisted by twelve high councilmen would conduct both spiritual and temporal affairs of the Church in northern Missouri and also act as a negotiating agency for a peaceful settlement of the Jackson County affair.

When they parted from their friends, Joseph gave George A. Smith expense money with which to get home, the unused part of which was returned when the boy arrived in Kirtland.

Three months had passed since Hyrum had left Kirtland and there was general rejoicing on his return. Hyrum inquired about the work on the temple, how the crops were doing, and in-

quired about the names of the several families of newcomers.
There was much work to be done, and his family needed attention—a replenishment of food and clothing was necessary.

No sooner had he settled into the routine of home life and
church responsibilities than he was called to attend several meetings with the high council. Sylvester Smith had made some
grave charges against the Prophet Joseph Smith while on their
recent trip to Missouri. After several meetings, Sylvester Smith
recanted his charges and repented of his evil complaints.

As a member of the building committee of the temple,
Hyrum was gratified to have the fine co-operation of the brethren,
even Joseph worked with his hands. Speaking of this he wrote:
"September 1, 1834, I continued to preside over the Church and
in forwarding the building of the house of the Lord in Kirtland.
I acted as foreman in the Temple stone quarry, and when other
duties would permit, labored with my own hands."[1] The Prophet called a meeting in Kirtland and bestowed blessings upon those
who had been working on the temple.

In September, Jared Carter, a member of the building committee who had erred in criticizing certain of the brethren, was
brought before the high council. During the trial, Hyrum arose
and expressed himself as to how Brother Carter had sinned. He
pointed out how pride had engendered in Elder Carter's heart a
desire to excel, and the spirit of meekness was withdrawn, and he
was left to err. . .because he was not yet perfect. But he erred in
understanding, and his words were wrong; yet the spirit of his
heart. . .might be good in the main.

At this time at Kirtland much time was taken up with
problems arising among members who transgressed and needed
trial and correction before the high council. William Smith,
brother to the Prophet, brought a charge against a Brother Elliot
for whipping his fifteen-year-old daughter. The usual procedure
of a trial before the church court was resorted to. When Mother
Smith, a witness, arose to testify, Joseph cautioned her about ir-
relevant information being unnecessary. William objected to

---

[1]Joseph Smith, *History of the Church*, vol. II, p. 161.

Joseph's interference, and a bitter quarrel ensued. Father Smith realized that tension was developing and counseled Joseph not to leave the meeting. The trial was brought to order, and the defendant confessed his error.

The next day, William wrote the Prophet justifying his actions, whereupon, Joseph wrote a reply requesting William to come to his office. On Saturday, October 31, William came to see the Prophet. Hyrum happened to be present, having come he said, ". . .Because he had been troubled all night and had not slept any. . . ." Hyrum excused himself, saying he had to go to the store but would return. William wanted to proceed at once to discuss their trouble, but Joseph asked him to wait until Hyrum returned. Soon Hyrum returned and the subject of their difficulties was taken up. Joseph proposed that Hyrum and Brother Parrish decide the matter. William continued to justify himself but finally agreed to have Hyrum and Brother Parrish be the adjudicators. Joseph confessed that he was willing to make amends for any wrong he might have been guilty of.

After he [William] got through, Joseph later wrote, "Brother Hyrum began to make some remarks in the spirit of meekness. He (William) became enraged. I joined Brother Hyrum in trying to calm his stormy feelings, but to no purpose, he insisted that we intended to add abuse to injury, his passion increased, he arose abruptly, declared he wanted no more to do with us. He rushed out at the door. We tried to prevail on him to stop, but all to no purpose. . . . He went home and spread the leaven of iniquity among my brothers, and especially prejudiced the mind of Brother Samuel." Later the Prophet wrote of William, . . ."I obtained a testimony that my brother William would return to the Church, and repair the wrong he had done.[2]

On Wednesday, December 16, a debate was held at William Smith's home between Joseph, William, and others on the subject of revelation being necessary for one's happiness. The Prophet, taking the affirmative, provoked the antagonism of William to the extent that violence was the result of the debate.

The Saturday following, Hyrum received a letter from William asking forgiveness for the abuse he had given Joseph. Hyrum, again acting as a peacemaker, called on Joseph bringing

---

[2]*Ibid.*, pp. 297-298.

the letter, and spent most of the forenoon discussing the difficulty between Joseph and William. Referring to this occasion Joseph wrote:

He, [Hyrum] said that he was perfectly satisfied with the course I had taken in rebuking William in his wickedness, but he is wounded to the very soul, because of the conduct of William; and although he experienced the tender feelings of a brother toward him, yet he can but look upon his conduct as an abomination in the sight of God. And I pray in my heart that all my brethren were like unto my beloved brother Hyrum, who possesses the mildness of a lamb, and the integrity of a Job, and in short, the meekness and humility of Christ; and I love him with that love that is stronger than death, for I never had occasion to rebuke him nor he me, which he declared when he left me today.[3]

The Prophet Joseph had also received a repentant letter from William. He confessed his sins and asked his brother to consider his withdrawal from the Quorum of the Twelve, because his iniquity would undermine the effectiveness of the quorum. He complained of ill health and felt that someone else could take his place to better uphold the office. He also expressed a desire to remain a member in order to enjoy the fruits of the gospel. He said he had been called by his quorum to answer for his misconduct.

Joseph after reading the letter wrote a reply. He reminded William that he had helped build the house in which he was then living, had given him flour and supplies, and that as brothers they should have natural affection for each other. He said that even though their parents were living with them and shared the ownership of the house, in due time he (William) would own it. There should be due respect for their parents because as children they had been raised from the cradle through periods of sickness and poverty. Therefore, the children should not bring the parents' gray hairs down with sorrow to the grave. Joseph reminded him that "After the school closed, Brother Hyrum requested the privilege of speaking; you objected; however, you said if he would not abuse the school he might speak, and that you would not allow any man to abuse the school in

---

[3]*Ibid.*, p. 388.

your house. Now, you had no reason to suspect that Hyrum would abuse the school; therefore my feelings were mortified at these unnecessary observations. . . .

. . .I desire brother William for you to humble yourself. I freely forgive you. . .you know the doctrine I teach is true, you know that God has blessed me. I brought salvation to my father's house, as an instrument in the hands of God when they were in a miserable situation. . . .

And now may God have mercy upon my father's house; may God take away enmity from between me and thee, and may all blessings be restored and the past forgotten forever. May humble repentance bring us both to Thee, O God, and to Thy power and protection, and a crown, to enjoy the society of father, mother, Alvin, Hyrum, Sophronia, Samuel, Catherine, Carlos, Lucy, the Saints, and all the sanctified in peace, forever, is the prayer of your brother, Joseph Smith Junior.[4]

During the late fall and winter months of 1834, there was sufficient lull in hostilities toward the Mormons to permit them to push the construction of the temple.

The economic conditions of the frontier were such that a system of barter made the distribution of goods possible. Farm produce was exchanged for books, clothing, furniture. Each trade transaction, however, was appraised in terms of dollars and cents. About a year before this, the Prophet owed his brother Hyrum $203.00 for certain items he had purchased. Perhaps that was one reason why Joseph, on December 4, 1834, in company with Vincent Knight and Hyrum, went to Painesville and drew $350 from the Painesville Bank on three months credit. Co-signers were F. G. Williams and Colonel N. K. Whitney, John Johnson, and Vincent Knight. With this money, he later wrote: "settled with Brother Hyrum and paid V. Knight $250."[5]

The long winter evenings of 1834 were spent by Hyrum and the brethren in the pursuit of knowledge. The "School of the Elders," later the "School of the Prophets," was well attended. In his record Joseph wrote: "December 8, at home. Read Hebrew in company with Dr. Williams, President Cowdery, Brother

4Ibid., pp. 341-343.
5Ibid., p. 324,

Hyrum and Orson Pratt." Oliver Cowdery was, on December 5, 1834 ordained[6] an assistant-President to Joseph Smith; but because of long periods spent in Missouri, Oliver, Second Elder in the Church, was unable to act in his important office.

There were three items uppermost in the minds of Hyrum Smith and the brethren at the close of 1834. First, the trouble in Missouri had not been settled. Governor Dunklin had presented their case to the state legislature, but no action had been taken upon it. Second, there was the urgency of moving ahead on the temple construction, which involved labor, money, and planning. Third, was the School of the Prophets by which the leaders desired to raise the literacy of the missionaries and members of the priesthood in order that they might be more effective in their various callings.

It was Saturday, February 14, 1835, that Hyrum Smith attended a special meeting, at which all who had gone up to Zion to assist in its redemption the previous season were present. Since June, 1829, it had been known that there soon would be called twelve special witnesses of the name and mission of the Lord Jesus Christ—a body of twelve apostles. (See D&C 18:37.)

This occasion was another important scene in the dramatic development of the Church. The field was ripe, ready to harvest, and laborers were sorely needed. On Sunday, February 8, the Prophet called Joseph Young and his brother Brigham to his home where he related a vision to them, telling them that he saw the organization of the Church, Brother Brigham chosen as one of the witnesses. He told him to notify all the brethren in the immediate branches to be present on February 14. He appointed Joseph Young to be the President of the Seventies. This office was new to this generation but Moses had chosen Seventy Elders of Israel, and Jesus chose seventies to help in the ministry during the Meridian of Time.

When the time came to open the meeting, Hyrum Smith, seated on the stand, noticed that the assembly room (located in

---

[6]The term "ordain" here is misused. "Set apart" is more appropriate considering the office.

the new school building under the printing office) was filled.
After the opening exercises, the Prophet Joseph spoke, acknowl-
edging the blessings of the Lord. He then told of the journey to
Zion by members of the camp and promised a crown of glory for
those of the brethren who had died with the cholera. He then
read to the congregation the fifteenth chapter of John after which
he asked that all members of Zion's Camp arise. (They were by
pre-arrangement, seated together.) He said that from these
would be chosen the Twelve Special Witnesses because they had
already proved their faith by their willingness to die for the
Church, and had made as great a sacrifice as Abraham. He
asked the congregation to raise their right hands if they agreed to
this proposal. The vote was unanimous. He made it clear that
the Lord had commanded him to hold this meeting and proceeded to organize the Quorum of the Twelve and also the
Seventies.

Complaints were made by some because they had not been
able to fight on their arrival in Missouri. Joseph explained that
it was not the purpose of the Lord to have them fight.

President Hyrum Smith prayed, after which they sang the
hymn entitled "Hark, Listen to the Trumpeters." At the close of
the hymn the meeting was adjourned for one hour.

The first item of business after reassembling and an opening prayer was the choosing of twelve men. The three witnesses,
Oliver Cowdery, David Whitmer, and Martin Harris, united in
prayer and then were blessed for this occasion by the laying on of
hands by the First Presidency. Then these three according to
previous commandment, proceeded to choose twelve men as follows:

1. Lyman E. Johnson	7. Wm. E. M'Lellin
2. Brigham Young	8. John F. Boynton
3. Heber C. Kimball	9. Orson Pratt
4. Orson Hyde	10. William Smith
5. David W. Patten	11. Thomas B. Marsh
6. Luke S. Johnson	12. Parley P. Pratt

The twelve were later listed in order of their age which revised the above list.[7]

Two weeks later, on February 28, 1835, the seven presidents of the seventy were chosen. These seven were to work under direction of the twelve and to serve primarily as missionaries in all the world. Seven presidents would later be called to preside over quorums as they were organized among the stakes. Seventy men were then called and ordained by the First Presidency as the First Quorum of Seventy. These too were selected from members of Zion's Camp in accordance with a revelation.[8]

During the following months several great revelations were given, the most important perhaps being those on the priesthood.[9] The leaders made no effort to organize or establish rules and laws without first being given specific instructions from God in revelations in the most minute detail. The revelations were carefully recorded and copies of them made for the use of missionaries until a collection could be compiled and published.

Hyrum Smith felt a great upsurge of enthusiasm for missionary work as he listened to President Oliver Cowdery charge the missionaries with the great obligations of their office and calling. Among other things, they were to be fearless like the apostles of old, a traveling high council to preach among the gentiles until he (God) called them to go to the Jews. Joseph followed by saying that they (the missionaries) were to hold the keys of this ministry, to unlock the door of the kingdom of heaven unto all nations and preach the gospel to every creature. This was the power, authority, and virtue of their apostleship.

The good office of Hyrum during periods of crisis was frequently sought. His summation at the trial of Jared Carter revealed the depth of his wisdom and understanding — part of which was: "... he was left to err because he was not yet perfect. But he erred in understanding, and his words were wrong; yet the spirit of his heart ... might be good in the main."

---

[7]*Ibid.*, pp. 180-200.
[8]*Ibid.*, pp. 201-204.
[9]The revelations were sections 107, 108, 109, 110, and 111.

His name was beginning to appear in the records as one having addressed the departing missionaries. He was aware of the importance of the new quorums and the added power and prestige they would give to the Church. His greatest desire was to keep close to all activity so that he could lend his guiding influence and offer his advice when it was needed. It was becoming more apparent as the church organization grew and inexperienced men, having no precedent to follow, would be more apt to exhibit weaknesses of judgment and personality. A little authority may prompt many to exercise unjust dominion over others. Therefore, until a sense of protocol could be established, there was evidence of bickerings, complaints, envy, and jealousy among the brethren. Fortunately there were those individuals mature enough to prevent such men from destroying the Church. Recent events in Kirtland reveal the emerging influence of Hyrum Smith as an arbitrator, counselor, and a peacemaker — a role he was destined to assume frequently during times of trouble and crisis.

CHAPTER XV

HYRUM AT HOME

January and February of 1835 was a period of taking stock for Hyrum and his family. The cold weather brought the family inside their comfortable home where they loved to be together. Here Hyrum counted his many blessings, grateful that there was little sickness and an abundance of love and affection in his home. Material needs were adequately provided, and this gave a feeling of security. Outside his home the walls of the temple were rising to the square. Materials and many willing hands had seemed to multiply, literally speeding the temple toward completion. The temporary lull in its construction would end when the warmer weather of March and April arrived. Meanwhile, seldom a day passed without Hyrum's making a careful inspection of the work. Stone and lumber were in good supply. The co-ordination of the workmen on the various projects was inspiring to see and a constant source of joy to the zealous chairman of the building committee. Even work on the temple was not allowed to impede missionary activity, and Hyrum was still a missionary, subject to active duty at any time; however, he was now more a temple builder than a missionary.

On February 14, 1835, the twelve were called to go to mission fields. At that time, Hyrum was assured that those working on the temple were to remain on the job until the project was completed for theirs was also a mission. Like those leaving to go abroad, the builders had a similar zeal for doing the work of the Lord. About a week after the twelve were called as missionaires, Hyrum recorded in his diary the following:

"February 21, 1835, a meeting was called to (thank the Lord) for the blessings that (have come) to Zion (and those who) were driven (from their) homes." Three days later, in his Day

Book,[1] he recorded incomplete entries of baptisms, subscriptions received on the temple and labor performed.

Before the winter was over the newly selected traveling high council were on their way to the mission field in the Eastern States. It was necessary for the Church to help the needy missionaries with clothes and money. George A. Smith, a member of the first quorum of seventies, describing his call to preach the gospel in the East, wrote: "Joseph and Hyrum gave me some gray cloth to make me a coat and a (snuff-tobacco-colored) vest and pantaloons. Brother Charles Thompson cut them out and Sister Eliza Brown made them up for me."[2]

There was little time for Hyrum Smith to spend with his family: Lovina, John, and Hyrum, Jr. The death of his second child, Mary, on May 29, 1832, had been a sore trial for Hyrum and Jerusha, but two more daughters were yet to bless their union: Jerusha and Sarah. Hyrum's was an affectionate and happy home where culture and refinement were characteristic qualities which emanated from this family circle to bless the Saints.

In the fall of 1835, Hyrum and Jerusha invited Lydia Goldthwait to their place to help Jerusha with her work during the remainder of her pregnancy. While there, Lydia met Newel Knight, an old friend of the Smiths, and a romance developed.

It was the advice of both Hyrum and Jerusha that the marriage take place at once, and when Lydia's objections were overruled, preparations were made immediately. A wedding supper was included in the plans and on the afternoon of November 22, Hyrum set out to invite the friends of the family. Going to Father Smith's he asked them all to be present. Hastening on to Joseph's house, he acquainted him with what was to take place the following day, and then asked Joseph to be present. As Hyrum was hurrying away, Joseph called out: "Stop, Brother Hyrum, don't be in such a hurry, where are you going now?"

---

[1]Hyrum's *Day Book*, size 3" x 4¼", well preserved paper cover, writing in ink. Entries dated Feb. 24, 1835; Aug. 5, 1835, and Oct. 30, 1837.
[2]George A. Smith, *Memoirs*.

"Oh, I can't say, I must make haste, as I have to go down and ask Seymour Brunson to perform the ceremony."

"It won't be necessary, Hyrum," replied Joseph, "for I intend to marry the couple myself." Hyrum looked at his brother with astonishment at this announcement. . . .

"Very well," replied Hyrum, "you know best. We will be very glad to have you do so."[3]

The next evening (November 23), about a dozen intimate friends of the family gathered in Hyrum's parlor. The young couple stood up and the Prophet arose and commenced the ceremony, at the close of which he pronounced them husband and wife by the authority of the priesthood he held. This was the first marriage ceremony performed by the Prophet Joseph.

The Smiths gave Brother and Sister Knight a hearty invitation to remain with them during the winter and advised them not to set up housekeeping until they removed to their Western home. The Knights gladly accepted the offer and spent several happy months in this pleasant home.

In the spring Hyrum Smith provided the newlyweds with a team and driver to take them to the Ohio River, where they embarked by steamer for their home in Clay County, Missouri. The Knights never forgot Hyrum's acts of hospitality. From them later came a description of and a tribute to Hyrum Smith expressed in the words of their biographer as follows:

When Lydia went to his home he (Hyrum) was between thirty-five and forty years of age, tall, well-framed, with a fine, handsome countenance, and blue eyes and his face was full of intelligence and spirit. His manner was dignified; but, he was amiable, and vivacious, withal exceedingly courteous and fascinating to all with whom he ever had intercourse. He was really a worthy brother of the Prophet, and together they were a worthy pair.[4]

---

[3]Susa Young Gates, *Lydia Knight's History,* Juvenile Instructor Office, Salt Lake City, Utah. (1883), p. 35. Note—Lydia Goldwaithe had married Calvin Baily at 16 and had had a daughter. After 3½ years he deserted her, and she married Brother Knight at 23.
[4]*Idem.*

As the temple neared completion, the temple committee (with Hyrum as its chairman) was gratified with the rapid progress made in building this house of the Lord. They felt that it was appropriate to publish a long list of donors. Soon the upper rooms would be ready for the School of the Prophets. The "fame" of this holy edifice was spreading far and wide, and a public journal made it a subject for comment. From M.M. Noah of the New York *Evening Star* came the following:

"Heathen Temple in Lake Erie — That boldfaced imposter, Jo Smith, of God Bible and Mormon memory, has caused his poor fanatic followers to erect on the shores of Lake Erie, near Paines- ville, Ohio, a stone building, 58 by 78 feet, with dormer windows, denominating the same 'The Temple of the Lord.' We should think this work of iniquity extorted out of the pockets of his dupes, as it reflects its shadows over the blue Lake, would make the waters crimson with shame at the prostitution of its beauti- ful banks to such an unhallowed purpose."[5]

Hyrum could only pity such lack of understanding. Actually the Kirtland Temple was tangible evidence of the Saint's loyalty to their faith in Hyrum and Joseph Smith. It symbolized the Lord's work and helped to authenticate the fact that there was revelation in modern times. Such a concept was new, and it clashed with the catechisms of the various sects which stated that visions and revelations had been done away with, that the Bible was the complete word of God, and that the gifts of the Holy Spirit ceased with the holy apostles. Would not this disturbing person, Joseph Smith and his Church go the way of other fanatics and, like a tornado, blow themselves out? The Christian socie- ties waited for the Church, to them a fraudulent institution, to fail and vanish away. Such failure would reveal to the world the true nature of the organization. But instead of failing it seemed to flourish. News filtered through from Ohio and Missouri that Mormonism was persisting. Every report of the church's activity was a disappointment to its detractors because the so-called fraud was succeeding. People were believing and joining; missionaries,

---

[5]Joseph Smith, *op. cit.*, vol. II, p. 351.

ever increasing in numbers, were going abroad. Still, enemies of the Church felt that it could not last because it was contrary to the logic of God and the Bible. It was, therefore, they reasoned, a man's duty to expose it and label it for what it really was.

During the latter part of 1835, the growth of the organization and its doctrine experienced an upsurge. Hyrum Smith was an apt student of the scriptures and the new revelations. He had studied Joseph's revision of the Bible and was now looking forward to the time when he could study the writings of Abraham. This recent addition to the scriptures had been the result of one Michael Chandler's bringing several Egyptian mummies to Kirtland for the purpose of getting Joseph, the Mormon Prophet and Seer, to decipher some ancient writing on papyrus rolls which had been found with one of the mummies.

Hyrum and the family, with some friends, made arrangements to purchase several of the embalmed bodies in order to obtain the ancient scrolls. After Joseph had successfully translated some of the inscriptions, Mr. Chandler was willing to part with the specimens. The Smith family and the Saints were proud to know that soon the book of Abraham would be added to the developing body of scripture. The work of the ancient Patriarch Abraham proved to be a message of great importance coming out of the remote past.

This important discovery was termed, by Joseph, to be a result of divine favor. This new revelation would, in time, be put with the scriptures of the visions of Moses, and the record of Joseph Smith's first vision and calling, to make up a volume of scripture known as the Pearl of Great Price.

The Lord had fortified the infant Church by bestowing upon its members such gifts of the Spirit as revelation, visions, inspiration, discernment of spirits, testimony, and faith. He had also given them new scriptures and the Holy Priesthood, and had authorized the building of a temple. Thus, as the year 1835 came to an end, there was much for Hyrum and his family to be thankful for. The temple, soon to be occupied, was a monument to Hyrum's faith and devotion. His spirit of encouragement and determination had inspired many to greater effort.

Hyrum spent Christmas and New Year's Day with his family. Then on Sunday, December 27, he met with the Saints in worship at the schoolhouse, which was their usual meeting place at that time. In this meeting Hyrum shared the time at the pulpit with President Cowdery and Bishop Partridge. Joseph, who was present, wrote of this occasion: "Each [gave] a short and interesting lecture."

Hyrum and Jerusha celebrated the arrival of the new year (1836) with the family, in a gathering at Joseph's place. Several members and friends, including Uncle John Smith and Martin Harris were in attendance. A part of the festivities was to make some resolutions. Those present covenanted with each other: "In the sight of God, and the Holy Angels, and the brethren to strive hence-forward to build each other up in righteousness in all things; and not to listen to evil reports concerning each other, with our grievances, in the spirit of meekness, and be reconciled, and thereby promote our happiness, and the happiness of the family; and, in short, the happiness and well-being of all."

Hyrum had shared Joseph's anxiety over the trouble which had developed in the family, for both sensed an evil influence seeking to weaken and undermine the Church from within. Prayers and supplication had been regularly addressed to God that he would bless the family and the Church with the spirit of love and unity. And William's return to the family fold and to activity in the Church was the source of great rejoicing.

The history of this period reveals the tremendous responsibility of Joseph and Hyrum. So many people brought their problems and quarrels before the high council that dealing with such problems became routine. There were constant reports of the teaching of false doctrine. These could not be ignored, and so the offenders were called in and set straight. Even so, in view of the heterogeneous background and diversified philosophies of the converts, it was amazing how unified the infant church had become in so short a time.

Hyrum and the Prophet were like two skilled craftsmen, welding on an anvil, the divergent human elements into one unified whole. They realized the importance of withstanding the fierce disintegrating forces which were threatening the destruction of all they stood for, and they found that their most powerful weapons against the forces of evil were the missionaries of the Church and the temple being gradually completed there in Kirtland.

CHAPTER XVI

HYRUM THE TEMPLE BUILDER

The beautiful new temple with its spire facing east was the first tangible representation of the Church, architecturally. The brethren often admired and commented about its New England design, its beauty and symmetry. The thick gray limestone walls were being plastered over and the woodwork of the windows, eaves, and doors painted.

The congenial spirit of Hyrum typified the harmony among the people as 1836 was ushered in. The work of building the temple had promoted a spirit of brotherhood and well-being, and such a structure gave the Church added prestige, as did the newly organized Quorums of Apostles and Seventies who were fulfilling in every way the charges placed upon them as prophets, seers, and revelators.

At the conference in Kirtland, January 13, 1836, Hyrum Smith was ordained to the Presidency of the high council, and several vacancies were then filled by ordination under the hands of Joseph, Hyrum, and Sidney Rigdon. During the closing period of the conference, Brother Rigdon became ill, and requested that Hyrum Smith and David Whitmer lay their hands on him and rebuke the disease. This they did, and he recovered.

Even before the temple was completed, various meetings of the Saints were held in the finished rooms. Hyrum, on his visits to the temple, noticed children and a few adults conducting themselves in a manner unbecoming to Saints in the house of the Lord, and he urged that a committee be appointed to draw up some rules of conduct. Therefore a committee met in the council room in the printing office to complete a set of rules.

The schools known as of the elders and the prophets moved into the upper rooms of the temple. There Hyrum witnessed many marvelous spiritual manifestations and participated as blessings were pronounced on the heads of many of the presiding brethren. He, himself, anointed and set apart Don Carlos Smith as president of the high priests and then watched as Don Carlos in turn anointed the quorum.

The close-knit Smith family met together Friday afternoon, January 29, 1836, for a feast, and to strengthen the bonds of fellowship. The oldest son, Hyrum, sensed the need for these periodic get-togethers. Among this family there was a deep concern over each others welfare, as was evidenced when Hyrum, while cutting wood, during early February, fell on his ax and cut a deep gash in his left arm. Dr. Frederick G. Williams sewed up the wound (about four to five inches in length), and when Joseph heard of the misfortune he rushed to Hyrum's side. Writing of this incident later Joseph declared, "And I feel to thank God that it is no worse, and I ask my Heavenly Father in the name of Jesus Christ to heal my brother, Hyrum, and bless my father's family, one and all with peace and plenty and eternal life."

Hyrum later mentioned in his journal a similar accident: "George Grant left October 30, 1837, for a little trip out to Antewarp. Visited Aunt Fannie. Stayed at Fannie's, fell on my arm, deep wound."[1]

This mention of a visit to "Aunt Fannie" reveals another side of Hyrum's character. He was tireless in his efforts to convert his kinsmen and have them identified with the Church. He visited his Uncle Silas, in obedience to a revelation, and said, "Uncle Silas, I have come, the Lord has sent me to baptize you for the Lord has seen the integrity of your heart, but knows your fears in regard to your family." Silas was baptized.[2]

Toward the end of March, the temple received its final inspection and was pronounced sound and well-built. No doubt the building committee exhibited great pride and satisfaction at the conclusion of such a formidable undertaking. The structure stood out in bold relief against a background of budding trees and

---

[1]Hyrum Smith, *op. cit.*
[2]From an old diary, author unknown, pp. 38-39. B.Y.U., Provo, Utah.

flowering shrubs. The approaching day of dedication would be very significant because the edifice would be the first to receive such distinction since the dedication of the ancient temple of Solomon in Palestine. It was a time of triumph, marking another step in the establishment of the restored Church. The building itself was evidence that the revelation of God's will had been put into action.

The day set for the dedicatory rites was Sunday, March 27, 1836, and it dawned with clear skies and bright sunshine which seemed an omen of the great blessings yet to come. When the appointed hour arrived, the temple was crowded to capacity, with the priesthood seated in their proper places. It was indeed, a solemn occasion.

As Hyrum sat with the First Presidency he felt caught-up in a spirit of exaltation and ecstasy as he reflected on the toil and sacrifice which had made this day possible.

This momentous occasion marked the beginning of the administration of holy ordinances necessary for the salvation of mankind. The Presidency of heaven and the hosts abiding with them were evidently pleased and gave evidence by way of many spiritual manifestations which were wituessed by those present.

The following Tuesday at 11:00 a.m., Hyrum Smith attended a meeting in the temple with the First Presidency and Oliver Cowdery to deliberate on certain problems. At that meeting a revelation was given concerning the dedicatory exercises— two more meetings were to be held in order that all who desired might attend. The Tuesday meeting continued through the day and the following night, and on Wednesday, the priesthood quorums assembled for the rites of the washing of feet. It was a time of great spiritual manifestation; a day of pentecost, of great rejoicing, for important blessings were poured out upon the members of the Church.[3]

In accordance with the revelation, a second dedicatory exercise was held Thursday, March 31, and a third on Sunday, April

[3]Joseph Fielding Smith, *Life of Joseph F. Smith*, pp. 431-433.

3, 1836. There was no variation in the procedure except for certain important spiritual manifestations. It was during this final session that the Prophet and Oliver Cowdery were visited by the Lord, who accepted the house (temple), and by Moses, Elias, and Elijah, who delivered to them important keys of the priesthood.

The temple represented a mighty work initiated by the Heavenly Father in a new dispensation of time. The primary objectives for its construction had now been realized. The keys of the priesthood were now restored.

* * *

The few months following the dedication of the temple was a period of peace and felicity for Hyrum and his family. Their faith and prayers were answered by the coming of Father Smith's relatives to Kirtland. The first to arrive in May 1836, was cousin Elias Smith from St. Lawrence County, New York. Elias said that his father (Asael Smith) and family, and his Uncle Silas Smith and family were also coming to Kirtland, and that their grandmother Mary Duty Smith (wife of the first Asael Smith), was at Fairport on Lake Erie. Hyrum immediately made ready the family carriage to bring Grandma Smith to live with them. She was ninety-three, and had not been baptized mainly because of the attitude of her eldest son Jesse, who had always been an enemy to the work. The family rejoiced at her arrival. She had come five hundred miles to see her children and recognized all whom she had previously met. Upon being introduced to her great-grandchildren, she expressed pleasure and gratification to see them.

Grandfather Asael Smith had died October 31, 1830, but had predicted long before that there would arise a prophet in his family, and Grandmother Smith was fully satisfied that the prediction had been fulfilled in the Prophet Joseph.

Silas Smith and his family arrived from the East on May 18, and then there was a joyful family gathering with Father Smith and three of his brothers in attendance, the first such gathering for many years. Joseph later wrote: ". . . It was a happy day for me, for we had long prayed to see our grandmother and uncles in the church."[4]

About sunset on May 27, 1836, within a few days after visiting with her children, Grandmother Smith died quietly, without sickness, pain, or regret. Sidney Rigdon preached a brief funeral sermon, and she was buried in the little cemetery near the temple. She had buried one daughter, Sarah; two sons, Stephen and Samuel; and her husband, and was survived by five sons — Silas, Jesse, John, Joseph, and Asael — and three daughters — Jessie, Priscilla, and Susanna.

The passing of Mary Duty Smith brought to an end a short period of happy association, for she had been an inspiration to her posterity. Her children had bestowed their most kind and tender affection upon her, and when she breathed her last it was a time for reminiscing. She had lived to see her illustrious grandchildren, and to partake of the blessings of the gospel. Hyrum was grateful to her for the heritage she had bequeathed them; his faith removed the sting of losing her so soon, for it assured him that he would see and be with her again.

Shortly after the death of Mary Duty Smith dark clouds began accumulating over Kirtland. At the moment they were only dark specks on the horizon. The work of Hyrum had settled into a comfortable routine of activity. With the final completion of the temple and the end of his chairmanship on the temple committee, came new opportunities for church service.

While petitions were being exchanged between the local citizens and the Mormons of Clay County, Missouri, for and against the Mormons' removal to other locations, the leaders of Kirtland were busy arranging missionary excursions into the Eastern States.

On Monday afternoon, July 25, 1836, Hyrum left his family to accompany the Prophet Joseph, Sidney Rigdon, and Oliver Cowdery on a mission to Massachusetts. The first part of their journey was by boat via Buffalo to New York. After meeting Elders Orson Hyde and Moses C. Nickerson, at the Farmer's

[4]*Ibid.*, pp. 442-443.

Hotel, they proceeded by boat to Utica. From Utica they took the train making eighty miles in six hours. The following day the party took a steamer the Erie to New York. Another steamer, the *Rochester,* going to the same direction signalled a race. The *Rochester* won by a few minutes. Joseph described the final outcome in these words: "By such undue pressure of steam lives of thousands may have been sacrificed, and I thank God that myself and friends were safely landed."[5]

This mission was like a vacation for Hyrum, because in contrast to that of the western frontier, he was enjoying the culture and conveniences of large cities and the companionship of Joseph and the leading brethren. The trip to New York was exciting. While in this city they went sightseeing. They visited a district where six months before a fire destroyed seventeen million dollars worth of property. From New York they went by steamer to Providence and then boarded a steam train to Boston, thence to Salem where they arrived early in August. Here they rented a house and did missionary work from house to house, preaching publically whenever the opportunity presented itself.

While in Salem, where they remained for over a month, they visited places of historical importance, those rich in the memory of Pilgrim Fathers. They recalled how the settlers, having fled from the old country to avoid persecution and death, had themselves become persecutors by denying religious liberty to the Baptists and Quakers, who like themselves, had fled from tyranny to a land of freedom. The town fathers of Salem from 1692 to 1693 had whipped, imprisoned, tortured, and burned to the stake, and hung many of their citizens for supposed witchcraft.

While at Salem, this group received a visit from Brothers Brigham Young and Lyman E. Johnson. Brother Young with his brother, Joseph, had been through New York, Vermont, Massachusetts, doing missionary work and had baptized many into the Church.

The apparent tendency of the missionaries to combine business with pleasure brought a censure from the Lord, for while

---

[5]*Ibid.,* pp. 463-464.

at Salem, on August 6, Joseph received a revelation in which the Lord said he was not displeased with Joseph's journey to this place notwithstanding his follies, and gave general counsel about the missionary work.

The records are silent about the success of this mission and the details of their return trip to Kirtland. It is supposed they returned home sometime in September. It is quite probable that the missionaries took note of the social and economic conditions along the eastern seaboard, and also, made an appraisal of the religious temper of the people. This knowledge would help facilitate missionary activity.

When Hyrum Smith and the brethren arrived home there were three problems needing their attention: First was the settling of the Missouri Saints on new territory in order to relieve the citizens of Clay County; second, the task of settling the new converts converging on Kirtland; and third, the establishment of a banking system to help facilitate the financial security of the Church. The country was experiencing a period of inflation and land speculation.

Before the end of 1836, the Shoal Creek territory attached to Ray County was taken up in Northwest Missouri which was subsequently to be divided into several counties. Caldwell County was designated early in December.

At this time the attention of the country was focused on the west with its opportunities for land and new business. This attraction, coupled with the gospel message helped to fire the imagination of new members to move west, many before they were adequately prepared. To meet this situation the brethren instructed the missionaries in the field to have the families moving to Kirtland to first send someone in advance to secure a place for them to live. All indications pointed to an economic boom in real estate values in this prosperous agricultural area.

By January 1, 1837, all preliminary arrangements had been made to establish the Kirtland Safety Society. Unable to secure a charter of incorporation, they decided to operate the banking institute on an independent basis. The Prophet called on all who could to support the institution and thus help to build and further the great work of the Lord.

What the brethren hoped would be a benefit to the new Church later proved to be a source of great trouble, for a spirit of speculation developed among some of the brethren who hoped for quick wealth. Notes and currency were over-issued against the total amount of legal specie on reserve. Then, during the early part of 1837, the nation's economy began to collapse, and a money panic swept the country causing the failure of many banks.

In Kirtland, the trend toward uncontrolled inflation and booming investments alarmed Joseph, but his warning went unheeded by most of the stockholders. Unable to stem the tide and sensing imminent failure, Joseph and Hyrum withdrew from the banking firm, but their withdrawal failed to prevent the losers from incriminating them as contributors to the ensuing catastrophe.

A series of events coming in rapid succession during the year 1836-1837 kept Hyrum Smith active in his role of shepherd of the flock in Kirtland, Ohio. The seeds of disaffection and apostasy were creeping in among the Council of Twelve.

With the Kirtland era reaching its climax, Hyrum's voice was frequently heard among the priesthood quorums, which met in the temple. On April 6, 1837, Hyrum addressed the assembly on the temporal affairs of the Church. He censured those who, without authority to do so, encouraged converts to move to Kirtland. He also alluded, in terms of disapprobation, to the practice of some individuals, of getting money from the brethren that came in, when such money should have been used to discharge heavy debts that were then hanging over the heads of the Church, or for the benefit of the Saints in that place.[6]

The illiteracy in the Church won Hyrum's hearty approval of the temple's being used as a school. Already over 140 had been enrolled at one time, divided into three departments: the Classics, where the languages only were taught; the English Department, where mathematics, common arithmetic, geography, English

---

[6]Joseph Smith, *op. cit.*, vol. II, pp. 478-479.

grammar, writing, and reading were taught; and third, the Juvenile Department.[7]

The gospel must be preached by missionaries with training in the liberal arts as well as in the scriptures and principles of the gospel. The loss caused by pruning the dead wood (apostates) from the Lord's vineyard must be compensated by grafting new branches. To meet this contingency a policy of missionary expansion was agreed upon, and inspiration came to open a mission in the British Isles.

The call of Heber C. Kimball met with sneers and opposition from apostates who formerly were members of the Quorum of Twelve. To the faithful Saints the call was divinely inspired. Speaking of this occasion, Elder Kimball wrote: "Hyrum, seeing the condition of the Church, when he talked about my mission, wept like a little child; he was continually blessing and encouraging me, and pouring out his soul in prophecies upon my head, he said: 'Go and you shall prosper as not many has prospered.' "[8]

In Kirtland that summer of 1837, Hyrum became increasingly alarmed over rumors that Joseph Smith was a fallen prophet. The "Kirtland Safety Society" was failing and Joseph had been stricken with ill health at the time the missionaries were leaving for England. His illness, the people reasoned, was a curse of God placed on him for his transgressions.

The reports coming from Missouri demanded attention. All was not well among the presiding brethren there, and the condition required the immediate attention of the First Presidency. Hyrum realized that he must make preparations to accompany Joseph, which meant that he must leave his family for a trip that would require two to three months. He worried about Jerusha who was expecting their sixth child. Lovina, now ten years old, helped to lift the load of household chores. John was almost five; Hyrum, Jr., was three; and little Jerusha was about twenty months old. Hyrum's departure although necessary was most difficult for him. A spirit of foreboding depressed him, and

---

[7]Ibid., pp. 474-475.
[8]Orson F. Whitney, The Life of Heber C. Kimball (Salt Lake City, Utah, 1888) p. 105.

it was with tears of affection that he assured his family he would return at the earliest possible moment. He was unaware that he was never again to see his beloved wife in mortality.

Not many days after his departure, while he was still following the now familiar route through rough and primitive country to Northern Missouri, his wife died, October 13, 1837, eleven days after the birth of a baby girl whom they named Sarah. Jerusha had stood by her husband through many dark periods of poverty and persecution. Her faith and devotion to Hyrum and the Church was without malice or complaint. She supported, complemented her husband, and strengthened his hand during every crucial period of the Church. Her death was a shock to the family and to the Church; and to Hyrum her loss was a staggering blow.

Of her death, Joseph the Prophet wrote: "My brother Hyrum's wife, Jerusha Barden Smith, died on the 13th of October while I was at Terre Haute, and her husband at Far West. She left five small children and numerous relatives to mourn her loss; her demise was severely felt by all. She said to one of her tender offspring when on her dying bed, 'Tell your father when he comes that the Lord has taken your mother home and left you for him to take care of.' She died in full assurance of a part in the first resurrection."[9]

There seemed to be no limit to the severity of the trials Hyrum was called upon to endure. Always a devoted husband and father, he was over a thousand miles away helping to put the Church in order when his bereaved and lonely family were laying away their mother. In Missouri, Hyrum was patient with his brethren. They had accepted the suggestions of kind friends in Clay County, Missouri, to move into new territory in the region of Shoal Creek. Hyrum met with Joseph (who had arrived a few days before) and a group of leading elders at the townsite to be known as Far West, later to become the county seat of Caldwell County. Here a conference was called for November 6, 1837. Hyrum noted at this meeting were present four of the

---

[9]Ibid., p. 519.

Twelve: Lyman E. Johnson, Thomas B. Marsh, William E. Mc-Lellin, and William Smith; also the high council. Among the problems discussed by these brethren was the laying out of the city of Far West and the size of the city blocks, which should be four acres. The building of the Lord's house (temple) would be postponed until the Lord should reveal it to be his will to have it commenced.

Another session of the conference was held the next day, at which time Hyrum was set apart as second counselor to his brother the Prophet in place of Frederick G. Williams, who was released because of insubordination. Certain brethren voted against him. Sidney Rigdon's nomination of Hyrum to fill this vacancy thus caused was unanimously accepted by the vote of those present. This new appointment removed Hyrum from the position he had held since September 3, 1837 as assistant counselor to Joseph Smith, jointly with Oliver Cowdery, Joseph Smith, Sr., and John Smith.

The crucial conference was concluded when Hyrum assisted in the ordination of Isaac Morley to the office of Patriarch.[10]

Hyrum, with his brother Joseph, Sidney Rigdon, and others, returned to Kirtland after an absence of about two months. It was a difficult homecoming. He was griefstricken at the news of Jerusha's passing. It is quite likely that Annie Grinolds, a charity member of his household came to live with the family at this time and remained as a domestic for many years. The Smith families had co-operated and been most kind in giving needed aid and comfort to the bereaved family.

Many tasks awaited Hyrum's attention after his long absence, and the press of many responsibilities, such as providing for the needs of a large family, and trying to solve problems in the Church was a heavy load indeed. His wife who had been a pillar of strength had been snatched from him. His burdens seemed insurmountable, and he sought out Joseph for advice. Part of the solution to his troubles would be to find a helpmate, some eligible young woman for a wife.

---

[10]*Ibid.*, p. 509.

A series of events coming in rapid succession during the year 1836-1837 kept Hyrum Smith active in his role of shepherd of the flock in Kirtland, Ohio. The seeds of disaffection and apostasy were creeping in among the Council of Twelve.

At this time there were living in Kirtland, Mary Fielding and her sister Mercy Rachel Fielding. The sisters from Toronto, Canada, were converts of Elder Parley P. Pratt. Their brother, Joseph Fielding, was then on a mission to England.[11] They had themselves emigrated from England to Toronto.

Hyrum had known them for sometime. They were both pretty, personable with light brown hair and of medium stature. Mary, who had taught school in Kirtland during February, 1837, was Hyrum's choice. He spent little time on courtship, and his early proposal was made on the basis of expediency. As Hyrum later remarked: "It was not because I had less love or regard for Jerusha, that I married so soon, but it was for the sake of my children." Then, too, his brother Joseph had advised such a course for the sake of his children, and he felt that it was the will of the Lord.[12]

Mary Fielding[13] did not hesitate to accept the proposal of so handsome and prominent a man. He was nearly thirty-eight and she thirty-six. The marriage was solemnized December 24, 1837, at Kirtland, Ohio. Mary was surely the most significant Christmas gift to bless that household! She was loved and respected by the Smith family, and her devotion to Hyrum's children rivaled that of their own mother, Jerusha.

---

[11]*Ibid.,* p. 492.

[12]Joseph Fielding Smith, *Life of Joseph F. Smith,* Deseret News Press (Salt Lake City, Utah, 1938.)

[13]Mary Fielding Smith, born July 21, 1801, in Honiden, Belfordshire, England, sixth child of a family of ten: John, James, Thomas, Joseph, Ann, Mary, Martha, Benjamin, Mercy Rachel and Josiah (stillborn). Parents were John and Rachel Ibbotson Fielding - born Halifax, Yorkshire, England, he eight years her senior. John, her father, was Duke Fielding; his mother, Elizabeth Dison.

Earlier, John Fielding had married Sarah Kitson. To this union were born seven children, five of whom died soon after birth. A daughter, Sarah, who never married, died in her forty-sixth year. She belonged to the Saint Neots Circuits of the Methodist Church, of which she was a consistent and steady member. A young brother, Marmaduke Fielding, died at the age of eleven. After the death of the first wife, John Fielding married Rachel Ibbotson in 1790, when she was twenty-three years old.

Mary Fielding emigrated to Canada in 1834, where she jointed her sister, Mercy Rachel, who proceded her to Canada.

(Courtesy of Marion Fluckigar.)

The optimism and good feeling among the Saints at the beginning of 1837 was shattered as the year came to a close. To Hyrum, the man second only to Joseph in the hearts of the people, the year had been a period of great worry and strain. The loss of his wife who had been a companion and sweetheart, leaving him with five young children to care for increased his burden. No doubt his sense of mission and his devotion to a great cause sustained him during the family crisis. He had known death before. There had been the loss of Alvin, his older brother, and his own little daughter, Mary. These had helped to condition him but could not soften the blow of Jerusha's death.

His long trip to the Eastern States and the journey to Missouri had been made at the request of the Prophet Joseph. He had been asked to give aid and counsel when others in high places were faltering. He mourned over the loss of good men who had been led astray and over the mounting enmity and cruelty heaped upon his revered brother, Joseph, by traitors in the Church. However, he would not look back and be discouraged; the drama of the great revelation was unfolding and trials of greater magnitude were yet in store. With the completion of the temple and the restoration of important keys of the priesthood, came also greater faith and devotion from the membership. The brief period of school pointed toward the importance of education and an enlightened priesthood. The enthusiasm of Hyrum for education was expressed in his letter to cousin Silas when he wrote that after four weeks study of Hebrew he was able to translate the Hebrew Bible fluently.

CHAPTER XVII

A NEW HOME

At the beginning of 1838, the conditions at Kirtland, Ohio, were coming to a climactic close for Hyrum Smith. Conditions beyond his control were forcing him to anticipate drastic action if necessary. There was very little he could do to prevent the hostility against the Church. Apostasy within the higher echelon of the Church was spreading at an alarming rate. The enemy, also, sensing the trouble among the church leaders, began to take action, but prosperity and the unity of the membership kept hostilities from flaming into open conflict.

A similar situation to that at the close of the New York period was now developing for the Smiths. The pattern of attack by the enemy was painfully familiar. The events prior to Hyrum's departure for the West had a significant bearing on the welfare of him and his family.

The favorite method of their persecutors was to bring civil suit for debt against members of the Smith family, then if the defendants were unable to pay, either their property was seized or they were sent off to prison. For a debt of fifty dollars against the Prophet Joseph, the mob threatened to take the Egyptian mummies, but the strategy of the family kept them from being harmed or destroyed.

In view of the critical situation, Hyrum met with others at his father's home on the night of January 12. Here they were somewhat reassured to hear Joseph say: ". . . But one thing, Brethren, is certain, I shall see you again, let what will happen, for I have a promise of life five years, and they cannot kill me until that time has expired."[1]

This pronouncement did not lessen the efforts to guard against grave dangers to members of the family. The following day word was received by Hyrum that his brother, Joseph, had

---

[1]Lucy Mack Smith, *op. cit.*, pp. 247-248.

left town during the night. He had been warned by the Holy
Spirit to arise from his bed and leave. He arose immediately and
waked Sidney Rigdon, and within moments the two had left their
families and were headed toward Missouri on horseback. It was
later learned that they rode sixty miles to Norton Township,
Medina County, Ohio, where they stayed among brethren for
the three days which elapsed before the arrival of their families.
Several of the mob then followed them for many days. Brigham
Young and his family joined them, and the three families traveled
by covered wagon, in extremely cold weather, to Far West, Missouri.[2]

The day following Joseph's departure from Kirtland, Luke
Johnson an apostate constable, served a summons on Hyrum's
father for marrying a couple without a proper license. Ignoring
the pleas of Mother Lucy Smith, the constable took Father Smith
to have him released on bonds. At that time, Hyrum was summoned by Mr. Johnson, and a plan was devised for Brother
Smith's escape. With the help of John Boynton, Hyrum made
good the liberation of his father. In a few days word was
brought to Mother Lucy of the whereabouts of her husband, and
she sent Don Carlos to him with money and clothes. Returning
from the errand to his father, Don Carlos was discovered by the
mob which unsuccessfully attempted to arrest him on the same
charges as those made against his father. Soon after this incident Don Carlos moved his family to New Portage, and later
joined the family of his father in moving to Missouri.[3]

Hyrum too began to make preparations to leave Kirtland for
Missouri. After the winter frost was out of the ground and the
snow melted away, the Saints would all be able to leave. There
had been a council meeting to arrange for the removal of church
records and other valuable items to Missouri. Hyrum fortunately
did not become the object of enemy action and was free to give
direction to an orderly movement westward.

On March 6, 1838, the seventies met in the temple to make

[2]Joseph Smith, *op. cit.*, vol. III, p. 2.
[3]Lucy Mack Smith, *op. cit.*, p. 248-249.

plans to go in a body to Zion. Hyrum felt that moving the Saints from Kirtland to the land of Missouri was in accordance with the commandments and revelations of God, and it seemed practical for a quorum of seventies to locate in as compact a body as possible in a spot where they could receive counsel from the twelve and the First Presidency in matters pertaining to their mission.

The morning session of their meeting was held under the supervision of President Hyrum Smith. They asked him to open with prayer and proceeded to formulate what they called the "Constitution for the Organization and Government of the Camp."

Another meeting for further planning was held March 17, just prior to the departure of Hyrum and his family. At this gathering Hyrum counseled them about their movement to Zion. The commandment had been given for "the honest in heart to rise up and go up into that land." He stated that what he had said and done about chartering a steamboat was for the purpose of moving the Church as a body. He told them, however, that this he had done according to his own judgment, without reference to the testimony of the Spirit of God. He said also that he had recommended the plan and advised the high council and high priests to adopt it, acting solely upon his own wisdom. It had seemed to him that the whole body of the Church in Kirtland could be removed with less expense in the way he had proposed. He said further that the Saints often act in relation to temporal affairs, upon their own responsibility, without any reference to the testimony of the Spirit of God.[4]

Hyrum declared that he knew by the Spirit of God that the plans made by the seventies for their removal and journey were according to the will of the Lord. He advised all others who were planning to go up to Zion, whose circumstances would permit, to join the seventies and go with them. If he were so situated he said, he would join the camp and go with them and comply strictly with the rules adopted for the regulation of the camp on the journey. It would be to his delight as an individual, he said,

---

[4]Joseph Smith, *op. cit.*, vol. III, p. 87-8.

to go without having any concern whatever in the management of affairs, either directly or indirectly, during the journey.

In answer to an inquiry concerning the difficulties that might attend the movements of so large a body, Hyrum observed that no fears need be entertained by any on that score, for, said he, "There would be no difficulty attend the camp if there should be 5,000 persons in it. The more the better; and the advantages of their going all together would be greater than they could possibly be if they should go in smaller companies. Food, clothing, and other provisions could be purchased much cheaper in large quantities."[5]

In closing, President Hyrum Smith advised the camp not to discriminate against those not living the word of wisdom, and to secure the assistance and advice of the high council in carrying out their plans for the move and organizing the camp.[6]

It was a miserable March day when Hyrum and his family bade farewell to Kirtland. They were leaving a comfortable and commodious home to face the cold of spring rains and an implacable enemy. It took great faith and courage to leave a well-regulated routine of good living and face the hazards of establishing a home in a primitive land.

Hyrum was endowed with a keen sense of loyalty and obligation, and had already shown marked ability as a leader. With this move to Missouri he was unconsciously playing his part in the rapid unfolding of God's plan for the Church. But it cost him heavily.

Just thinking of the Kirtland Temple brought a flood of memories of the toil and worry, and the spiritual blessings resulting from its erection. As his little caravan started westward, Hyrum swept a last long look over the familiar surroundings of this village nestled among rolling, verdant Ohio hills. This place had been their home for seven years, and leaving it excited mingled emotions.

Across the street from the temple stood Sidney Rigdon's now-

---

[5]*Ibid.*, p. 90.
[6]*Ibid.*, p. 90.

vacant home. A little farther on, the well-traveled road descended a gradual slope to the north, past the frame home of his parents; to the right, across the way, was the tavern-inn where the Prophet Joseph's son Joseph III had been born.[7] Nearby was the store of Gilbert and Whitney, now managed by its new owners. The bridge running in a westerly direction over the creek through well-cultivated patches of land, reminded Hyrum of the many times he had gone this way with loads of grist, flour and lumber to and from the mills erected along the water course.

Hyrum Smith realized now that Kirtland had never been meant to remain the hearquarters of the Church. The infant Church was not a year old when Hyrum and Joseph had been commanded by a revelation to leave the state of New York and go to Ohio. During the first year in Ohio, Parley P. Pratt had returned from his mission to the western borders of Missouri and had described to Hyrum and the Prophet Joseph the fertile region lying westward. Upon Joseph's inquiry the Lord had revealed to him the significance of this new area, which was geographically located near the center of the North American continent. Here would be located, eventually, the city of Zion, or the New Jerusalem, and the headquarters of the Church.

However, Kirtland was first to be built up. The Lord, in a revelation had said: ". . . I, the Lord, will retain a strong hold in the land of Kirtland . . . in the which I will not overthrow the wicked, that thereby I may save some. . . . After that day, I, the Lord, will not hold any guilty that shall go with an open heart up to the land of Zion." (D&C 64:21-22.)

This revelation gave sanction for the Saints to emigrate to Missouri. The Colesville Branch had gone on to get settled, and the law of consecration had been established among them.

Hyrum reflected on the progress made during the few short years at Kirtland and his status in contrast with that of seven years before. His success could be judged by the progress of the Church. The Church had grown rapidly. A President and two

---

[7]Interview, Thomas Gale, resident of Kirtland, Ohio. (1954)

counselors had been set apart to be known as "The First Presidency"; a Quorum of Twelve Apostles and a Council of Seventies had been added. A local organization had been effected, this to be called a stake, a term taken from Isaiah, and meaning "support the church like a great tent." This organization also had a president and counselors, a high council, bishops, high priests, seventies, and elders. There had been revealed a comprehensive organization of the priesthood, both Melchizedek and Aaronic — the latter to have quorums of priests, teachers, and deacons.

During the period at Kirtland, about sixty-two revelations had been given and recorded, the Bible had been revised and the book of Abraham had been translated. From this new scripture emerged new principles and doctrines of the gospel.

Surely, no other period had been so fruitful of growth and development of polity (form of government) in the Church. Hyrum had been a part of it all. But now he resolutely turned his face from the past to the new life beyond the western horizon. There could be no turning back.

The journey to Far West, Missouri, was a two months' trek, a distance of over a thousand miles. Later, when speaking of this journey, Hyrum said, "I left Kirtland in the spring of 1838, having the charge of ten individuals,[8] weather very unfavorable, roads poor which increased expenses and caused delays. After much suffering and privation we arrived safely in Missouri. I sent all household furniture and some implements via water, amounting to several hundred dollars, having made purchase of several hundred acres of land to settle on. Took a house in Far West. Heard rumors of mob action but couldn't believe because we had broken no law."[9]

Hyrum's mother, Lucy Mack Smith, described their journey as one of hardship. They camped out in tents, in driving storms, traveled on foot through marshes and quagmires, and were soaked many times with rain. Being without any changes of clothing or

---

[8]The ten were: Hyrum's wife (Mary Fielding Smith), Lovina, Hyrum, John, Jerusha, Sarah (children), Grandma Grenolds, George Mills, and Robert Thompson and wife, Mercy Fielding Thompson.
[9]*Journal History*, Historian's Office, Salt Lake, Utah.

warm bedding, they suffered greatly when colds and sickness resulted.

When Hyrum and his family arrived at Far West they were amazed to see a fast-growing community. The Saints had moved north from Clay County, Missouri, in 1836, after the local citizens had met and passed a resolution urging them to move. They had selected this town site in Caldwell County.

By the autumn of 1838, the exiles had established two thousand farms and paid the government $318,000 for land, which at the minimum price for government land would give them over 250,000 acres.[10] There were 150 houses, constructed from native lumber, 4 dry-goods stores, 3 family groceries, 6 blacksmith shops, and 2 hotels. The excavation for the temple had been made, and by the fall of 1836 a commodious schoolhouse had been erected on the public square. This structure was also used as a town hall and courthouse, as well as a schoolhouse. It first stood in the southwest quarter of the town, but upon the establishment of the county seat, it was removed to the center of the square.[11]

Far West was situated on a rolling plain covered by a stand of prairie grass cut by intermittent water courses which were lined with native shrubs and timber. Wild game, such as deer, turkey, and prairie hens was abundant. The land was good, just waiting to be tilled before it could yield its strength to feed the multitudes that would soon begin to gather there from all corner of the globe.

There was much to be done at Far West: The Church had to be strengthened; the civil government had to be established (the Federal Government would provide sufficient land for settlement on a large scale); and a house needed to be erected unto the Lord. A revelation mentioning Hyrum's name had been received by the Prophet Joseph the latter part of April. This revelation read in part:

> . . . my servant Joseph Smith, Jr., and also my servant Sidney Rigdon, and also my servant Hyrum Smith, and your counselors who are and shall

---

[10]George A. Smith, Church Historian, History of Mo., "American Commonwealths" p. 181. From *History of the Church*, vol. III, p. XLIII.
[11]*History of Caldwell County*, (National Historical Company, 1886) Ref. *Hist. of the Church*, vol. 3, p. XLIII.

be appointed hereafter; . . . and unto all the . . . Saints scattered abroad into all the world; my church shall be called in the last days . . . "The Church of Jesus Christ of Latter-day Saints."[12] Verily, I say unto you all, arise and shine forth, that thy light may be a standard for the nations. . . . Let the city Far West, be a holy and consecrated land unto me, and it shall be called most holy; Therefore I command you to build an house unto me, for the gathering together of my Saints, that they may worship me.[13]

This announcement no doubt pleased Hyrum and the brethren, for now a permanent home for the Church could be established. But before Missouri could become a "most holy" land, the Church must be put in order. The disaffection and apostasy at Kirtland had spread like an epidemic to Far West. Before Hyrum had arrived at Far West, trouble had arisen among the church leaders there. David Whitmer, the stake president at Far West, and his two counselors had been tried for mishandling church funds; and Thomas B. Marsh and David W. Patten had been named to head the Church until Joseph should arrive.

Soon afterward David Whitmer was excommunicated from the Church, and then Oliver Cowdery was cited before the high council on nine separate counts, three of which were later withdrawn; but the remaining six he answered only partially. He defended himself for the sale of his land in Jackson County, Missouri, on the ground that it was his personal right under the Constitution. Of his complicity with the apostates in Kirtland or his charges against the Prophet, he said nothing. William E. McLellin was brought before the council for apostasy. He said he had lost confidence in the head of the Church and had stopped praying and keeping the commandments of the Lord. He also was excommunicated from the Church at Far West.[14]

Among the first things Hyrum did, after locating his family, was to go north about fifteen or twenty miles with Joseph and a company of the brethren to seek a location for another city. On their way they met Sidney Rigdon and company, who were re-

12The Church has been called: "The Church of Christ," "The Church of Jesus Christ," and "The Church of God." *History of the Church*, vol. III, p. 24.
13D&C sec. 65.
14Joseph Smith, *op. cit.*, vol. III, pp. 30-31.

turning to Far West from a similar scouting trip.[15] The town of
Far West was fast becoming the hub for several settlements, such
as Adam-ondi-Ahman, Hawn's Mill, Millport, DeWitt, Wight's
Ferry, and Gallatin.

On this trip north on Monday, May 28, Joseph and Hyrum
and company visited Adam-ondi-Ahman. On Wednesday, May
30, Hyrum returned home, and on Friday the Prophet also returned to Far West. On June 2, Hyrum and family were happy
to hear that Joseph's household had been blessed with another
member — born that day — whom they had named Alexander
Hale Smith.

The following Monday, June 4, Hyrum with Joseph and
others returned to Adam-ondi-Ahman and stayed with Brother
Moses Dailey overnight and the following day went in the rain
to Colonel Lyman Wight's home. For several days they continued surveying and locating plots for houses, working until their
task was completed.

The immediate problem was to obtain homes for newcomers
by locating sites for towns where they could build more housing;
and a defense against mounting mob action must be organized.
John Smith and six families were soon to arrive and would settle
at Adam-ondi-Ahman. A Canadian company and the Kirtland
Camp, expected sometime in July, would also be directed to this
new town site north of Far West.

*   *   *

Adam-ondi-Ahman was located to the north of Grand River,
in Daviess County, Missouri, about twenty-five miles north of Far
West. It was situated on an elevated spot of ground overlooking
the river, which rendered the place as healthful and beautiful as
any other in the United States. The following is a description of
the altar site written by one Chapman Duncan:

> I think the next day (after arriving the night before) he (Joseph) said
> to those present, Hyrum Smith, Bishop Vincent Knight, myself and two or
> three others, "get me a spade and I will show you the altar that Adam of-
> fered sacrifice on." . . .We went forty rods north of my house. He placed

---

[15]*Ibid.*, pp. 37-38.

the spade with care, placed his foot on it. When he took out the shovel full of dirt, it bared the stone. The dirt was two inches deep on the stone I reckon. About four feet or more was disclosed. He did not dig to the bottom of the three layers of good masonry well put wall. The stone looked more like dressed stone, nice joints, ten inches thick, eighteen inches long or more. We came back down the slope, perhaps fifteen rods on the level. The Prophet stopped and remarked that this place where we stood was the place where Adam gathered his posterity and blessed them, and predicted what should come to pass to later generations. The next day he returned to Far West.

Independence day, July 4, 1838, was celebrated at Far West in appropriate style. This day had special significance for a people who had been subjected to persecution by mobs who had driven them from their homes, destroyed their property, and threatened their lives.

An excavation on a suitable location was ready at this time for the laying of the cornerstone of a new temple. It was a little over two months (April 26, 1838) since they had been commanded by revelation to build a house unto the Lord; the Saints had organized a committee and laid plans to build a temple, which was to be 110 feet long and 80 feet wide.

The day, which dawned fair, had as its first event a colorful parade at 10:00 a.m. The parade was led by the military unit, which was followed by the leaders of the Church. These leaders included the brethren who were in charge of the day's celebration: Joseph Smith; Hyrum Smith; Sidney Rigdon, orator of the day; and Reynolds Cahoon, Chief Marshal; also the Twelve Apostles, presidents of stakes, High Council, Bishop and Counselors, Architects, and assorted ladies and gentlemen. The cavalry brought up the rear of the large procession, which marched to music and formed a circle, with ladies in front, around the temple excavation.

The southeast cornerstone of the Lord's house was then laid by the presidents of stakes assisted by twelve men; and the southwest stone was laid by the presidents of elders' quorums, assisted by twelve men. After the oration by Sidney Rigdon there was a shout of "Hosanna," and a song composed for the occasion by

Levi W. Hancock was sung by Solomon Hancock. The most perfect order prevailed throughout the day.

Word from William Smith was received by Hyrum and Joseph on July 6, stating that William, Don Carlos, Joseph Smith, Sr., and three other families were having considerable trouble on their journey to Far West. Their horses were sick and lame, and their money had run out. They had failed to acquire sufficient cash before leaving Kirtland, because it was not available, and they had only $25.00 among them on which to make the remaining journey of 500 miles. "But," wrote Don Carlos, "our courage is good, and I think we shall be brought through. I leave it with you (Joseph) and Hyrum to devise some way to assist us to some more expense money. . . . Poverty is a heavy load, but we are all obliged to welter under it. . . ."[16]

The shifting and moving of the Saints made the economic phase of their existence very difficult. There seemed never to be enough money. On July 8, 1838, the Prophet approached the Lord in prayer with these words, "O Lord, show unto thy servant how much thou requirest of the properties of thy people for a tithing."

In reply the Lord said in part:

Verily thus saith the Lord, I require all their surplus property to be put into the hands of the bishop of my church of Zion. For the building of mine house and for the priesthood, and for the debts of the Presidency of my church; And this shall become the beginning of the tithing of my people; And after that those who have thus been tithed, shall pay one-tenth of all their interest annually, and this shall be a standing law unto them forever, for my holy priesthood, saith the Lord.[17]

Shortly after this time, a meeting was held and resolutions were passed to meet the financial needs of the presiding brethren. Hyrum, Joseph, and Sidney Rigdon were kept busy directing the arriving Saints to the various settlements and in the council meetings that were necessary to conduct the affairs of the people.

Increased activity of the Saints aroused mob action against

---

[16]*Ibid.*, pp. 41-44.
[17]D&C sec. 119.

them. While the business of organizing an orderly government went on, the mob element was busy inciting the old settlers against the Mormons. Already plans were laid to prevent the Saints from voting at the polls at Gallatin, Daviess County, Missouri. On the day the voting took place a skirmish occurred with the Mormons obtaining the upper hand. The Missourians feared the loss of their suffrage.

The following day rumors spread that several casualties among the brethren had occured and that Missourians had been prevented from voting, and that the majority of the citizens of Daviess County were determined to drive the Saints from the county. Immediately, Hyrum left for the West with the Prophet and Sidney Rigdon for Gallatin to investigate affairs. They were soon joined by fifteen or twenty men armed for their own protection, and further along the way to Gallatin they were joined by others. That night, they arrived at Colonel Wight's place. To their great relief and joy they learned that none of the brethren had been killed, although several had been severely wounded.

The next day Hyrum and Joseph, with the posse, called on Adam Black, justice of the peace-elect for Daviess County, who had joined the mob forces to prevent the Saints from settling in the county. When they asked him outright whether he was for or against the Mormons, and whether he would administer justice; they politely requested that he sign an agreement to uphold the law. He refused to sign the document but agreed to write one himself to their satisfaction and sign it. He agreed to follow a neutral course avoiding taking sides.

The above incidents gave the enemy a chance to misrepresent conditions, by lying and deceit, to arouse the citizenry of Missouri against the Saints.

On Thursday, August 9, Joseph, Hyrum, and Sidney Rigdon met at noon at Adam-ondi-Ahman with certain representative citizens for the purpose of drawing up a covenant of peace in order to preserve one another's rights and to deliver offenders to be dealt with according to law and justice; after this meeting

hoping that things would be worked out satisfactorily. For safety, families at Gallatin were moved to Diahman and Far West. On Monday, August 13, some of the brethren on their way from the forks at Grand River, were chased by evil men for ten or twelve miles. After successfully eluding them, the brethren were met eight miles from Far West by some other brethren who informed them that Judge King had issued a writ for the arrest of the Prophet Joseph and Lyman Wight on trumped up charges growing out of their visit to Adam Black on the night of August 8 to obtain his signed agreement to uphold the law and help bring peace.[18]

Soon afterwards the sheriff of Daviess County came to Far West to serve the writ, but after an interview with the Prophet, he demurred on the grounds of seeking more evidence, and the writ was never served.

By the last of August, Governor Lilburn W. Boggs of Missouri, as commander-in-chief of the state militia, made a proclamation to General David R. Atchison which read: "Ready four hundred mounted men. . . and form into companies according to law. Indications of Indian disturbances on the immediate frontier and the recent civil disturbances in the counties of Caldwell, Daviess, and Carol, render it necessary as a precautionary measure." A similar letter was addressed to Major Generals John B. Clark, Samuel D. Ducas, David Willock, Lewis Bolton, Henry W. Crowther, and Thomas D. Grand.[19]

The Prophet Joseph and Lyman Wight were brought to court and bound over on a $500 bond on the basis of many false accusations, not because they were guilty, but to satisfy the mob. Every precaution was made to avoid any undue provocation.

On Saturday, September 8, word was received that Adam-ondi-Ahman had been attacked.[20] The following day a company of mounted men were sent from Far West to its defense. When it was learned that a wagon load of arms had been sent to the Daviess County mob, Captain William Allred, with ten mounted

---

[18]Joseph Smith, op. cit., vol. III, pp. 55, 60-63.
[19]Ibid., pp. 64-65.
[20]Adam-ondi-Ahman had 500 in habitants. Journal History, vol. XII, p. 199.

men, was sent to intercept it. Two men were arrested and, with their guns, taken to Far West for trial. Captain Allred acted under the civil officers of Caldwell County. The next day, the prisoners were ordered by Judge Black to be liberated. Nevertheless, a trial was held the following Wednesday which proved that the arms were being taken to the mob.

Reports continued to come in that Mormons captured by the mob were being tortured to death in the most cruel manner. These reports were circulated to bait the Mormons into making reprisals, and thus give the enemy justification to accuse them of acts of violence.

A letter was sent from Daviess County to Governor Boggs containing all the falsehoods and lies that the mob could devise against the Mormons. Also, orders were sent that General Atchison, by the solicitation of the citizens and the advice of the judge of the circuit court, was to order out four companies of fifty men each from Clay County, and a like number from Ray County, to proceed immediately to the scene of excitement and insurrection.

When an investigation was made of the trouble, a report was sent by General Atchison and General Alexander Doniphan to the governor that the reports already made to him were invalid and false; that the Mormons who lived on the east of Grand River should return to their homes and the militia be disbanded.[21]

After the disbanding of the militia in Daviess County, the discharged soldiers gathered at DeWitt, Carol County—located fifty miles southeast of Far West near the junction of the Grand and Missouri rivers—and threatened vengeance against all Saints without regard for age, sex, or condition. On Tuesday, October 2, 1838, they opened fire on the Saints.

In the meantime at Far West, Hyrum, with the leading brethren, traveled several miles out to extend a welcome to the Kirtland Company and escort them into the city. The company had traveled eleven miles that last day, having come 860 miles from Kirtland. Many were hungry, for food had been at a

---

[21]Joseph Smith, op. cit., pp. 82-85.

minimum for several days. Sidney Rigdon furnished beef for the camp and took care of the sick ones. They camped on the public square at Far West directly south of and close to the excavation for the Lord's house. It was a scene of greeting old friends and praising the Lord for their safe arrival. Concerning the arrival of the Kirtland camp Joseph wrote:

> The camp continued their journey to Ambrosial Creek, where they pitched their tents. I went with them a mile or two, to a beautiful spring on the prairie accompanied by Elder Rigdon, brother Hyrum and Brigham Young, with whom I returned to the city.

The next day was a day to be remembered by that part of The Church of Jesus Christ of Latter-day Saints, called The Camp, or Kirtland Camp, No. 1, for as they arrived at their final destination and began to pitch their tents about sunset, one of the brethren living in the place proclaimed with a loud voice:

> Brethren, your long and tedious journey is now ended; you are now on the public square of Adam-ondi-Ahman. This is the place where Adam blessed his posterity, when they rose up and called him Michael, the Prince, the Archangel, and he being full of the Holy Ghost predicted what should befall his posterity to the latest generations.

Over five hundred Saints had journeyed from Kirtland to Zion enduring many hardships during the three months' trek; insufficient food for themselves and feed for their animals, sickness and the spirit of rebellion in some, adverse weather and poor wagons, which had often to be repaired all made it a period of extreme hardship. Their faith in the gospel had been tried to the breaking point, and during the last several weeks of the journey, many withdrew to remain by the wayside.

The mounting force of evil like a tidal wave was about to sweep over them. In Hyrum's family, now located in a comfortable house at Far West there was a feeling of tension and uneasiness. Conditions were not favorable. Mary Fielding Smith, Hyrum's wife, was soon to become a mother, and the worry and concern endured by Hyrum for his wife and family was almost overwhelming. What was in store for him and his loved ones? The next few months would tell.

CHAPTER XVIII

DRIVEN FROM FAR WEST

When Hyrum Smith first arrived in Far West, the threats he heard made by the enemy to drive the Mormons out of Northern Missouri puzzled him. He was disturbed because the Saints were citizens of the United States and had done nothing to warrant such threats and treatment. They had acquired virgin territory by legal means and had spent considerable money for improvements.

Since Hyrum's arrival the threats of molestation had become a reality. It had been necessary for him to visit the outlying settlements and spend much time attending council meetings trying to solve the difficulties. Then came the alarming reports of an attack on the Saints in Carroll County.

The governor of Missouri had turned a deaf ear to their entreaties for help. Dr. Austin and Captain Bogart, a Methodist minister, one of the worst of the mobocrats, distinguished themselves as leaders of the mob militia which had been laying seige to the settlement of DeWitt for several days. They guarded the roads, intermittently firing guns and a cannon into the village. General Clark of the state troops had written to General Atchison that the Saints were on the defensive and that unless he could get reinforcement to control the mob, the Mormons would be forced to flee the country. Reinforcements did not come, and on Thursday, October 12, 1838, the mob drove the Saints of DeWitt, Carroll County (about seventy wagons of them), from their homes and out of town.

An agreement to reimburse the Mormons for their losses was never honored. Cattle were slaughtered and used by the mob; houses were burned and goods destroyed. The sick and the weak died and were buried by the wayside without coffins or funeral sevices. The caravan made about twelve miles that first day, a pitiful and stricken company journeying to Far West.

The victorious mob of Carroll County then made plans to move their forces to Daviess County to dispossess the Mormons there of their property and repossess the land that had been purchased and improved to make farms. About eight hundred mobbers from different sections converged on Adam-ondi-Ahman. Some deliberately fired their own homes to make it appear that the Mormons had done it—an old trick successfully used five years before in Jackson County. The leaders of the mob also wrote to the governor, blaming the Mormons for the blackest of deeds.

For self-protection, the Saints called for volunteers to join the Caldwell militia. On Monday, October 15, one hundred men volunteered under the leadership of a Mormon officer, Lieutenant-Colonel George M. Hinkle (an arrangement agreed to by General Doniphan), and marched to the defense of Adam-ondi-Ahman.[1] They found conditions of suffering, fear, and evil similar to those at De Witt. Isolated houses were burning; cattle, hogs, and horses were being driven off; and people were fleeing into the town for safety, destitute of clothes, fearing for their very lives. A snowstorm on October 18 and 19 added to the suffering.

The mob showed no mercy. Women and children, ordered out of their comfortable homes, were forced to stand and watch their homes burn to the ground. The experience of Agnes M. Smith, wife of Don Carlos Smith, was typical. Don Carlos was at that time serving as a missionary for the Church. His wife and two small children fled from their burning home toward the settlement. Sister Smith carried her little ones across Grand River,

---

[1]Chapman Duncan, a member of the Mormon Militia, described what happened; "The bugle sounded, and by the time I was ready there were three-hundred men mounted early to start. We arrived in Adam-ondi-Ahman after sun rise the next morning. The Mormons went down to Millport through the mob. Three-hundred men buried their cannon and left. They started after burying their cannon in the road and got corn and scattered over it. An old sow in rooting after the corn bared the end of the cannon. So the brethren, as they called it, raised the dead. We placed the cannon on an high elevation as was and went to firing it. By this time Joseph the Prophet had come out. After the shooting he made a very mild speech." *Biography of Chapman Duncan*, BYU, Provo, Utah.

wading in water up to her waist. In all she walked more than three miles over ground covered with snow.

When word of these acts was received at Far West, the first judge of the county, Elias Higbee, ordered Lieutenant Colonel Hinkle to send a company to disperse the mob. About midnight, seventy-five volunteers under Captain David W. Patten met on horseback at the town square to commence their march.

After traveling for several hours they approached the Crooked River Ford, in the vicinity of the enemy. Drawing near, the volunteer company dismounted, leaving several of their number behind to look after the horses while the others proceeded on foot. As they ascended a rise near the river bank, their figures were silhouetted against the eastern sky in the early dawn; Bogart's men fired upon them. Of the several who were felled by the burst of fire, Brother Patrick O'Bannion was killed.

Captain Patten then ordered a charge and the volley roared as he shouted the watchword, "God and Liberty." The enemy returned the fire and retreated; and as the volunteers pursued them, a mobber stepped out from behind a tree, wheeled, and shot, mortally wounding Captain Patten. After the battle the volunteers counted 11 casualties: 3 dead and 8 wounded. Bogart reported one killed.

The wounded were taken in wagons to Far West, and the men who had been taken prisoners by the enemy were released. The Prophet, Hyrum, and Lyman Wight met the returning company near Log Creek. The sight of the dead and wounded made them sick at heart. The stricken Captain Patten was being carried in a litter to Brother Winchester's place, three miles from Far West. As they moved along the road with him, his suffering was so intense that he pleaded with his bearers to leave him by the side of the road. But his faith was undaunted, and his last words to his wife were, "Whatever you do else, oh! do not deny the faith."

Captain Patten, then President of the Quorum of Twelve, died as he had lived, a man of God and strong in the faith. And, as Joseph the Prophet later wrote: "How different his fate to that of the apostate, Thomas B. Marsh. . . ."

The battle of Crooked River climaxed the crisis between Mormons and Missourians. Captain Bogart falsely reported that ten of his comrades had been killed, many wounded, and the rest taken prisoner; that the Mormons were preparing to plunder, sack, and burn Richmond; and that in anticipation of such an attack from the Mormons, men, women, and children had began fleeing in all directions, many going to nearby Lexington. He said too that at that moment one hundred armed Mormon milita men were converging on Richmond. These and other false charges were repeated the next day.

The second day after the battle of Crooked River, after receipt of a lying report to Governor Boggs at Jefferson City, Missouri, the governor dispatched an order to General John B. Clark, telling him to mobilize the state militia for immediate action against the Mormons. The communique contained further misinformation: "The Mormons have burned and pillaged many homes, driven off stock, and are destroying the crops. The towns of Gallatin and Millport are in ashes." The message was concluded with instructions that the General go well-equipped with sufficient supplies and wagons.

On Saturday, October 27, 1838, Governor Boggs, without first making an investigation into the reports, issued at Jefferson City what has appropriately been called "The Exterminating Order." This order sent to General Clark was to drive the Mormons from the state and was the signal for widespread depredations.

That dreadful order from Governor Boggs became the signal for an unrestrained attack on the Mormons. It had been issued at the precise moment when the enemy of the Saints was in its ugliest mood, and thus it was that the little hamlet of Haun's Mill on Shoal Creek became the site of a premeditated attack.

The persecutions had only one ray of light and of relief in an otherwise bleak persistence—the courage of General Doniphan who stalwartly refused to follow orders to shoot the Mormon leaders.

Following the massacre, the enemy detachment (a part of the main army under the supervision of Colonel Ashby but under the immediate command of Captain Nehemiah Comstock) rejoined the main body of the army camped outside Far West.

To Hyrum Smith, the atmosphere supercharged against the Church was nothing short of astounding. He returned with Joseph to Far West after witnessing the distressing situation at Diahmon and dispatched some documents by messenger to General Atchison, stating the facts as they did exist and praying for assistance. A petition was sent to the governor setting forth the alarming situation. In the meantime the presiding judge of the county court, acting upon affidavits made to him by the citizens, issued orders to the sheriff of the county to order out the militia of the county to stand in constant readiness night and day to prevent the citizens from being massacred.

The perfidy on Colonel Hinkle's part to deliver up the Mormon leaders to General Lucas as prisoners is well known. It was a temporary triumph for Lucas and the mob militia. The temper of the military toward the prisoners is revealed by what followed.

It was learned later that General Clark had written General Lucas to have the "royal prisoners" sent to him at Richmond for execution. But Lucas, ignoring the order, made haste to show off his prisoners to the people of Jackson County. On this journey, the Prophet Joseph received assurance by revelation that not one of them would perish but would live to join again with the Saints.

The caravan arrived at Independence a little past noon, in the midst of a great rainstorm, which failed however to keep people from lining the streets to witness their arrival and to hear the bugle blast of triumphant joy. Hyrum describing this event, later wrote:

After our arrival at Independence, we were driven all through the town for inspection, and then the following day we were all permitted to go to the tavern to eat and to sleep, but afterwards they made us pay our own expenses for board, lodging, and attendance . . . for which they made a most exorbitant charge.

We remained in the tavern about two days and two nights, when an officer arrived with authority from General Clark to take us back to Richmond, Ray County, where the General had arrived with his army to await our arrival there; but on the morning of our start for Richmond, we were informed by General Wilson that it was expected by the soldiers that we would be hung up by our necks on the road while on the march to that place and that it was prevented by a demand made for us by General Clark, who had the command in consequence of seniority, and that it was his prerogative to execute us himself, and he should give us up into the hands of the officer, who would take us to General Clark, and he might do with us as he pleased.

During our stay at Independence, the officers informed us that there were eight or ten horses in the place belonging to the Mormon people, which had been stolen by the soldiers, and that we might have two of them to ride if we would cause them to be sent back to the owners after our arrival at Richmond. We accepted of them, and they were ridden to Richmond, and the owners came there and got them.

We started in the morning under our new officer, Colonel Price of Keytsville, Chariton County, Mo., with several other men to guard over us. We arrived there on Friday evening, the ninth day of November, and were thrust into an old log house, with a strong guard placed over us. After we had been there for the space of half an hour, there came in a man who was said to have some notoriety in the penitentiary, bringing in his hands a quantity of chains and padlocks. He said he was commanded by General Clark to put us in chains. Immediately the soldiers rose up and pointing their guns at us, placed their thumb on the cock and their finger on the trigger and the state's prison keeper went to work putting chains around the leg of each man, and fastening it on with a padlock, until we were all chained together, seven of us.

In a few moments came in General Clark. We requested to know of him what was the cause of all this harsh and cruel treatment. He refused to give us any information at that time, but said he would in a few days, so we were compelled to continue in that situation—camping on the floor, all chained together, without any chance or means to be made comfortable, having to eat our victuals as they were served to us, using our fingers and teeth instead of knives and forks.

While we were in this situation, a young man of the name of Grant, brother-in-law to my brother William Smith, same to see us and put up at the tavern where General Clark made his quarters. He happened to come in time to see General Clark make choice of his men to shoot us on Monday morning, the twelfth day of November; he saw them choose their rifles, and load them with two balls in each; and after they had prepared their guns, General Clark saluted them by saying, "Gentlemen, you shall have the honor of shooting the Mormon leaders on Monday morning at eight o'clock!" But in consequence of the influence of our friends, the heathen General was intimiated so that he durst not carry his murderous design into execution; and sent a messenger immediately to Fort Leavenworth to obtain the military code of laws. After the messenger returned, the General was employed nearly a whole week examining the laws, so Monday passed away without our being shot. However, it seemed like foolishness to me that so great a man as General Clark pretended to be, should have to search the military law to find out whether preachers of the gospel, who never did military duty, could be subjected to courtmartial.

However, the General seemed to learn the fact after searching the military code, and came into the old log cabin, where we were under guard and in chains, and told us he had concluded to hand us over to the civil authorities, as persons guilty of treason, murder, arson, larceny, theft, and stealing. The poor deluded General did not know the difference between theft, larceny, and stealing.

Accordingly, we were handed over to the pretended civil authorities, and the next morning our chains were taken off, and we were guarded to the courthouse, where there was a pretended court in session; Austin A. King being the judge and Mr. Birch the district attorney, the two extremely and very honorable gentlemen, who sat on the court martial when we were sentenced to be shot.

Witnesses were called up and sworn, at the point of the bayonet, and if they would not swear the things they were told to do so, they were threatened with instant death; and I do know, positively, that the evidence given in by those men, whilst under duress, was fake. This state of things was continued twelve or fourteen days, and after that we were ordered by the judge to introduce some rebutting evidence, saying if we did not do it, we would be thrust into prison. I could hardly understand what the judge meant, for I considered we were in prison already, and could not think of anything but the persecutions of the days of Nero, knowing that it was a religious persecution, and the court an inquisition.[2]

While the Mormon leaders were enduring a mock trial at Richmond, Brigadier-General Robert Wilson marched on Adam-ondi-Ahman with his troops and arrested all the men and put them under guard, at the same time patrolling all roads to prevent

---

[2]Joseph Smith, *op. cit.*, vol. III, pp. 417-418.

any person passing in or out without his consent. A court of inquiry was set up having as its judge Adam Black, an attorney belonging to General Clark's army, who was also a leader of the mob in Daviess County.

After three days' investigation every man was honorably acquitted. Thereupon General Wilson ordered every family to be out of Diahman in ten days and granted permission for them to go to Caldwell County (Far West) and remain there until spring, when they must leave the state under pain of extermination.

In obeying the order of General Wilson, the Saints had to leave their crops and houses, and to live in tents and wagons, even though the weather was bitterly cold. As for their flocks and herds, the mob had already stolen them—thereby relieving the Saints of the trouble of taking care of them, or from the pain of seeing them starve to death. The casualties from mobbing included about thirty dead, many wounded, about a hundred missing, and sixty awaiting trial—for what they knew not.[3]

The court proceedings at Richmond, Missouri, were a travesty of justice, a rank violation of the spirit of free America. The words of Hyrum Smith paint a picture of "Make-believe justice":

. . . We gave him (Judge King) the names of forty persons, who were acquainted with all the persecutions and sufferings of the people. They made out a subpoena, and inserted the names of those men, and caused it to be placed in the hands of Bogart, the notorious Methodist minister, and he took fifty armed soldiers and started for Far West. I saw the subpoena given to him and his company when they started.

In the course of a few days, they returned with most of all those forty men, whose names were inserted in the subpoena and thrust them into jail, and we were not to bring one of them before the court; but the judge turned upon us, with an air of indignation and said, "Gentlemen, you must get your witnesses or you shall be committed to jail immediately, for we are not going to hold the court open on expense much longer for you, anyhow."

We felt very much distressed and oppressed at that time. Colonel Wight said, "What shall we do? Our witnesses are all thrust into prison or probably will be, and we have no power to do anything; of course we

---
[3]*Ibid.*, pp. 207-208.

must submit to this tyranny and oppression; we cannot help ourselves." Several others made similar expressions, in the agony of their souls, but my brother Joseph did not say anything, he being sick at the time with a toothache, and ague in his face, in consequence of a cold brought on by being exposed to the severity of the weather.

However, it was considered best by General Doniphan and Lawyer Reese that we should try to get some witnesses before the pretended court. Accordingly, I, myself gave the names of about twenty other persons; the judge inserted them in a subpoena and caused it to be placed in the hands of Bogart, the Methodist priest, and he again started off with fifty soldiers to take those men prisoners as he had done to the forty others. The judge sat and laughed at the good opportunity of getting their names, that they might the more easily capture them and so bring them down to be thrust into prison in order to prevent us from getting the truth before the pretended court of which himself was the chief inquisitor or conspirator. Bogart returned from his second expedition with one prisoner only whom he thrust also into prison.

The people at Far West had learned the intrigue and left the state, having been made acquainted with the treatment of the former witnesses. But we, on learning that we could not obtain witnesses whilst privately consulting with each other what we should do, discovered Mr. Allen, standing by the window on the outside of the house; we beckoned to him as though we would have him come in. He immediately came in. At that time Judge King retorted upon us again, saying, "Gentlemen, are you not going to introduce some witnesses?"; also saying it was the last day he should hold the testimony open for us, and if we did not rebut the testimony that had been given against us, he should have to commit us to jail.

I had then got Mr. Allen into the house, and before the court, so called. I told the judge we had one witness, if he would be so good as to put him under oath; he seemed unwilling to do so, but after a few moments consultation the state's attorney arose and said, he should object to that witness giving in his evidence and being sworn in, stating that this was not a court to try the case, but only a court of investigation on the part of the state. Upon this, General Doniphan arose, and said he would be d----d, if the witness should not be sworn; and that it was d----d shame, that their defendants should be treated in this manner; that they could not be permitted to get one witness before the court, whilst all their witnesses, even forty at a time, have been taken by force of arms and thrust into the "bull pen" in order to prevent them from giving their testimony.

After Doniphan sat down, the judge permitted the witness to be sworn, and enter upon his testimony. But as soon as he began to speak, a man by the name of Cook, who was a brother-in-law to priest Bogart, the Methodist, and who was Lieutenant and whose place at that time was to superintend the guard, stepped in before the pretended court and took him by the nape of his neck and jammed his head down under the pole or log of wood that was placed up around the place where the inquisition was sitting to keep the by-standers from intruding upon the majesty of the inquisitors, and jammed him along to the door and kicked him out of doors. He instantly turned to some soldiers who were standing by him and said to them, "Go and shoot him, shoot him."

The soldiers ran after the man to shoot him—he fled for his life, and with great difficulty made his escape. The pretended court immediately arose and we were ordered to be carried to Liberty, Clay County and there to be thrust into jail. We endeavored to find out for what cause, but, all that we could learn was, because we were "Mormons."

The next morning a large wagon drove up to the door and a black-smith came into the house with some chains and handcuffs. He said his order from the judge was to handcuff us and chain us together. He informed us that the judge had made out a mittimus and sentenced us to jail for treason; he also said the judge had done this that we might not get bail; he also said the judge stated his intention to keep us in jail until all the "Mormons" were driven out of the state; he also said that the judge had further stated that if he let us out before the "Mormons" had left the state, that we would not let them leave, and here would be another d——d fuss kicked up. I also heard the judge say myself, whilst he was sitting in his pretended court, that there was no law for us, nor the "Mormons" in the state of Missouri; that he had sworn to see them exterminated, and to see the governor's order executed to the very letter, and he would do so; however, the blacksmith proceeded and put the irons upon us, and we were ordered into the wagon, and were driven off for Clay County, and as we journeyed along the road, we were exhibited to the inhabitants. And this course was adopted all the way, thus making a public exhibition of us, until we arrived at Liberty, Clay County.

There we were thrust into prison again, and locked up and were held there in close confinement for the space of six months, and our place of lodging (log building) was the square side of a hewed white oak log, and our food was anything but good and decent. Poison was administered to us three or four times. The effect it had upon our system was that it vomited us almost to death, and then we would lie some two or three days in a torpid, stupid state, not even caring or wishing for life. The poison being administered in too large doses, or it would inevitably have proved fatal, had not the power of Jehovah interposed on our behalf to save us from their wicked purpose. . . .[4]

---

[4]*Ibid.*, pp. 419-428.

It was ironic in a town named Liberty to behold the laws of justice flouted and mobocracy hold sway. But there was no hesitancy on Hyrum's part to uphold principles and demand the rights of his people. To compromise in the least degree with the enemy would result in eventual apostasy. If he had ever interpreted the suffering and sorrow of the Saints as evidence of God's ill-will toward them, he might have deserted the cause. But he was not one to yield to expediency. If he had yielded to the side which seemed to hold the upper hand at the moment, his life's story might well have been similar to that of Thomas B. Marsh, W.W. Phelps, John F. Boynton or David Whitmer.

However, the primary motive for Hyrum Smith's migration to Missouri was not economic advantage but rather to assist God in establishing the church.

But the constant worry and the strain on Hyrum since his arrival at Far West about six months before had affected his health. The soldiers had callously and rudely torn him from his family and had placed him face to face with death. His concern over Mary Fielding Smith who was then expecting their first child, his realization of the dependency of his and Jerusha's four small children upon him, his knowledge that his home needed work done on it to make it comfortable, his grief over the plight of the Saints, and his own imminent peril, were almost overwhelming. But throughout his ordeal Hyrum exhibited a faith which the enemy could not destroy, a faith which reconciled him to his fate. To him, God was still in control and would overrule all things for the Saints' best good.

When the prison doors of Liberty Jail closed upon the prisoners there came to a close one of the most intensely stirring scenes in the life of Hyrum Smith. The events in northern Missouri had ended any hope for him to remain in Far West. And, had it been possible for him to blot from his memory the horrors of the past few weeks, he would, no doubt, have done so.

But Hyrum could not forget. He remembered the details of the pretended court proceedings under Judge King. He had had to be spokesman for the group when Joseph was ill. He had been the object of curious people who gazed at him as if he were some queer and unfamiliar creature. He recalled the clanking of the leg chains and the foul language of the guards, and the grief of leaving his family at the mercy of the mob. He relived the anguish of seeing his brother, Joseph, march off and become enveloped in a sea of howling demons and then be ignominiously and disrespectfully treated, being forced to lie on the ground all night like an animal without a covering to shield him from the rain and cold.

These and many other inhuman acts could never be erased from his mind. And here in Liberty Jail, Hyrum pondered how it would be possible for the Lord to build his Church under such conditions.

CHAPTER XIX

A PRISONER

Was the fate of Hyrum Smith sealed when the door closed and the key turned with an echoing thud in Liberty Jail? No doubt the mob militia of Missouri thought so, because their objective in driving out the Mormons had been achieved. Because of the nerve-shattering experience of becoming a prisoner and enduring the indignities of being arrested and threatened with death, Hyrum would never again be quite the same. He had been a missionary and a leader at Kirtland, but now was a felon before the law, not because he had broken the law, but, like Paul of old, for the sake of Christ. And, like the ancient prophets had stoically accepted his lot, and with a resigned spirit shifted the responsibility for his plight to the benevolence of God.

The forced exhibition of being paraded like animals along the route to Liberty Jail did not disturb him as much as did the welfare of his family at Far West. Could Hyrum have callously ignored his family by taking an indifferent resigned-to-his-fate attitude? No, not likely, because there were others outside the prison walls such as Brigham Young, John Taylor and Heber C. Kimball to aid the exiles in establishing a new home beyond the reach of the enemy. His hope of deliverance was not based on blind faith, nor did his calm demeanor reveal his intention of planning an escape. If he were to be an instrument in the hands of God to help build the kingdom, how was he to begin under such adverse circumstances? The way was hedged for the time being to establish the Church in Missouri or to help the membership of the Church to find a place of refuge from the enemy. Evil forces had triumphed, their objective had been achieved and the satanical forces like a hurricane had blown themselves out. The excitement simmered down to an attitude of wait-and-see.

How was this crisis going to affect the life and temperament of Hyrum Smith? Many of the faithful were made stronger; some became bitter and left the Church; others became disillusioned and returned to their native land. There was very little for the prisoners in Liberty Jail to rejoice about. The fast moving events of the past several months was a period of great trial and emotional upset in the lives of the Smiths. When the municipal court, later in Nauvoo, convened to put the record straight before the Saints and citizens of Illinois, Hyrum testified to what took place and expressed his feelings concerning the whole affair.

Like an attorney for the plaintiff, Hyrum was well versed in all of the details leading to the present impasse. He enumerated the events connected with the Gallatin affair and the perfidy of Judges Black and King. He described the atrocities at Millport and the part played by generals Clark, Atchison, and Lucas of the Missouri militia and how they yielded to the popular cry to drive the Mormons out. There was also General Doniphan, a man of courage who showed understanding and sympathy for the Mormons. His sympathy for Colonel Hinkle and Neil Gillium was non-existent, for these men were considered traitors to the people and to God. Other prominent citizens such as one Bogart and Sashiel Woods, Methodist and Presbyterian ministers respectively, he charged with robbery, driving off cattle, carrying off men, women, and children and threatening their lives; and subjecting them to all manner of abuse. He recounted the suffering of his brother's (Don Carlos) wife who was driven from her home and who escaped with her two children across Grand River to the home of Col. Wight; also how Col. Wight, the Mormon officer, put a stop to the mob's efforts to set fire to the houses of the Mormons.

In support of his brother Joseph, Hyrum said:

"I have been acquainted with him ever since he was born, which was thirty-seven years in December last; and I have not been absent from him at any one time not even for the space of six months, since his birth, to my recollection." Hyrum defended his brother against charges of treason or the violation of any other law in any state of the union; was never subject to military duty in any state, he being exempt because of the amputation and extraction of a bone from his leg; he was rather a minister of the gospel.

Hyrum ended his testimony in these words: "But I do know that whilst he was in the state of Missouri, the people commonly called 'Mormons' were threatened with violence and extermination."

Hyrum was in a favorable position to plead Joseph's cause, knowing his brother so intimately since his (Joseph's) birth and having shared the searing heat of mobocracy and malignancy of the enemy from within and from without. In Hyrum's mind there was no justification for the enemies' untoward action against his people. According to the law, both civil and moral, the Missourians were the offenders and should therefore be held accountable before the nation and the world. What he didn't realize was the nature of human psychology pertaining to the craving of self-preservation and economic and social security by the enemy. By fair or foul means the old settlers had expressed a desire to eliminate an imaginary threat to their security, this they could not achieve except by violence and war upon the Saints.

It is quite understandable for the leaders of the Church to condemn their enemies. The local and state newspapers and periodicals expressed a more objective viewpoint of the situation and on occasion asserted the side of the defendant. The Quincy *Whig* announced the end of the Mormon War and expressed a great concern for the 5000 exiles thrust on the charities of Illinois, Iowa, and Wisconsin. Hope was expressed for an impartial trial so that Missouri could maintain its dignity before its sister states and fellow citizens of the Union.[1]

From the *Sangamo Journal* of Springfield, Illinois, came an expression of sympathy and a suspect of sin somewhere between the Missourians and this misguided sect; it was difficult to fix the responsibility.[2] The St. Louis *Gazette* sympathized with the Missourians and spoke of the Mormons' taking things in their own hands, quoting a report from Judge King at Richmond. The newspaper at Liberty, *The Far West,* reported the order of General Lucas to have Joe and Hyrum Smith returned to Richmond for trial — and General Lucas' high regard for the correct

---

[1] Quincy *Whig*, Quincy, III, Nov. 17, 1838. By Bartlett and Sullivan.
[2] *Sangamo Journal*, Springfield, Illinois, Oct. 13, 1838.

conduct of his troops; also the stipulation under which the Mormons were to be removed from the state.

While the newspapers were taking sides, the legislature was passing resolutions. On January 3, 1839, three were passed: first investigate the cause of the disturbance and have the military stop them; second, have none of the documents published without the consent of the legislature; third, have a committee of both branches investigate and report to the governor. Testimony by the Mormons was lacking because most of them had left for Ohio and Michigan. And what would the world say if a committee read the testimony while the defendants were in chains, according to a Mr. McDaniels? A Mr. Ashley defended the citizens in the disturbed counties. He said the tears shed were crocodile tears and desired the documents of Judge King's court to be published. A Mr. Scott said that Judge King was the most unfit man for this purpose and wished that the legislature would remove King from office. He was against having a few individuals cooped up in jail.

Continuing, Mr. Scott said:

> The gentlemen said that "crocodile tears" have been shed over these poor Mormons. Sir, I would to God there were no occasion for shedding tears in these transactions; but sir, when we see the women, and the widows and orphans shedding tears over the mangled bodies of their dead husbands and fathers, there is occasion for tears, and they are not crocodile tears.

The senate, after much debate, adopted the first resolution by a vote of 27 to 3 and the second without opposition; the third was voted upon by a committee, which was negative, and the senate adjourned.[3] An effort was being made by representatives to see conditions in their true light. There exuded from the legislative halls an anxiety to maintain the dignity and self-respect of Missouri. At the moment the voices for an objective appraisal of the situation were in the minority. The two thousand dollars appropriated by the state to alleviate the distress of the Mormons was a gesture of good will. However, it was later charged that the money benefited the Missourians more than the Mormons.

---

[3]*Ibid.*, January 17, 1839.

or the money found its way into the hands of the Missourians because the Mormons were forced to buy food including meat stolen from them by their enemies.

From the *Missouri Republican* at Jefferson City came an article stating that the perpetrators of the war on the Mormons were inspired by selfish motives. It read in part:

> We have many reports herein, relating to the conduct of some of the citizens of Daviess and other counties, at the present land sale at Lexington: It is reported. . .that on a recent land sale, the lands of Caldwell and Daviess were brought into the market, and that some of the citizens who have been the most active in the excitement against the Mormons purchased a number of Mormon tracts of land. Where the Mormons had made settlements and improvements, the said citizens have purchased them for speculation. It is said that the town of "Adamon Diamond," [sic] a Mormon town in Daviess, in which there is several houses—a very valuable site for a town—was purchased at this sale for a dollar and a quarter an acre. It is further said that there is a company formed, embracing a number of persons, for the purpose of speculating in the lands of these people.
>
> It can hardly be expected that an editor in Missouri will come out fully and give the whole story of this base affair. Enough, however, is disclosed to cover that part of the state with lasting disgrace. Can men, women and children be driven from their homes to "hide the peltings of pitiless storm" of winter, many of them shot like wild beasts, for the purpose of obtaining their lands, without incurring public indignation?[4]

Public indignation over the plight of the hapless Mormons was not of sufficient force to tip the scales of justice in their behalf. The result of the legislature's inquiry was anticipated. A serious difficulty confronted the state in the trial of Hyrum Smith and his brethren. It was almost impossible to find an unbiased jury in the counties where the disturbances had taken place.

According to the editors of the *Sangamo Journal* in Springfield, Illinois, there was not a man to be found in the counties who had not formed an opinion of the case: "If the prisoners do not change the venue, the state cannot change it and I am well assured that such has been the excitement that no man in the counties of Ray, Carroll, Caldwell, and Daviess will be in a posi-

[4]*Idem.*

tion to serve as a juror. What will be the result of these persecutions, I am at a loss to say. This much is certain, the detention of those 36 prisoners under guard have to be fed and protected during the winter season which the state will feel before it's done. It cannot fail to be a very expensive affair for the state. The pay of the militia called out, the expense of helping such a number of prisoners, the cost of attending their trial, . . . etc., must amount to a large sum."[5]

It is evident from the foregoing newspaper accounts that there was much confusion and lack of information as to the true condition of the Mormons. Few among the news writers were able to discern the injustices heaped upon the exiles, and their voices calling for justice were feeble and faint amid the general hysteria of an inflamed and excited populace in northern Missouri.

The *Sangamo Journal* of Springfield, Illinois, viewed the trouble somewhat realistically. The editor forthrightly expressed his opinion regarding the state of Missouri in disgrace; the driving of defenseless people from their homes into the bitter storms of winter, many being shot like wild beasts for the purpose of seizing their lands without arousing public indignation; also, the failure of the courts to obtain an unprejudiced jury, and the Missouri editors for not telling the whole truth of the Mormon War.

Never before had Hyrum been in jail. The court and the officers of the state militia had not exhausted their list of Mormon leaders whom they hoped to arrest. No doubt the conversation of the prisoners included the hope that Brigham Young, John Taylor, Heber C. Kimball, Charles C. Rich, and Erastus Snow would not be captured and made prisoners. Perhaps conditions could be a lot worse. The frustration of men caught in a labyrinth of confusion made mostly by new and strange conditions beyond their control was very real. They must have time to take stock of themselves and view the shifting conditions of the times. The environmental conditions of the frontier were

---

[5]*Idem.*

not conducive to rationality and sound logic. The law of the jungle, might-makes-right and inhumanity-to-man, was firmly entrenched in the traditions of the people on the frontier of America. How long would conditions exist containing the ingredients of primitiveness? No one knew, perhaps as long as ignorance, jealousy, suspicion of men's motives, and intolerance existed. If Hyrum Smith had any ideas of solving the dilemma, he never recorded it. The details of events leading to his imprisonment were clear in his mind but how he was to escape was greatly obscured.

Perhaps at this point it would be well to relate the details preceding and during the imprisonment.

At Richmond, Missouri, late in 1838, the trial of Joseph and Hyrum Smith and the other brethren (Lyman Wight, Alexander McRae, Caleb Baldwin, and Sidney Rigdon) lasted sixteen days, before Judge Austin A. King. An ignorant man who knew no law, he finally stated the charges against them: "treason, murder, burglary, arson, robbery, and larceny." Not a single witness was allowed to testify in their behalf. On November 29, 1838, Judge King closed the trial and committed the prisoners to jail on the following mittimus:

State of Missouri
Ray County
To the keeper of the Jail of Clay County
Greetings: Whereas, Joseph Smith, Jr., Hyrum Smith, Lyman Wight, Alexander McRae, and Caleb Baldwin, as also Sidney Rigdon,—are committed into your custody in the jail of said County of Clay, there to remain until they be delivered there from by due course of law.
Given under my hand and seal the 29th day of November, 1838.
                                    /s/   Austin A. King

State of Missouri, Clay County
I, Samuel Hadley, sheriff of Clay County, do hereby certify that the above is a true copy of the mittimus to me, directed in the case therein named.
                                    /s/   Samuel Hadley, Jailer
Clay County, Missouri. By Samuel Tillery, Deputy Jailer.[6]

---

[6]Joseph Fielding Smith, *Life of Joseph F. Smith,* (Salt Lake City, Utah, 1938), p. 59.

The prisoners, in chains, were thrust into the primitive basement of a two-story structure, into a room whose dimension was about fourteen and a half feet square, with a ceiling about six and a half feet high and walls about four feet thick.[7]

At every opening and closing, the heavy wooden door, with its crude lock device and heavy iron hinges, emitted a nerve-shatering, soul-chilling screech which mocked their dignity and self-respect.   The high, iron-barred windows were little more than peepholes through which sunshine and very little fresh air could enter.

This dungeon with its smoke-smudged walls and ceiling and its burnt-oil-wick and stale-sweat odor became the scene of a living nightmare for the Lord's anointed.   They would transform this profane place into a hallowed spot, but for them the part it played in their education was to acquaint hearts and spirits with life in its most trying and degraded state.

The time in jail was tolerable only because of frequent visits from members of their families, friends and the mail service.   At intervals the jailer would Joseph for a turn about town.[8]

On January 16, 1839, Joseph wrote a letter to the apostles addressed to Heber C. Kimball and Brigham Young.   The letter began, "Salutations: Joseph Smith Jun., Sidney Rigdon, Hyrum Smith, prisoners for Jesus' sake; send greetings":

The message was one of hope and courage.   The twelve were to manage the affairs of the Church until the crisis was over. The blessing of the Lord were invoked upon them.[9]

In the meantime the homes of Hyrum, Joseph, and others at Far West had been looted by roving bands of mobbers. Hyrum was tortured by the news that his home had been pillaged by a mob led by Bogart, the infamous Methodist preacher who had been the cause of so much trouble to the Saints.

The mob had forced their way in amid the protests and cries of the family and had broken open Hyrum's trunk and carried

[7]Alma P. Burton, *Mormon Trail*, p. 50, (Salt Lake City, 1953).
[8]*Missouri Argus*, St. Louis, Missouri, vol. IV, No. 48, p. 2, March 19, 1839.
[9]Orson F. Whitney, *op. cit.*, pp. 237-238.

away papers and other valuables.   Joseph F. Smith, at that time
Hyrum's youngest child, later wrote of the incident.

> . . .I being an infant lying on the bed, another bed being on the floor,
> was entirely overlooked by the family, my mother being very sick.   The care
> of me devolved upon my Aunt Mercy and others of the family, during the
> fright and excitement. So when the mob entered the room where I was, the
> bed on the floor was thrown onto the other completely smothering me up;
> and here I was permitted to remain until after the excitement subsided.
> When thought of and discovered, my existence was supposed to have come
> to an end . . . their suppositions were erroneous, however well-founded. . . .[10]

Mary Fielding Smith, after the birth of her first child (which
occurred November 13, 1838) caught a severe cold and for four
months was too ill to do any work.   Her large family had to
depend on her sister Mercy who was a great comfort to all of
them.

Describing this melancholy scene Mercy later wrote:

> . . . At times I feared to lay my baby down (Mary Jane, born June 14,
> 1838) lest they (the mob) slay her." (Her husband, Robert B. Thompson,
> had fled ahead of the mob and was not heard of for three months.)   "About
> the first of February 1839, by the request of her husband, my sister (Mary)
> was placed on a bed in a wagon and taken on a journey of about 40 miles
> to visit him [Hyrum] in prison, her infant son Joseph F. then being about
> eleven weeks old.   I had to accompany her taking my own babe along, then
> near eight months old.   The weather being extremely cold we suffered much
> on the journey.
>
> We arrived at the prison in the evening.   We were admitted and the
> doors closed upon us, a night never to be forgotten.   A sleepless night.   I
> nursed the darling babes and in the morning prepared to start for home
> with my afflicted sister, and as long as memory lasts will remain in my
> recollection the squeaking hinges of that door which closed upon the noblest
> men on earth.   Who can imagine our feelings as we traveled homeward, but
> would I sell that honor bestowed upon me of being locked up in jail with
> such characters for good? No! No![11]

---

[10]Joseph Fielding Smith, *op. cit.*, pp. 123-124.
[11]Mercy Fielding Thompson, *Letter to My Posterity*, opened the Centennial Year,
April 6, 1930.

The visit of Mary Fielding Smith to see her beloved husband was a momentous occasion. The pitiful sight of his sick wife and his tiny son, whom he had never seen before, melted Hyrum's heart. The spare bedding and the food delicacies brought by the welcome visitors bespoke their loving devotion. The bleak winter weather of February and the threats of hostility plunged their hopes into an abyss of dark despair. Many tears were shed as the atrocious acts of the mobs were delineated. Never would Mary and Mercy Rachel forget the prayers uttered by Hyrum that night for the Lord to shed his power of mercy and protection in behalf of his loved ones. Surely words cannot describe their anguish when came the hour for the women to leave. The clumsy covered wagon lumbering into the distance, with Mercy and perhaps son John at the reins and Mary lying ill inside — was a scene Hyrum would never forget.

About February 7, soon after the visit of Mary and Mercy, food was brought to the prisoners by Brigham Young, Heber C. Kimball, Porter Rockwell, Don Carlos Smith, and George A. Smith. William Covey also visited them and brought each of the prisoners a new pair of boots. James Bleaven and daughters brought cakes, pies, etc., and handed them through the window. This food was most gratefully received for what they usually had was coarse and filthy.[12]

The experiences of Hyrum and the prisoners while incarcerated first at Richmond and then at Liberty may never be adequately told. There were times when conditions deteriorated to the point where the human spirit must assert itself or yield to utter debasement. While still in Richmond, prior to the Liberty experience, the Prophet Joseph had occasion to rebuke the guard. Parley P. Pratt, who was lying chained on the prison floor with the Prophet and the other prisoners described what happened:

It was one of those nights . . . we had lain as if in sleep till the hour of midnight had passed, and our ears and hearts had been pained while we listened for hours to the obscene jests, the horrid oaths . . . and filthy lan-

---

[12]*Journal History*, February 7, 1839. Taken from a letter of Alexander McCrae to the Deseret News, (Salt Lake City, Utah, October 9, 1854).

guage of the guards . . . as they recounted to each other their deeds of
rapine, murder, robbery, etc., while at Far West and vicinity . . . I could
scarcely refrain from rising upon my feet and rebuking the guards . . . On
a sudden, Joseph arose to his feet and spoke in a voice of thunder. . . .
"Silence, ye fiends of the infernal pit! In the name of Jesus Christ, I rebuke
you, and command you to be still; I will not live another minute and hear
such language. Cease such talk, or you or I die this instant."

Brother Pratt said he had seen majesty and dignity but once,
and that was when it stood in chains, at midnight, in a dungeon
in an obsucre village in Missouri.[13]

There seemed to be no good reason for Hyrum and Joseph
to have hope for survival. No friends were allowed to champion
their cause. If the state or the nation had sympathy for them no
one knew it. The enemy had succeeded in sealing off every
avenue of escape and had not overlooked any means of embar-
rassing and humiliating the prisoners.

Plans were even laid to kill the prisoners by serving them
spoiled and poisoned food. The crowded, stinking cell—cold and
unsanitary as it was and supplied with inadequate bedding—
added to their misery. The coming trial with the "court" being
what it was held little hope for acquittal on legal grounds. Reports
reaching them of the scattered and poverty-ridden Saints being
driven by a ruthless mob, together with their anxiety over the
safety and welfare of their families, were almost more than they
could endure.

What was the purpose of this ordeal? Was it necessary for
the Lord to exact such an extreme test of their faith? Joseph
went to the Lord with this pathetic plea, March 20, 1839.

O God, where art thou? And where is the pavilion that covereth thy
hiding place?

How long shall thy hand be stayed, and thine eye, yea thy pure eye,
behold from the eternal heavens, the wrongs of thy people and of thy servants, and thine ear be penetrated with their cries?

Yea, O Lord, how long shall they suffer these wrongs and unlawful op-

---

[13]Joseph Smith, *op. cit.,* vol. III, p. 208.

pressions, before thine heart shall be softened toward them, and thy bowels be moved with compassion toward them?

The Lord answered:

My son, peace be unto thy soul; thine adversity and thine afflictions shall be but a small moment;

And then, if thou endure it well, God shall exalt thee on high; thou shalt triumph over all thy foes.

Thy friends do stand by thee, and they shall hail thee again with warm hearts and friendly hands.

Thou art not yet as Job; thy friends do not contend against thee, neither charge thee with transgression, as they did Job. . . .

The ends of the earth shall inquire after thy name, and fools shall have thee in derision, and hell shall rage against thee;

While the pure in heart, and the wise, and the noble, and the virtuous, shall seek counsel, and authority, and blessings constantly from under thy hand.

And thy people shall never be turned against thee by the testimony of traitors.[14]

The eyes of God were upon his servants, and this crucial period, with all its hardships, had a definite purpose. The blessed coming of the great revelation, the establishment of the Church and kingdom of God, required all that they had endured. Joseph and Hyrum had been ruthlessly torn from their wives, children, mother, father, and friends, but the experience was not in vain. Their hearts were comforted with the Lord's words:

If thou art accused with all manner of false accusations; if thine enemies fall upon thee; if they tear thee from the society of thy father and mother and brethren and sisters; and if with a drawn sword thine enemies tear thee from the bosom of thy wife, and of thine offspring; and thine elder son, although but six years of age, shall cling to thy garments, and shall say, My father, my father, why can't you stay with us? O, my father, what are the men going to do with you? and if then he shall be thrust from thee by the sword, and thou be dragged to prison, and thine enemies prowl around like wolves for the blood of the lamb;

And if thou shouldst be cast into the pit, or into the hands of murderers, and the sentence of death passed upon thee; if thou be cast into the deep; if

---

[14]D&C 121:1-3, 7-10; 122:1-3.

the billowing surge conspire against thee; if fierce winds become thine enemy; if the heavens gather blackness, and all the elements combine to hedge
up the way; and above all, if the very jaws of hell shall gape open the
mouth wide after thee, know thou, my son, *that all these things shall give
thee experience, and shall be for thy good.*
   The Son of Man hath descended below them all. Art thou greater
than he?[15]

   Needless to say, Joseph and Hyrum took great comfort in
this personal and sacred counsel.
   But still the indolence of the civil authorities in taking action
to clear up the present impasse was most disheartening to the
prisoners. Escape seemed the only solution to an intolerable
situation and an escape attempt was made early in February. Of
this attempt Alexander McRae, one of their fellow prisoners,
recorded the following:

   After we had been there sometime, and tried every means we could to
obtain our liberty by the law, without effect (except Sidney Rigdon was
bailed out), and also having heard, from a reliable source, . . . by the most
influential men, that "the Mormon prisoners would have to be condemned
or the character of the state would go down," we came to the conclusion
that we would try other means to effect it.
   Accordingly on the 7th day of February, 1839, after counseling together
on the subject, we concluded to try to go that evening when the jailer came
with our supper; but brother Hyrum, before deciding fully, and to make it
more sure, asked Brother Joseph to inquire of the Lord as to the propriety of
the move. He did so, and receiving answer to this effect—that if we were
all agreed, we would go clear that evening; and if we would ask, we should
have a testimony for ourselves. I immediately asked, and had not more
than asked, until I received as clear a testimony as ever I did of anything in
my life, that it was true. Brother Hyrum Smith and Caleb Baldwin bore
testimony of the same: but Lyman Wight said we might go if we chose, but
he would not. After talking with him for some time, he said, "if we will
wait until tomorrow I will go with you." Without thinking we had no
promise of success on any other day than the one above stated, we agreed to
wait.
   When night came, the jailer came alone with our supper, threw the
door wide open, put our supper on the table, and went to the back part of
the room, where a pile of books lay, took up a book, and went to reading

---

[15]*Ibid.*, 122:6-8. (Italics author's.)

leaving us between him and the door, thereby giving us every chance to go if we had been ready. As the next day was agreed upon, we made no attempt to go that evening.

When the next evening came, the case was very different; the jailer brought a double guard with him, and with them six of our brethren to visit. Erastus Snow, William D. Huntington, Cyrus Daniels, David Holeman, Alanson Ripley and Watson Barlow. . . . The jailer seemed to be badly scared; he had the door locked and everything made secure. It looked like a bad chance to get away, but we were determined to try it; so when the jailer started out, we started too. Brother Hyrum took hold of the door, and the rest followed; but before we were able to render him the assistance he needed, the jailer and the guard succeeded in closing the door, shutting the brethren in with us, except Cyrus Daniels, who was on the outside.

As soon as the attempt was made inside, he, Daniels, took two of the guards, one under each arm, and ran down the stairs that led to the door, (the entrance to the jail was a door on the floor above, via the jailer's office), it being in the second story. When he reached the ground they got away from him; and seeing we had failed to get out, he started to run, but put his foot in a hole and fell, a bullet from one of the guards passed very close to his head, and he thinks the fall saved his life.

The scene that followed this defied description. I should judge from the number, that all the town and many from the country, gathered around the jail, and every mode of torture and death that their imagination could fancy, was proposed for us, burning us to death, tearing us to pieces with horses, etc. But they were so divided among themselves that they could not carry out any of their plans, and we escaped unhurt.

During this time, some of the brethren spoke of our being in great danger; and I confess I felt we were. But Brother Joseph told them not to fear, that not a hair of their heads should be hurt, and that they should not lose any of their things, even to a bridle, saddle, or blanket; but that everything should be restored to them; they had offered their lives for us and the gospel; that it was necessary the church should offer a sacrifice, and the Lord accepted the offering.[16]

The trouble ended when several of the brethren employed lawyers and a hearing. Erastus Snow pleaded his own case and was acquitted. Having no knowledge of law, his plea nevertheless won the admiration of the court.

With the passing days, the snow melted outside, and the warm spring breezes changed the landscape to green; but the

---

[16]Joseph Smith, *op. cit.*, vol. III, pp. 257-258.

prisoners grew gaunt, pale, and hollow-eyed. Still they hoped for something to happen soon to make their escape possible. Their crowded cell had become headquarters for the harassed Church. There had been much coming and going of friends and relatives; messages had been sent and received. And although the tide of evil and hatred threatened to engulf them, God was yet with them. He comforted them and gave them revelations, and their spirits remained unbroken. The heavens had not been closed; no man's puny arm could interfere with God's great purposes. The scene of their ordeal was drawing to a close, and Joseph and Hyrum, the main actors, were soon to be on their way to assume their roles in another episode even more climatic and providential than this had been.

CHAPTER XX

THE ESCAPE

The days in jail were endless to Hyrum. He compared his present misery with the days at Kirtland, thinking of their comfortable home and the relative tolerance of the enemy. Yet the present distressing situation had not resulted from any thoughtless decision to leave Ohio. They had moved to Missouri at the command of the Lord. Hyrum and his wife didn't question the wisdom of coming with the Saints to this frontier region, there to face a populace governed by a suspicion and hate unsurpassed in the history of America. There were times now, however, when Hyrum wondered why the Lord had called them thither and why he was so slow to extend his hand in their behalf.

Toward spring in 1839, Hyrum sensed from the word that filtered into their jail cell that the hateful passion of the mob element was beginning to subside a little, to blow itself out. This calm came, however, only after the enemy was satiated with murder, rapine, pillage, and theft. The deeds of the mob were recounted over and over by the jail guards, who in a spirit of jesting and mockery deliberately intended to wound the sensitivities of their listeners.

But ultimately the mob reached an impasse. Their prisoners could not be tried and acquitted; therefore, the case could not be brought to an "honorable" conclusion. The state of Missouri could not justify its actions before the court of public opinion or among her sister states of the union. The Mormon trouble hung like a dark cloud over Missouri. Perhaps the best solution would be to allow the prisoners in Liberty Jail to escape, ultimately.

When the ice began to break up on the streams and rivers, the attention directed toward the Mormons shifted from Missouri to Illinois, and like the coming of spring, new hope came to the exiles. The Missouri episode was drawing to a close, for by spring the Prophet and Hyrum, with the brethren in Liberty Jail, and another group in jail at Richmond, Missouri, were the only Mormons remaining in Missouri. The others, approximately fifteen thousand who remained loyal to their faith, had fled to Illinois. Many had renounced their faith and returned to former homes.

The prisoners justified their escape from prison because the machinery of justice had broken down. The judicial authorities were intimidated and threatened if they moved for an acquittal. The prisoners petitioned the Missouri supreme court for a writ of habeas corpus twice but were refused both times by Judge Reynolds, who later became governor of the state. They also petitioned the county judges for a writ of habeas corpus, which was granted three weeks afterwards, but they were not permitted to have any trial. The prisoners were only taken out of jail and kept out for a few hours and then remanded again.

After three or four days, Judge Turnham came into the jail in the evening, and said he had permitted Mr. Rigdon to get bail. He said Rigdon had to do it in the night, unknown to any of the citizens or they would kill him, for they had sworn to kill him if they could find him. As for the rest of them he dared not let them go for fear of his own life as well as of the prisoners' lives. He said it was hard to be confined under such circumstances, for he knew they were innocent men! And he said that the people also knew it.

Judge Turnham said the plan to hold the prisoners was concocted from the Governor down to the lowest judge, and that the Baptist priest, Riley, was riding down into town every day to watch the people, stirring up the minds of the people against the Mormons all he could, exciting them and stirring up their religious prejudices, for fear we would let them go. Mr. Rigdon, did however, get bail, and made his escape to Illinois.

The jailer, Samuel Tillery, Esq., told the prisoners that several of the Generals of the Missouri militia had met with the governor of Jefferson City in September to make plans to arrest the Mormon leaders, but now the governor was ashamed of the whole transaction and would be glad to set the prisoners free.

Some time in April a farcical court was held for the prisoners in Daviess County. Esquire Birch, the man who was one of the jury who sentenced the prisoners to death, was now the circuit judge. The grand jury that was impanelled were all at the massacre at Haun's Mill. They excused themselves for the barbaric act because the governor had ordered them to do it. The same men who sat as the jury in the daytime were placed as guards over them at night. Judge Birch made no effort to stem the abuse of the prisoners, and he said on one occasion within the hearing of the prisoners, that there was no law for the Mormons in the State of Missouri. After ten days of pseudo-court proceedings, the prisoners were informed that they were indicted for "treason, murder, arson, larceny, theft, and stealing."

At this point the prisoners asked for a change of venue from Daviess County to Marion County but were refused. However, the court, for some unknown reason, allowed them to change to Boone County. Therefore a mittimus was made out by Judge Birch, without date, name, or place. They fitted them out with a two-horse wagon and horses and four men, besides the sheriff, to act as guard.

In the words of Hyrum, the details of their escape are as follows:

We started for Gallatin, the sun about two hours high, a.m. and went as far as Diahman that evening, and stayed until morning. There we bought two horses of the guard and paid for one of them in our clothing which we had with us, and for the other we gave our note. We went down that day as far as Judge Morins, a distance of some four or five miles. There we stayed until the morning, when we started on our journey to Boone County, and traveled on the road about twenty miles distance. There we bought a jug of whiskey, with which we treated the company and while there the sheriff showed us the mittimus before referred to without date of signature, and said that Judge Birch told him never to carry us to Boone County, and never to show the mittimus, "And," said he, "I shall take a good drink of grog, and go to bed, you may do as you have a mind to."

The constituted judicial authorities of Northern Missouri were forced by public opinion to hold a make-believe court, knowing the prisoners were innocent but defied the citizens in allowing them to escape. The mob's objective of expulsion of the Mormons was complete, and the thirst for blood and craving for exultation over their sense of power to degrade and humiliate the Mormons. The persecuted and frightened Saints were being conditioned to seek a more effective way for self-preservation if a similar situation again should rise. Hyrum Smith became more wary of the designs of men and had a lesson in the depravity of mankind. Surely, he thought, how important was the message of the gospel in a world where only the law of the jungle prevailed.

When William Morgan, sheriff in charge of the prisoners, and ex-sheriff William Bowman returned to Gallatin and reported the escape of their prisoners, the people became very angry. The citizens of Gallatin abruptly rode the sheriff out of town on a rail, and Bowman was dragged over the town square by the hair of his head. They accused these men of complicity in the escape of the Mormon leaders and said that both had been well paid for their treachery.[1]

The escape of Hyrum Smith, his brother, and the others ended the crisis of imprisonment from November 1, 1838, to April 15, 1839 five months and a half—the prisoners had endured hardship, privation, and insult. The enemy seemed not to have overlooked any device to realize their evil aims. A mock court, treachery, false testimony, threats, abuse, indignities, attempted murder were all used to undermine, discredit, and if possible destroy, the Lord's anointed.

Later, the Prophet Joseph wrote of the reasons for their escape:

. . . Knowing that the only object of our enemies was our destruction, and likewise knowing that a number of our brethren had been massacred by them on Shoal Creek. . .and they sought every opportunity to abuse others who were left in that state, and that they were never brought to an account for their barbarous proceedings, which were winked at and encouraged by

---

[1] Joseph Smith, *op. cit.*, vol. III, p. 321. Taken from *History of Daviess County*, Pub. Birdsall and Deon, 1882.

those in authority, we thought that it was necessary for us, inasmuch as we loved our lives, and did not wish to die at the hands of murderers and assassins, and inasmuch as we loved our families and friends, to deliver ourselves from our enemies, and from that land of tyranny and oppression, and again take our stand among a people in whose bosoms dwell those feelings of republicanism and liberty which gave rise to our nation.[2]

The reaction of the Missouri press concerning the Mormon trouble from January to May, 1838, varied from being favorable to bad. At Jefferson City, February 2, a newspaper excused the Governor for issuing the Extermination Order on the ground that there was a general uprising among the people. A Mr. Corrill sent a memorial to the General Assembly asking them to rescind the "Exterminating Order." A Mr. Arthur of Clay County wrote a defense of the Mormons to the Legislature, saying "The citizens of Clay County were robbing the poor Mormons." He called the citizens "devils in human shape."[3] From St. Louis came an article from the *Missouri Argus* May 6, 1839, "Joe Smith, Golden Bible — migrating to the land of promise wicked and sinful enough to prevent the fulfillment of his prophecy." And from the St. Louis *Missouri Republican,* January 8, 1839, " . . . confident the trial before Judge King, of the Mormons would be a fair one." Dissatisfaction was expressed concerning the manner by which the money appropriated for the Mormons was being handled. Thus the Mormon trouble in Missouri came to an end with public opinion in a state of deadlock, a few "for" but most against.

While the trial of Hyrum Smith and his brethren was being enacted, his family had not been spared of mob action. The inclement weather during the exodus from Missouri made their suffering more acute. Had they been allowed to leave at their own discretion much suffering could have been avoided. The three previous moves had been made under much different circumstances, pleasurable in the main, but now the bleakness of their humble home and the vacant houses of Far West echoed a sor-

---

[2]*Ibid.,* pp. 320-324.
[3]*Jeffersonian Republic,* Jefferson, Mo., Saturday, Feb. 2, 1839.

rowful and depressed spirit of Hyrum's household as the journey commenced toward a new home in Illinois.

The exact date of the Smiths leaving is not known. However, it was only a few days after Mary Fielding Smith returned from seeing her husband in Liberty Jail. Quite likely the schedule and details of the departure for Illinois had been advised and planned by Hyrum. No doubt it was a strenuous undertaking and required the help of everyone. Mercy Fielding Thompson accompanied her sister, Mary, and the children, and other members of Hyrum's family on their long and hazardous journey. Years later, Mercy wrote her version of the move in these words:

Shortly after our return (from Liberty Jail) to Far West we had to leave our cold unfurnished house and start in lumber wagons for Illinois, my sister (Mary) again being placed on a bed in an afflicted state. This was about the middle of February, the weather extremely cold. I had still the care of both babies (Joseph and Mary Jane). We arrived at Quincy about the end of the month. My husband (Robert Thompson) had engaged a room for our accommodation but my sister was obligated to be with me on account of the baby.

The whole of Brother Hyrum's family of ten[4] remained with us until April when Brother Hyrum arrived in Quincy, Illinois. He soon made arrangements to move his family. I went along to Commerce, leaving my husband in Quincy, who followed in a few weeks and was employed by Joseph Smith as a private secretary, which office he held until his death which took place August 27, 1841. . . .[5]

The kindness and love of Mercy for her sister, Mary, illustrates the close bond of family ties and unity so characteristic of Hyrum's family. Within a few days after their arrival at Quincy, Illinois, William Smith wrote to Hyrum. A letter dated March 6, 1839, stated that Emma and children (Joseph's family) were living three miles from her (Quincy) and were in a tolerable

---

[4]The ten in Hyrum's family were Mary, his wife; baby Joseph Fielding, Lovina, John, little Jerusha, Sarah, Hyrum Jr. The three others Hyrum had taken in out of charity; these were Hannah Grinnels (Grinolds) an elderly woman; Jane Wilson, a younger woman afflicted with nervous spells (fits), very dependent; and George Mills, a British army veteran who joined the family in 1835. Mercy R. Thompson, *Letter to Posterity.*

[5]Joseph Smith, *op. cit.*, vol. III, p. 272.

good place. Also, that Hyrum's children and Mother Grinolds are living at present with father Joseph Smith, Sr. and were all well.[6]

Perhaps Joseph Smith, Sr., had moved in with Hyrum's family and the Thompsons. Joseph's family left Far West, February 6-7, 1839, with Jonathan Holmes and wife, under the care of Stephen Markham.[7]

It is supposed that the house obtained by Robert Thompson for Hyrum's family was located near that of Judge Cleveland, outside Quincy about seven miles. Edward Partridge had seen Mary Fielding Smith before Hyrum arrived and had reported to Hyrum that her health was very poor when she arrived at Quincy, but that she was improving.[8]

*   *   *

Hyrum and Joseph, free men once more, kept to the by-ways in order to avoid the Missouri officers. Several weeks before, Sidney Rigdon had arrived safely in Illinois. The other prisoners, Lyman Wight, Alexander McRae, and Caleb Baldwin had each taken his separate way in order to avoid capture; but all traveled toward the new gathering place of the Saints.

The families of Hyrum and Joseph were anxiously waiting at Quincy, Illinois, for their return. Some of the brethren had given up hope of ever seeing their leaders again, but not their families, nor their mother. It was Mother Smith who told Brothers Partridge and Morley, who were themselves doubtful of every seeing Joseph and Hyrum again, that she would see them before the following night. The Spirit had whispered to Mother Smith and given her this assurance. She asked the brethren to stay in town in order to witness the truth of her statement.

That night Lucy Smith had a more vivid manifestation, which she later described in these words:

After falling asleep that night I saw my sons in vision. They were on the prairie traveling and seemed very tired and hungry. They had but one

[6]Idem.
[7]Ibid., p. 256.
[8]Ibid., p. 272.

horse. I saw them stop and tie him to a stump of a burnt sapling, then lie down on the ground to rest themselves, and they looked so pale and faint that it distressed me. I sprang up and said to my husband, "Oh, Mr. Smith, I can see Joseph and Hyrum and they are so weak they can hardly stand. Now they are lying on the cold ground asleep! Oh, how I wish that I could give them something to eat!"

Mr. Smith begged me to be quiet, saying that I was nervous; but it was impossible for me to rest—they were still before my eyes—I saw them lie there full two hours, then one of them went away to get something to eat, but not succeeding, they traveled on. This time Hyrum rode and Joseph walked by his side, holding himself up by the stirrup leather. I saw him reel with weakness, but could render him no assistance. My soul was grieved; I rose from my bed and spent the remainder of the night in walking the floor.

Continuing, Mother Smith relates the fulfilment of her prophecy:

The next day I made preparations to receive my sons, confident that the poor, afflicted wanderers would arrive at home before sunset. Sometime in the afternoon, Lucy, (the youngest Smith daughter) and I went down stairs —she was before me. When she came to the bottom steps she sprang forward and exclaimed, "There is Brother Baldwin. My brothers—where are they?" This was Caleb Baldwin, who had been imprisoned with them. He told us that Joseph and Hyrum were then crossing the river and would soon be in Quincy. Lucy, hearing this, ran to carry the tidings to Hyrum's family, but the excitement was not sufficient to keep up her strength. When she reached the door she feel prostrate, but after recovering a little, she communicated the welcome news.[9]

Hyrum's seven-year-old John, later describing the Missouri scene said:

I left Ohio in the spring of 1838, and remembered much of the travel on the journey to Far West—remember that the Liberty Pole was struck by lightning on the 4th of July. I remember some of the suffering on our way to Quincy, Illinois; remember seeing my father (Hyrum Smith) when he

---

[9]Lucy Mack Smith,*op. cit.*, pp. 301-302. Hyrum and Joseph reached Quincy, Illinois, April 23, 1839, according to Susa Young Gates. *The Relief Society Magazine*, vol. III, No. 3.

came home from Liberty Jail. He had a full beard, his hair was long, and he was riding a small bay horse.[10]

The arrival of Hyrum and Joseph at Quincy was a signal for family rejoicing. When Hyrum clasped his wife in his arms and in turn his children, new strength flowed into his tired and emaciated body. There was for him no purpose in prolonged grief over the sight of their poverty and starvation. There must be no giving way to self-pity. All that mattered at the moment was that they as a family were again united. Their lives had been spared by the kind hand of divine Providence, and their health was sufficient for them to make plans and begin work to establish a new home. These plans began to take form on April 23, 1839, the day Hyrum arrived. The warm spring breezes changed the landscape from a winter vista to a season when mother earth puts on her new garb of green. Nature seemed to aid in bringing an upsurge of new hope to the Smith family.

The vast new region with its water courses, timbered swales and hillsides, and wild game, brought new hope and courage to the penniless exiles. Here, perhaps, another beginning could be made.

The momentum of conversions to the new society had lessened somewhat during the past year, and the bitter, sustained persecutions had thinned the ranks of the Church. Many problems awaiting the leadership must be attacked, studied, and eventually solved.

The Missouri period had been an intense, excruciating, and paradoxical period in the history of the American citizens known as the "Mormons." No such incident, involving thousands as it did, can be regarded as trivial. No doubt, this displacement of whole communities by forceful means, in a land dedicated to freedom of religion, is without a parallel in the history of man.

Hyrum and other truth-seeking and thoughtful individuals would have done well to analyze objectively the whole picture of

[10]John Smith, *Document* 7½ x 11½ inches—written longhand—black ink—dated February 9, 1909, Salt Lake City, Utah. A brief history of his life during Missouri and Illinois period. In possession of descendants.

the sad days of the 1830's. In so doing they might have erased from their memories much of the rancor and hate they experienced, and the outcome may have been less tragic. As some have expressed it, the degenerate element formed on the frontier of that period cannot be wholly blamed for what happened. It is true that many a criminal or man of notorious character sought protection from the law in the seclusion and relative safety of the frontier. But it is also true that some of the lawless element consisted of county and district judges, physicians, army captains, majors and generals, and many other high officials of the state, including the governor and lieutenant governor.

The state of Missouri was guilty of no greater crime when it persecuted the Latter-day Saints than were the countries which persecuted Saints during the barbarous Dark Ages of European history. When estimated in net results there may have been more murders and robberies, greater destruction of property, and more widspread suffering in those times than in Missouri.

When the New England Mormons and the old settlers of the Southern States met in Missouri, a clash of cultures resulted in a conflagration that could not be smothered. The hard-working northerners were looked down upon by southern gentlemen as people akin to the slave owning class. Many high positions among civil, professional, and military personnel were sought by unworthy gentlemen of the south. The Mormons had a strong puritanical background of religion, morality, and industry. Their ideas were in direct contrast to the established order of the easygoing, haughty spirit of southern hospitality.

And the Missourians were super-sensitive about the slave question. Missouri had been admitted to the union, 1818-1819, on a compromise which stated "That while Missouri. . .permitted slavery, it also prohibited free people of color from immigrating into the state." Therefore, in July 1833, when the Mormon paper, *Evening and Morning Star*, appeared, containing an article inviting free Negroes and mulattoes from other states to become Mormons, the old settlers wrote back in retaliation what was called "The Secret Constitution." Among other things it

said: "In a late number of the *Star*, . . .there is an article inviting free negroes and mulattoes from other states to become
Mormons, and settle among us." The Missouri Constitution
permitted the entry of free men of color only if they possessed a
certificate clearly indicating their status that had been issued by
a court of record. Otherwise they were expelled from the state.
Hence the Missourians' condemnation of the Mormons on this account was without foundation. In a special issue of the *Star* on
July 16, 1833, the Saints declared their intention not only to stop
free Negroes from coming into Missouri, but also to prevent their
becoming members of the church.

Another point of difference was political. The Mormon concept of government was world-wide, not local. Zion embraced the
whole world. The old settlers envisioned the Mormons eventually occupying the seats of government, and great fear came upon
them. This fear bore fruit in their refusal to permit Mormons to
vote at the polls in Gallatin, Daviess County, August 1838.

The Prophet Joseph Smith had said that the Constitution of
the United States was written to establish good order in society,
love of God, and good will to man. The standard of democracy
was to be exalted and priestcraft put down.

Another charge leveled at the Mormons was that they had
encouraged the Indians on the frontier to become Mormons, stating that the Indians were part of God's chosen people. The flyleaf of the Book of Mormon conveys the idea that the Lamanites
(Indians) were to be favored.

Then, too, many of the Saints were tactless in openly
declaring that Western Missouri was the land of Zion and that
the Lord would eventually favor his people by having them own
the whole of it; it was to become the Mormons' land of inheritance. Missourians were unaware that the Lord had said: "The
land of Zion shall not be obtained but by purchase. . . ."[11]

It is quite evident that the newly converted Saints were not
ready to establish Zion. Full sainthood had not been achieved,
for there were certain iniquities among them. The Lord had

[11]D&C 63:29.

pointed out that they were to observe the Sabbath day that there
was too much idleness among them, and that they failed to teach
their children correct principles. There were also jealousies and
bickerings. Hyrum Smith and Orson Hyde had sent the Saints a
letter from Kirtland, which read in part: "We feel more like
weeping over Zion than in rejoicing over her, for we know the
judgment of God hangs over her. . . ."[12]

The importance of the establishment of the new church was
not fully understood by many of the converts. Their previous
religious concepts and ideologies were deeply imbedded; hence
they had great difficulty in conforming to Mormonism.

The above reasons for the antagonism of the Missourians toward the Mormons were symptomatic of a deeper fear, a fear inspired by the very nature of this new religion. The Mormons
were called fanatics or knaves who communicated with God. The
citizens felt that nothing could dissuade the newcomers from their
"pretentions." This same fear prompted General John B. Clark
to say on the public square in Far West:

> I am sorry, gentlemen, to see so great a number of apparently intelli-
> gent men found in the situation you are. . . .I would advise you to scatter
> abroad, and never organize yourselves with Bishops, Presidents, etc. lest you
> excite the jealousies of the people, and subject yourselves to the same
> calamaties that have now come upon you.

In the minds of Hyrum and Joseph was the memory of what
Moroni had said years before, that the adversary was present in
the world, and that his objective was to overthrow the Lord's
work. Satan with his followers had been cast out of heaven to
reside upon the earth,[13] and there had never been a truce established between the opposing forces of good and evil. The war between the Saints and the Missourians was never settled, and
peace was never established.

Even when the Smiths moved to a new location, the peace
they had so long desired was only temporary. The escape from

---

[12]*Ibid.,* 68:29-34.
[13]Joseph Smith, *op. cit.,* pp. 102-110.

jail of Hyrum and Joseph was providential; their time to die had not yet arrived. Mary Fielding Smith had recovered her health, and her baby was doing well. Because many friendly hands gave them assistance, they had successfully escaped the threats of the enemy; and it was good to be once more near a friendly community. Surely the scars of conflict would fade in time. At any rate, there was no time for tears and bitterness.

Before Hyrum and his brethren lay a greater challenge; there was a home to build, and a church, and a city.

CHAPTER XXI

A NEW HOME IN NAUVOO

The gently rolling plains of western Illinois looked good to the Smiths as they made their way to the new Zion. This area, with its sparsely settled communities, was about two hundred miles southeast of Northern Missouri. Its people had been apprised of the conditions of the Saints by newspapers and by rumors, and the reports reaching them from Quincy, Illinois, and St. Louis, Missouri, had been favorable to the Mormons and critical of Missouri. Therefore, these people reacted sympathetically toward the Saints in somewhat the same way as they would have sympathized with homeless animals.

During the first few months of 1839, the refugees had made their way to Illinois, traveling in small companies and groups with many sick, maimed, cold, and hungry among them. Fortunately, their capable leaders organized the trek and helped to provide food, clothing, and transportation. A committee had been organized by Brigham Young, John Taylor, and others to put the more able among the Saints under covenant to help the less fortunate. On January 30, 1839, Brigham Young had obtained 380 signers of this covenant.[1]

In February, 1839, a meeting was called by William Marks and John P. Green at Quincy, Illinois to decide on a suitable place for a permanent settlement. Among the locations considered, and the most favored, was a section lying between the Mississippi and Des Moines Rivers, which was favorable for two dollars an acre. This section of land was situated about twenty-five miles north of Quincy, their temporary headquarters, and was owned by Dr. Isaac C. Galland who resided on the land at a frontier trading post called "Commerce."

Dr. Galland had heard from Elder Israel Barlow about the Mormon trouble in Missouri the fall before, when Elder Barlow

---

[1]Joseph Smith, *History of the Church*, vol. II, p. 251-254.

had fled from Missouri and settled above the mouth of the Des Moines River. Being in sympathy with the Mormons, Dr. Galland wrote to Governor Lucas of Iowa Territory and obtained his support for the Saints to occupy the section known as the "Half Breed Lands," across the Mississippi River to the west. Letters were then written to Elder Barlow and others to obtain a response to the idea of having the Mormons settle in Illinois. Sidney Rigdon, after leaving the prison in Missouri, made an investigation, and through his correspondence with the brethren in jail at Liberty, the proposal of Dr. Galland was accepted.[2]

It was gratifying to Joseph and Hyrum Smith to learn that on March 17 Brigham Young had called a meeting at Quincy to consider whether the Saints should scatter or settle in a body. Brother Young and others well remembered the plea made in Far West by General Clark when he urged them to cease organizing stakes, with presidents, bishops, etc., and to scatter out in order to avoid the wrath of the citizens. However, the Saints, in a community, had social contacts for mutual benefit and enjoyment and also provided a common defense against enemy pressure. Thus, the Lord's work could best be served by a civic institution whose members were in close proximity to each other. That way the evil forces could not succeed in dividing, then conquering. It was the duty of these Saints to build Zion, and they must maintain a united front.

The joy of Hyrum's reunion with his family after six months of enforced separation was ample proof to him that God had heard and answered the many fervent prayers addressed to him. The clouds of despair had parted, and once more the bright sunlight of hope shone through. Looking back, Hyrum felt that every mile lying between Illinois and their former home in Missouri meant greater security from the enemy. He saw in the kind acts of new friends and neighbors the hand of the Lord and became convinced that man cannot live alone. To be at the mercy of others and to receive aid in

[2]*Ibid.*, pp. 265-271.

time of great distress was for him a humbling experience which, in turn, developed in him a deeper love and understanding of his fellow men.

In the days following the arrival of Hyrum and Joseph (about April 23, 1839), the Smith families again enjoyed a close fellowship. The harrowing experiences of Missouri were often spoken of but always with the hope in mind that a secure future would dim the horrors of the past. This new country and its people seemed most hospitable.

Hyrum was astonished to have a company of Quincy Grays (militia) come to the house and salute the liberated prisoners in a most polite manner. It heartened him to observe that there was yet a spirit of human kindness and moral integrity among men, and this kindly and respectful act was to him an omen of future peace and good will.

The decisions of the brethren regarding a possible location for settlement north of Quincy was very satisfactory to Hyrum. Within a few days of their arrival he, with Joseph and several of the brethren, was on his way to view a possible location for the settlement recommended by Bishop George Miller. The virgin territory held a strange fascination for them, seeming to beckon them onward as they rode over one high knoll after another. Then, as the mounted party topped a promontory, they beheld a landscape falling away to the west in a gradual slope; and Hyrum's feeling was the same as that of the others: this site was a unanimous choice. It seemed to them that nature had put on her loveliest dress in order to impress her visitors. Their return trip to Quincy was a joyous one for the prospect of a new homesite, for the penniless refugees had now become a reality.

They spent very little time preparing to move to the new location, other than long enough to make an agreement to purchase one farm containing 135 acres from Hugh White at Commerce for $5,000, and to buy the western tract owned by Dr. Isaac Galland for $9,000. The acreage extending to the east would provide space for an expanding metropolis.

Before Hyrum and others could move their families, however, a number of church matters had to be settled. A conference convened (May 6) to decide how best to help the arriving Saints get located. Missionaries had to be called for foreign missions, a petition must be dispatched to the federal government for redress of losses suffered in Missouri, and a presiding elder should be sent to New York to encourage the scattered Saints there.

Within a week after this conference Hyrum's family was happy to be on their way to a new home, with their scanty belongings stacked high on lumber wagons. The presence of Joseph and Hyrum as free men among them comforted the Saints. Their voices, offering counsel and encouragement, strengthened the morale of the entire group. Troubles seemed suddenly to have vanished; all seemed right again. The Church had not been destroyed but was growing stronger with every passing day. Once more the Saints began to feel secure.

Both Hyrum and Joseph were able to locate their families in abandoned log houses in Commerce.[3] During the days that followed, the voice of the ax, the hammer, and the saw was constantly heard; the river wharf received a constant stream of building supplies and emigrants; the whole place was swarming with busy, happy people, and Joseph and Hyrum were familiar figures moving about them. The brothers frequently met in counsel with the brethren in a log cabin which had become the temporary headquarters of the Church. Quincy became a supply base for the building of Nauvoo as well as for the establishment of the Church. Frequent business trips to and from Quincy by the brethren accelerated the work of building a new city. The scanty capital available among the Saints for the purchase of land and building material was supplemented by the issuing of promissory notes. The losses suffered by the Saints in Missouri in terms of money alone, can never be known, and it was money needed desperately now in order to re-establish themselves.

---

[3]Lucy Mack Smith, *op. cit.*, p. 302.

Reconstruction plans were formulated in the humble log cabins occupied by Joseph, Hyrum, and Sidney Rigdon; and the task of welding and rebuilding the Mormon society went steadily forward. Meetings were held; the gospel was preached; and new sites were selected where cities and towns would be organized to take care of the influx of Saints and converts. On Tuesday, July 2, 1839, Hyrum Smith accompanied Joseph, Sidney Rigdon, Bishops Whitney, Knight, and others across the river to the Iowa side to inspect a purchase lately made by Bishop Knight as one of these townsites. The site was selected and the name designated as "Zarahemla."

During the afternoon of July 2, Hyrum, busy with his work as a leader, addressed members of the twelve and seventies who had been called on missions. Directing his remarks to the twelve he said:

Remember the nature of your mission, be prudent and humble and use care in the selection of subjects for preaching. Never trifle and take lightly your office and calling and hold strictly to the importance of your mission. At all times remember your position before the Lord and hold in high esteem and respect the priesthood you bear.[4]

At the conclusion of much instruction and advice, Elders Wilford Woodruff and George A. Smith, having been ordained apostles to fill vacancies in the twelve, were set apart for their respective missions. The immediate needs of a people in dire distress did not becloud the vision of the leaders in Zion. They saw the constant need of missionaries. They realized that the Great Designer had brought his Church out of the furnace of persecution and that powerful blows must be made while the iron of the Spirit was hot.

The health of Hyrum, Joseph, and the brethren was also poor. Many members of the flock were often bedridden. The heat of July brought swarms of mosquitoes and other insects from the marshes along the river, and the hapless refugees, with resistance lowered by malnutrition and poor housing fell easy prey to the dreaded malarial fever. The homes of Hyrum

---

[4]*Journal History,* Vol. 13, No. 3, p. 383.

and Joseph and other leaders became homes of refuge to many of the most critical cases.

Hyrum's youngest sister, Lucy, and his eldest daughter, Lovina, contracted the disease. William Smith, Hyrum's brother, came on a visit and offered to take Lovina back to his home at Plymouth, Illinois, hoping that the ride would benefit her, but she continued to decline; and fearing she would die, William sent for her father. When the messenger arrived, Hyrum was so ill that he was unable even to sit up, and Mother Smith decided to take Lucy and go to Lovina's bedside. Much to their relief, they found Lovina greatly improved, and in a short time she regained her health.[5]

By the latter part of July, during a rainy season, the number of sick had increased to include members of the twelve and other leading brethren. On Monday and Tuesday, July 22 and 23, the sick were administered to with great success. The Prophet Joseph arose from his own bed, made his way to other sick people lying in their tents, dugouts, and shanties, and administered to them in the name of the Lord, healing them in a miraculous way.

Following this miraculous time of healing, the number of sick decreased.

On Sunday, July 28 Hyrum Smith and his family sat in Sacrament meeting and listened to the Prophet Joseph admonish the members of the church to set their houses in order, and to meet on the next Sabbath to partake of the Sacrament, ". . . that we might be enabled to prevail with God against the destroyer and that the sick might recover." By the eighteenth of August, the Prophet wrote: "This week I spent chiefly visiting the sick, sickness much decreased."[6]

At the semiannual conference held at Commerce on October 6, 7, and 8, a proposal was made to organize a stake of Zion for a gathering place at Nauvoo. William Marks was made president and three wards were organized with respective

---

[5]Lucy Smith, *op. cit.*, pp. 303-305.
[6]Joseph Smith, *op. cit.*, vol. IV, p. 7.

bishops. It was also decided that a news sheet was to be published, to be known as the *Times and Seasons;* Emma Smith was called to select hymns appropriate for publication for the use of the Church; and plans were laid to construct an office for President Joseph Smith, a schoolhouse, and a boarding house. Again their lack of funds hampered them. They thought bitterly of the wrongs perpetrated against them in Missouri.

Throughout the Missouri persecutions, and since their coming to Illinois, Hyrum and Joseph had made plans to appeal the Mormon case to the federal government in Washington, D. C. Surely, they reasoned, the parent government, if fully informed, would take action to have the state of Missouri reimburse the stricken Saints for their losses. There should be no time lost in making this appeal, now that a new place had been found for the gathering of the refugees. They needed their lost funds to expedite the building of a new community.

Accordingly, on October 28, Hyrum voted with others to sent Joseph Smith, Sidney Rigdon, and Elias Higbee as delegates to Washington, D. C., to importune the President and Congress for redress.

Prior to their leaving for Washington, D. C., the Prophet gave Hyrum advice and instruction on matters of the Church, and on October 29, with Porter Rockwell driving their two-horse carriage the trio left for the nation's capital. Elder Rigdon was ill at the time and grew no better, so that the following Friday, traveling toward Springfield, Illinois, they obtained medical aid from Doctor Robert D. Foster, a member of the Church, who kindly consented to accompany the group in order to aid Brother Rigdon. The journey of about 800 miles was fraught with considerable difficulty. While going through the hill country toward Washington, the coach team ran away and the Prophet Joseph displayed the courage of a hero, risking his life to save its passengers. The occupants of the coach had nothing but praise for his actions and wanted to reward him for valor, until they learned of his identity.[7]

---

[7]*Ibid.,* pp. 23-23.

In Nauvoo during this time, the high council had met at the home of Oliver Granger and voted that Hyrum Smith, George W. Harris, and Oliver Granger act as a committee to send a petition to the state legislature to define the new boundary lines of the city of Nauvoo, and of Commerce. Hyrum Smith was to furnish the maps and plates for the alteration, and Seymour Brunson was to circulate the petition for signatures.

On the day of their arrival in Washington the Prophet and Brother Higbee after much looking, finally secured a place to stay in the capital city, which then had a population of about 50,000, and on Friday of the next week, the Prophet mailed the following letter to Hyrum:

Washington City, Corner Missouri and 3rd St's., December 5, 1839. Dear Brother Hyrum, President, and to the Honorable High Council of The Church of Jesus Christ of Latter-day Saints to whom be fellowship, love, and the peace of almighty God extended, and the prayer of faith forever and ever. Amen. Your fellow laborers, Joseph Smith, Jr., Elias Higbee, and agents as well as the servants that are sent by you to perform one of the most arduous and responsible duties . . . we arrived in this city on the morning of the 28th of November, and spent the most of that day looking up a boarding house . . . we found as cheap boarding house as can be had in this city.

On Friday morning, 29th, we proceeded to the house of the President. We found a very large and splendid palace. . . . We went to the door and requested to see the President [Martin Van Buren], when we were immediately introduced into his parlor, where we presented him with our letters of introduction. As soon as he read one of them, he looked upon us with a kind of half frown and said, "What can I do? I can do nothing for you! If I do anything, I shall come in contact with the whole state of Missouri."

But we were not intimidated, and demanded a hearing, and constitutional rights. Before we left him, he promised to consider what we had said, and observed that he felt to sympathize with us on account of our suffering.

The Prophet, continuing, told about hunting up the representatives in order to put the case before them, and how the gentlemen from Illinois had cordially treated them; but he added: "Yet there is prejudice, superstition, and bigotry of an ignorant generation to contend with. There is but little solidity and honorable deportment among those sent to Washington to represent the people; but a great deal of pomposity and show."

The Prophet had received a letter from Sidney Rigdon, who because of illness had been left along the way. His health was improving, and he was soon to arrive in Washington. They could draw on him to publish their book (hymnbook), and there should be some money deposited at the Branch Bank in Quincy and the receipt forwarded to them. Money from the sale of books would help. Their anxiety about money was expressed as follows:

We cannot accomplish the things for which we were sent without some funds. You very well know, brethren, we were contented to start, trusting in God, with little or nothing.

In closing he wrote:

For God's sake, be wide awake and arm us with all the power possible, for now is the time or never. We want you to get all the influential men you can of that section of the country, of Iowa, and of every other quarter to write letters to members of Congress, using their influence in our behalf, and to keep their minds constantly upon the subject.

Please forward this to our wives. Yours in the bonds of the everlasting covenant, signed, Joseph Smith, Jun., and Elias Higbee.

In the postscript, the Prophet wrote about Congress and some seats being contested in the New Jersey delegation. He mentioned the disposition of some members of Congress to show off their oratory on the most trivial occasions, and to insist on so much etiquette, bowing and scraping, twisting and turning to make a display of folly and show, more than of substance and gravity, such as becomes a great nation like ours. ("However," he said, "There are some exceptions.")

Mention was made of Joseph's stopping the runaway team driven by a drunken Missourian, and how Elias Higbee jumped out of the stage before the team stopped to assist them in stopping and hurt himself. He told of their interview with the President and of his questions as to how they differed from other religions; and how he answered the questions, telling the President of the mode of baptism and the gift of the Holy Ghost by laying on of hands, all other considerations being contained in the gift of the Holy Ghost. He deemed it unnecessary to preach the gospel to the President, although he gave him his testimony.[8]

* * *

In Nauvoo, Hyrum Smith was conducting the affairs of the Church—meeting regularly with the high council and advising on various problems brought before the Church. The high council of Nauvoo voted that Bishop Knight provide for the families of Joseph Smith, Jr., Sidney Rigdon, and Orrin Porter Rockwell during their absence in Washington.

About the middle of December, Hyrum Smih wrote a long epistle entitled "To the Saints scattered abroad," giving an account of his suffering in Missouri. Much of the content was the same as had already been published in the *Times and Seasons*, with the exception of his testimony to the truth of the Book of Mormon, and of his being one of the eight witnesses of the Nephite plates from which the record was translated.

Hyrum's feelings toward the Book of Mormon and toward his recent suffering are expressed in the following:

> Having given my testimony to the world of the truth of the Book of Mormon, the renewal of the everlasting covenant, and the establishment of the kingdom of heaven in these last days, and having been brought into great affliction and distresses for the same, I thought that it may be strengthening to my beloved brethren to give them a short account of my sufferings, for the truth's sake, and the state of my mind and feelings, while under the circumstances of the most trying and afflicting nature. * * * I had been abused and thrust into a dungeon and confined for months on account of my faith, and the testimony of Jesus Christ. However, I thank God that I felt a determination to die, rather than deny the things which my eyes had seen, which my hands had handled, and which I had borne testimony to, . . . wherever my lot had been cast, and I can assure my beloved brethren that I was enabled to bear as strong a testimony

---

[8]*Ibid.*, pp. 41-42.

when nothing but death presented itself, as ever I did in my life. My confidence in God was likewise unshaken. I knew that He who suffered me, along with my brethren, to be thus tried, that He could and that He would deliver us out of the hands of our enemies, and in His own due time He did so, for which I desire to bless and praise His holy name.[9]

On December 22, Hyrum sent a letter to Parley P. Pratt at New York in answer to Brother Pratt's inquiry about printing an edition of the Book of Mormon in New York. Hyrum advised him that such an important decision must await the consideration of Joseph and others, that he, Hyrum must acquiesce to the idea of publishing the Book of Mormon also in Europe. This observation would also apply to the publication of the Book of Doctrine and Covenants, hymnbook, etc. He wrote that the families of the twelve were generally well but not altogether comfortable.

After receiving word from Joseph about the necessity for raising funds, Hyrum succeeded in depositing three hundred dollars with Messrs. Holmes and Co., merchants of Quincy, subject to the order of Judge Young to be applied to the Prophet's account.

In his letter to the Prophet January 3, 1840, he said, referring to raising money on the sale of city lots: "In consequence of my health, which has been poor and the coldness of the weather, I have not been able to attend to it myself." Hyrum mentioned the printing of the Book of Mormon and the Doctrine and Covenants and Parley P. Pratt's offer to have the printing done in New York. Near the close of the letter Hyrum wrote:

I want a letter from you, brother Joseph, as soon as possible, giving me all the instructions you think necessary. I feel the burden in your absence is great. . . . The Mississippi is frozen up. The weather is very cold, and a great quantity of snow is on the ground and has been for some time. Your family is in tolerable good health, excepting one or two having the chills occasionally. . . . You may expect to hear from me again. I sent you a copy of the deposit I made in Holmes and Co., which I hope you will receive safe. I am very affectionately, signed Hyrum Smith.[10]

---

[9]Ibid., p. 46. *Times and Seasons*, vol. I, pp. 20-23.
[10]Ibid., pp. 51-52.

Judge Elias Higbee remained in Washington, D. C., to meet with congressional committees in order to bring before the highest legislative body the grievances of the Saints against the state of Missouri. The Prophet Joseph Smith, after visiting several branches of the Church, preached and counseled the various bretheren who where on their way to their appointed fields of labor as missionaries and returned to Nauvoo, March 4, 1840, after a very difficult trip.

There remained much to be done to build up this wilderness country, where the Saints could consolidate their position. The postoffice at Commerce had its name changed to that of Nauvoo, taken from a Hebrew term signifying a beautiful place.[11]

During the month of March much correspondence was received from Judge Higbee on developments in Washington. Prejudice and misunderstanding among the nation's lawmakers made it impossible to obtain satifactory results. Sidney Rigdon was still under a physician's care in New Jersey and seemed unable to assist Brother Higbee. His able help at home was greatly missed by Hyrum and Joseph.

At the general conference at Nauvoo, April 6, 7, 8, the results of the mission to Washington were related by the Prophet Joseph. It was a time of taking stock, making decisions, and giving counsel. Reports from the British Mission were very favorable. Brigham Young who was in England, became President of the Quorum of Twelve.[12] Willard Richards was ordained an apostle to fill the vacancy made by the advancement of President Young. Orson Hyde and John E. Page were assigned to go to Palestine to dedicate that land for the return of the Jews. A number of grievances among the Saints were taken care of. The case of Frederick G. Williams was presented by Hyrum Smith, and it was recommended that he be forgiven for his misconduct in Missouri. His re-instatement was unanimously

---

[11]*Ibid.*, p. 121.
[12]Thomas B. Marsh was excommunicated, March 17, 1839, which made Brigham Young President of the Twelve.

approved. Seventy-five persons had been baptized during the conference and fifty ordained into the seventies quorum.[13]

Again, slowly but surely, the star of hope was rising for the outcast Saints. They were gathering to a new state. The original settlers were friendly. The state of Illinois was anxious for new settlers who were thrifty and who could be relied upon to help liquidate the state's bonded indebtedness. Hancock County in western Illinois could boast of a new city named Nauvoo. The year 1840 would prove to be the beginning of a new era, a period of consolidation and growth.

During the early months of 1840, Hyrum spent many hours in thoughtful consideration of what was best to do for the welfare of the people. He had made a selection of a plot of ground for a home of his own in Nauvoo, and the cold weather pointed up the need for improved housing facilities for his family. But his personal needs were never permitted to make demands upon the time and energy required for the fulfilment of his duty to the Church.

---

[13]Joseph Smith, *op. cit.*, pp. 102-110.

CHAPTER XXII

HYRUM'S ADMINISTRATION

Three days of April conference at Nauvoo cleared the atmosphere of many vexatious problems. Hyrum Smith had endorsed the plan of acquiring land on the Iowa side of the river for a place of gathering for the Saints and had also supported the advice of the Prophet to the brethren to pay off the debt on the town plots for an inheritance to the poor. He heard again a report of the proceedings at Washington, D. C., and of the action of the Senate on the memorial which was presented to them. Elders leaving for the mission field were advised to see that their respective families were provided for, and to teach the "Gathering of Israel" as set forth in the Holy Scriptures.

During the week following the conference the brethren were concerned with getting the missionaries ready to depart for their field of labor. The call of Orson Hyde and John E. Page to Palestine marked the commencement of the Lord's work of gathering the remnants of the House of Israel. Joseph Smith had said: "The Jewish nations have been scattered among the Gentiles for a long period of time, and in our estimation, the time of the commencement of their return to the Holy Land has already arrived."[1]

It was believed by the brethren and others that the gathering of the Jews to their homeland and of the converted Saints to Illinois was a fulfilment of prophecy prerequisite to the second coming of the Messiah, and by April 15, the Palestinean missionaries were on their way. Being without funds they worked their way from city to city. It was heartening to the leaders to witness the faith and devotion of the elders of the Church, and to hear that Elders Brigham Young, Wilford Woodruff, John Taylor and others had established several

[1]Joseph Smith, op. cit., vol. IV, p. 112.

branches of the Church in England. The success of the English mission was partly due to the conversion of a group of Anglican dissenters, called the "United Brethren," including their ministers. This event did not escape the notice of the London newspapers nor of the American press: One article entitled "Mormonism" in the Philadelphia Gazette, read: "We perceive by the London papers . . . Missionaries in England preaching with considerable success."[2]

The reality of the gathering of Israel was evidenced to the brethren when they read the following press release on November 14, 1840: "Announcement — 49 cabin and 200 steerage passengers belonging to a sect called Latter-day Saints, bound fo Quincy. . . . 2000 next spring will embark for that place."[3] These and similar reports were forerunners of more to follow. The field was ripe and ready to harvest and there was but a need now for more missionaries to thrust in their sickle with all their might.

The successful establishment of Nauvoo within so short a time was sensational. The vigorous growth of this frontier town had a sobering effect on certain dissenters and curious onlookers. During July, 1840, a letter was received from William W. Phelps, an apostate who had been a stalwart during the Ohio and Missouri period, begging forgiveness and a restoration of his membership.

Phelps had turned traitor to Joseph, Hyrum and the brethren during the crisis at Far West. But in the face of his repentance, their hearts retained no rancor. Their feelings on the matter are reflected in a reply to his letter dated July 22, 1840: "You may in some measure realize what my feelings, as well as Elder Rigdon's and Brother Hyrum's were when we read your letter." The Prophet manifested a forgiving spirit in these closing lines: "Believing your confession to be real and your repentance genuine, I shall be happy once again to give you the right hand of fellowship."[4]

---

[2]*Sangamo Journal*, Springfield, Ill., Dec. 8, 1839, vol. 8, No. 7, Whole No. 371, p. 2.
[3]*Quincy Whig*, Quincy, Ill., vol. 3, No. 29, p. 1.
[4]Joseph Smith, *op. cit.*, vol. IV, pp. 162-163.

A few days later came a letter from one John C. Bennett who had achieved some degree of importance as a physician and a professor and was then a military man, a brigadier-general who had been appointed quarter-master general of the state of Illinois in 1840. He professed a desire to be identified with the Saints and live in Nauvoo. He said in part: ". . . I shall likewise expect to practice my profession, but at the same time, your people shall have all the benefits of my speaking powers and my untiring energies in behalf of the good and holy faith. . . ."[5] Several letters were exchanged prior to Bennett's coming to Nauvoo; but the innate weakness of his character and his evil motives were not detected because of his seeming sincerity. Not until later was his treachery exposed, to the great sorrow and suffering of the people.

Nauvoo was like a magnet which drew Mormons and non-Mormons alike. Saints and sinners, rich and poor gravitated to this boom town. Hyrum realized the need of locating new townsites near Nauvoo in order that the virgin territory could be cultivated and made to sustain an expanding economy. Eventually villages, towns, and cities would fan out from Nauvoo like the spokes of a huge wheel. Already several communities had been established across the river west in the territory of Iowa, and Joseph and Hyrum decided to spend several days among the Iowa Saints.

On Sunday, August 16, Hyrum addressed the congregation in Lee County, Iowa, on "The Eternal Judgment." The following Sunday he visited Nashville, three miles southeast of Montrose, and while there voted with the people to build a city near Nashville.[6] The Church had purchased 20,000 acres for this purpose. A stake had been organized at Ramus, and Hyrum ordained Joel Hills Johnson its stake president.[7] Later (October 23), another stake was organized at Lima, Adams County, Illinois. Here Hyrum ordained Gardiner Snow a bishop.[8]

[5]Ibid., p. 168.
[6]Ibid., 182.
[7]Joel Johnson Diary, 1802-1883.
[8]Journal History, op. cit.

Each time Hyrum returned with his companions to Nauvoo from across the river they expressed joy at the growth of the city. The terrain, enclosed at the river's edge, extended about six miles up to a central prominence, with wide streets running at right angles. Many new homes were in the process of construction, and the whole scene elicited a feeling of peace and satisfaction. To them, no other city was quite so picturesque or so strikingly beautiful. Near the end of August, the population had grown to about three thousand. And people continued to pour in, some to make their homes and others as tourists. Hyrum, as one of the founders of this commonwealth, was intrigued by the visits of many unique personalities and was interested in their comments.

To the Saints it was important news when something favorable was published about Nauvoo. Such a column appeared October 17, 1840. The article, "A Glance at the Mormons," written by a correspondent about a year after he had visited the Mormon settlement, reflected the gentile view. It appeared in the Alexandria *Gazette* and read in part:

Since the Mormons were expelled from the state of Missouri, they have purchased the town of Commerce, a situation of surpassing beauty at the head of the lower rapid on the Illinois shore of the upper Mississippi River. The name of the place they recently changed to Nauvoo, the Hebrew term for fair or beautiful. Around this place, as their center, they are daily gathering from almost every quarter, and several hundred new houses erected in the past few months attest to the passing traveller the energy, industry, and self-denial with which the community is imbued. They have also obtained possession of extensive lands on the opposite side of the river, in that charming portion of Iowa Territory, known as the "Half Breed Reservation" and there on the rolling and fertile prairies, they are rapidly selecting their homes and opening their farms. As the traveller now passes through those natural parks and fields of flowers which the hand of the creator seems to have originally planned there for the inspection of his own eye, he beholds the cabins dotted down in the most enchanting perspective either on the border of the timber or beside the springs and streams of living water, which are interspersed on every hand.

Nor are they unmindful of their interests abroad while they are accomplishing so much at home. No sect with equal means has probably ever suffered and achieved more in so short a time. Their elders have not only been commissioned and sent forth to every part of our country, but they have left their families and friends behind them and gone to Europe and even to the Holy Land to reveal the wonders of the "New and Everlasting Covenant" to preach the dispensation of the fullness of time.

They do not doubt but that they shall be endued when necessary, with power from on high to proclaim to all the nations of the earth in their own tongues, the wonderful works of God.

The signal success which everywhere attends their exertion, proves how well their religious system is adapted to give expression to the various forms of enthusiasm that pervade the religious sentiment of the day. Retaining many truths which are held in common by different denominations of Christians and covering their own absurdities with imposing forms and lofty pretensions, their system opens a winning asylum for all the disaffected or dissatisfied or other persuasions, and much that is congenial to almost every shade of erratic or radical religious character. As an illustration, it is stated, in the last number of their *Times and Seasons*, that, on a single occasion in England, one of their Elders lately baptized, among others, no less than thirteen preachers of one denomination of Christians.

There had been some talk among the brethren of a temple at Nauvoo. To Hyrum Smith such talk brought memories of his experience at Kirtland, and he felt impelled to make mention of it several times to Joseph, for he sensed a personal involvement in the planning of such a building. In a message from the First Presidency, August 31, 1840, to the scattered Saints, a statement was made, among others, about the erection of a divine edifice in order that the Saints might secure the blessings of heaven. . . . "The time has now come to erect a house of prayer, a house of order, a house of worship to our God, where the ordinances can be attended to agreeably to His divine will in this region of the country."[9]

Hyrum's interest and his feeling were reflected in the general epistle. The Saints were urged to put forth their strength for the upbuilding of Zion, and to arm themselves with courage, They were urged to feel an individual responsibility and to show as much interest as though the whole labor depended on themselves alone.

---

[9]Joseph Smith, *op. cit.*, vol. IV, p. 186.

Those who could assist in this project were urged to come to Nauvoo. The printing and circulation of the Book of Mormon, Doctrine and Covenants, a hymnbook and other new scriptures would help not only to sweep away the cobwebs of the superstition and error but also to finance the building of God's house. But a temple was only one among the many buildings needed in Nauvoo.

The leaders of the Church did not minimize the importance of full co-operation of its members in a gigantic building program. They had visions of future needs and an expanding membership. Amid other plans for buildings, Hyrum also made plans for a new home to be constructed on his acre not far from Joseph's house. He had been deeply concerned about his parent's comfort, too, and was happy for the new house Joseph had built them. Hyrum supported the construction of a city hotel to accommodate visitors who were coming more frequently. As Nauvoo grew, the demand for housing and for public buildings would naturally increase.

During the hot busy days of summer, Hyrum found time for frequent visits to his aging parents. His father was very feeble, having failed steadily for some time; and the stifling heat of early September 1840, was taking a terrible toll of his strength. Even the many prayers for the aging patriarch, and the medical aid and loving care of his family failed to relieve him except temporarily.

Mother Smith wrote of her husband's illness, telling how Joseph, after his return from Washington, D. C., had administered to him and brought about a temporary recovery.

Father Smith's condition worsened steadily and Mother Lucy sent for Hyrum and Joseph. They arrived on a Saturday night and gave their father something which alleviated his distress. The next day Joseph came and assured his father that he (Joseph) would not for the time being be troubled by the Missourians who had begun an attempt to rearrest Joseph as an escaped prisoner. Joseph then explained to his father the principle of work for the dead. This information was comforting to the weakened patriarch, and he requested Joseph to be baptized immediately for his brother Alvin.

As it became evident that their father was dying, the children all gathered to receive a father's blessing. He first gave his wife, Lucy, a blessing and then, beginning with Hyrum, gave a blessing to each in his turn, down to the youngest.

Before receiving his blessing, Hyrum bent over his father and said: "Father, if you are taken away, will you not intercede for us at the throne of grace, that our enemies will not have so much power over us?" The father then laid his hands upon Hyrum's head and said:

My son, Hyrum, I seal upon your head your patriarchal blessing, which I placed upon your head before, for that shall be verified. In addition to this, I now give you my dying blessing. You shall have a season of peace, so that you shall have sufficient rest to accomplish the work which God has given you to do. You shall be as firm as the pillars of heaven unto the end of your days. I now seal upon your head the patriarchal power, and you shall bless the people. This is my dying blessing upon your head in the name of Jesus. Amen.

To Joseph he said:

Joseph, my son, you are called to a high and holy calling. You are even called to do the work of the Lord. Hold out faithful and you shall be blest and your children after you. You shall even live to finish your work; at this Joseph cried out, weeping, "Oh! my father, shall I?" "Yes," said his father, "you shall live to lay out the plan for all the work which God has given you to do. This is my dying blessing upon your head in the name of Jesus. I also confirm your former blessings upon your head, for it shall be fulfilled. Even so, Amen."

When he had blessed Lucy, the youngest, he spoke to his wife, praising her for her steadfastness in rearing their children, saying that she should not mourn but live to be a comfort to the children and that her last days would be her best days.

He then paused for some time, being exhausted. After which he said in a tone of surprise, "I can see and hear as well as ever I could." Pausing again; "I can see Alvin"; another pause and "I shall live seven or eight minutes." Then, straightening himself, he laid his hands together; after which his breathing shortened and in about eight minutes stopped altogether without any sign of struggle or even a sigh.[10] Joseph Smith, Sr., was buried in Nauvoo, in a plot whose exact location is unknown. At his death his oldest living son, Hyrum Smith, was made presiding Patriarch to the Church. The young Church provided a successor by following the patriarchal order of father to son, thereby setting a precedent to be followed in perpetuating this office.

Joseph Smith, Sr., had been an old man at sixty-nine. He had endured the hardships of pioneering and bitter persecutions. But his faith had remained undaunted during adversity. He had ridden out the storm and lived to see his people gain a state of comparative security and well-being.

After the funeral, Hyrum and Joseph were forced to maintain a constant vigilance against the threats of arrest and imprisonment made by some Missouri officers who were seeking to take the escaped leaders back to their home state. The *Times and Seasons* under date of Tuesday, September 15, announced that the governor of Missouri, after a silence of two years, had at last made a demand on Governor Carlin of Illinois for Joseph Smith, Jr., Sidney Rigdon, Lyman Wight, Parley P. Pratt, Caleb Baldwin, and Alanson Brown as fugitives from justice.

The article stated that the sheriff visited Nauvoo to arrest these men, but due to the tender mercies of a kind Providence, they were not found. The governor of Missouri had at one time permitted the mob militia to drag the prisoners from everything dear and sacred to them; and he had countenanced their being tried by a court-martial which condemned them to be shot. In part, the *Times and Seasons* article read:

What a beautiful picture Governor Boggs has presented to the world, after driving twelve to fifteen thousand from their homes and murdering innocent men, women and children; then, because a few made their escape

---

[10]Lucy Mack Smith, *op. cit.*, pp. 306-314.

from his murdering hand and have found protection in a land of equal rights so that his plans and designs have all been unfruitful to the extent that he has caused "Mormonism" to spread with double vigor, he now has the presumption to demand them back, in order that his thirst for innocent blood may yet be satisfied.[11]

Hyrum's name was not listed as one of the fugitives from justice. Perhaps the Missouri court felt that Hyrum was not a key figure. This fact was important to the Saints as future events will show. Hyrum would be needed to keep a firm hand on affairs while his brother Joseph maneuvered to avoid capture by a relentless foe. The action of Missouri against the Mormon leaders, coming so soon, was a complete surprise to Hyrum and Joseph. The warrant for the arrest of Joseph and the others shocked and angered the Saints, and they resolved to thwart the enemy with every available means.

It is quite logical to suppose that a state in the position like that in which Missouri found herself, smarting under a cloud of infamy, and desiring to vindicate her cause and clear her name, would strive to destroy the Mormon movement. Only in this way could she regain her respectability among her sister states. Thus it was that when reports reached Missouri telling of the success of the people whom they had banished beyond their borders, fear and evil forebodings aroused its citizens to take action.

While the enemy was plotting and scheming to wreck the Church, Hyrum and others sat in general conference during October 3, 4, and 5, 1840, at Nauvoo. These meetings gave them new hope and revived their faith. Since the previous conference in April, noticeable progress had been made in missionary work. Hyrum was chosen as one of a committee of three to organize stakes between Nauvoo and Kirtland wherever the church membership justified it. He gave some general instructions and spoke on a problem he had observed for some time. He said that there were several individuals who, in moving to Nauvoo had not settled with their creditors and had no recom-

---

[11]Joseph Smith, *op. cit.*, vol. IV, pp. 198-199.

mend from the branches of the Church where they had resided. On motion, it was resolved that "The persons moving to this place, who do not bring a recommend, be disfellowshipped." Hyrum was also appointed on a committee to liquidate the debts on the city plot.[12]

As had been previously stated, the death of his father brought to Hyrum the office of presiding Patriarch, because he was the oldest living son of his father's family. This additional responsibility he assumed in a quiet and modest manner; and his appointment met with the immediate favor of the Saints, for he was much beloved of all who had come under his benign and understanding personality.

As the year 1840 drew to a close, Hyrum and his family were happy to acknowledge their blessings. As a father, Hyrum found joy and satisfaction in his family. They were devoted and co-operative, and he was glad to see their material needs well supplied. As a leader of his people he marveled at the faith and devotion of the church membership. He felt a powerful strength of faith among his immediate associates and many who had been called to go abroad as missionaries. He had never been more sure that the cause he had espoused was of divine origin and that he was blessed by a kind and benevolent Heavenly Father, and he resolved anew to carry out every command and duty pertaining to his holy office in the restored Church of God.

---

[12]*Idem.*

CHAPTER XXIII

A YEAR OF DECISION

Early in January, 1841, Hyrum sat with the First Presidency at Nauvoo, Illinois, to write a proclamation to the Saints in all the world. From time to time it was deemed necessary to make a statement about existing circumstances and prospects of the Church, and also to give such instructions as might be necessary for the well being of the Saints.

In this message the leaders congratulated the membership of the Church on the progress of the great work. Encouraging reports had continued to come in from abroad concerning missionary work and the establishment of branches and stakes, and in glowing terms the brethren wrote:

. . . For not only has it spread through the length and breadth of this vast continent, but on the continent of Europe, and on the Islands of the sea, it is spreading in a manner entirely unprecedented in the annals of time.

All this had happened in the short time since the Mormons had been driven unmercifully from Missouri. Many citizens of the country had been led to rejoice because of the seeming triumph of the enemy over the Mormons. The Saints acknowledged that the Lord of Hosts was with them and had delivered them from the hands of bloody and deceitful men. The state of Illinois had welcomed them, and here they found an asylum among people worthy of the character of free men. The citizens of Quincy, like the good Samaritan, poured oil into their wounds, and contributed liberally for their necessities. Those most responsible were mentioned by name. The legislature without respect to parties, freely, openly, boldly, and nobly came to their assistance and owned them as citizens and friends, took them by the hand and extended blessings of civil, political, and religious liberty. Under date of December 16, 1840, one of the most liberal charters, with the most plenary powers ever conferred by a legislative assembly on free citizens, was granted for "The City of Nauvoo," the "Nauvoo Legion" and the "University of the City of Nauvoo."

The meaning and origin of the name "Nauvoo" was explained; the site of the city described as having the Mississippi River bounding it on the north, west, and south, with a vast prairie to the east. The place had been made healthy by drainage of the swamp area. The population numbered in excess of 3000, and the opportunities for agriculture and manufacturing were most favorable. All Saints who had been blessed of heaven with the possession of this world's goods were advised to dispose of them as fast as circumstances would possibly permit, without making too great a sacrifice, and remove to their city and county, to establish and build up manufacturing in the city, or purchase and cultivate farms in the county. Those with riches were urged to come—help should be given to the poor. The elders were to instruct the Saints to come without delay, and these instructions were from the Lord.

Soon to be constructed was a temple of the Lord, where the Saints would be able to worship the God of their fathers according to the order of his house and the powers of the Holy Priesthood. The Nauvoo Legion would enable them to perform their military duty by themselves, and thus afford them the power and privilege of avoiding one of the most fruitful sources of strife—oppression from the world. It would enable them to show their attachment to the state and nation. And as a people, whenever the public service required their aid, thus proving whenever the public service required their aid they could prove themselves obedient to the paramount laws of the land and, be ready at all times to sustain and execute them.

The "University of the City of Nauvoo" would enable the Saints to instruct their children in all knowledge and learning, in the arts, sciences, and learned professions. The future importance of this institution was expressed in these words:

We hope to make this institution one of the great lights of the world, and by and through it to diffuse that kind of knowledge which will be of practicable utility, and for the public good, and also for private and individual happiness. . . . This corporation contains all the powers and prerogatives of any other college or university in this state.

The membership was urged to more united action, in these words:

By a concentration of action and a unity of effort, we can only accomplish the great work of the last days which we could not do in a . . . scattered condition, while our interests, both temporal and spiritual, will be greatly enhanced, and the blessings of heaven must flow unto us in an uninterrupted stream; of this, we think there can be no question.

It was to be understood that the Saints, when they came to Nauvoo, should not expect perfection, or that conditions would be only harmonious, peaceful, and lovely. If they did they would undoubtedly be deceived, for there were, in Nauvoo, too, people from different states and countries who retained their prejudices. There were also those who crept in, unawares, to sow discord, strife, and animosity, and by so doing, brought evil upon the Saints. There should be a determination among those who came to keep the commandments of God and not be discouraged by the things enumerated. Great exertion must be made to erect the temple of the Lord in order that he might accept it. In it his power and glory would be manifest.

The proclamation closed in a democratic spirit, declaring that the writers claimed no privileges that they could not share with their fellow citizens of every denomination. All were invited to come and settle among them, for they would be treated as citizens and friends. The Saints would consider it not only a duty but a privilege to reciprocate the kindness they had received from the benevolent and kind-hearted citizens of the state of Illinois. The Proclamation was signed Joseph Smith, Sidney Rigdon, Hyrum Smith — Presidents of the Church, Nauvoo, January 15, 1841.[1]

---

[1] Joseph Smith, op. cit., vol. IV, pp. 268-273.

Thus the infant movement known as The Church of Jesus Christ of Latter-day Saints gathered momentum. The stage was set to establish the kingdom of God firmly upon the earth. The blessings of heaven were poured out upon a much injured and maligned people. A proclamation of the gospel was to be made to all the kings of the world as well as to all the governors of the nation and to all the nations of the earth. The proclamation was to be written by Robert E. Thompson, clerk to the Prophet Joseph, in a spirit of meekness and by the power of the Holy Ghost.

Out of the budding and flowering of the restored gospel gradually evolved a new approach toward religion. Hyrum Smith became an apt student of the fundamental gospel principles as they were revealed and expanded. Upon his sturdy shoulders had been placed the responsibility for helping to shape the course of this new society. Hyrum always felt a need to have the membership of the Church manifest a spirit of dignity and a sense of mission. This sense of mission was doubly necessary at this time because before them lay a most formidable task: the work of building the "Nauvoo House" and a temple.

The position of Hyrum Smith in the supreme councils of the Church had not been defined since the death of his father. No new revelation had been given to the Church since the imprisonment of its leaders in Liberty Jail, almost twenty-one months before. Thus, it was not surprising that the beginning of 1841, the Lord gave some important instructions, which included a declaration of his esteem for Hyrum and also defined his authority and duties. (D&C 124.) The revelation, in part, says:

And again, verily I say unto you, blessed is my servant Hyrum Smith; for I, the Lord, love him because of the integrity of his heart, and because he loveth that which is right before me, saith the Lord. (verse 15.)

Continuing, the Lord spoke of the building of the temple in order that baptisms for the dead might be performed; also regarding the erection of a house for the weary traveler to be known as the "Nauvoo House." The revelation continued:

> ... Let my servant Hyrum Smith put stock into that house as seemeth him good, for himself and his generation after him, from generation to generation.

It had been about two years and nine months since Hyrum Smith had been referred to in a revelation as a counselor in the First Presidency. He had nobly filled the vacancy made by the withdrawal of apostate Frederick G. Williams.

As associate President with his Prophet brother, he had fully shared the privations and sufferings of his brother and had been a pillar of strength in the council during the most trying period of the church. But now his new appointment was defined in the revelation as follows:

> And again, verily, I say unto you, let my servant William (Law) be appointed, ordained, and anointed, as counselor unto my servant Joseph, in the room of my servant Hyrum, that my servant Hyrum may take the office of Priesthood and Patriarch, which was appointed unto him by his father, by blessing and also by right.
>
> That from henceforth he shall hold the keys of the patriarchal blessings upon the heads of all my people.
>
> That whosoever he blesses shall be blessed, and whosoever he curses shall be cursed; that whatsoever he shall bind on earth shall be bound in heaven; and whatsoever he shall loose on earth shall be loosed in heaven.
>
> And from this time forth I appoint unto him that he may be a prophet, and a seer, and a revelator unto my church, as well as my servant Joseph;
>
> That he may act in concert with my servant Joseph; and that he shall receive counsel from my servant Joseph, who shall show unto him the keys whereby he may ask and receive, and be crowned with the same blessing, and glory, and honor, and priesthood, and gifts of the priesthood, that once were upon him that was my servant Oliver Cowdery;
>
> That my servant Hyrum may bear record of the things which I shall show unto him, that his name may be in honorable remembrance from generation to generation forever and ever. (verses 91-96.)

The revelation further stated that the Prophet Joseph must be given greater assistance:

Behold, I say unto you, I have a mission in store for my servant William, and my servant Hyrum, and for them alone; and let my servant Joseph tarry at home, for he is needed. The remainder I will show unto you hereafter. Even so. Amen. (verse 102.)

In the revelation too was advice to Counselor Sidney Rigdon that he was to humble himself and remain in Nauvoo and not think of moving to the eastern lands.

And then the Lord speaking to the Saints at large, said:

And hearken unto the counsel of my servants Joseph, and Hyrum, and William Law, and unto the authorities which I have called to lay the foundation of Zion, and it shall be well with him for ever and ever. Even so. Amen. (verse 118.)

* * *

A few days later on Sunday, January 24, 1841, Hyrum Smith was sustained as Patriarch to the Church, and William Law as a Counselor.

The patriarchal office required Hyrum to give individual blessings to the members of the Church, blessings which were carefully recorded by a scribe and given to the recipient. A special office for this work was to be constructed near Hyrum's home. However, his new duties did not remove him from the council of the First Presidency, for the Lord had designated him, as well as Joseph, "prophet, seer and revelator." He was to work in concert with Joseph and have all the blessings, glory, and honor, priesthood and gifts of the priesthood that were once conferred on Oliver Cowdery. Hyrum was to fulfill the role next to Joseph, as an associate President of the Church.

The following day, Monday, February 1, 1841, Hyrum was elected to the City Council of Nauvoo. Two days later he heard John C. Bennett, Mayor-elect, deliver his inaugural address, and he approved Bennett's eloquent and scholarly address. Bennett's concluding remarks emphasized a determination to execute all state laws and city ordinances to the very letter, even should it require the strong arm of military power to enable him to do so. As a public official he would be partial to no man; the peaceful, unoffending citizen was to be protected in the full exercise of all his civil, political, and religious rights, and the guilty violator of the law was to be punished, without respect to persons.

On Thursday, the following day, Hyrum signed his name with that of Joseph, Don Carlos Smith, and Charles C. Rich as members of the city council. They solemnly swore in the presence of Almighty God that they would support the Constitution of the United States and that of the state of Illinois, and would truly perform the duties of Councillors of the city of Nauvoo, according to the law and to the best of their ability.[2]

This was the beginning of Hyrum's experience in civil affairs, and he championed the several developments needed to make Nauvoo a first rate municipality. Before the month of February was gone, a corporation, with Hyrum as a member, was formed to promote agriculture and manufacturing in Hancock County. On Monday, March 1, the city council divided the city into four wards designating the blocks and boundary lines. The wards were to be known as First, Second, Third, and Fourth. Ordinances were passed upon by the City Council pertaining to the "Nauvoo Legion," "Religious Liberty in Nauvoo," "Ordinances to choose additional city officers," etc. Military commission was given to the offices of the Nauvoo Legion by Governor Thomas Carlin of Illinois.

Following the work of organizing Nauvoo, preparations were made to lay the cornerstone of the Nauvoo Temple on April 6, 1841. A central location above the city to the east, about a mile from the Mississippi River, had been chosen. Many visitors were present to witness the ceremony. The Quincy newspaper, a week later, reported that there were present between seven and eight thousand; and some said 12,000. Also present was the Nauvoo Legion of 650 men. Sidney Rigdon spoke energetically for an hour; there was good order, no accidents; General Bennett commanded the Legion under Joseph Smith.[3]

---

[2]Joseph Smith, op. cit., vol. IV, pp. 294-295.
[3]Quincy Whig, vol. III, no. 52, quoted from Warsaw World, April 7, 1841.

Another newspaper stated: "The Mormons had a great military display last week at Nauvoo. The cornerstone of the temple was laid, with great military pomp and array by the Nauvoo Legion. . . . One or two of the Fort Madison visitors came nigh being put under guard during the ceremonies."[4]

Hyrum was not present on this significant occasion. While the Prophet Joseph and others were laying the southeast cornerstone and listening to Sidney Rigdon's address, Hyrum was presiding over a conference in Philadelphia, where a branch was organized with a president and two counselors. Many branches were represented at this gathering.[5]

No mention is made of Hyrum's return to Nauvoo from Philadelphia. It is assumed that he returned around May 1, 1841, for he made a report (May 4, 1841) of his journey and proceeding in the East which had been pleasing and satisfactory.[6]

No sooner had Hyrum returned to Nauvoo than another trip East was proposed for important business reasons. This time he must be careful of his health, for the recent trip had been a grueling one, and the trip the year before with Oliver Granger and the one more recently with Dr. Isaac C. Galland had been arduous and fatiguing. On this journey he and William Law were to sell stock in the Nauvoo House, and collect donations for the building of the temple. Their written authorization said in part: "They are vested with full authority pertaining to their business transactions." Joseph commented further that "the Saints should place confidence in them. Hyrum has long been known for his virtue, patience, and every principle that can adorn a Christian character."[7]

Prior to Hyrum's departure for the East he warned Joseph of the dangers of being taken by Missouri officers for a trial based on charges of being a fugitive from justice. The following events and news items reveal the intensity of feeling among the

---

[4]*Hawkeye and Iowa Patriot,* vol. 2, n. 46, p. 2, April 15, 1841, Burlington, Iowa. I. T.
[5]Joseph Smith, vol. IV, *op. cit.,* pp. 326-331.
[6]Journal History, *op. cit.*
[7]*Ibid.,* February 15, 1841.

enemy against Joseph and the Saints and also reveal the tactics they employed to get the Prophet involved again in endless lawsuits.

Shortly, Missouri Governor Boggs demanded of Governor Carlin of Illinois that he deliver the head of the Mormon Church for trial. Agitation for the arrest of Joseph was made soon after his escape from Missouri and persisted. The fall before, the press at Springfield, Illinois, had said: "Governor Carlin issued a process for the arrest of Joe Smith and Sidney Rigdon, and their delivery to the Missouri officers."[8] About the same time the newspaper at Burlington, Iowa, quoted an article from the Quincy *Whig*, concerning the suggested giving up of Smith and Rigdon to Missouri. It was an affair between Carlin and Boggs.[9] The editors were opposed to another trial in Missouri, and also to plotting to maneuver Joseph Smith to justify taking him to Missouri.

Perhaps Hyrum Smith should have delayed his eastern assignment in order to aid Joseph in thwarting the enemy. The following episode reveals the shallow soil supporting the opposers of Mormonism, the methods used by evil forces in fighting the growth of the new church, and the sinister forces arrayed against this new society which in time would challenge the Brethren's utmost ingenuity for self-protection.

On Tuesday, June 1, Joseph accompanied Hyrum Smith and William Law as far as Quincy, Illinois, on their way east. Before returning to Nauvoo, Joseph made a courtesy call on Governor Carlin who treated him with the greatest kindness and respect. Shortly after leaving the governor's residence, however, he was arrested at Heberlin's Hotel, Bear Creek, about twenty-eight miles south of Nauvoo by a posse of officers headed by Sheriff Thomas King of Adams County, Illinois, and an officer from Missouri, sent by Governor Carlin for the purpose of delivering the Prophet to the Missouri authorities. Joseph returned to Quincy to obtain a writ of habeas corpus

---

[8]*The Sangamo Journal*, vol. 9, no. 361, Friday, September 5, 1840.
[9]*Hawkeye and Iowa Patriot*, vol. II, no. 17, p. 2, October, 1840.

from Charles A. Warren, Esq., Master in Chancery. Judge Stephen A. Douglas happened to come to Quincy that evening and granted a request for a hearing on the Tuesday following at Monmouth, Warren County, where the court would then give a regular term.

The trial at Monmouth lasted for over a week amid great excitement. Judge Douglas acquitted the Prophet after a stirring defense by attorney O. H. Browning who described in eloquent words the suffering of the Mormons when they were driven from Missouri. His speech, one of the most eloquent ever made in defense of Joseph Smith, caused the spectators to weep, even the honorable judge himself, and most of the officers shed tears. The co-editor of the *Times and Seasons* wrote:

> . . . we have listened to one of the most eloquent speeches ever uttered by mortal man in favor of justice and liberty by O. H. Browning, Esq., who has done himself immortal honor in the sight of all patriotic citizens who listened to the same.

This crisis in the absence of Hyrum brought to a satisfactory conclusion was a great relief to the Saints. The feelings of the Prophet were expressed in these words:

> This decision was received with satisfaction to myself and the brethren. . . . It is now decided that before another writ can be issued, a new demand must be made by the Governor of Missouri. Thus have I once more been delivered from the fangs of my cruel persecutors for which I thank God, my Heavenly Father.[10]

Hyrum Smith and William Law had met Elder George A. Smith while they were visiting the Saints in Chester County, Pennsylvania. Elders Young, Kimball, and Taylor arrived at Nauvoo, July 1, amid a large gathering of friends and received the hand of fellowship and the commendation of the Prophet for a mission that was highly satisfactory.

And from Elder Orson Hyde came word of his eventful journey to Palestine to dedicate that land for the return of the Jews. Hyrum Page had deserted him at New York.

---

[10]Joseph Smith, vol. IV. *op. cit.*, pp. 364, 360, 369, 370-371.

On Saturday, August 7, 1841, Hyrum and Joseph again suffered a heavy loss when their beloved brother Don Carlos died at his home in Nauvoo. Don Carlos' life had been closely knit with that of his brothers. He had performed valiant missionary service for the Church; had been associated with the *Elders Journal* in Kirtland and had later assisted with the publication of the *Times and Sessions* at Nauvoo. At nineteen he had married Agnes Coolbirth and had subsequently become the father of three daughters. And now at twenty-six he was dead, a victim, it was thought, of the dampness in the basement where he worked on the newspaper.[11]

The spectre of death haunted the Smiths that August of 1841. Don Carlos' death on August 7 was followed a week later by the death on August 14 of Joseph's infant son, Don Carlos (fourteen months old), and two weeks later by the death on August 27 of Robert Blaskel Thompson, Hyrum's brother-in-law, then thirty years of age. But the climax of sorrows for Hyrum came on September 25 with the loss of his own next oldest son, Hyrum, who was then just over seven years of age.[12] Neither the circumstances nor the causes of these deaths are known.[13]

To Hyrum it seemed that he lived constantly on the edge of disaster; each day or week brought its joy or sorrow. On the more hopeful side of life's ledger was the return of the apostles from England. The presence of such stalwarts as Brigham Young, John Taylor, and Wilford Woodruff lightened the heavy load borne by the Prophet and Hyrum. Meetings were called and certain authority delegated to the Quorum of the Twelve. The Prophet wrote:

> . . . I also requested the Twelve to take the burden of business of the church in Nauvoo, and especially as pertaining to the selling of church lands.

---

[11]*Ibid.,* pp. 393-394. Press notice: "Don Carlos Smith's death notice" — "One of the publishers of the *Times and Seasons* died 7th of August at 26. He was universally respected. Younger brother of the Prophet." Quincy *Whig,* vol. 4, no. 19, p. 2.
[12]Joseph Smith, *op. cit.,* vol. IV, p. 411.
[13]Mary had died in Hyrum's arms at Kirtland, Ohio, May 29, 1832. Hyrum now had five children: Lovina, John, Jerusha, Sarah, and Joseph Fielding.

In order to relieve his brother Joseph of as much responsibility as possible, Hyrum made it a point to be part of welcoming committees whenever a demand for one arose. At this time word had been received at Nauvoo that a large number of Sac and Fox Indians were encamped at Montrose, Iowa. On Thursday, August 13, a ferryman brought a number of them to visit the Prophet. A squad of the Nauvoo Legion and the military band were on hand to escort them to the grove, and Hyrum went to welcome them. But they refused to come ashore until Joseph came down. At the landing, Hyrum introduced the Prophet to Keokuk, Kis-ku-kosh, Appenoose, and about one hundred other chiefs and braves of the above-mentioned tribes, with their families.

After conducting them to the meeting grounds in the grove, Joseph instructed them in many things which the Lord had revealed to him concerning their fathers and told them of the promises that were made concerning them in the Book of Mormon. He advised them, through an interpreter, to cease killing each other and warring with other tribes, also to keep peace with the whites.

Keokuk replied that at his wigwam he had a Book of Mormon which Joseph had given him some years before. Speaking to the Prophet, he said: "I believe you are a great and good man; I look rough, but I am a son of the Great Spirit. I have heard your advice—we intend to quit fighting and follow the good talk you have given us."

After the conversation they feasted on the green with good food, dainties, and melons grown by the brethren, and they entertained the spectators with a specimen of their dancing.[14]

Hyrum had assumed many duties of a routine nature hoping to relieve his younger brother for more important work.

[14]Of this solemn occasion the press at Fort Madison sarcastically wrote: "Chief Keokuk with 50 or 60 of his warriors, squaws, and papooses visited Nauvoo. The distinguished strangers were received with marked attention. The Nauvoo Legion—ever ready to honor the great ones of the earth who came to pay homage to the Prophet — escorted them from the landing to the Temple where in the august presence of the Twelve Apostles, and twelve oxen, these almighty chiefs held converse for the space of half an hour." *Fort Madison Courier* vol. I, no. 7, p. 3, September 1841.

And, too, there was always the possibility that Joseph would be forced into absenting himself from Nauvoo to defend himself from the enemy. If such a situation should suddenly arise who would take his place? This problem had been much in the minds of Hyrum and Joseph since their coming to Nauvoo. And so at one of the meetings held at this time, the Prophet spoke on the seniority of authority among the First Presidency and the twelve. He said that "the time had come when the Twelve should be called upon to stand in their place next to the First Presidency. They should attend to the settling of the emigrants and the business of the church in the Stakes. The Twelve," he said, "should have an opportunity of providing for themselves and families and at the same time relieve him so that he might attend to the business of translating" (the papyrus which had come with the Egyptian mummies).

During the semiannual conference in October, 1841, Patriarch Hyrum Smith occupied the stand in the bowery atop the hill in front of the temple whose walls were slowly rising. The morning session had been presided over by President Brigham Young while members of the First Presidency were laying the cornerstone of the Nauvoo House. Saturday, October 2, 1841, was a chilly fall day; but all seats were taken, and many were standing. Many nonmembers had also gathered and were scattered among the members to witness the proceedings. With the several quorums seated in their order, the gathering was an impressive affair, and a spirit of friendliness and well-being filled the air. The brethren on the stand manifest a cordiality and love which created just the right atmosphere for a successful conference.

A letter from Elder Orson Hyde on the success of his mission was read and various vacancies in church offices were filled. Then some general advice was given by the several speakers. Patriarch Hyrum Smith made plain his disapproval of the course of some elders in attempting to discourage immigrants from coming to Nauvoo and enticing them to settle at places not approved for gathering.

During the later sessions of this conference the importance of baptism for the dead was stressed at length by the Prophet, and he explained the role of angels, ministering spirits, translated bodies, etc. Hyrum was called upon to offer the benediction at two sessions of the conference. At the conclusion of the conference the Prophet wrote:

> Although the conference commenced under discouraging circumstances owing to the inclemency of the weather, yet a vast number of the brethren and visitors from abroad were present, and on Saturday and Sunday, the weather having become favorable, the congregation was immense.[15] The greatest unanimity prevailed; business was conducted with the most perfect harmony and good feelings, and the assembly dispersed with new confidence in the great work of the last days.[16]

The good feeling prevailing among the Saints at the conference persisted afterward. There had been a frank appraisal of general conditions in the Church. Their economic situation had been evaluated, and solutions to problems proposed. And their zeal for missionary work remained unabated. The Quorum of Twelve met to make missionary assignments to various centers of population in the Middle West and East.

It was agreed among the brethren that the Church would negotiate all land sales to the emigrants to prevent speculators from profiteering and to provide the needed source of revenue for the Church. This policy would not only be carried out at Nauvoo but also at Zarahemla, Warren, Nashville, and Ramas.

Land located north of Nauvoo along the River had been purchased from Horace R. Hotchkiss of New Haven, Connecticut, and some also to the south, which included the best steamboat landings, but it was very unhealthy. Mr. Hotchkiss who had received no interest on the agreed terms of the land sale wrote to Joseph Smith, explaining that he had failed to contact Hyrum Smith and Dr. Galland when they were in the East. A verbal agreement with Mr. Hotchkiss allowed to the

---

[15]The Prophet, in a letter to Smith Tuttle, said that there were about 10,000 present.
[16]Joseph Smith, op. cit., vol. IV, p. 429.

Saints five years grace should conditions be unfavorable and prevent their paying for the land.

The situation at Nauvoo concerning the Hotchkiss land trouble was described by the Prophet in a letter to Smith Tuttle, Esq.

> . . . Cold weather is now rolling in upon us. I have been confined here this season by sickness and various other things which are beyond my control.
> . . . Having been demanded by the Governor of Missouri, of the Governor of this state, and he did not have moral courage enough to resist the demand . . . I accordingly was taken prisoner and they put me to some ten or eleven hundred dollars' expense and trouble such as lawyer's fees, witnesses, etc. etc., before I could be redeemed from under the difficulty. But I am now clear of them once more.

From what followed in this communique it appeared that Dr. Galland had not yet reported to Nauvoo the details of his mission east to take care of the Hotchkiss real estate transaction. He had been instructed either to trade some church property located in the East or to obtain money in some other way to pay Mr. Hotchkiss. Hyrum Smith, who had accompanied Dr. Galland, had become ill and been forced to return home. It had been his hope to pay off both the Hotchkiss principal and the interest, even though it was not due until some time later. Toward the end of the message Joseph said:

> As to the growth of our place, it is very rapid, and it would be more so were it not for sickness and death. There have been many deaths which leaves a melancholy reflection, but we cannot help it. When God speaks from the heavens to call us hence, we must submit to his mandates.[17]

No doubt, the coming of cold weather and the winter soon to descend upon them brought memories of persecution, suffering, and want. The year 1841 had been a trying one for Hyrum Smith. At forty-one years of age he was beginning to realize the limitations of his physical capacities. Exposure

---

[17]*Ibid.*, p. 432.

to the inclement weather and long months of imprisonment with foul food, besides the constant pressure of enemy threats of violence and death, took their toll. He had to guard his health. Hyrum had worked long hours away from home a good part of the time Joseph was absent in Wasington. He had gone to Quincy, Illinois, to arrange for money to help carry the Saint's appeal to the Federal Government for redress for their losses in Missouri.

The death of his beloved father had been a great trial, as had that of his brother Don Carlos, whom he had dearly loved. The grim reaper had spared neither Joseph's nor his own immediate family; both had been bowed by grief over the loss of their little ones. He had himself spent anxious days and nights standing vigil over the sickbeds of his loved ones, and had also offered prayers of supplication to the throne of grace for his sick friends. The many calls of his benevolent faith and prayers had not gone unheeded.

But in the midst of this travail he had been greatly blessed. The Lord had called him to be Presiding Patriarch, giving him great power. He had been designated as a prophet, seer, and revelator and had been called to hold the position next to the Prophet that was formerly held by Oliver Cowdery, that of assistant to the President. He was more nearly equal to Joseph in authority than any other man. He enjoyed the complete confidence of the First Presidency. He had made two long tedious trips East on important church business. Only the failure of his health had prevented him from successfully completing the second venture.

His voice had been heard in important councils establishing the city government of Nauvoo, the Nauvoo Legion, and city ordinances. He had had a voice in the erection of the Nauvoo House and the temple, and a part in the organization of new stakes, wards, and towns. He had given patriarchal blessings, extended advice to missionaries abroad and offered a solution to many vexing problems arising in the establishment of a civic and religious organization.

After the grief of losing his little son had somewhat subsided, Hyrum resumed his work with a more mature zeal and with complete self dedication. He was fully aware that in the months ahead there lay more problems to be solved and more work to be accomplished.

CHAPTER XXIV

A PROPHECY

On October 31, 1841, the Sunday after conference Hyrum Smith unlocked his new office for a meeting which was to transact important business. Soon, others arrived including Brother Joseph and members of the Quorum of Twelve. At this meeting the Prophet instructed those present on many principles of the gathering of the nations and the fate of the wicked and downtrodden of this generation.

Hyrum mentioned that he had written a letter to the Saints still in Kirtland, Ohio, concerning the building up of that place. The minutes of a conference held in Kirtland, Ohio, October 2, 1841, were then read. They included a proposal to have Saints living in that vicinity contribute to the establishment of a religious paper, entitled *The Olive Leaf*.

There had been much concern among the brethren over the affairs at Kirtland, Ohio. The Kirtland Stake President, Almon W. Babbitt, had taken a mistaken attitude about the leaders returning to Kirtland. In a letter to Nauvoo he referred to his impression that he was to prepare the way for men of greater counsel and wisdom. He had understood that Brother Hyrum Smith, with his family, was to have returned to Kirtland by the spring of 1841, although Hyrum had made arrangements with Brother Babbitt to exchange a piece of land in Clayton for the Carter house and had made many other arrangements of like nature.[1] Apparently Brother Babbit had a misconception of Hyrum's intentions.

Kirtland, Ohio, would never again become the headquarters of the whole Church. The sacred temple had been defiled and the spirit of evil was there. The Saints of Kirtland had not even expressed their sympathy or regrets to Hyrum and Joseph while they were prisoners in Missouri. The Lord had

---

[1]Journal History, *op. cit.*, October 18, 1841.

completed his designs in Kirtland during that period of five years when the Prophet had made his headquarters there, and he now had other plans for that city.[2]

During that October 31 meeting, Hyrum Smith read for the brethren's approval a letter he had prepared for Kirtland. This letter contained Hyrum Smith's prophecy concerning Kirtland, which is not contained in the Doctrine and Covenants.

All the Saints that dwell in that land are commanded to come away, for this is "Thus saith the Lord"; therefore pay out no moneys nor properties for houses nor lands in that country, for if you do you will lose them, for the time shall come that you shall not possess them in peace, but shall be scourged with a sore scourge; yet your children may possess them, but not until many years shall pass away; and as to the organization of that branch of the church, it is not according to the Spirit and will of God; and as to the designs of leading members of that branch relative to the printing press and the ordaining of Elders, and sending out Elders to beg for the poor, are not according to the will of God, and in these things they shall not prosper, for they have neglected the House of the Lord, the baptismal font, in this place in Nauvoo wherein their dead may be redeemed and the key of knowledge that unfolds the dispensation of the fullness of times may be turned and the mysteries of God be unfolded upon their salvation and the salvation of the world and the redemption of their dead depends, for thus saith the Lord, there shall not be a general assembly for a general conference assembled together until the House of the Lord and the baptismal font shall be finished, and if we are not diligent the church shall be rejected, and their dead also, saith the Lord.

Therefore, dear Brethren, any proceedings of the Saints otherwise than to put forth their hands with their might to do this work, is not according to the will of God, and shall not prosper; therefore, tarry not in any place whatever, but come forth unto this place from all the world until it is filled up, and polished, and sanctified according to my word, saith the Lord. Come ye forth from the ends of the earth that I may hide you from mine indignation that shall scourge the wicked, and then I will send forth and build up Kirtland, and it shall be polished and refined according to my word: therefore, your doings and organizations and designs in printing, or any of your councils are not of me, saith the Lord, even so, Amen. Signed Hyrum Smith, Patriarch for the whole church.[3]

---

[2]In Doctrine and Covenants, 124:83, the Lord warned William Law not to return to Kirtland for he had a scourge prepared for the inhabitants thereof.

[3]*Sangamo Journal,* vol. 10, no. 13, whole no. 533—p. 2, Springfield, S. Francis, (Ill. Nov. 19, 1841). Also *Church History,* vol. IV, pp. 443-444.

The Lord made it plain that a scourge was to fall upon Kirtland and its inhabitants but said also that after many years should pass away, their children would possess the blessings promised. Today, the latter part of this prophecy is beginning to be fulfilled, for the membership of the church is increasing in the vicinity of Kirtland and Northern Ohio.[4]

The above revelation also expressed the feeling of urgency to complete the Nauvoo Temple. There was no room left for doubt in the minds of the Saints regarding the importance of this temple project.[5]

November 1841 was cold, but Hyrum Smith's family was comfortably housed not far from the main street of Nauvoo and only a short distance from the Prophet's home, which was later to be referred to as the "Homestead."[6] As winter approached that year Hyrum found that giving patriarchal blessings and attending council meetings were only part of his duties. As a city councilman he was aware of the undesirable element being swept into Nauvoo by the rising tide of immigrants and that the atmosphere of the city was charged with the spirit of speculation, heightened expectancy, and novelty that accompanies the growth of any boom town.

The thoroughfares of the bustling frontier city were crowded with strangers, notable because of their wearing apparel, their language, and their manners. And it was only natural that among these strangers should be some of unscrupulous character. Many of these were speculators from St. Louis, New

---

See Artel Ricks "Hyrum's Prophecy," *The Improvement Era*, vol. 59 (May, 1956), p. 305.

[5]The above meeting was held in Hyrum Smith's new office. The *Times and Seasons* — in an October, 1841, issue quoted by the *Sangamo Journal* of Springfield, Illinois — said: "The brethren are here notified that our well beloved brother Hyrum Smith, Patriarch of the whole church, has erected a comfortable office, opposite his dwelling house, where himself together with his scribe and recorder (James Sloan) will attend regularly every Monday, Wednesday and Friday during the entire day, or, upon any other day if urgent circumstances require it, to perform the duties of his high and holy calling. "A copy of the blessing can be received immediately after being pronounced so that the brethren who live at a distance can have it to take with them." *Sangamo Journal, op. cit.*, also *Times and Seasons*, Nauvoo, Ill., October number, 1841.

[6]The Prophet's new home "The Mansion House" located across the street was then under construction. John William Smith's father worked on it in July, 1841, and lived in an old blacksmith shop. *Biography of John Wm. Smith, 1826-1905.*

Orleans, and other points east and south, brought in either by vessels plying the Mississippi River or the overland routes. Some of these undesirables had gained negative impressions about the Mormons from false reports. Others felt that quick wealth could be had by outwitting a people who were simple, naive, and trusting. One of their methods was to blame the Saints for crimes committed and circulate rumors that their leaders endorsed their dishonesty.

To counteract these rumors Hyrum, with the consent of Joseph and the brethren, issued the following statement to the public condemning the idea that the brethren sanctioned crime:

Whereas it has been intimated to me by persons of credibility that there are persons in the surrounding country who profess to be members of The Church of Jesus Christ of Latter-day Saints who have been using their influence and endeavors to instil into the minds of good and worthy citizens in the State of Illinois and the adjoining states that the First Presidency and others in authority and high standing in said church, do sanction and approbate the members of said church, in stealing property from those persons who do not belong to said church, and thereby to induce persons to aid and abet them in the act of stealing and other evil practices; I therefore, hereby disavow any sanction or approbation by me, of the crime of theft, or any other evil practice in any person or persons whatever, whereby either the lives or property of our fellow men may be unlawfully taken or molested; neither are such things sanctioned or approbated by the First Presidency or any other person in authority or good standing in said church, but such acts are altogether in violation to the rules, order, and regulations of the church, contrary to the teachings given in said church and the laws of both man and God. I caution the unwary who belong to the aforesaid church, and all other persons against being duped or led into any act or scheme which may endanger their character, lives, or property, or bring reproach upon the church, and I certify that I hold my person and property ready to support the laws of the land in the detection of any person or persons who may commit any breach of the same. To which I subscribe my name and testify this 26th day of November, 1841.

Signed

Hyrum Smith

Sworn to and subscribed before me this 26th day of November, 1841, Ebenezer Robinson, J. P."[7]

---

[7]Joseph Smith, *op. cit.*, vol. IV, pp. 460-461.

Mary Fielding Smith, wife of Hyrum Smith

Patriarch John Smith, son of Hyrum and Jerusha Barden Smith.
(Courtesy of Ralph Smith.)

As the Christmas season neared, the Saints enjoyed the preparations for the usual festivities. The families of Hyrum and Joseph were closely knit. Much visiting and exchanging of gifts among them promoted love and good will. On Sunday evening, the day after Christmas, Hyrum attended a public meeting at Joseph's home, at which he, President Young, and the Prophet were the speakers. The congregation was very attentive to the subject of Faith and Spiritual Gifts as explained from 1 Corinthians 13, 14. The Prophet said that the gift of tongues was necessary in the Church . . . to enable servants of God to preach to unbelievers. He said that when devout men from every nation should assemble to hear the things of God, the elders were to preach to them in their own mother tongue, whether it was in German, French, Spanish, or Irish, or any other, and those who understood the language spoken in their own tongue were to interpret. This would be done by the gift of tongues.

Hyrum's family was happy to see Joseph's new store building across the street, a half block east from their place. Christmas had come and gone with some regrets over not having sufficient supplies for the celebration. But now, the wagons were arriving loaded with merchandise, and the citizenry would be able to obtain a belated supply. On Saturday (New Year's day), Hyrum's children saw their Uncle Joseph, with several others, go into the store to unpack the boxes of groceries and dry goods and arrange them on the newly built shelves.

It seemed to Hyrum that this was an opportunity for Joseph to strengthen his economic position by establishing a mercantile business. Why should Joseph not take advantage of the times for such a venture rather than have the outside speculators enrich themselves at the expense of the Saints? Hyrum himself was too involved in other affairs and lacked the necessary capital for such a venture. The store building had been in the course for construction for several months. Its red-brick walls had been extended vertically, high enough for a second story

where Hyrum and Joseph had planned sufficient space for a
council room and an office for Joseph, and perhaps a larger
room for school classes and for storage purposes.

The wisdom of such planning was later proved, for in the
upper rooms of the storehouse many important events transpired.
Hyrum spent many hours in Joseph's second story office, where
a place for the Egyptian mummies had been provided and the
work of translating the Book of Abraham from the papyrus
went forward. Here, too, the proofs of the new book of modern
scripture were checked prior to publication in the *Times and
Seasons*. School was held for a time in these rooms, and sacred
temple ordinances were revealed and performed.

The ground floor of the building served as the store, but
only for a limited time because Joseph was no merchant. Such
a mundane occupation was beyond the province of his calling.
His kindhearted liberality disqualified him as an astute businessman.

Nevertheless, despite evil rumors and mutterings drifting
in from Missouri, the Smith families at the beginning of 1842,
were enjoying a period of comparative peace and prosperity.
There was no room for pessimism, thought Hyrum, when there
were so many things on the credit side of the ledger which
were favorable to the Saints. One of the most favorable aspects
was the progress made on the temple and on the Nauvoo House:
large cargoes of lumber had been brought on barges from the
mills in Wisconsin; on February 1, two large stones for doorsills
for the Nauvoo House were landed; and the font in the temple
was sufficiently complete to be used for baptisms.

Then too, when tithing days were designated at regular
intervals, the Saints responded in a gratifying manner. Thus,
the debts of the Church were being met, thereby relieving the
tension of threatened lawsuits; and the success of the missionaries
abroad was phenomenal. Church immigrants pouring into
Nauvoo were of the sturdy middle class—thrifty, hardworking,
skilled in the crafts and building trades. It seemed to Hyrum
that conditions were ripe for success in the building of Zion.

The ideal place, the time, the natural resources, and the skilled manpower necessary to complete the task were all available.

These and other blessings gave Hyrum and his brethren cause for true rejoicing. The disappearing snow and melting of the ice on the river during March and April of 1842 signalled an increase of activity. Hyrum's large home was noted for its warmth and hospitality. The hitching posts in front, almost always in use, were an indication of the traffic that came to his door. Horses and carriages were there every day and often late into the evening. Newly arrived immigrants stared curiously and were duly impressed with the importance of the place. Serious-faced officials, farmers, workmen, families came and went.

And the sudden growth of Nauvoo did not go unnoticed. The spiraling population caused by immigration, principally from England, brought the Mormons more and more into the spotlight; and Hyrum found himself becoming an object of curiosity. As a leader of the people he was forced to share the limelight with his brother Joseph the Prophet.

Toward the end of March, Masonic Grandmaster Jonas visited Nauvoo; and, like the other prominent personages, who came out of curiosity to get a first hand glimpse of the Mormons, their leaders, and their city, he was entertained by the Prophet Joseph. After a visit of several days, this Masonic official returned to his home at Columbus, Adams County, Illinois, and reviewed his experiences in an article appearing in the *Advocate*, addressed to the Editor of the newspaper:

Mr. Editor—Having recently had occasion to visit the city of Nauvoo, I cannot permit the opportunity to pass without expressing the agreeable disappointment that awaited me there. I had supposed, from what I had previously heard, that I should witness an impoverished, ignorant, and bigotted population, completely priest-ridden and tyrannized over by Joseph Smith, the great Prophet of these people.

On the contrary to my surprise, I saw a people apparently happy, prosperous and intelligent. Every man appeared to be employed in some business or occupation. I saw no idleness, no intemperance, no noise, no riot—all appearing to be contented with no desire to trouble themselves with anything except their own affairs. With the religion of these people I have nothing to do; if they can be satisfied with the doctrines of their new revelation, they have the right to be so. The constitution of the country guarantees to them the right of worshipping God according to the dictates of their own conscience, and if that can be so easily satisfied, why should we who differ from them complain?

But I protest against the slanders and persecutions that are continually heaped upon these people. I could see no disposition on their part to be otherwise than a peaceable and law-abiding people, and all they ask of the country is to permit them to live under the protection of the laws, and to be made amenable for their violations. They may have among them bad and desperate characters, and what community has not? But I am satisfied the Mormon people, as a body, will never be the aggressors or violators of the law.

While at Nauvoo I had a fine opportunity of seeing the people in a body. There was a Masonic celebration and the Grand Master of the state was present for the purpose of installing the officers of the new lodge. An immense number of persons assembled on the occasion variously estimated from five to ten thousand persons, and never in my life did I witness a better dressed or a more orderly and well behaved assemblage. Not a drunken or disorderly person to be seen and the display of taste and beauty among the females could not well be surpassed anywhere.

During my stay for three days, I became well acquainted with their principal men, and more particularly with their Prophet, the celebrated "Old Joe Smith." I found them hospitable, polite, well informed, and liberal. With Joseph Smith, the hospitality of whose house I kindly received, I was well pleased; of course, on the subject of religion we widely differed, but he appeared to be quite as willing to permit me to enjoy my right of opinion as I think we all ought to be to let the Mormons enjoy theirs, but instead of the ignorant and tyrannical upstart, judge my surprise at finding him a sensible, intelligent, companionable, and gentlemanly man. He appears to be much respected by all the people about him, and has their entire confidence. He is a fine looking man about thirty-six years of age, and had an interesting family.

The incorporated limits of Nauvoo contains, it is said, about seven thousand persons; the buildings are generally small and much scattered. The temple and Nauvoo House now building, will probably, in beauty and design, extent and durability, excel any public building in the state and will both be enclosed before winter.

From all I saw and heard, I am led to believe that before many years the city of Nauvoo will be the largest and most beautiful city of the west provided the Mormons are unmolested in the peaceable enjoyment of their rights and privileges and why they should be troubled while acting as good citizens, I cannot imagine, and I hope and trust that the people of Illinois have no disposition to disturb unoffending people who have no disposition but to live peaceably under the laws of the country and to worship God under their own vine and fig tree.[8]

The above provides a partial appraisal of the Mormon community, but even in its favorable remarks it is apparent that the negative criticism of this people was wide spread. Even this author was surprised and "agreeably disappointed" to find many complimentary and praiseworthy qualities among them. The Masonic official looked on them with benign favor, having an understanding spirit which helped him to observe conditions in a true light. Jonas' interest in the church leaders is understandable because Joseph and Hyrum had a few weeks before become members of the Masonic fraternity,[9] for reasons not fully determined or understood.

During the two weeks prior to the general conference which was to convene Wednesday, April 6, 1842, Patriarch Hyrum Smith was unusually busy. A number of problems were developing which needed immediate attention. Hyrum had been aware of severe poverty among some of the Saints and the inclement weather during the winter had emphasized a need for action. To help alleviate the suffering of the people, the "Female Relief Society" was organized March 24, 1842, with Emma Smith, the Prophet's wife, as President, assisted by two counselors. The purpose of this society was to relieve the poor, the destitute, the widow, and the orphan, and to serve all benevolent purposes.[10] The first auxiliary organization of the Church was organized to meet a specific need among the Saints and was destined to prove its worth for generations yet unborn.

There was also another situation developing which disturbed Hyrum. Rumors of immorality among the leaders of the Church, especially Joseph Smith, were being circulated,

---

[8]*Ibid.*, pp. 565, 566.
[9]Hyrum Smith received his first three degrees of Masonry in Ontario County, N. Y. Joseph and Hyrum were Master Masons. Taken from Orson F. Whitney, *Life of Heber C. Kimball*, (Salt Lake City, 1888), p. 11.
[10]Joseph Smith, *op. cit.*, vol. IV, p. 567.

When the day arrived for the conference, Hyrum, with others, was summoned to the home of Joseph Smith to receive instructions concerning current problems and the conference. The Prophet was ill and unable to attend. And here, before leaving Joseph's home for the conference, Hyrum and the others—Elders Brigham Young, Heber C. Kimball, and Willard Richards— testified that they had never heard Joseph Smith teach any principle but those of the strictest virtue, either in public or in private.[11]

When the conference convened, Hyrum was on the rostrum prepared to present to the Saints the thoughts uppermost in his mind. The topics discussed by the speakers at this conference reflected the conditions of the time. When Hyrum spoke, he gave expression to that which was closest to his heart—the blessings of the temple, and the value of obtaining the blessings of the endowment when the temple should be completed. He reminded the Saints that the missionaries who went from Kirtland, were called in at the dedication of that temple to receive their washings and anointings and that with the completion of the Nauvoo Temple, the missionaries could again receive their endowments and go forth into the world clothed with mighty power. He continued his sermon by refuting slanderous rumors about himself and the Prophet, Brigham Young, Willard Richards, and others of the twelve.[12]

The conference made Hyrum aware that dissatisfaction was creeping in among the leading brethren. The names of Sidney Rigdon and William Law were conspicuously deleted from the record of those called to take part in the conference. At the final meeting on Sunday, April 10, Joseph was present and preached: "Notwithstanding, this congregation profess to be Saints, yet I stand in the midst of all (kinds of) characters and classes of men."[13] The meaning of this observation was not at that time clearly understood; only time would make it clear. But temporarily at least the conference sessions seemed to clear

---

[11]*Ibid.*, pp. 582-583.
[12]*Idem.*
[13]*Idem.*

the air, bringing problems into the open where they could be dealt with.

Then, close on the heels of the conference came another vital issue pressing for attention. The brethren had worried much regarding old claims against themselves and the Church; but now claimants were clamoring for immediate payment, many without valid claims at all, and, as usual, the attacks were upon Joseph.

The Saints from Missouri had endured hardship and the loss of property. But they had already held a meeting and agreed to forgive each other their debts and to pay what they could for the erection of the temple. And so at this time Hyrum and the others endorsed the use of the bankruptcy law recently enacted by the Congress of the United States. The Prophet, like Hyrum, had been robbed of property time after time in various places; and they were unable, because of the bankruptcy law, to collect from those who owed them; so there remained no alternative for them but to use the law to extricate themselves.

On Monday, April 18, 1842, Joseph, Hyrum, and Samuel Smith went to Carthage, Illinois, where they declared their insolvency before the clerk of the county commissioner's court. Dr. Willard Richards went along as the Prophet's clerk.[14]

In due time both Hyrum and Joseph were granted legal release from the encumberance of debt both to themselves and to the Church. But this move was pounced upon by their enemies as an act of dishonesty, and they were accused of using the law as a means to enrich themselves at the expense of their creditors. It must be made plain that in taking this course neither Hyrum nor Joseph repudiated their legitimate debts to those in Nauvoo and neighboring counties.

During the long spring and summer evenings, Hyrum and Joseph would often visit the temple site together. Contemplating its erection and purpose gave them an upsurge of faith and hope. The clouds of calumny and distrust were dispelled as they

---
[14]Ibid., pp. 594-600.

gazed on its walls slowly rising. The baptismal font in the basement was now completed and in use.

The temple scene held for Hyrum and Joseph a special significance, for here had developed new religious doctrine, a doctrine which gave all mankind an opportunity to obtain eternal salvation.

The font made possible baptismal work for the dead, an ordinance which had only recently been explained in sermons and writings. The temple represented the work of the priesthood, the keys of the work having been given by the hand of Elijah the prophet, turning the hearts of the fathers to the children, and of the children to the fathers. (Malachi 4:5-6.) The basis for this unique doctrine was that the new church was the sole custodian of the priesthood which held the sealing power to preside in behalf of the dead as well as for the living. Therefore, the living descendants of those who had died before the restoration of the gospel could now be baptized (by proxy) for their dead. This was the same ordinance, now restored, which was spoken of by Apostle Paul when he said: "Else what shall they do, they that are baptized for the dead, if the dead rise not at all. . . ." (I Corinthians 15:29.) Following his crucifixion Christ preached to the spirits in prison (I Peter 3:18-19), for he had said to the thief on the cross: "Today shalt thou be with me in paradise." Thus during the time between death and resurrection the spirits of men were to have a chance to hear the gospel. The same principles which saved the living could also save the dead.

When the realization of this glorious principle burst upon the Saints, there was renewed vigor to complete the building of the Lord's house. With such a principle the great family of the Father could be linked together. The past could be joined to the present and the present to the future, for all generations to come. This principle revealed God the Father as a loving Father, the same yesterday, today, and forever.

Every man-hour of work on the temple, every stone, every piece of timber, and every nail used in its construction added to the permanency and strength of the young Church which was surely the kingdom of God on the earth.

Hyrum felt that the work of building the temple was a race against the enemy. Would the Saints win? Perhaps, by a very close margin. The Patriarch kept careful watch. He was well aware of the cynicism in the Lee County *Democrat* from Fort Madison, which said: "The population of Nauvoo has increased to 8000; walls of the temple going up—many wealthy neophytes are coming into the church . . . doubtless making it a 'profitable business.' "[15] The increasing population of Nauvoo and the steady progress of the temple incited the jealousy of the apostates and many of the gentiles. To the Saints it was evidence of God's work in their behalf.

There was no mistaking the fact that evil forces were using every device to impede the work of the Church and eventually overthrow it. Hyrum realized this and was not surprised to hear increasing rumors of immorality among the leaders of the Church.

The ancient order of patriarchal marriage had been revealed and a command given from the Most High to practice it; but how was the commandment to be obeyed when the cultural background of the people and their established mores made them antagonistic toward it. To obey the commandment provided a choice opportunity for disgruntled members and the enemies of the Church to consider the holy principle a product of Satan, and the leaders of the Church Satan's tools. But at that time this lack of understanding among a few members could not be cleared up openly, even though Joseph and Hyrum and a few others understood the new principle and its implications. There was no immorality and no sensual living. There was nothing in the principle contrary to the ancient law of chastity. Joseph and Hyrum set their wills like flint to counteract the evil rumors.

---

[15]Quincy *Whig*, vol. IV, no. 39, p. 2, Jan. 22, 1842.

CHAPTER XXV

THE ENEMY FROM WITHIN

With the beginning of May, 1842, certain events began to unfold which revealed plottings from within against the Prophet Joseph's life.

On Wednesday, May 4, Hyrum went to the Prophet's general business office in the upper part of the store. This private office was where the sacred writings were kept, translations made, and revelations received. Soon after he arrived, General James Adams from Springfield, Bishop Newel K. Whitney, George Miller, President Brigham Young, Elders Heber C. Kimball, and Willard Richards also arrived; and during the several hours that followed, the group listened to the Prophet explain and instruct them in the intricacies of the Holy Endowment,[1] including its sacred ritual. Joseph's words concerning this occasion are descriptive: "In this council was instituted the ancient order of things for the first time in these last days."

At the end of that day Joseph and Hyrum administered the endowment and communicated the keys from those pertaining to the Aaronic Priesthood up to the highest order of the Melchizedek Priesthood.

The following day the same council, with the exception of General Adams, met in a continuation of the previous meeting. Here again was re-enacted, in behalf of Joseph and Hyrum, the same rites that they had communicated to the council the day before. Hyrum Smith acted jointly with the Prophet, having the necessary keys to effect the ancient rites for and in behalf of the council present. These ceremonies were an integral part of the great "restoration of all things" in this last dispensation,

---

[1]The endowment pertains to man's journey from his premortal state of existence through mortality, and into eternity. Certain covenants, tokens, and signs are made known by which he may, when the time comes, pass by the angel to his place in the celestial kingdom.

the Dispensation of the Fulness of Times, and were to become the foundation of the sacred ritual of the temples.

With this new doctrine came added responsibilities for the leaders. The Saints, facing the challenge of the new doctrine, had to be oriented by the brethren, who had first to study and comprehend the full meaning and application of many newly revealed principles before they could teach them to the Saints.

To Hyrum it had been evident for some time that many of the Saints were ignoring the word of wisdom (Doctrine and Covenants 89), the health code given under inspiration in 1833. This principle had proved to be a test of faith to the new members. English converts were prone to have their tea; the southerners, their liquor; the New Englanders their tobacco; and some were reluctant to abstain from any of the forbidden stimulants. Sufficient time had to be allowed for recent members to understand the evil effects of age-old habit, and thus it had been necessary from time to time, for the leaders to define this new way of life.

Now, however, the growing disregard of this fundamental principle moved Hyrum Smith, on Sunday, May 1842, to discourse on the subject. In his characteristic way, speaking under the inspiration of the Lord, he explained what the Lord meant by "hot drinks" stating specifically that these included coffee and tea. These things, he stated firmly, were forbidden by the Lord. Hyrum's interpretation of that day was subsequently adopted by the Church and has been adhered to ever since.

About two weeks later the mayor of Nauvoo, John C. Bennett, resigned his position. He had been charged with other apostates with plotting against the Prophet and resigned in order to defend himself before the city council, which had summoned him and Hiram Kimball, Robert D. Foster and Chauncey Higbee. The ex-mayor declared before the council that he had nothing against Joseph Smith and that in time he hoped to be restored to full fellowship in the church. The conduct of various civic leaders had worried Hyrum for some time, and finally culminated in charges being brought against them after the Nauvoo

Legion under the command of John C. Bennett staged a sham battle[2] following a parade of about two thousand of the Legionnaires on May 7.

Hyrum, who was ever on guard lest some danger threaten Joseph, became alarmed as he saw the Prophet, without a bodyguard, stationed at a point of vantage to witness the army maneuvers. The incident passed, however, as Joseph's bodyguard under Captain A. P. Rockwood countermanded the order of Mayor Bennett and took up a position close by the Prophet. Could this have been a plot to assassinate the Prophet? Joseph's feelings about this occasion made him suspicious of the true motives of John C. Bennett and led to the Mayor's resignation to face charges brought against him. The Prophet himself succeeded Bennett as mayor and Hyrum became vice-mayor.

During the weeks that followed the sham battle, a series of events revealed the perfidy of this former officer of the quartermaster corps of Illinois. Hyrum's testimony at Bennett's trial before the judicial body of the Church led to Bennett's excommunication from the Church. Bennett's persistence in immoral practices forced him to leave Nauvoo under pressure of public censure; whereupon he joined the enemies of the Saints to seek vengeance. Afterward, rumors were circulated that he would lead an uprising from Galena, Illinois, to come against Nauvoo. Bennett's final blow against the Church, however, was his book, *The History of the Latter-day Saints,* in which he chronicled all his grievances. His feelings were summed up in the statement:

---

[2]Among the visitors were Governor Thomas Carlin and the editorial staff of the Sangamo *Journal* of St. Louis, Missouri, who were invited to attend by the Nauvoo Legion. A description appearing in the Lee County *Democrat,* Vol. 1, No. 43, p. 2, follows: "Nauvoo Legion parade in Nauvoo, about 1500 troops—3000 ladies and gentlemen from surrounding country attended. In afternoon a sham battle ensued . . . in which a dreadful slaughter would have ensued if the cowardly legs of the infantry had not carried their valiant bodies with great celerity out of the contest. Altogether it was a rare scene of the young and aspirant after military glory. . . .

 "To hero bounce for battle strife
 Or hard of martial Ley
 'Twere worth ten years of peaceful life
 One glance at their array!"

My reason for joining the church was to effect the salvation of my country. . . . I learned that the Mormons intended to revolutionize and involve in a Civil war, the whole of the western country, and to prevent such a catastrophe, I joined them and became acquainted with their secrets for the sake of exposing them.[3]

The Bennett incident gave rise to calumny and hate against the Mormons. The various media of communication took up the chant of annihilation for the followers of Hyrum and Joseph Smith. Journals and newspapers of the region were sensitive to the evil reverberations coming out of Nauvoo. From June until December of 1842, the presses seem to work overtime perverting the truth. Articles such as the following did not go unnoticed by Hyrum Smith.

General John C. Bennett is on his way to Missouri to expose Joseph Smith.[4] Rumor—Joe Smith had a revelation that he would be bodily absent from Nauvoo for 10 years.[5] A battle between Mormon and non-Mormon Anti-Mormons driven back—can do nothing against 900 well armed soldiers—20-30 killed, many wounded—Governor with 300 left for War-saw. Nothing but the destruction of Nauvoo will restore peace to this part of the state. Mormons leaving for Europe in crowds—looking for suspension of hostilities in Nauvoo.[6] It is supposed that Joseph Smith has gone to Olny, LaHarpe, Hancock Co., gives reasons why he is withdrawing from the Church. . . . They cannot stay the tide which is setting against the Mormon imposture. Public opinion has decreed its own downfall.[7]

However, the press hysteria against the Church was not accepted at face value by all citizens, partially because of the apparent lack of unity among the editors of the various publications. But during July, Hyrum himself became greatly upset over a news item pressing for the indictment of Joseph, accusing him of being implicated in the assassination of ex-governor Boggs of Missouri. Hyrum urged Joseph to take measures to avoid possible arrest by police officers from either Illinois or Missouri.

---

[3]Quincy *Herald*, *op. cit.*, vol. 1, no. 49, August 25, 1842.
[4]Alton *Telegraph*, July 30, 1842.
[5]Quincy *Whig*, August 20, 1842.
[6]Quincy *Herald*, August 25, 1842.
[7]Lee County *Democrat*, September 24, 1842.

The danger was very great because Governor Carlin of Illinois had made threatening remarks against the Prophet. Orrin Porter Rockwell was cited by the paper as the actual assassin, being Joseph's henchman who had committed the deed. He was warned to avoid arrest but later fell into the hands of Missouri officers. After his release from prison he made his way to Nauvoo, where his account of the suffering and abuse he had suffered at the hands of his Missouri captors brought Joseph to the point of tears.

At this time, with the Bennett episode over and Porter Rockwell released from prison, the turmoil subsided somewhat. Nauvoo was in the capable hands of Joseph and Hyrum. The brethren all felt that John C. Bennett had been sincere at first but that later, because of his immorality, had lost his faith. His so-called "Expose of Mormonism" in his book was certainly insincere.[8]

The foul charges made by Bennett against the church leaders should not detract from the importance of the commandment of the Lord concerning the law of plural marriage. (Doctrine and Covenants 132). Documentary evidence confirms the reality of the above revelation being given as early as 1831. The very nature of the commandment made it necessary that the Prophet Joseph communicate its contents only to certain people under certain conditions. Perhaps the very secrecy surrounding the revelation on plural marriage lent credence to the charges of immorality.

On Friday, August 5, Hyrum, with the Prophet and others, crossed the river to Montrose to witness the installation of the officers of the Rising Sun Lodge (a unit of Ancient York Masons) in a meeting conducted by General James Adams, Deputy Grand Master of Illinois. To the brothers the future looked especially gloomy because of the ever-rising tide of slander, threats, and infidelity. Hyrum and the others, while waiting for the installation services to begin, listened to Joseph and con-

---

[8]Joseph Smith, op. cit., vol. V, pp. 77-81.

versed about the persecutions in Missouri and the constant annoyances which had followed them to Illinois.

To their astonishment they heard the Prophet prophesy that the Saints would continue to suffer much affliction and would be driven to the Rocky Mountains where many would apostatize, be put to death, or lose their lives as a result of exposure and disease. He also said that some would assist in making settlements and building cities and some would see the Saints become a mighty people in the midst of the Rocky Mountains.[9] Anson Call standing nearby watched the Prophet take a drink from a barrel of ice water sitting in the shade of a block house. After the Prophet drank the water he stood holding the tumbler in his hand and said: "I prophesy that the Saints will go to the Rocky Mountains, and this water tastes much like that of the crystal streams that are running from the snow-capped mountains."

Later, Brother Call, describing this scene wrote: "I had before seen him in vision, and now saw while he was talking, his countenance changed to white, not the deadly white of a bloodless face, but a living brilliant white. He seemed absorbed in gazing at something at a great distance, and said: 'I am gazing upon the valleys of the mountains.'" Then he turned to Anson Call, promising him that he would live to go west to help build cities from one end of the country to the other.[10]

* * *

On the afternoon of Monday, May 8th, Hyrum Smith, as vice-mayor and president pro-tempore of the Nauvoo City Council, met with the council and passed an ordinance stating the mode of procedure in case of habeas corpus demanding that they appear before the municipal court. The ordinance stated that if such a writ, after an examination into its origin, were found to be illegal or was issued through private pique or with malicious intent it should be quashed and considered of

---

[9]*Ibid.*, pp. 84-85.
[10]*Ibid.*, pp. 86.

no force or effect, and the prisoner, or prisoners, should be released. This ordinance was signed by Hyrum Smith.[11]

This action resulted directly from the arrest that morning of the Prophet and Porter Rockwell by the Sheriff of Adams County, on a warrant issued by Governor Carlin. The warrant was founded on a requisition from Governor Reynolds of Missouri, the charge being that they had been accessories to the shooting of ex-governor Boggs of Missouri. When a writ of habeas corpus was issued for a trial before the municipal court, the officers could not concur until they had consulted with Governor Carlin. The Prophet and Rockwell left with the local marshall, pending further action.

Again it was necessary for the Mayor of Nauvoo to go underground, leaving Hyrum to fill the office and discharge its duties. By the end of the week, Hyrum, Joseph's wife, William Law, Newel K. Whitney, and others met the Prophet after dark in a skiff on the river to hold a council meeting. Joseph had gone to Zarahemla to visit with Uncle John Smith and had asked them to meet him so that they could determine what to do about the illegal warrants that had been issued for his arrest.

To avoid arrest the Prophet had to move from one secluded place to another, and the loyal brethren decoyed the sheriff away from his hiding places. On Saturday, May 13, Hyrum received a letter from Elder Hollister at Quincy, stating that Governor Carlin had admitted that his proceedings were illegal and that he would not pursue the matter any further. Reports came from over the river that several companies of men were searching for the Prophet at Montrose and Nashville in Keokuk County. His horse had been seen going down the river the day before. A reward of thirteen hundred dollars which had been offered for him and Rockwell had increased the determination to find them. Threats were even circulated by the sheriff that unless the Prophet could be found Nauvoo would be burned to ashes.

---

[11]*Ibid.*, pp. 87-88.

Under such circumstances it was extremely difficult for the church leaders to maintain the necessary daily contact with the Prophet. On the fifteenth, at nine o'clock, Hyrum Smith, and others of the brethren, walking in different directions to elude the vigilant officers, arrived at Joseph's hiding place to make a report of conditions and to receive advice and instruction. A variety of subjects were discussed. They were cautioned about being overly wrought-up over the plotting of the enemy. All of them felt encouraged after the meeting, for there was present a spirit of love and unity.

The council broke up at 2:00 a.m. and its members returned home. Hyrum had received special instructions to be carried out in the event that a militia came to search for Joseph.

The dark period of isolation from the familiar scenes of home and family brought periods of great depression and melancholy to the Prophet. But he received consolation and hope from loyal and righteous brethren. Erastus H. Derby offered Joseph the kindest of hospitality. Then there was Emma, whom Joseph never ceased to praise for her unwavering devotion and deep concern. And of Hyrum Joseph wrote:

> There was Brother Hyrum who next took me by the hand—a natural brother. Thought I to myself, Brother Hyrum, what a faithful heart you have got! Oh may the Eternal Jehovah crown eternal blessings upon your head as a reward for the care you have had for my soul!
>
> Oh, how many are the sorrows we have shared together, and again we find ourselves shackled with the unrelenting hand of oppression. Hyrum, thy name shall be written in the book of the law of the Lord, for these who come after thee to look upon that they may pattern after thy works.[12]

The designs of the enemy at this time were frustrated, and the tension eased. Within a few weeks the Prophet appeared again among the Saints at Nauvoo. Hyrum Smith called a special conference to be held in the grove near the temple on Monday, May 29, 1842, the purpose of which was to counteract the malicious charges made against the Saints by John C. Ben-

---

[12]*Ibid.*, pp. 107-108.

nett. More missionaries were asked for as well as vigor in the construction of the temple and the Nauvoo House. Toward the close of Hyrum's address, the congregation was elecrified by the sudden appearance of the Prophet on the stand. President Hyrum Smith was visibly moved by the Saints' show of affection and love for their beloved leader, and his powerful testimony set the scene for Joseph's speech. When Hyrum had closed his remarks, the Prophet arose with all eyes upon him and ears strained to receive a renewed assurance that all was well. He addressed the Saints in his familiar way and congratulated them on his victory over the Missourians. He promised that if they followed his counsel there would be no lives lost.

Joseph promised to fight with the broad sword of the spirit, and to send Hyrum to call conferences everywhere throughout the states to show the world the corrupt and oppressive conduct of Boggs, Carlin, and others, so that the public might have the truth laid before them. He was sending the twelve abroad to support the Prophet, the Lord's anointed, and if they upheld his character, they would prosper. He concluded by saying that he had the best of feelings toward his brethren, but to the apostates and enemies he would give a lashing and a curse.[13]

On this high note, the conference closed. Approximately 380 elders volunteered to go immediately on the proposed mission. Preparations were begun to send Hyrum Smith and William Law to the eastern states on church business. Many meetings were held and arrangements made so that the Prophet could go into hiding should the enemy again appear with illegal warrants of arrest.

The weeks that followed found Hyrum Smith and Wilson Law visiting among the branches of the eastern states, attempting to determine the evil effects of John C. Bennett upon the progress of the Church in that region. In Nauvoo, a careful watch was maintained to preserve the Prophet from capture by his enemies.

---

[13]*Ibid.*, pp. 138-139.

When Hyrum returned from the East, he was happy to see the interior of the temple gradually rising above the foundation. The workmen were laying a temporary floor and installing benches within the enclosure of the massive stone walls. Extensive work on the temple had momentarily come to a halt because of a charge of unequal distribution of iron and steel tools and lumber. It was time, too, to award the contract to the lowest bidder for construction of the first course of stone around the temple. Hyrum Smith was asked to represent the defendants in the case involving the workmen on the temple. Both sides were given a hearing and after several hours the trouble was settled. Hyrum advised those aggrieved to realize the difficulties involved and to show a spirit of understanding and charity. The Prophet gave the final verdict that the temple committee remain as it had been before.

Another problem needing attention at this time was the postal service at Nauvoo, which was so poor that the Prophet, as mayor, requested the resignation of the postmaster, Sidney Rigdon. Letters had not been delivered and important mail had been pilfered, and the Prophet accused the postmaster and his confederates of unlawful practices. The service improved after the appointment of a new postmaster.

Pressure of the enemy from Missouri against the Prophet during the fall and winter of 1842 kept Hyrum constantly on the alert. He took every precaution to prevent his brother Joseph from being taken to Missouri. Only the fact that Joseph and Porter Rockwell were granted by the Nauvoo municipal court a writ of habeas corpus, saved them from trial in Missouri.

This action by the municipal court of Nauvoo and other special privileges granted under the Nauvoo Charter prompted Governor Thomas Ford of Illinois in his inaugural address Thursday, December 8, 1842, to say among other things: "The municipal charter of Nauvoo is too liberal and should be modified so that the inhabitants of Nauvoo should have no greater privileges than others."[14] To have the charter of Nauvoo changed

---

[14]Ibid., p. 200.

would lead to its abolishment by the state lawmakers. Such a move would weaken the Mormon's bulwark against the enemy and their chances for self-preservation.

The news of the governor's speech alarmed Hyrum and his brethren. And since some other business also demanded attention, Hyrum decided that they should leave immediately for the state capital. Therefore, the day after the Governor's speech they left Nauvoo for Springfield, Illinois.

The journey was slow and laborious, the weather being very cold, and after thirty-four miles of travel, they stopped in Plymouth with Samuel Smith who kept a public house. The next day they continued their journey to Springfield. Having arrived at the capital, Hyrum presented his and Joseph's petition of bankruptcy and evidence to prove that Joseph was in Illinois when the attack was made on ex-governor Boggs of Missouri.[15]

Hyrum and his party remained in Springfield to hear the proceedings of the House of Representatives on the Nauvoo charter issue. A resolution had been introduced which urged the repeal of the charter. It had been urged that the state arms consisting of three six-pound cannon, a few score of muskets, swords, and pistols be taken from the Nauvoo Legion.

As a representative from Hancock County Hyrum's brother William assured the legislative group that they were laboring under undue apprehension about the Nauvoo Charter. He made it clear that the Charter of Nauvoo contained no special privileges not found in other charters in cities such as Quincy and Springfield.

The delegation waited upon the new governor to obtain an annulment of the writ issued by ex-governor Carlin. Upon receiving the request of the governor of Missouri for the Prophet's arrest on the charge of shooting Boggs, Governor Ford asked the state Supreme Court to make a decision. He felt that he should not change the verdict of his predecessor.

Hyrum Smith received his discharge in the case of bankruptcy on Thursday, December 16. The Prophet's case was

---

[15]*Ibid.*, pp. 200-204.

continued with a plea that he must write to the office at Washington.[16] Hyrum was easier now, for he felt freed of the illegal and fraudulent debt claims of his enemies.

With a change in the office of chief executive of the state, some hope was expressed that the Prophet might secure a release from the illegal charges that had been brought against him. When Hyrum and the others returned to Nauvoo, they brought letters from Governor Ford, Justin Butterfield, and James Adams, advising Joseph to go to Springfield at his earliest convenience to have a hearing before the state court. He was assured of protection against mob violence.

As he told Joseph about the details of the trip, Hyrum noted a spirit of optimism rise in the Prophet at the prospect of again being a free man. Plans were made for him to make an immediate trip to the state capital, accompanied by Hyrum and others of the brethren; and within a few days they commenced another long tedious journey to Springfield, Joseph having submitted to arrest in order to clear his name. The weather continued cold. The party stopped again in Plymouth at Samuel Smith's the first night and then continued on, arriving four days later at their destination. It was Friday, December 30, at two-thirty o'clock when they arrived at Judge Adams.[17] Joseph and Hyrum Smith were the center of attention. They had been measured for height by the brethren at Rushville, the second night after leaving Nauvoo. They were of equal stature — six feet — and were handsome, dignified, and inseparable.

The Nauvoo party, on arriving at Springfield, caught the gaze of the local inhabitants. Hyrum alighted from his mount to follow the Prophet up the front steps of Judge Adams' home, and was followed by Wilson Law, who had custody of the Prophet. Others followed — serious-faced, intelligent, able, men of vigor — including Dr. Willard Richards, John Taylor, William Marks, Levi Moffit, Peter Haws, Lorin Walker, and Orson Hyde. In a few minutes others stopped and went in. These

---

[16]*Ibid.*, pp. 202-205.
[17]*Ibid.*, p. 211.

included William Clayton, Henry C. Sherwood, Edward Hunter, Theodore Turley, Dr. Tate, and Shadrach Roundy.

Hyrum Smith listened to Justin Butterfield, Esquire, United States District Attorney, tell the Prophet that Judge Pope had continued the court two days because of this case and would close it tomorrow. He assured the Prophet that his case would be tried on its merits and not on any technicality. It was agreed that Joseph be arrested on the original writ which had previously been demanded by King and Pitman, the officers of Adams County. The Missouri persecutions were rehearsed by the Prophet. Later, the court interviewed William Smith, who was a member of the legislature. The evening was spent at Judge Adams', and all were made comfortable for the night in his large home.

The following day, Saturday, December 31, 1842, set the scene for civil action to release the Prophet from the cloud of suspicion which had blighted his life for months past. But good friends and a strong spirit of justice and humanity were needed.

At nine o'clock, Attorney General Butterfield called to inform Joseph that Sheriff King had the original writ. However, rather than have Joseph arrested on this original writ, the Attorney General agreed that a new petition be signed by Joseph for Governor Ford to issue a new writ on which Joseph should be tried. The writ was granted, and at eleven o'clock Joseph was arrested by Mr. Maxey in the presence of Mr. Butterfield, his attorney, who immediately wrote a petition to Judge Pope for a writ of habeas corpus which Joseph signed. At half-past eleven he stood before Judge Pope.

Mr. Butterfield read the petition and stated that the writ and warrant were different from the requisition of the governor of Missouri. He then read Governor Ford's warrant, Watson's affidavit, Governor Reynolds' requisition on the governor of Illinois, and the proclamation of Governor Carlin, showing that Governor Reynolds had made false statement, since nothing appeared in the affidavit to show that the Prophet was in Missouri. He also stated that all the authority of transportation of persons from one state to another rests on the Constitution and the law of Congress. He asked for habeas corpus because the papers were false, and because they could prove that Joseph Smith was in Illinois at the time of the crime, not in Missouri.

The writ was granted, returned, and served in one minute. The habeas corpus was read, and the court granted a move to allow Joseph bail until a hearing could be held. Generals James Adams and Wilson Law each put up bail of $2,000 for the Prophet, and the Monday following was set for the trial.

The news of the trial had spread and the courtroom was crowded. The spirit of mobocracy was manifest when Joseph, Hyrum, and the others left the courtroom preceded by William Law. As Law came to the head of the stairs, a man in the crowd below remarked, "There goes Smith the Prophet, and a good looking man he is."

"And," said another, "as damned a rascal as ever lived."

Hyrum, overhearing the remarks, replied, "And a good many ditto."

"Yes," said the man, "ditto, ditto, G— D— you, and every one that takes his part is as damned a rascal as he is."

Then at the foot of the stairs, General Law said, "I am the man, and I'll take his part."

Whereupon, the man answered, "Your are a damned rascal, too."

"You are a lying scoundrel," replied Law; and the man, cursing and swearing began to strip off his clothes and ran out into the street. Mr. Prentice, the marshal, interfered and with great exertions quelled the mob.[18] Following the trial, Joseph and Attorney Butterfield called on Governor Ford who was ill. They learned that the governor had received a requisition from the Governor of Missouri to continue the persecution, but Governor Ford seemed to realize that the old charges were dead.

During the afternoon, while the legislature was in session, a team ran away and went past the state house. A cry was

---

[18]*Ibid.*, pp. 210-213.

raised, "Joe Smith is running away," which produced great excitement and a sudden adjournment of the House of Representatives.

The following day, Sunday, January 1, 1843, the speaker of the House of Representatives offered the hall for preaching services. At 11:30 A.M., a respectable congregation assembled. Elders John Taylor and Orson Hyde delivered the sermons. Most of the members of the legislature and the various departments of state were in attendance. The congregation listened with good attention notwithstanding the great anxiety to "see the Prophet."

On Monday, court convened at 9:30 a.m., at which time it was decided to continue the Prophet's case until the following Wednesday. From the remarks of several individuals it was felt that a more favorable spirit toward Joseph Smith was manifest. Out of curiosity, several women acquaintances of Judge Pope accompanied him on the bench, which was the first time during his term.

The decision of the court on the following Wednesday was to dismiss the case on the ground that no state upon the requisition of its governor can call upon the governor of another state to deliver up a criminal if it cannot be proved that the so-called criminal is a fugitive from justice. In this case the Prophet had supporting evidence, through affidavits and testimony that on the day of the shooting of Boggs, May 7, 1842, he was reviewing the Nauvoo Legion in the presence of thousands of people.

The tension relaxed when the decision of the court became known and there was great rejoicing among Joseph's party. Both Hyrum and Joseph were overjoyed. In the late afternoon the Prophet, accompanied by General Law and Elder Orson Hyde, went to the home of Mr. Prentice where they had been invited for dinner. Others present were Judge Douglas; Esquires Butterfield, Lamborn, and Edwards; Judge Pope's son, and many others. It was like a feast of triumph for the Saints. A feeling of good will, the sparkling wit, and several anecdotes made the dinner a pleasurable occasion.[19]

Friday, January 6, with the affairs of the trial ended, the Prophet was released. Many gathered around him in the courtroom, conversing and asking questions on religion and a variety of other subjects. Mr. Butterfield, on handing Joseph his discharge papers, said, "You must deposit these in the archives of the temple when it is complete." Joseph received many invitations to visit distinguished gentlemen in Springfield and a ticket from the theatre manager to attend the theatre.

The return trip to Nauvoo commenced Saturday morning, January 7. On the way the horses on the large carriage became unmanageable and slipped off the icy road, over a six-to-eight-foot embankment cracking the fore axletree and top of the carriage. Luckily, Lorin Walker and Dr. Richards escaped injury. They repaired the axletree with wood from a small tree —joking meanwhile that Lilburn W. Boggs ought to have to pay the damages.

The return of Joseph and Hyrum was a signal for general rejoicing in Nauvoo. And where Joseph was, there also was Hyrum—at the trials, hiding to elude officers, initiating new rites and ceremonies, rejoicing over dangers past, planning to meet new dangers—whatever joy or sorrow life brought to one was shared by the other as they strove valiantly to fulfil their divine callings.

---

[19]*Ibid.*, pp. 221-223.

Chapter XXVI

THE FAMILY

Faithful Hyrum, whose home was located a short distance from Joseph's homestead and the store, continued to act as the Associate President of the Church. Mary Fielding Smith was a dutiful wife and mother to their six children. Martha Ann, the baby, born May 14, 1841, was a constant source of joy, and her health was carefully guarded. Joseph Fielding had been born in Far West, Missouri, during the height of persecution and mob action. Of Hyrum and Jerusha's children Lovina— now sixteen and budding into womanhood—was a reliable and dutiful daughter; John, just past ten, was a growing boy much like his father; Jerusha, six, was active and helpful, reminding Hyrum often of her dear dead mother; and Sarah, four and a half, was a little mother to the younger children.

The spring months of 1843, were happy with father at home. Their Uncle Joseph, going about his business without fear of arrest, came often to visit them. He bounced Martha, the baby, on his knees and exclaimed over her dimpled cheeks and plump little arms and legs. He drew young Joseph to him remarking what a fine lad he was and spoke to the others endearingly.

The children were known among the Saints of Nauvoo as they went about their errands—walked to church—or visited their friends. Everyone seemed gracious, often remarking what a fine family they were. The neighbors manifested their interest and affection which reflected their love for the Patriarch. Therefore, the older children soon realized the responsibility of belonging to an important household. This was borne in upon them when they witnessed the constant stream of visitors to their father's office, when they saw him in full officer's uniform before the Nauvoo Legion, and when he occupied the stand at church gatherings. They noticed the likeness between their father and their Uncle Joseph, and noted also that Hyrum's profile was somewhat thinner and sharper and that his full head of brown hair was somewhat darker than the Prophet's. Hyrum's gray eyes were kind, and his firm voice had a pleasing pitch that was warm and friendly.

Hyrum and the Prophet were natural leaders. At conferences Hyrum often presided or conducted and always occupied the pulpit to discourse on the gospel, or to give general counsel on current problems confronting the church. To avoid offense he was deliberate and careful in his remarks. If some of the brethren happened to make tactless remarks, he called them to one side, and, in a kindly tone, cautioned them.

The history of Hyrum Smith continued to be intertwined with that of the Prophet. When the Prophet occupied the center of the stage, Hyrum was usually in the background like a guardian fortress. There was a spirit of harmony between them, a meeting of minds. This inseparable bond gave both of them strength when it was greatly needed, so that the enemy sought in vain to undermine their morale and faith. Their united strength was felt like a sturdy pillar throughout the membership of the Church, lending support to the apostles, the priesthood, and to the membership in general.

The rapid growth of Nauvoo and the spread of Mormonism became an increasing source of alarm to the gentiles. If this vigorous new Church should continue to grow, the enemy reasoned, what would become of the country? On the surface all seemed calm, but underneath there were sinister rumblings which bode ill for the Church and its leaders. Evil forces, fearing righteousness and morality and blinded by hate were ready to strike.

The carefully documented history written by the Prophet provides the best source of information about the fast-moving events of the months that followed. And it provides a faithful glimpse into the life of Hyrum by reviewing some of the more important problems, movements, and decisions of the time, all of which he was concerned with.

At 5:00 p.m. on Friday, May 26, Hyrum Smith, with the Prophet, Brigham Young, Heber C. Kimball, Willard Richards, Judge James Adams, Bishop Newel K. Whitney and William Law met in the upper room above Joseph's store. The Prophet gave them their endowments, and some instructions in the priesthood, and on the new and everlasting covenant.[1]

The thirteenth year of the young Church witnessed the last of the major doctrinal concepts to be revealed. There was an urgency to place responsibility and keys of authority on the potential leaders of the future. The sacred rites, when once established, would lend the spiritual strength necessary to weather the storm of a new crisis during the years ahead. And when the ordinances of the Holy Priesthood were housed within the walls of the gray limestone structure on the brow of the hill, the combination would be a symbol of the Church's foundation. It would become like the rock upon which the Savior told Peter he would found his Church and against which the gates of hell should not prevail.

Hyrum and Joseph continued to weld into definite form a mighty Church, whose author was God. However, the winds of adversity were still strong against it. Weak members had to be made strong. Those who erred were counseled to improve their ways. If a member proved to be rebellious, unfaithful, and unrepentant, he must be severed from the society in order to protect it. Therefore, from time to time a pruning had to take place.

When it was necessary to hold a church court to try an erring member, Hyrum Smith was usually one of the judges and sometimes a member of the jury that was called upon to decide on the more important cases. Then as now much care had to be taken in resolving problems of apostasy, especially among the ranks of leaders. Each had his following who would be sympathetic, and because of personal devotion, would be influenced negatively against the church. Hyrum Smith sensed more keenly the gravity of the situation, therefore advocated

---

[1]Joseph Smith—*History of the Church,* vol. V, p. 409.

mercy and would be on the side of the offender allowing him the benefit of the doubt until his guilt was fully determined.

* * *

Early in the evening of Sunday, June 18, a message arrived at Nauvoo for Hyrum Smith, the contents of which aroused Hyrum to action. The Governor of Missouri (Reynolds) had been urged by the grand jury of Daviess County, Missouri, to serve a warrant for Joseph's arrest on the old Missouri charges. One Samuel C. Owens had written to Governor Ford about a week before concerning this warrant and his (Owen's) correspondence with John C. Bennett. He claimed that Bennett had made arrangements with Harmon T. Wilson of Carthage, Illinois, to obtain a writ from the Governor (Ford) in order for Wilson to serve it and bring this man, Joseph Smith, to that justice which "the magnitude of his crime merits."[2]

The previous Tuesday, June 13, Joseph, with Emma and the children, had left Nauvoo to visit Emma's sister, Mrs. Wasson, who lived near Dixon, Lee County, Illinois, some 210 miles distant. Fearing that the Prophet was in danger of being arrested and taken to Missouri, Hyrum immediately contacted William Clayton and Stephen Markham, urging them to leave at once to inform Joseph of his danger. They left Nauvoo at about half-past twelve at night and by continuous travel, except for brief pauses to rest and feed their mounts, met the Prophet between Wasson's and Dixon after 4:00 p.m. Wednesday, having ridden 212 miles in 66 hours. The Prophet told them not to be alarmed, saying, "I have no fear, I shall not leave here; I shall find friends, the Missourians cannot hurt me, I tell you in the name of Israel's God."[3]

A plot had been carefully laid by his enemies to arrest him and take him to Missouri. Fortunately the plans were frustrated by the quick action of Hyrum Smith and others who made a dramatic rescue from the custody of two sheriffs. Apparently the enemy failed to realize the loyalty of Joseph's friends

---

[2]Orson F. Whitney, op. cit., p. 422.
[3]Joseph Smith, op. cit., vol. V, pp. 438-439.

and the efficiency of members of the Nauvoo Legion in guarding all roads and waterways to prevent his abduction. Several points of law were violated by the sheriffs in their anxiety to accomplish their purpose: Personal damage, bruising Joseph's side by the muzzles of their pistols and attempting to deny the prisoner legal counsel, and by refusing to allow a writ of habeas corpus to try the prisoner in a local court. The sheriffs were arrested by the sheriff of Lee County, Mr. Campbell, and were taken to Nauvoo for trial.

The events leading to Joseph's liberation began at Nauvoo a week after the first alert of danger. Hyrum Smith who was administering the affairs of the Church and the community of Nauvoo was not aware of the extreme danger of his brother. As an official of the ancient accepted York Masons as Worshipped Master, laid the cornerstone of the new Masonic Temple located on Main Street. He had been advanced to its leadership and took a prominent part in its establishment in Nauvoo. There had been much work in planning for a fit celebration, which was held on Saturday, June 24, 1843. Hyrum was pleased with the procession as it marched in true Masonic order from the lodge room to the new site. Following the ceremony, two Masonic hymns were sung, after which they proceeded to the grove near the temple where an oration was delivered by Brother John Taylor. From thence they went to Mr. Warner's where about two hundred sat down to an excellent dinner. The company broke up early in the afternoon, highly delighted with the day's proceedings.

The following day, Sunday afternoon, June 25, while meeting was being held at the temple, Hyrum went to the stand while Elder Maginn was preaching and asked to make an announcement. He requested the brethren present to meet him at the Masonic Hall in thirty minutes. The lodge room could only accommodate about a fourth of the number who came, whereupon they assembled to an adjoining green and formed a hollow square where Hyrum told them of the circumstances of Joseph's arrest. Elder William Clayton had arrived about two o'clock with the message. He asked that a company go to Joseph's assistance, to see that he had his rights. The desired number were chosen from three hundred volunteers.

Hyrum remained in Nauvoo to see that everything was done to guarantee Joseph's safety. The dramatic rescue of the Prophet from his enemies was as follows:

On Thursday, June 29, General Wilson Law and William Law and about sixty men came up in several little squads. The meeting was described by Joseph in these words: "I walked out several rods to meet the company. William and Wilson Law jumped from their horses and unitedly hugged and kissed me, when many tears of joy were shed."

It was decided to by-pass Quincy and to go directly to Nauvoo. The lawyers told him that Nauvoo was the nearest place to obtain a writ of habeas corpus. A messenger was sent ahead to tell the citizens of Nauvoo of the approaching company. That evening they camped on Honey Creek at Mr. Michael Crane's where a feast of turkey and chicken was prepared for over a hundred men. The company feasted, sang, and had a happy time that night.

Early the next morning was the beginning of a day of triumph for Joseph, Hyrum, and the Saints. On this memorable day Joseph wrote the following:

Friday, 30. A messenger started from my company in the night, and arrived in Nauvoo early in the morning, saying that I and the company would be in the city about noon. Dr. Willard Richards and Wilford Woodruff arranged the seats in the court-room, preparatory to my arrival.

At half-past ten o'clock, the Nauvoo Brass Band and Martial Band started with Emma and my brother Hyrum to meet me; also a train of carriages, containing a number of the principal inhabitants. . . .

When the company from the city came up, I said I thought I would ride a little easier; got out of the buggy, and, after embracing Emma and my brother Hyrum, who wept tears of joy at my return, as did most of the great company who surrounded us, (it was a solemn, silent meeting) I mounted my favorite horse, "Old Charley," when the band struck up "Hail Columbia," and proceeded to march slowly towards the city, Emma riding by my side into town.

At Nauvoo, a petition of the municipal court was issued in lieu of Joseph H. Reynold's refusal to submit to a writ of habeas corpus. The Nauvoo Charter granted the right to act on the writ of habeas corpus, thus placing Joseph under the jurisdiction of the local court for trial. With this action he asked to be excused in order to address the Saints. Permission was granted; the court was adjourned until eight o'clock the next morning.

Hyrum's heart was full as he sat with a large gathering to hear the Prophet speak. He acquiesced to all the Prophet had to say about what had happened the past several days. And surely Joseph was right when he said forbearance ceases to be a virtue when tyranny exists and that the Saints were justified in taking up the sword to defend their rights, and that he would be willing to spill his blood rather than to yield to mob rule. The Saints, Joseph continued, must not, however, be the aggressors. He spoke of the Nauvoo Charter, its strength, and its legality. To go against the charter was to oppose the Constitution of the United States, for Illinois had obtained its charter from the parent government at Washington, D. C.

The threat against Joseph's life was also a threat against Hyrum and the brethren. The crisis had passed successfully but not without its implication of that which was to follow. Hyrum remained alert and ready for any emergency.

Joseph F. Smith
Son of Hyrum and Mary Fielding Smith and the sixth president of the Church.

Martha Ann Smith Harris, daughter of Hyrum and Mary Fielding Smith. Taken on her 60th birthday. (Courtesy of Richard Harris.)

Chapter XXVII

HYRUM THE PROPHET

It had been but a few months since Hyrum and Joseph had returned from Springfield, Illinois, with an acquittal of all the Missouri charges. Now if their enemies continued to secure new warrants on the old charges what might eventually be the outcome? Were law and justice to be ignored? Was anarchy to triumph?

Sheriff Joseph H. Reynolds of Missouri and Harmon T. Wilson of Carthage were enraged over the final acquittal of the Prophet by the Municipal Court of Nauvoo. They immediately proceeded to Carthage and laid the plans to petition Governor Thomas Ford of Illinois to raise a military force and move upon Nauvoo and take Joseph Smith into custody. To counteract this move, 900 citizens of Nauvoo signed a petition to be forwarded to the governor to abide by the court's decision. A copy of the proceedings of the local court were made and sent to Springfield in order for the governor to be apprised of the testimony and details of the trial.

When the case was reviewed by Governor Ford, he decided to abide by the court's decision. Later, Governor Ford, when asked by Sheriff Reynolds of Missouri to use a military force to capture Joseph Smith, replied:

. . . Now, sir, I might safely rest my refusal to order a detachment of militia to assist in retaking Smith upon the grounds that the laws of this state have been fully exercised in the matter. . . . The governor has no other authority in calling out the militia than which is contained in this section; by which it appears that there must be . . . an actual or threatened invasion or some extreme emergency to warrant the governor in exercising his power. No one of these contingencies has arisen.[1]

---

[1]Joseph Smith, *History of the Church,* vol. V., pp. 533-535.

Sunday evening, July 2, 1843, at 6 o'clock, Hyrum was seated in Joseph's office above the store when he glanced out the window and noticed a large gathering in the street. He answered a knock on the door and ushered in several brethren who announced their return on the *Maid of Iowa*. They had been on a scouting trip up the river to safeguard the Prophet from his enemies. The remainder of the group formed a hollow square in the street below, and Joseph called out the window for them not to break ranks until he came down and spoke to them. Of this occasion he wrote, "My brother Hyrum and I went into the hollow square and directed them not to allow their ranks to be broken. I then shook hands with each man, blessing them and welcoming them home."

Joseph enumerated the experiences which had restored his freedom; and while he was speaking, a stranger, heavily cloaked, broke through the south line of the ranks. Immediately the orderly sergeant took the stranger by the nape of the neck and thrust him outside the ranks, telling him not to come in again. No stranger must be permitted to get close to the Prophet.

About dusk, Joseph dismissed the company, blessing them in the name of the Lord; and before they departed, Hyrum also bestowed his blessings on them commending them for their diligence and their attention to the instructions he had given them before their departure.

It had been a busy Sabbath. Hyrum told Joseph about welcoming several Pottawattamie Indian chiefs in the basement of the Nauvoo House. They had refused to talk to Hyrum or communicate their feelings until they could see the great Prophet. They had waited to deliver their message. The meeting was held in the courtroom with about thirty of the brethren present. During the interview, the Indian spokesman arose and said among other things:

We have talked with the Great Spirit and the Great Spirit has talked with us. We have asked the Great Spirit to save us and let us live, and the Great Spirit has told us that he had raised up a great Prophet chief and friend who would do us great good and tell us what to do, and the Great Spirit has told us that you are the man (pointing to the Prophet Joseph).

The Spirit of God rested upon the Lamanites, especially the orator. Joseph was much affected and shed tears. He arose and said unto them:

I have heard your words. They are true. The Great Spirit has told you the truth. I am your friend and brother, and I wish to do you good. Your fathers were once a great people. They worshipped the Great Spirit. The Great Spirit did them good. He was their friend, but they left the Great Spirit and would not hear his words or keep them. The Great Spirit left them and they began to kill one another and they have been poor and afflicted until now.[2]

The Prophet told the chiefs to cease their warfare and killing and to live in peace. The Indians seemed well satisfied and returned to their homes after receiving a gift of beef and several horses.

The most pressing problem at the moment was the need to present to the public the truth concerning the Prophet's recent arrest. On Monday, July 3rd, a meeting was called at the Grove, where it was decided to send elders throughout the various counties of Illinois. Over a hundred special missionaries were called and dispatched. In the afternoon, the relief expedition of Charles C. Rich sent out by Hyrum before Joseph's return, came home, and met the Prophet, as had the others. After singing a song and shaking the Prophet's hand they received his blessing for a task well done.

The history of the Missouri persecutions from the testimony by Hyrum, previously given, was reviewed. An affidavit by the Prophet briefly recounted the events of his time spent in Missouri, showing that he had neither been a soldier nor borne arms in any military action which would make it possible for him to be guilty of treason against the state of Missouri.

---

[2]*Ibid.*, pp. 479-480, taken from Wilford Woodruff's *Journal*.

No action must be left undone that would help to counteract the evil reports about the Prophet and his people abroad.

The press reports kept the citizens of Illinois informed on developments at Nauvoo. From January to August 1843, notices concerning such things as the Prophet's arrest in the Boggs case, the legal counsel of Mr. Lamborn for the state and of Mr. Butterfield for Joseph Smith, the requisition by the Governor of Illinois, and the acquittal by Judge Pope were printed. *The Gazette and Advertizers* of Burlington, Iowa, noted the arrival of 1252 English and German immigrants at St. Louis, all of them bound for Nauvoo. From Springfield, a press notice condemned the verdict of acquittal of Joseph Smith and described the ladies who sat on the judge's bench ot the trial as having come to see a licentious prophet.

A notice in the Lee County *Democrat* said "Emigrants arriving. Steamer *Dension*—large number of Mormons—English —Nauvoo bids fair to become a large city."

Reports were made on the election of Joseph Smith to the mayorship of Nauvoo with Hyrum Smith as one of his counselors, and also, that the Prophet had heard that there was an indictment out for him and Hyrum on old Missouri charges.[8]

At the general conference at Nauvoo, the first of April, 1843, Hyrum Smith was sustained as Presiding Patriarch over the whole church. In this office, whose duty was to bless the membership of the Church, he succeeded his father, Joseph Smith, Sen., as his eldest son would in turn succeed him upon his death. The Lord, through a revelation, had named the office of Patriarch as that of "Evangelist."[4]

Among the many who came for their patriarchal blessings was Elias Harmer. In his office across the street from his home, and with James Sloan, the scribe, copying in legible handwriting, Hyrum blessed Brother Harmer telling him that he was of the lineage of Naphtali.[5]

---

[8]*Journal History,* March 17, 1843.
[4]*Ibid.,* April 6, 1843.
[5]Original copy written in black ink on paper 7½ by 12½ inches in size. Owned by descendants.

The ice in the Mississippi River was breaking up, the weather chilly and windy when the general conference convened on Thursday, April 6, 1843, to continue—two sessions a day—until Sunday, April 9.

Hyrum Smith occupied the stand throughout the conference and listened to the Prophet speak regarding the building of the Nauvoo House. Interest in working for its completion was greatly lagging, the emphasis being placed on the temple. Money donated by members of the Church to the traveling elders had not been accounted for, and it was therefore decided to discontinue this manner of obtaining money. From then on only the apostles were authorized to accept monetary offerings.

There were charges made by the enemy that the Church allowed its members to steal from gentiles. These were vehemently denied. Charges made against members of the temple committee revealed that some of the committee members either spent the funds unwisely or were guilty of poor bookkeeping.

When the conference convened at three o'clock, April 6, Patriarch Hyrum Smith spoke about thieves saying that he had some communication to make to the conference on stealing.

I have had an interview with a man who formerly belonged to the church. He revealed to me that there is a band of men and some who pretend to be strong in the faith of the doctrine of the Latter-day Saints, but they are hypocrites and some who do not belong to the church who are bound together by secret oaths, obligations, and penalties to keep the secret, and they hold that it is right to steal from any one who does not belong to the church, provided they consecrate one-third of it to the building of the temple. They are also making bogus money.

This man says he has become convinced of the error of his ways and has come away from them to escape their fury. I wish to warn you all not to be duped by such men, for they are Gadiantons of the last days. . . .

I will mention two names—David Holman and James Dunn. They were living in my house.[6] I went to them and asked them if they were stealing for a livelihood. Holman confessed that he had stolen from the world, not from the brethren. I told them to get out of my house. David asked me to forgive him, and he lifted his hands towards heaven and swore,

---

[6]Hyrum's household included as many as twelve to twenty in all. Out of pity the patriarch continually housed and fed certain elderly and unemployable persons.

if I would forgive him, he would never do so again. Soon after he went to Montrose where he was found stealing salt. He then stole a skiff and came across the river, stole a barrel of flour that had just been landed from a steamer, rowed down the river to Keokuk and sold the flour for $2.00, saying he had picked it up in the river, and it was likely to be a little damaged, got his pay, and went his way. Dunn would not promise to quit stealing but said he would go to St. Louis. I tell you today, the men that steal shall not long after be brought to the penitentiary. They will soon be brought to condign punishment. I demand in the presence of God, that you will exert your wit and your power to bring such characters to justice. If you do not, the curse of God will rest upon you. Such things would ruin any people. Should I catch a Latter-day Saint, he is the last man to whom I would show mercy.

With the growing boldness of the unscrupulous in Nauvoo, the troubles of the Saints increased. There were also complaints about the temple committee because of the lack of materials such as nails, glass, etc., and money to buy the necessary furnishings. When the temple committee met on Saturday for a hearing, Patriarch Hyrum Smith said:

I feel it my duty to defend the committee as far as I can, for I would as soon go to hell as be a committee-man. I will make a comparison for the temple committee. A little boy once told his father he had seen an elephant on a tree; the people did not believe it, but ran out to see what it was; they looked and it was only an owl.

On July 4, 1843, the patriotic Saints noted the anniversary of the founding of the United States with all due respect. However, the day dawned upon Nauvoo that year at a time when the very principles which established the country whose birth they celebrated were being grossly violated by the enemies of the Church. As the sun rose on this picturesque city of ten to fifteen thousand inhabitants, tension was present beneath the calm exterior. Its people did not know what move their enemies were to make next. At one o'clock that morning Messrs. Walker, Patrick, Southwick—lawyers of the Prophet—together with Stephen Markham and Lucien Woodworth, had left Nauvoo for Springfield, Illinois, with affidavits, a petition, and a record of the proceedings of the Nauvoo Municipal Court which had freed Joseph.

The day was well planned. Following the advice of Hyrum Smith, the committee of the day had selected Orson Hyde to address the morning gathering. Elder Hyde had been called to go to Russia on a mission. At 2:00 p.m. Elder Parley P. Pratt delivered a masterly discourse to the nearly 15,000 who had assembled. The Saints needed the reassurance of their rights as citizens which such an occasion provided. Just prior to the afternoon meeting a volley of artillery was heard coming up from the river. It came from a large group of visitors (800 to 1,000), in a holiday mood, who had just landed at the Nauvoo River wharf. Three steamers, one each from St. Louis, Quincy, and Burlington, had landed. Two companies of the Nauvoo Legion were escorting them. The Prophet met them and invited them to listen to an oration.

The impression of the Saints obtained by these visitors at the celebration was summed up by a Quincy citizen in these words:

> The large concourse of people assembled to celebrate the day which gave birth to American independence convinced me that the Mormons have been grossly slandered, and that they respect, cherish and love the free institutions of our country and appreciate the sacrifice and bloodshed of those patriots who established them. I never saw a more orderly, gentlemanly and hospitable people than the Mormons, nor a more interesting population as the stirring appearance of their city indicates. Nauvoo is destined to be, under the influential enterprise of such citizens as it now contains and her natural advantages, a populous, wealthy, and manufacturing city.

> The services of the day were opened by a chaste and appropriate prayer by an Elder whose name I do not know, which was followed by rich strains of vocal and instrumental music. Then followed the oration which was an elegant, eloquent, and pathetic one, as much so as I ever heard on a similar occasion.

> We started home about six o'clock, all evidently much pleased with Nauvoo and gratified by the kind reception of her citizens.
> > Signed,
> > A citizen of Quincy.[7]

---

[7]Joseph Smith, op. cit., vol. V, pp. 491-492.

In the early journals of the Saints is recorded an account of the institution of plural marriage. Joshua R. Clark recorded the following:

. . . When the Prophet received the revelation on plural marriage it was first read in father's home by Hyrum Smith to a few close friends back of closed doors. Father's younger brother, Samuel, was very sick upstairs but his spirit stood behind Hyrum and read the revelation over Hyrum's shoulder. My sister, Rachel, crept downstairs and sat on the steps and heard it read.[8]

Certain periodicals of the Ohio, Missouri, and Illinois period of the Church, alluded to the advocacy of plural marriage. The Warsaw *Signal,* April 5, 1844, wrote: "Spiritual wife doctrine taught in 1836, Kirtland, Ohio." This article was used against the Prophet in his campaign for President of the United States.

During the storm which followed the revelation on plural marriage, Hyrum was a bulwark of strength to the Prophet. He was invited to Joseph's office, rode with him through the city, and walked with him at night along the river bank, giving always of his understanding strength and supplying what advice he could. Both brothers knew that the cunning of Satan motivated those who could not or would not understand the full significance of the doctrine of celestial marriage. Pressures both from without and within the church were increasing.

The following Sabbath (July 16, 1843) Hyrum sat on the stand in the Grove and listened to Joseph preach concerning a man's foes being those of his own household; and about the everlasting covenant of marriage:

Joseph said in part:

The same spirit that crucified Jesus is in the breast of some who profess to be Saints in Nauvoo. I have secret enemies in the city intermingling with the Saints, etc., saying that I should not prophesy anymore, and proposing Hyrum to hold the office of Prophet to the Church as it was his birthright.

---

[8]Joshua R. Clark and Mary Louisa Woolley Clark, *Diaries and Records,* 1840-1928, BYU, Provo, Utah.

I am going to have a reformation and the Saints must regard Hyrum, for he has the authority that I might be a Priest of the Most High God; and slightly touched upon the subject of the everlasting covenant, showing that a man and his wife must enter into that covenant in the world, or he will have no claim on her in the next world. But on account of the unbelief of the people, I cannot reveal the fullness of these things at present.[9]

During the following week, repercussions of Joseph's speech were heard. Did Joseph resign from being Prophet? The following Sunday, July 23rd, he again addressed the Saints. He spoke on love and friendship; and about the great burden he was called upon to carry and the call made upon him by his Heavenly Father to lay the foundation of this great work and kingdom in this dispensation. He was subject he said, to the same passions as other men, like the prophets of olden time. He said:

Last Monday morning certain brethren came to me and said they could hardly consent to receive Hyrum as a prophet, and for me to resign. But I told them, "I only said it to try your faith, and it is strange, brethren, that you have been in the church so long and not yet understand the Melchizedek Priesthood."[10]

Between the conference meetings, Hyrum, William Law, and Willard Richards were called to come to Joseph's home and administer to him. The Prophet had become ill from too much outdoor speaking at the grove, but soon recovered.

The building of the temple had been progressing satisfactorily. Each day Hyrum took careful notes of its progress. He felt an almost inexplicable urgency to get the new structure fully completed. Somehow it symbolized a bulwark against the enemies of the Church, and he directed his energies toward the positive side of building the kingdom. He reflected on the gains made in Nauvoo since its founding, and noted the success of the missionaries in Philadelphia. The Sabbath meeting following con-

---

[9]Joseph Smith, op. cit., vol. V, p. 510.
[10]Ibid., pp. 517-518.

ference gave Hyrum a chance to address the Saints and retaining his optimistic mood, he spoke words of encouragement.

The Saints, including their Prophet had a high regard for Hyrum's integrity, as was evident on Sunday, August 6, 1843, when Joseph said: "Brother Hyrum tells me this morning that he has had a testimony to the effect it would be better for the people to vote for Hodge, and I never knew Hyrum to say he ever had a revelation and it failed." Following Joseph's discourse, Hyrum spoke at some length on the coming election.

Meanwhile the enemies of the Church continued with their work of trying to destroy the Church.

On Saturday, August 19, 1843, an anti-Mormon meeting of the citizens of Hancock County convened at the courthouse in Carthage. A committee was chosen and a date set (September 6, 1843 at 1:00 p.m.) for the next meeting. However, the late August showers that fell on Nauvoo seemed not only to revive the vegetation but also to soothe the tension. Elder Jonathan Dunham returned from an exploration trip to the West and reported to the brethren.[11] The Prophet learned of Sidney Rigdon's conspiracy to deliver him into the hands of his enemies, the Missourians, and had him publically disfellowshiped. In the evenings Hyrum, with others, met at Joseph's for prayer meeting.

Hyrum Smith would never replace his brother the Prophet as head of the Church even though their enemies were circulating the erroneous report of Joseph's fall from the grace of God. The Saints were assured, by the presence of their leaders in their midst and by their testimony of the divinity of the work, that all was well. At a meeting in the Grove, Sunday, July 9, Joseph had remarked that all was well between him and the heavens; that he had no enmity against anyone.[12]

---

[11] Elder Jonathan Dunham was appointed to visit the Pottawattamie Indians settled on the Missouri River 300 miles west of Nauvoo. The Prophet Joseph had on Aug. 6, 1843, predicted that the Saints would become a great and mighty nation in the Rocky Mountains. Elder Dunham's journey was about 600 miles attended by an Indian guide. He most probably was prospecting a possible trail and locating resting places for the Saints when engaged in a great westward movement. See B. H. Robert's comment. *History of the Church*, vol. V, pp. XXVII-XXVIII.

[12] Joseph Smith, *op. cit.*, vol. V, p. 498.

However, if Joseph were to die, Hyrum, by virtue of his position would take his place. The remark that Joseph had made about Hyrum becoming the Prophet was the object of comment. Willard Richards happened to meet Hyrum on the street one day and remarked: "I am writing to the brethren; has our new Prophet anything to say to them?" and Hyrum answered, "Give them my respects."[13]

The seership of Joseph the Prophet made it possible for him to sense the activity of evil forces closing in upon him and the Saints. He knew that the political climate was not right. Earlier, the people of western Illinois had welcomed the Mormons because they needed more people to develop their natural resources and strengthen their economy.[14] And too, with the natural sympathy of most people for an outcast, they had extended a helping hand to the Mormon exiles. But as time elapsed and the newcomers gained the balance of power politically, each of the major powers courted the majority potential to assure their election. The party that was defeated cursed the Mormons and vowed reprisal. The party that won the election was on the spot to support the Saints. When public sentiment began to turn against Nauvoo and the Mormons because of the failure to arrest the Prophet and of the way the municipal court of Nauvoo had exercised its powers in acquitting the Prophet, the incumbent party weakened in their loyalty to the Mormon cause.

Hyrum and Joseph, in counsel with the brethren, had to

---

[13]*Ibid.*, p. 513.

[14]When the Saints entered Illinois in 1838, the state was sparsely settled, and needed people to subdue her wilderness and cultivate her rich lands, especially people desirous of making homes and becoming permanent citizens. Recently, Illinois had launched into an extensive system of internal improvements by state aid. The system included 1,300 miles of railroad in the state, besides improvement of the navigation of the Kaskaskia, Illinois, Great and Little Wabash, and Rock rivers, also, the construction of a canal from Lake Michigan to the navigable waters of the Illinois River, a distance of more than one hundred miles (from Chicago to Peru). To carry out this system of internal improvements, the state legislature of 1836-37 had appropriated the sum of $12,000,000; and to raise the money state bonds were placed on the stock markets of the Eastern States and in England. It is evident that it would have been the height of folly for the people of the state to do other than give hearty welcome to the Mormons, so rich in labor power; so full of wealth-producing energy. Joseph Smith, *History of the Church*, vol. IV, pp. XX-XXL. B. H. Roberts.

act to forestall a crisis from this direction. The state's lawmakers were agitating for a repeal of the Nauvoo Charter. The politicians had assured the Saints every legal protection and advantage through the charter, but now when adverse winds were blowing, the true status of the Saints under the charter became evident. Of what value would the Nauvoo Legion be if, by order of the chief executive, they were ordered to disarm or if the courts and law enforcement agency were nullified.

In addition to the political aspect there were other causes of strife—social and economic—and false brethren within. The next few months would bring to the surface the evil forces which had worked so long for the overthrow of the whole Mormon movement. Hyrum's cherished dreams of completing the temple and achieving peace for himself and his people would not see fulfilment in his day.

CHAPTER XXVIII

HYRUM AND THE TEMPLE COMMITTEE

On September 20, 1843,[1] when Hyrum Smith with his brother Joseph visited the former's farm, located a mile east of the city, Hyrum was pleased to see his crops looking better. A heavy rain the week before, the first since June 1, had somewhat revived the scrubby vegetables, corn, and other crops, but the early potatoes were scarcely worth digging. The storm had broken the summer heat as well as the drouth and given notice that fuel must be secured for the coming winter.

Thinking of wood for winter comfort reminded Hyrum of the crackling of the wood fire in Joseph's private office above the store the week before. He had been summoned by Joseph to meet with several brethren to discuss some urgent matters of business. With most of the Quorum of Twelve away on missions, a special council had to be organized.

The uncertainty of the times and the many pressing problems required a council of men with sound, mature judgment, and Hyrum approved a list including himself and Uncle John Smith, Newel K. Whitney, George Miller, Willard Richards, John Taylor, Amasa Lyman, John M. Bernhisel and William Marks. Thursday, September 28, this council met in the room over Joseph's store at Nauvoo and chose the Prophet president; whereupon Joseph led them in prayer, asking that he might be prolonged until his mission on the earth was accomplished, that all their households might be blessed, and also the Church and the world, and that he might have dominion over his enemies.[2]

Such a council, thought Hyrum, was especially needed at this time, to lend strength to the leadership of the church. The spirit of dissension and criticism was gaining headway among some of the most trusted of the brethren. Former Counselors

---

[1]Joseph Smith, *op. cit.*, vol. VI, p. 35.
[2]*Ibid.*, p. 39.

Sidney Rigdon and William Law were conspicuously absent from the newly formed council, and their names had been deleted on official letters from the office of the President. This change in the membership of the First Presidency of the Church was evident on October 3, 1843, when only the names of Joseph and Hyrum under "Presidents of the Church of Jesus Christ of Latter-day Saints" appeared on the letter appointing George J. Adams to fill a mission to Russia.[3]

But the good fellowship of Hyrum and Joseph's friends was expressed when their special council meetings and parties were held. There was much to be thankful for. In their awareness of enemy threats and imminent danger ahead, they found it good to meet together often in the autumn months of 1843.

When Hyrum received an invitation for him and his wife to attend a party at the Mansion House on October 3, they made plans to attend. Hyrum realized the need for such social gatherings, and his family had on several occasions been the recipients of Joseph and Emma's graciousness and warm hospitality. When they arrived at the appointed hour, they were surprised to see over a hundred couples already crowded into the spacious parlor and living room of the first lady and gentleman of the city of Nauvoo and of the Church. Even with this extra large crowd, however, there was a warm outpouring of friendship and sociability. As usual, the evening began with a multiple-course dinner served personally by Joseph and Emma as host and hostess. Following the dinner the guests appointed a committee to draft some resolutions, which included a manifestation of thanks to Joseph and Emma for such a festive occasion.

The following resolutions drafted at that time reveal the loyalty and kindly spirit of Hyrum and the brethren toward the Prophet:

Resolved, General Joseph Smith, whether we view him as a Prophet at the head of the church, a General at the head of the Legion, a Mayor

[3]*Ibid.*, p. 41.

at the head of the city council, or as a landlord at the head of his table, if he has equals, he has no superiors.

Resolved, Nauvoo, the great emporium of the West, the center of all centers, a city of three years' growth, a population of 15,000 souls congegated from the four quarters of the globe, embracing the intelligence of all nations, with industry, frugality, economy, virtue, and brotherly love, unsurpassed by any age in the world, a suitable home for the Saints.

Resolved, Nauvoo Legion, a well disciplined and faithful band of invincibles, ready at all times to defend their country with this motto, *Vive la Republique.*

Resolved, Nauvoo Charter, like the laws of the Medes and Persians, an unalterable decree by a patriotic band of wise legislators for the protection of the innocent.

Resolved, Thomas Ford, Governor of Illinois, fearless and faithful in the discharge of all duties, long may he live and blessing attend his administration.[4]

This party proved to be a most enjoyable occasion, for it lifted the morale of both Hyrum and Joseph and assured them of the love and high esteem in which the Prophet was held by his friends. Hyrum himself, as Patriarch to the Church and Associate President, continued to hold a significant position in the councils of the Church. And he and his wife were especially favored at a prayer meeting at Joseph's home on Sunday evening, October 8, 1843. Of this occasion the Prophet wrote: "My brother Hyrum and his wife were blessed, ordained and anointed."[5]

The special conference of the Church which had been set for October 6, 7, and 8 was interrupted by stormy weather, and had to be postponed until Monday, October 9, at 10:00 a.m. Monday dawned fair, and the outdoor facilities in the Grove were filled to capacity by the faithful saints. The Prophet and Hyrum occupied most of the time. Among several problems taken up was that of Sidney Rigdon and his collusion with the Missourians at the time of Joseph's arrest at Dixon. Elder Almon W. Babbitt and President William Law made remarks in defense of Sidney Rigdon. On motion of William Marks,

---

[4]*Ibid.*, pp. 42-43.
[5]*Ibid.*, p. 46.

seconded by Patriarch Hyrum Smith, the conference voted that Elder Sidney Rigdon be permitted to retain his station as Counselor in the First Presidency. Whereupon, Joseph Smith arose and said: "I have thrown him off my shoulders, and you have again put him on me. You may carry him, but I will not."[6]

Hyrum arose and in his kindly characteristic way spoke on the attributes of the mercy of God, who influences, controls, and conquers, and the propriety and importance of the Saints exercising the same attributes toward their fellows, especially toward the aged and fellow servants in the cause of truth and righteousness.[7] No one, said Hyrum, should be unjustly accused of wrongdoing. And if someone were suspected of any offense there should be ample time allowed to establish fully his innocence or guilt. A person was innocent until proved guilty.

After conference, Hyrum inspected the partially built temple. He felt responsible to do all he could to complete this building, for there was a great need for the Saints to obtain their endowments and other important blessings, which could only be received in a house of the Lord. There was at the moment a lag in the construction of the edifice. The great concern of Hyrum for its completion was reminiscent of his experience years before at Kirtland. As he pondered on the problem he little realized that he was to receive an appointment to help speed its construction.

The appointment of Hyrum to the temple committee came unexpectedly, when Judge Elias Higbee, a member of the committee passed away, and Hyrum was selected to fill the vacancy. Of this occasion the Prophet wrote: "My brother Hyrum was appointed by the voice of the Spirit, one of the Temple Committee in place of Judge Elias Higbee, deceased."[8] Hyrum was also appointed Trustee in Trust of the building committee. The news of Hyrum's appointment met with many favorable comments. And when he went on the job October 23, as chairman

---

[6]*Ibid.*, pp. 39-49, *Journal History*, October 23, 1843.
[7]*Idem.*
[8]*Ibid.*, p. 53.

of the committee, he got a great hand from the workers. A universal feeling of good will resulted from his appointment.[9]

The supply of available materials and skilled labor increased, and the unity of the Saints became increasingly evident. The blessings of heaven seemed to be with them in a greater degree than ever before. Large cargoes of lumber from the pinery in Wisconsin began to arrive regularly at the wharf at Nauvoo. The Prophet noted the volume in terms of thousands of feet and the number of shingles on each barge which arrived.[10]

During the weeks that followed, Hyrum kept close to the project, encouraging the workmen. At the suggestion of Mercy Rachel Thompson, the penny-fund was instituted by the Women's Relief Society to buy glass and nails for the temple. Hyrum had approved this project and had encouraged the sisters both at home and in the foreign missions to contribute.[11]

While reports of enemy mass meetings against Nauvoo and rumors of the enemy's action against the Church continued to come in, Hyrum Smith was quick to note any news of a favorable nature about his people. Thus it was that his attention was called to an article appearing in *The Nauvoo Neighbor*, entitled "Nauvoo and Joseph Smith," and taken from the New Haven (Connecticut) *Herald*. The article said that a man from New Haven had recently visited Nauvoo, and that he spoke of the industrious, moral, and well-ordered town, where there was freedom of religion, a diversity of society, and two-thirds of the population were Mormon. He considered that Joseph Smith was an agreeable man in conversation and more sinned against than sinning. In Nauvoo, said the visitor, education was by no means neglected; proper schools and teachers were provided and temperance reigned throughout. At Nauvoo, a city of 15,000 to 18,000 inhabitants, four or five steamboats stopped each day. The man wished that he could speak so well of his native town as he could of Nauvoo.[12]

---

[9]William Clayton's *Journal*, quoted from *Journal History*.
[10]*Ibid.*, pp. 143, 298-299.
[11]*Idem.*
[12]Joseph Smith, *op. cit.*, vol. I, pp. 32-33.

And there were other events which Hyrum found favorable
to the Church. Among the more important of these were the
release of Orrin Porter Rockwell from prison in Missouri and
the safe arrival in England of Elder Reuben Hedlock, who
was to take charge of the British mission. The success of the
brethren on missions in the Eastern States and of the recent
conference at Boston, and the general response of the Saints
in that area was also most encouraging. There were missionaries
being sent to Russia, to the Islands of the Pacific, to Canada,
and into the local and neighboring states.

But all was not brightness. There were also problems for
Hyrum to solve at this time. The lowering temperatures were
a warning of approaching winter, and there were always those
who would need fuel, clothing, bedding, and adequate housing
to see them comfortably through the cold. The Relief Society
was functioning and could be relied upon to help meet this
need. But another problem was the constant stream of emigrants. The city was literally bursting at the seams; new sub-
divisions had to be plotted and lots made available for new
homes. Also, jobs had to be found to utilize new skills, talents,
and muscles. Many of the newcomers would need temporary
relief to get started in this new land.

The influence of Nauvoo was being felt throughout the
frontier region of Illinois, Missouri, and Iowa. Economically,
socially, and politically this "City Beautiful" was stealing the
spotlight from other centers of population. It was becoming
the hub of a great wheel where all roads converged, and such
a center of business and culture brought hordes of inquisitive
people, many of them questionable in character, fugitives from
justice, horsethieves, counterfeiters, swindlers, gamblers, and
ruffians who preyed upon the people. To safeguard the populace, Hyrum had voted, as a member of the city council, to
pass a law making it legal to question any vagrant or stranger
concerning his business and place of residence, and anyone
caught on the streets after a certain hour at night was under
suspicion.

Always present were the newsmen from the daily press of eastern cities, there to confirm or disprove the rumors concerning the Mormons and Nauvoo. Representatives of the leading churches and sects of the day came to satisfy their curiosity concerning the Prophet and stayed at his home, now transformed into a hotel with a dining hall and a lobby. Mayors, governors, army officers, writers, industrialists, and just plain people trekked to the city to look the situation over; and many were disappointed to see only industry, sobriety, intelligence, friendliness, brotherhood, and a prophet without affectation. Their preconception hadn't prepared them for this youngish man of thirty-eight and his brother Hyrum, forty-three. They were not tyrannical in appearance, with an austere swagger in their walk and actions. They hadn't any long gray beards and black broadcloth costumes to set them apart. The visitors scrutinized closely their deportment, manners, and speech, in an effort to discover the course of their influence, but the power was hidden; they couldn't discover it. Some left with fear of what the outcome would be if this people were left unmolested; others marveled and wrote about their wonderment; and some swore vengeance against an imaginary evil they expected to come upon the country.

Many were guests of Hyrum and Joseph on occasions when the Nauvoo Legion maneuvered and paraded to martial music. They saw the well-drilled squads of infantry and cavalry, with their new equipment—cannons, rifles, sabers, uniforms—and a serious glint in their eyes. The soldiers were young, intelligent, healthy—full of *esprit de corps*. The officers rode in full uniform upon fine-looking mounts saddled with the latest and best, with Lieutenant General Joseph Smith and his brother Hyrum at their head. Commissioned army officers with every military rank in their order, moved down the main thoroughfare of Nauvoo in a never-to-be-forgotten sight. Nauvoo was like a sovereign state within a state, having unusual powers of rank and authority.

But what was the real purpose of all this display and authority? To the Saints it meant security; to the non-Mormon it spelled danger. The Missourians were frankly alarmed. What would happen to them if this threat of power from Hancock County, Illinois, should gain momentum? And their alarm spread like a cloud to Illinois where the people began to ask themselves if the sovereign state of Illinois had granted the Mormons too much power. If so, something must be done. There were those who began to murmur that welcoming the Mormons to Illinois had been a mistake. The Mormons, they concluded, had become potential liabilities to the state.

How could Carthage, Quincy, Warsaw, Burlington, and even St. Louis grow when land values remained dormant, business was hindered, and financial capital flowed to this new metropolis? Having a thriving new city mushroom from a swamp in 1839 to a city over 15,000 population in four short years (and still increasing rapidly) was just too much to contemplate. Like a too sudden change in customs, styles, inventions, discoveries, the shock jolted the inert non-Mormon element, arousing its resentment.

The history of the months following this time reveal the forces of evil becoming increasingly ferocious. Every means was used by the enemy to stem the growth of this thriving Mormon metropolis and of the Church itself. Hyrum Smith was sensitive to the tension mounting against Nauvoo and understood its underlying causes. He felt it his duty to keep abreast of the times so that he would be ready to act should the need arise.

On Saturday, September 2, 1843, a notice appeared in the *Lee County Democrat* at Fort Madison, which was typical of the temper of some:

Notice of Expulsion. A meeting was held in Hancock County in which they [the citizens] declared the Mormons shall either peaceably leave the state or they will forcibly be driven away. It is said that the notices to that affect have been posted in public places in the county.[13]

---

[13]*Lee County Democrat*, vol. 3, no. 7. Whole no. 111, Fort Madison, I. T. R. Wilson and Albright-Editors, July 29, 1843.

Prior to this time the same paper referred in part to Hyrum Smith, brother of the Prophet, mentioned the arrest of Joseph Smith by Illinois authorities and his release by writ of habeas corpus before the municipal court of Nauvoo, as being well-known and said:

We do not presume to pass upon the merits of the issue of this case, nor to judge of the more ancient rupture between the Missourians and the Mormons. Perhaps both parties will find it difficult to clear their skirts of all blame, but which will in the end be able to say, "I can wash my hands of the blood—guiltless, we will not venture a judgment."

Jo Smith, the Mormon Prophet, is doubtless one of the most remarkable men of the present, or in fact, of any other age. He is now, as we are advised, but thirty-seven years old, and if our memory serves us well, it is not yet fifteen years since he first gave motion to the doctrine of Mormonism. He was uneducated, of an obscure parentage, poor and the very last man in the world who would have been called out to lead and direct one of the most anomalous revolutions in religion the world has ever experienced. He has now upward of two hundred thousand followers in this country and his missionaries in Europe seem to meet with success there, only paralleled in times when Luther and Melancthon stormed the "*papalsee*," and Protestantism, struggling against the clouds "of the dark ages," burst the darkling gloom of idolatrous popery and espoused of the affairs of human events.

Our astonishment, however, at events so strikingly strange, so apparently anomalous in the provinces of the great disposer of all events has been lessened by the reflection, that He (Christ) appeared at an age when darkness, idolatry and superstition cast upon the world the shadows of mental stupor and moral death. How different stands the case of Jo Smith, the Prophet, and apostle of Mormon. He appears in the middle of the eighteenth century. The full glory of brightness and revelation is in the very zenith of the Christian firmament, and in a country, too, most distinguished for enlightenment, and the least prejudiced of bigotry and fanaticism, ancient manners, and inherited forms of religion. Still his success is no less remarkable, although in an age so much less susceptible to the wicked designs of Priesthood and the designing schemes of ambitious men.

We make these remarks entertaining neither jot nor tittle of belief in Mormonism, or in our friend Joseph the Prophet, as a *divine teacher*. Nevertheless, we shall be disposed to show to the public a fair expose of the matters of controversy between our Mormon neighbors and their inveterate enemies across the Mississippi, the Missourians.[14]

---

[14]*Ibid.*, vol. 3, no. 2. Whole no. 106, p. 2.

The above reflects the thoughts of men striving to be fair and measuring Joseph Smith and his work in an objective manner. A comparison of the Mormon movement was made with the reformers of medieval times and a contrast of this enlightened age with the corrupt and evil conditions of the sixteenth century. Perhaps some progress had been made since those earlier times, but the will to malign, persecute, and kill was the same; only the methods were more modern. Due recognition was awarded the Prophet for his rise from a lowly station in life to that of leader of hundreds of thousands.

Press releases during September spoke of a pleasure trip to Nauvoo on board a new steam ferryboat:

> . . . At about ten o'clock in the morning she left our wharf crowded with men, women, and children, in all between two and three hundred, and after passing our town (Fort Madison) in a beautiful style, proceeded on her way downward to the city of "Latter-day Saints. . . . "
>
> After the landing of the boat at the wharf, many of the ladies and gentlemen paid a visit to the temple, while others paid a visit to the circus, others partook of the good things which are at all times found in the city of Nauvoo. . . .[15]

From the same publication there appeared the following:

> Tempest in a Teapot. Announcement of an anti-Mormon meeting in Carthage. A committee to warn the Mormons to move—two to three thousand qualified voters—rather a great number to be much alarmed by their Carthagenian brethren. Wouldn't it be amusing if the county seat should be removed from Carthage to Nauvoo? This we predict will be the result of this anti-Latter-day Saint movement.[16]

Continuing three weeks later:

> The leaders of the anti-Mormon movement make fools of themselves.
>
> Those who are believers in the Mormon faith have little to fear from the *lions* like these. We understand that the Prophet is ready for any attack that may be made upon him or his people. Let them beware.

---

[15]*Ibid.*, vol. 3, no. 8. Whole no. 112, p. 2 Saturday, September 9, 1843.
[16]*Ibid.*, Saturday, September 1, 1843.

An ordinance in *Nauvoo Neighbor* that marriages can be performed by any minister of the Gospel, mayor, alderman, justice or judge, without a license which is required by the state. Under age must get consent of guardian.

Those of our young people who are unable to procure a license had best to go to the city of the Latter-day Saints to have those solemn rites performed.[17]

On October 21, 1843, there appeared the following: "Another anti-Mormon meeting at Warsaw, a resolution was passed to ask the governor to withdraw the state arms from the hands of the Mormons and the citizens be allowed to form themselves into independent companies in case of emergency."[18]

The editor of the Burlington *Hawkeye*, wrote:

The Mormons: The prairie between Fort Madison, Warsaw, and Carthage has changed from dreary prairie to one studded with houses and good farms. Seven years ago along the old Rock Island Trace, a dreary waste, were fields, good sod fences, six miles long. As long as the Mormons are harmless they should be treated well. We shall never convince them that they are a deluded people, in as far as their religion is concerned in any other way.[19]

The expressions from the newspapers indicated an admiration for the Mormons, and also a great alarm because people thought these frugal, industrious people were deluded, and that all their religious principles were based on fraudulent concepts. They supposed it impossible that good could come out of such a corrupt source. They forgot to judge the tree by its fruits.

The Savior said,

Ye shall know them by their fruits. Do men gather grapes of thorns, or figs of thistles?

Even so, every good tree bringeth forth good fruit; but a corrupt tree bringeth forth evil fruit. . . .

Wherefore by their fruits ye shall know them.[20]

---

[17]*Ibid.*, vol. 3, no. 11. Whole no. 115, p. 2, Saturday, September 30, 1843.
[18]*Idem.*
[19]Burlington *Hawkeye*, vol. 5, no. 11, p. 2, Burlington, Iowa, October 19, 1843.
[20]Matthew 7:16, 17, 20.

If there were evils in the Church, then a pruning would be in order. The new Church, like a vigorous, healthy growing tree was not becoming corrupt. Hyrum and Joseph watched for blight, and infected branches, and cut out the objectionable parts in order to build the Church strong and true.

And the pruning process was very difficult for Hyrum because his kindly nature shrank from taking action against suspects, whether Saint or gentile. But he knew that Nauvoo could not present a united front against an enemy from without if the home front was weak and its position undermined by traitors from within.

As the year 1843 drew to a close, only the blessings of heaven made it possible for Hyrum to bear the tremendous burden which was his as combined Associate President of the Church, Presiding Patriarch to the Church and chairman of the Nauvoo Temple building committee. His responsibilities were great, but he carried them humbly and without shirking.

CHAPTER XXIX

A NEW POLITICAL PARTY

The latter part of October 1843 brought the first evidence of winter. Two-thirds of an inch of ice froze on small bodies of water. When Hyrum rode out to the prairie with Joseph and returned at 3:00 p.m., snow was on the ground. There was a cold east wind, and the storm continued all day.[1] On Sunday, two weeks before, the Apostles—Brigham Young, Heber C. Kimball, and George A. Smith—who had been laboring in the East, returned home. Hyrum and Joseph Smith were pleased with their report of increased activities among the Saints and of the spirit of gathering manifest by them. Collections of tithing and donations to the temple and the Nauvoo House fund were sufficient to permit their ordering from St. Louis the groceries and various other items necessary for the temple and its workmen.

At 10:00 a.m. Thursday, November 2, the council sat with Hyrum and Joseph to consider current business matters. Joseph L. Heywood had sent a letter concerning a Colonel Frierson who desired to help the Mormons by petitioning Congress in their behalf. Brother Heywood stated in the letter that he knew of some honorable men in Missouri who desired to wipe out the stain that rested upon Missouri by making a just reparation. He stated also that he, with others of the Saints, preferred John C. Calhoun as a candidate for President of the United States rather than Martin Van Buren. He hoped that Colonel Frierson could obtain the endorsement of the Mormons to memorialize Congress in their behalf. If the leaders approved, he (Brother Heywood) would come to Nauvoo to assist in writing the memorial.

The council decided to write a letter to each of the five candidates who were then campaigning for the Presidency of

[1]Journal History, op. cit., October 31, 1843.

the United States to inquire what his feelings were toward the Saints as a people and what his course of action would be, should he be elected, regarding the cruelty and oppression that the Saints had suffered in the state of Missouri.

To the letter sent to Martin Van Buren, a postscript was added asking whether his views had changed since the subject matter of the present communication was presented to him in his then official capacity at Washington in the year 1841, a subject treated by Van Buren with coldness, indifference, and neglect bordering on contempt.[2]

Letters were mailed to Lewis Cass, Richard M. Johnson, Henry Clay, as well as Calhoun and Van Buren. During the months ahead the Saints would have to make a choice of a candidate on either the Democratic or Whig ticket. Perhaps it would be necessary to withdraw, to avoid taking sides, and create a party of their own.

By the end of November, Colonel Frierson had arrived at Nauvoo and had met with Hyrum, Joseph, and the twelve. The Prophet had seen that a careful history of the Church was kept even though death and apostasy had claimed several of his scribes, and precious records had been stolen. Frierson studied the history of the Missouri troubles and the leaders read to him the affidavits concerning the expulsion of the Saints from Missouri, made by Hyrum Smith, Brigham Young, and others at the time of their testimony before the municipal court at Nauvoo.

Colonel Frierson wrote a memorial to Congress, setting forth a review of the trouble of the Saints in Missouri. In it he called upon Congress to take into consideration the wrongs perpetrated against this greatly maligned people and to grant them such relief as, by the Constitution and laws, they have power to grant.

The colonel took a copy of the memorial with him to Quincy to obtain signatures and endorsements, and a com-

---

[2]Joseph Smith, *op. cit.*, vol. VI, p. 65.

mittee was appointed to obtain signatures from citizens residing in Nauvoo.[3]

The leaders of the Church had come to feel that the Mormons were being maneuvered into a position where justice could never be obtained. President Van Buren had said, "Your cause is just, but I can do nothing for you," and Governor Ford of Illinois, being a politician was inclined to favor only those forces which would support his position. Memorializing Congress for help seemed futile, but they were willing to try anything. Perhaps an appeal for help to Hyrum and Joseph's native state would help to solve the problem.

They therefore drew up an appeal to the "Green Mountain Boys of Vermont," a lengthy treatise imploring the liberty-loving sons of Vermont to come to the aid of their fellow citizens. Examples from the Bible were cited: Abraham had rescued Lot in the days of Sodom and Gomorrah. And France and Holland had come to the aid of the thirteen American Colonies during the revolution. Copies of this appeal were made, and Parley P. Pratt was granted the right to distribute them in all the towns of Vermont.

Elder Parley P. Pratt addressed an appeal for aid against the enemy to his native State of New York. At a public meeting in the hall above the store the appeals[4] were read, and the Prophet addressed those present for two and a half hours, reviewing circumstances in Missouri. Already he had thirty-eight law suits and had paid Missouri $150,000 for land. The Prophet made a motion that every man at the meeting should write his native country, and the motion carried.

It was also determined that the Nauvoo Legion was to enforce justice. However, the state auditor would not honor the warrants on the state treasury to pay the legion. Under the charter the legion was to be part of the state militia and were liable to call, yet attorney-general Josiah Lambourn disallowed any money for the legion. The only consideration would be to

[3]*Ibid.*, pp. 83-88.
[4]These appeals were the memorial to Congress, the appeal to the Green Mountain Boys, and P. P. Pratt's appeal to the state of New York.

furnish them state arms. The state auditor, J. N. McDougall ruled that the Nauvoo Legion was an independent military establishment designed to sustain the municipal authorities of Nauvoo. The Prophet realized that prejudice against the Saints because of their religion was the main cause for the withholding of their portion by the state.

The seriousness of the situation was not minimized by Hyrum, for very soon something of a drastic nature would have to be resorted to to help stem the tide of opposition. Hyrum accompanied the Prophet on trips to the prairie and met with him often to plan strategy to cope with the enemy. Reports were beginning to come to their attention concerning the increased boldness of certain men harassing the Saints in Nauvoo. A report came from David Avery and his son Philander that they had been kidnapped by the Missourians and were being held in jail.[5] This act indicated a plot by the enemy to get more of the Saints into their hands. General Wilson Law received orders to have a part of the Nauvoo Legion on hand for immediate service in case of an emergency. Also a force of from forty to fifty men were made policemen to protect Nauvoo against the subversive element which might slip into the city for evil purposes. A petition to Congress was prepared asking the government to recognize the Nauvoo Legion as part of the United States militia.

By December 14, Philander Avery, (son of Daniel Avery) arrived in Nauvoo, having escaped from his kidnapers in Missouri. Also a letter had been received from Governor Ford informing President Smith that it was not lawful to call out a part of the legion to re-inforce the police in guarding against an invasion from Missouri or against any group from that quarter who attempted to take Joseph Smith into custody. The governor advised the citizens of Nauvoo to be peaceful towards the people of Missouri. He stated further that the many affidavits he had received concerning the trouble had not been read, and

---

[5]*The Illinois Statesman*, Jacksonville, Illinois, vol. 1, no. 35, p. 2. Mormon kidnapped— great excitement. Governor of Missouri called on to make arrest.

perhaps would not be read unless he felt the necessity to do so, that is unless new demands from Missouri were made for the arrest of the Prophet.

This communique from the chief magistrate once again revealed an utter lack of sympathy and sense of justice toward the Saints. The feelings of Joseph were expressed in these words:

> . . . Oh reason, where art thou fled! O humanity, where has thou hidden thyself? Patriots of '76 has your blood been spilt in vain, that in 1843 the executive of a great republican state can coolly say, "I have not yet read them (affidavits) and probably never will." Is liberty only a name? Is protection of person and property fled from free America? Let those answer who can.[6]

Constable King Follet arrested John Elliott, a schoolmaster for kidnapping Avery and brought his prisoner to Nauvoo for trial. At his trial the Prophet gave him a lecturing to and dismissed him. A warrant was issued at this time for the arrest of Colonel Levi Williams on the charge of kidnapping Daniel Avery. General Wilson Law was asked by Lieutenant General Joseph Smith to detach one hundred men from the Nauvoo Legion to help carry out the writ. A report was received that over one hundred men had assembled at the home of Colonel Williams at Warsaw to prevent any disorder. The report said that Colonel Williams had ordered the lower part of the county to mobilize a force, send runners to Missouri to excite the Missourians, and have them join the forces at Warsaw for the purpose of making an attack on Nauvoo. It was deemed advisable not to try to arrest Colonel Williams at this time, but to have General Law place the legion in readiness to repel any such invasion.

Affidavits concerning this warlike preparation of the mob, were duly sworn to and forwarded to the governor; even though he might never read them, he would be left without an excuse.

The city of Nauvoo drew up a lengthy memorial to Congress to which Hyrum Smith signed his name along with that of the Prophet Joseph, the counselors, the aldermen, the recorder, and

---

[6]Joseph Smith, *op. cit.*, vol. VI, pp. 113-115.

the marshal. Reports of robbery and of Saints' homes being burned indicated to the brethren the increasing boldness of the mob element.

* * *

In Hyrum's household, preparations were completed for the Christmas holidays. Saturday and Sunday, December 23 and 24, were days for the family to be at home.

Early Christmas morning (Monday), Hyrum and his household were awakened by serenaders singing Christmas carols. He arose from his bed and went out to shake hands with the group consisting of a blind English widow, Lettie Rushton, who had lost her sight ten years previously, three of her sons with their wives, her two daughters with their husbands, and several of her neighbors. Hyrum blessed each one of them in the name of the Lord and said that he had thought at first that a cohort of angels had come to visit them; it was heavenly music to him. The Prophet said of the song, "Mortals, Awake! with Angels Join," which awakened him at 1:00 a.m. "It caused a thrill of pleasure to run through my soul. All of my family and boarders arose to hear the serenade, and I felt to thank my Heavenly Father for their visit and blessed them in the name of the Lord."[7]

The Christmas festivities centered at the Mansion House. The spirit of love and kindness was, as always, a part of the Prophet's household; but somehow this holiday time had about it a special significance. Joseph's thirty-eighth birthday had been duly observed on Saturday, two days before. Perhaps for Joseph Christmas day was a continuation of his own birthday observance and enhanced by the Savior's birthday. The Prophet at 2:00 p.m. seated fifty couples at dinner. Later in the evening a large party again seated themselves for supper, which was followed by music and dancing.

Hyrum and Mary were present. They had brought their five-year-old son, Joseph Fielding, and seated him on the orchestra platform during the party.[8] This lad, who later became the

---

[7]*Ibid.*, p. 134.
[8]Preston Nibley, *Joseph Smith the Prophet,* (Salt Lake City, 1944), pp. 488-489.

President of the Church remembered the occasion. He remembered that a man with long hair falling over his shoulders and apparently drunk came in and acted like a Missourian. Joseph, describing the affair later, wrote:

> I requested the captain of the police to put him out of doors. A scuffle ensued and I had a chance to look him full in the face, when to my surprise and joy, untold, I discovered that it was my long-tried, warm, but cruelly persecuted friend, Orrin Porter Rockwell, just arrived from nearly a year's imprisonment without conviction in Missouri.[9]

Orrin Porter Rockwell, a lifelong friend of the Prophet enumerated the events of his arrest and imprisonment in Missouri, and the story was a revelation of man's inhumanity to man. He had been shackled with irons, thrust into a filthy prison without benefit of bedding or heat during the winter months. His life had been threatened. He had refused a bribe to decoy the Prophet into the hands of the Missouri officers. When he had heard the plot to arrest the Prophet at Dixon, his dread and fear of what might happen had made the flesh on his bones twitch until a dove flew several times into the grating of his cell and cooed, and he knew that it was an omen to him Joseph would be safe, and he himself would be liberated. His liberation came soon, when his mother brought $100.00 to pay for the service of attorney Doniphan. The court was unable to find sufficient grounds for a conviction and decided to acquit him of complicity in the shooting of ex-Governor Boggs. His return to Nauvoo was a source of great satisfaction to the brethren.

It was also learned on this day that Daniel Avery had been released from imprisonment in Missouri. The Prophet felt that his (Avery's) release had been due to their vigilance in communicating with the Governor and continually making public the conduct of Missouri. Whatever the cause, they rejoiced in the freedom of these two good brethren.

At this time, sixteen-year-old Lovina, Hyrum's oldest daughter was growing into womanhood and had become the object for

---

[9]Joseph Smith, op. cit., vol. VI, pp. 135-142.

several suitors. Joseph Jackson, a newcomer to Nauvoo was one who attempted to court Lovina. He asked Hyrum for permission to become his son-in-law and was refused. Thereupon he asked the Prophet to use his influence in his favor; and failing in this request, too, he applied to William Law, who became a secret enemy of the Smith family to help Jackson steal Lovina from her father. The attempt failed, and Jackson then tried to persuade a number of the enemy to join him in a conspiracy to murder the whole Smith family. Later, a Mr. Eaton exposed Jackson's evil schemes along with the names of others who became open enemies to the Prophet and Hyrum.[10]

Soon after the Christmas festivities, the Prophet appointed forty men to act as police officers. There was an uneasy feeling among the brethren that all was not well among some of the top leaders. Rumors were about concerning the infidelity of William Law, counselor to the Prophet, and William Marks, president of the stake.

On January 3, at a meeting of the special city council, the case of William Law was taken up. William Law had told Hyrum Smith that the police had been secretly instructed by the Prophet to put Law out of the way. This accusation was denied by the Prophet. Councilor Hyrum Smith said that William Law had told him that the police had sworn him (Law) to keep the secret, which was that he was to be put out of the way in three months. On cross examination, William Law named the man who had told him of the intention of the police. The man in question was brought in and the cross-examination continued. All this had grown out of an erroneous interpretation of the Prophet's remarks about a Judas in General Smith's cabinet, who stood next to him and must be taken care of.

Hyrum considered the matter very alarming. Recalling Dr. Sampson Avard and John Carl's treachery and false-swearing in Missouri, he rehearsed what had been said by the mayor to the police in the former council. The council lasted all day. William Law cross-examined all the police but discovered nothing but

---

[10]Lucy Mack Smith, op. cit., pp. 320-321.

imaginings which had grown out of a surmise by one Daniel Carn. William Law was mollified and shook hands with Joseph, declaring he did not believe a word of the story, and would stand by the Prophet to the death. He then called upon the whole council and the police to witness his declaration.[11]

Such a declaration temporarily restored William Law into the full confidence of Hyrum and Joseph. However, during the weeks ahead, a number of situations helped to reveal the true character of Joseph's counselor.

With Nauvoo under heavy police protection, the work on the temple continued at a steady rate. Hyrum Smith endorsed the penny fund donation, made to the temple by the sisters of England. An article in the *Millennial Star* complimented the English sisters, and Mary Fielding Smith, Hyrum's wife, with her sister Mercy Thompson, wrote to the women in England, informing them of the allotment of the fund in Nauvoo. A weekly amount of one penny and a half-penny had been subscribed to by over a thousand, and more were expected to join. On the bottom of the letter was written the following: "Nauvoo, Dec. 25, 1843. The ladies' subscription to the temple, of one cent a week, is fully sanctioned by the First Presidency. Signed, Hyrum Smith."[12]

The weather was cold with intermittent snowstorms. But the city of Nauvoo even under the tension of expected persecution was the scene of many socials, house parties, and sleighing. Hyrum and his family were welcome guests with many others at the Mansion House.[13] Among the Saints was a spirit of peace and confidence that everything would be all right, even though evil rumors were about. There had been so much trouble because of persecutions and threats that the conditions now did not seem to warrant any alarm. All went about their daily work, proud of Nauvoo. The presence of the temple under construction, the colorful Nauvoo Legion, and the constant arrival of immigrants

---

[11]Joseph Smith, *op. cit.*, vol. VI, pp. 152-165.
[12]*Ibid.*, p. 143. Mercy Fielding Thompson initiated the suggestion of the penny fund.
[13]Lee County *Democrat*, *op. cit.*, vol. 3, no. 26. Whole no. 133, p. 2. Joseph Smith rented the Mansion House to Ebenezer Robinson, formerly editor of *The Times and Seasons*.

from abroad were all a source of pride which gave a feeling of security and well-being. The leaders, Hyrum and Joseph, had been preserved in health; they had succeeded in being liberated from the enemies. Nothing, the Saints felt, could change this situation.

Hyrum and Joseph were happy to note the confidence and the peaceful, happy feeling among the Saints. However, like a ship's officers on their vessel at sea, they could read the barometer and sense the direction and strength of the wind. For them the lowering clouds in the distance bode little good. The age-old conflict of tyranny versus justice was to reach new heights during the new year (1844) which had just dawned.

On Friday, January 5, 1844, a special session of the city council met at 11:00 a.m. again to allay the fears of William Law and Marks. There had been many rumors circulated concerning the fate of these men. Again witnesses were called in and it was finally decided that the reports were false. During the investigation of the rumors against Brothers Law and Marks, it was revealed that a Brother Sobey had testified on a basis of mere rumor to the effect that Joseph Smith was going to get revenge against Brothers Law and Marks. The stir among the brethren at such charges was illustrated by Hyrum Smith who remarked:

> . . . Sobey makes me think of an old Dutchman that had an ox—the first animal he ever owned in his life, and he broke him to ride; then he filled a sack with rocks and laid it on the ox's back, got on himself, and told his son to hide by the roadside and when he came along to jump out and yell boo, as he wanted to know how well his ox was broke. The son did accordingly. The ox was frightened and threw the old man off. "Father," said the son, "I did as you told me." "Yes," said the old man, "but you made too big a boo."[14]

At the end of the meeting which adjourned because of a lack of candles, Joseph had been again assured by a person of questionable loyalty, this time, General Wilson Law, who said: "I am Joseph's friend; he has no better friend in the world. I am ready

---

[14]Joseph Smith, *op. cit.*, vol. VI, p. 168.

to lay down my life for him." Upon this the mayor and General Law shook hands.[15]

The winter of 1843-44 wore on, extremely cold. The council chamber over the store was often so cold that it was necessary to transact business in the Mansion House. And the inclement weather seemed to symbolize the present impasse of the political scene for the Saints. Three replies had come to the letters sent to possible candidates for the presidency. John C. Calhoun of South Carolina stated that "the case of Missouri does not come within the jurisdiction of the Federal Government"; Henry Clay of Kentucky had advised the Mormons to migrate to Oregon; and Lewis Cass' reply was equally unsatisfactory.

The problem now was to determine which course to take. Why should the Saints vote for a man whose policy, based on expediency, might lead to a war of extermination against the Mormons? The Saints could not stand aloof from either political party and refuse to cast a vote for the candidate of their choice. Under these circumstances a meeting of the brethren was called at the mayor's office Monday, January 29, to determine what the course of the Saints should be in the coming presidential election. The candidates for President of the United States at that time were Martin Van Buren and Henry Clay. A discussion by the Prophet, Hyrum Smith, and the twelve brought about a resolution to form a party of their own, which must be done in full confidence of success. The twelve, with missionaries, would have to carry the campaign to the electorate. Such a campaign would be the means of bringing their views of government before the people.

When the time came for nominations for President on an independent electoral ticket, Willard Richards arose and nominated Joseph Smith to be that candidate, and the nomination was unanimously accepted. This important decision gave great hope of obtaining justice and correcting gross political abuse in high places. The Prophet outlined the procedure of electioneering.

[15]*Ibid.*, pp. 169-170.

The states were each assigned to members of the twelve. Among other things, the Prophet said:

> If I ever get into the Presidential chair, I will protect the people in their rights and liberties. I will not electioneer for myself. Hyrum, Brigham, Parley, and Taylor must go. . . . The Whigs are striving for a king under the garb of Democracy. There is oratory enough in this church to carry me into the Presidential chair the first slide.[16]

During the next days, Hyrum was called in for consultation to decide on appropriate action. Plans must be ready by April 6, general conference time, for after this conference the missionaries would go forth with a message of good government supported by revealed principles of religion. On Tuesday, February 6, the Prophet wrote,

> Very cold day. I spent the evening with my brother Hyrum, Sidney Rigdon, and the twelve and their wives at Elder John Taylor's, took supper and had a very pleasant time. Wednesday, 7th, an exceeding cold day. In the evening I met with my brother Hyrum and the Twelve Apostles in my office, at their request, to devise means to promote the interests of the General Government. I completed and signed my "Views of the Powers and Policy of the Government of the United States."[17]

In this lengthy treatise one may gain a glimpse of the mind of the Prophet Joseph Smith. Here the insight, magnitude, and nobility of his soul is effectively portrayed in his great regard for the founding fathers of this nation—George Washington, Thomas Jefferson, and others—and in the importance he placed on integrity and regard for all peoples no matter of what color, creed, or race. He mentioned needed reforms: the foul prisons ought to be turned into seminaries of learning; slaves could be purchased and freed with money obtained from the sale of public lands; Texas should be annexed and Mexico and Canada share the blessings of this great republic; banking reforms should be made and the pay to members of Congress reduced.

---

[16]*Ibid.*, p. 188.
[17]*Ibid.*, pp. 197-209.

The Prophet's grasp of the problem and what ought to be done was eloquently expressed in these words:

> The wisdom which ought to characterize the freest, wisest, and most noble nation of the nineteenth century, should, like the sun in its meridian splendor, warm every object beneath its rays, and the main effort of her officers, who are nothing more than the servants of the people, ought to be directed to ameliorate the conditions of all, black or white, bond or free. . . .[18]

This lengthy document was read and reread before the council. Many copies were made and published at home and abroad. The missionaries carried copies to be referred to from time to time. Perhaps, thought Hyrum and Joseph, "this action would be the means of arousing public sentiment in support of our people."

Governor Thomas Ford had recently written an article in the Warsaw *Signal* placing the responsibility for keeping the peace upon the citizens of Hancock County, including the Mormons. The members of the twelve were each making an appeal to his native state to recognize the injustice of a sister state (Missouri) toward 15,000 expelled citizens who had been deprived of homes, land, and property, and had suffered persecutions in the form of insults, exposure during inclement weather, intimidation, torture, rape, and murder.

No response was forthcoming from Congress. The move on the part of the brethren to organize a new political party to elect a President of their own was merely a stop-gap gesture. The Saints must exercise their franchise as citizens without becoming embroiled in conflict with either political party. But running their own candidate for President was not the answer to their difficulties. There was little chance for a new party to succeed under the circumstances. The only value to be derived from this was to plead the cause of an injured people and place the views of a modern Prophet before the citizens of the country. Perhaps at some place and time the scales of justice might be moved to ameliorate a persecuted and maligned citizenry.

---

[18]*Idem.*

If these moves for self-preservation failed, what then was to be the alternative? Hyrum knew not where the answer lay. But he was a peace-loving man who stood always for justice and forbearance, and put his trust in Almighty God. Somehow, in the end, the forces of righteousness would triumph.

CHAPTER XXX

HYRUM AND JOSEPH LOOK WESTWARD
FOR A NEW HOME

Hyrum Smith and his family noticed the ice breaking up on the Mississippi River during February of 1844. It had been an unusually cold winter, and there had been many problems to worry him. As Patriarch he felt he had to have a tentative solution to the conspiracy rising within the ranks of the Church. Something had to be done very soon to safeguard the Church from internal enemies in high places.

Another problem soon to come before the brethren was the organizing of manufacturing companies. They needed some means to relieve the poverty of the Saints and the Church. And when rumors reached Nauvoo that mass meetings were being held at Warsaw and Carthage threatening the wholesale expulsion of the Saints from Illinois, Hyrum and Joseph began to think of the possibility of moving the Saints west.

The idea of moving to the Rocky Mountains as a solution to their problem grew even more appealing. Mention had already been made to Anson Call about the part he would someday play in establishing the Church and its members in the great basin.[1] If this idea to move west were to be realized, there remained the work of exploration and a preliminary survey of the vast regions of California and Oregon. Plans must be laid in advance to meet the impending crisis.

The brethren were painfully aware of the dilemma of the Saints. A report had come from Carthage that a mass meeting had been held at the courthouse and that a resolution had been passed to hold a "wolf" hunt the second Saturday of March, which day (March 17) had been set aside for fasting and prayer for the destruction of Joseph Smith.

---

[1]*Supra* (before quoted) chapter XXV.

The problems were discussed in a council meeting held Tuesday, February 20. Among the first topics considered was the possible location for the ultimate removal of the Saints. The council concurred with the Prophet's remarks to the twelve:

> I would like you to send out a delegation and investigate the locations of California and Oregon, and hunt out a good location where we can remove to after the temple is completed, and where we can build a city in a day and have a government of our own, get up into the mountains where the devil cannot dig us out and live in a healthful climate, where we can live as old as we have a mind to.[2]

The following evening, Wednesday February 21, another meeting was held for the purpose of selecting a company to explore Oregon and California in order to find a site for a new city of the Saints.

So urgent was the need for a western expedition that Hyrum was summoned to a third meeting on Friday, February 23. The minutes of this meeting, written by Joseph, contain the following: "Met with the Twelve in the assembly room concerning the Oregon and California Exploring Expedition, Hyrum and Sidney present. I told them I wanted an exploration of all the mountain country. Perhaps it would be better to go direct to Santa Fe. Send twenty-five men, let them preach the Gospel wherever they go. Let that man go that can raise $500, a good horse and mule, a double barrel gun, one barrel rifle, and the other smooth bore, a saddle and bridle, a pair of revolving pistols, bowie knife, and a good sabre. Appoint a leader and let them beat up for volunteers. I want every man that goes to be a king and a priest. When he gets on the mountain he may want to talk to his God; when with the savage nations have power to govern, etc. If we don't get volunteers, wait till after the election."[3] A move to the west would take time. The Saints would have to be prepared.

The following Sunday morning Hyrum and Joseph addressed the Saints at the temple block; and in the evening at a

---

[2]Joseph Smith, *op. cit.*, vol. VI, p. 222.
[3]*Ibid.*, pp. 223-224.

prayer meeting in the assembly room, the Prophet made an important announcement which he describes thus:

> . . . I prophesied that within five years we would be out of the power of our enemies, whether they were apostates or of the world, and told the brethren to record it, that when it comes to pass they need not say they had forgotten the saying.[4]

This prophecy would see the Saints established in the West with President Brigham Young as their leader and caravans of immigrants moving in an unending stream to their new home in the mountains. Did Hyrum and Joseph foresee the cost, the disaffection and desertions of some of the leaders, the rage of their enemies, the shedding of blood? The suffering and privation that lay ahead may not have been seen. And what of Hyrum's own family? What would be their attitude; would they face the challenge under new leadership?

By the end of February, 1844, the river was cleared of ice enough for navigation. River steamers began passing on their way to the various settlements. Seasonal rains had helped to melt the ice and snow. At the moment the affairs of the temple occupied the mind of Hyrum. With navigation on the river restored, lumber, stone and building materials could be supplied.

While feverish preparations were made to explore the West and to complete the temple, a scandalous rumor was circulated around the city concerning Hyrum Smith and certain females of Nauvoo. None of the malicious reports heretofore circulated had had such an effect on Hyrum as did this one. An immediate investigation resulted in the arrest of Orsimus F. Botswick for slander. At the Mansion House, Monday, February 26, the court fined him fifty dollars. Francis M. Higbee, Botswick's attorney, gave notice that he would appeal to the municipal court and then to the circuit court. He was warned by the mayor, Joseph Smith, that if he did so and took the matter to Carthage, it would stir up the mob and bring them upon Nauvoo.[5]

[4]*Ibid.*, p. 225.
[5]*Idem.*

Hyrum Smith could never have been guilty of the charges made against him. Those who knew the integrity of his soul and the purity of his heart were outraged at such charges. Hyrum's life had been exemplary. The only criticism one might make would be of his living secretly the celestial law of plural marriage. Perhaps publishing the new doctrine and presenting it to the Saints for their acceptance would have allayed the many evil implications and false rumors. It seemed, however, that the new doctrine was so revolutionary and contrary to the established marriage mores of the western world that the very idea would have touched off an explosion which might have retarded, if not actually destroyed the struggling young Church.

Volunteers were making application to join the western exploration expedition. Also, at the regular council meetings the various cases of apostasy were taken up. The guilty were called in and given a chance to repent; those who failed to repent were excommunicated. Some of these apostates had persuaded some of the elders to re-baptize them without first going through the proper procedure of confession, repentance, and making full amends to the injured parties concerned. The elders who had done the rebaptisms had to be properly instructed.

By March 1, James Arlington Bennett of Long Island, New York, a recent convert to the Church, became the vice-presidential candidate on the Reform Party ticket with Joseph Smith, and the plans for electioneering took precedence over other things. The twelve met in council to make plans and assure each other of the importance of this campaign.

The first warm days of March turned the attention of the temple committee to their responsibility. Thursday, March 7, was a splendid day for a general gathering. Over eight thousand Saints assembled at 9:00 a.m. at the temple. After a hymn by the choir and the invocation by Parley P. Pratt, Hyrum Smith arose and addressed the vast assembly. His talk reflected their attitude toward completing the House of the Lord.

In a clear strong voice he said:

The object of the meeting is to stir up your minds by way of remembrance. It is necessary to have a starting point, which is to build the temple.

With the assistance of the sisters, we expect to get the nails and glass, and with the assistance of the brethren, we expect to do the rest. I will proclaim in public and in private that the sisters bought the glass and nails by penny subscriptions. "Choose ye this day whom ye will serve."[6]

We shall call upon this vast multitude for a donation to buy powder and fuse-ropes to blast the rocks in the quarry. We want the brethren to do at least as much as the sisters.

We do not intend to finish the Nauvoo House this season, but to take all the hands and finish the temple this summer, or the walls of it, and get the roof on by December, and do off the inside next winter, and about a year from this spring we will dedicate it.

We can do anything we undertake. We have power and we can do great things. In five years the work will progress more than it has done for ten years past. . . .[7]

When Hyrum had finished, the Prophet spoke to the people about the difficulties encountered by the police in enforcing the law. He reminded the citizens that they were the makers of the laws and that the officers were their servants. He named several members of the Chuch who were guilty of stirring up strife.

The meeting continued with W. W. Phelps' reading of General Smith's "Views of the Powers and Policy of the General Government of the United States." President Brigham Young and John Taylor spoke on the necessity of contributing to the temple fund, and the meeting concluded with the Prophet's speech about the feasibility of annexing Texas, Mexico, and Canada, and liberating the Negro by indemnifying their owners. After the choir sang, Brigham Young gave the closing prayer.

The warm March weather brought out the buds and made the grass grow enough so that meetings could be held out-of-doors near the temple. On Sunday, March 10, 1844 Wilford Woodruff

---

[6]From William Clayton's *Journal*, B'k 28. Until his death, Hyrum Smith kept a record of the women's penny fund with the aid of Sister Mercy Thompson. Some paid a year in advance. Nearly $2000 had already been realized, with contributions coming in daily.

[7]Joseph Smith, *op. cit.*, vol. II, pp. 236-237.

recorded the lengthy sermon Joseph delivered on the importance of the work of Elias, Elijah, and the Messiah. That morning, the prophet's friend, King Follet, had been buried with full masonic honors. Brother Follet had been killed the day before when an accident occurred while he was digging a well. His death turned the Prophet's thoughts to the great mission of Elijah and temple work. In this sermon the Prophet spoke under the inspiration of heaven. He made it clear how those living cannot be saved without their dead, and vice versa. He also said there was no forgiveness for those who shed innocent blood, and related that the Lord had told him once that, what he asked for, he would have. Continuing, he said:

I have been afraid to ask God to kill my enemies, lest some of them should peradventure, repent.

I asked a short time since for the Lord to deliver me out of the hands of the Governor of Missouri and if it needs to be accomplish it, to take him away. The next news that came pouring from there was that Governor Reynolds had shot himself. I would now say, "Beware, O earth, how you fight against the Saints of God and shed innocent blood, for in the days of Elijah, his enemies came upon him and fire was called down from heaven and destroyed them. . . ."

The Prophet, referring to the doctrine of revelation said:

We cannot be perfect without the fathers, etc. We must have revelation from them, and we can see that the doctrine of revelation far transcends the doctrine of no revelation; for one truth revealed from heaven is worth all the sectarian notions in existence.[8]

At this time a letter was received from Lyman Wight, member of the twelve, written from Black River Falls, Wisconsin, February 15. He, with other brethren, had been sent to the pinery of Wisconsin to secure lumber for the temple and the Nauvoo House. He spoke encouragingly of being able to get out over a million feet of lumber by July, enough for both projects. He complained of having to transport, clothe, and feed too many lazy

---

[8]*Ibid.*, pp. 252-254.

men who pretended to assist in the work. He spoke of the friendly Chippewa and Menomanee Indians and their willingness to allow them to cut lumber. He also told of their desire to hear the gospel.

Brother Lyman mentioned the proposition of moving the Saints to Texas and the Southwest. He visioned a great work to be accomplished in taking the gospel to the natives of this region. He said he would await counsel from the brethren at Nauvoo.

The brethren at Nauvoo were hard-pressed for money to provide for the men at the pinery. Attempts were made to raise some cash by borrowing from individuals who had some to lend. The laziness of the men who had been sent for lumber may have been due, at least in part, to the inability of the Church to meet the regular payroll.

The First Presidency sent Elder Orson Pratt to the national capital and Elder Amos Fielding to England. Both were to collect money for the temple by presenting a certificate of authorization bearing the corporation seal, and the signatures of Joseph and Hyrum Smith over the words: "Presiding Elders of the whole Church of Jesus Christ of Latter-day Saints."[9]

Spring brought boat loads of immigrants from England, and many visitors. The Prophet's "Powers and Policy of the General Government of the United States" was being published and had received comments from publishing firms and politicians alike. Of the Prophet some said that he was "more forthright than Henry Clay." He was termed the "Great Mormon Prophet." The eyes of the country were drawn more toward the Mormons and Nauvoo. When visitors came, as others had done the year before, they were astonished at what they beheld in the horseshoe bend of the Father-of-Waters. Such integrity, thrift, and industry demanded their respect.

The river traffic had increased its tempo. The saws, hammers, and trowels heard over the city were busy on new construction. The temple was moving ahead and the farmers were preparing the soil for seeding. The Prophet at this time wrote in

[9]*Ibid.*, pp. 263-264.

exultation: "Almost every stranger that enters our city is excited
with astonishment that so much has been done in so short a time,
but we flatter ourselves from the known industry, perseverance
and diligence of the Saints, that by the return of another winter
so much more will be accomplished that his astonishment will be
increased to wonder and admiration."[10]

*   *   *

About this time, March 26, Hyrum and Joseph learned of a
conspiracy going on among the brethren in higher circles. William Law, Counselor to the First Presidency; his brother Wilson
Law, an officer in the Nauvoo Legion, together with Chauncey
L. Higbee, Francis M. Higbee, Dr. R. D. Foster, and Joseph H.
Jackson were plotting the destruction of the Saints. An affidavit
concerning the above plot was sworn to before Justice of the
Peace, Daniel H. Wells, at Nauvoo. The Prophet was also told
how two youths, Dennison L. Harris and Robert Scott, had attended the meetings held by the plotters and when they were
asked to take the oath against the Prophet, they refused. The
plotters thereupon threatened to take the boys' lives.[11]

Characteristically, the Prophet Joseph stood at the pulpit and
publicly denounced the plotters for what they were, declaring
that he had no fear for what they could do, and saying: "I won't
swear out a warrant against them, for I don't fear any of them;
they would not scare off an old setting hen. I intended to publish
all the iniquity that I know of them. If I am guilty, I am ready
to bear it. . . . I am willing to do anything for the good of the
people."[12] The Prophet was as bold as a lion against his enemies.

There was a chance for the conspirators to repent, at least
for the time being. Sidney Rigdon had been accused of traitorous
acts and had pleaded his cause and regained, for the moment, the
full confidence of the brethren.

Even though great progress was made at this time in popula-
ting Nauvoo and the neighboring settlements, there was a feeling

---

[10]*Ibid.*, pp. 265-266.
[11]See full account in *The Contributor*, April, 1884.
[12]Joseph Smith, *op. cit.*, vol. VI, p. 272.

of impending disaster. The council meetings discussed various proposals. Something had to be done. The mind of the Prophet had been on the acquisition of territory such as Texas and Oregon. If the Saints were to be moved out of their place, perhaps a way could be opened by an appeal to Congress. The government could assist the Saints and at the same time bring into the union valuable new territory and thus strengthen the nation.

The council accepted the Prophet's suggestion to memorialize Congress to allow Joseph Smith to raise one hundred thousand armed volunteers, as a United States Army officer, and proceed to Oregon and other bordering territory and make it part of the United States. This should be done to promote a peaceful occupation of these relatively non-occupied territories. Such a move would help facilitate colonization and protect citizens with the pioneer spirit who were beginning now to move into these virgin territories. The peace of any country would not be disturbed, and all treaties between other countries and the United States would be observed.

A few days later, on March 20, the Prophet addressed a Memorial to John Tyler, President of the United States, embodying in it the same sentiments as was contained in the Petition to Congress. Elder Orson Hyde was delegated to take the Memorial to Congress. The Petition was introduced by Mr. Wentworth to the House. Before its reading by Mr. Wentworth was finished, it was objected to by Mr. J. R. Ingersoll. After some discussion it was decided to let a committee, which had been appointed, go into the whole matter of the Oregon Bill. It was evident that Congress was then considering some action on the northwest region of the American continent. No further consideration was given the Prophet's proposals.[18]

During the latter part of March and the first of April, Hyrum had been very busy. Among his extra responsibilities was that of assisting with the dedication of the recently completed Masonic Temple. On Friday, April 5, the day prior to the annual confer-

---

[18]*Ibid.*, pp. 281-282. Note — Orson Pratt and John E. Page assisted Elder Hyde in obtaining Congress attention.

ence of the Church, over 550 members of the Masonic fraternity
assembled from various parts of the world. A procession was
formed at Henry Miller's house and was accompanied to the
temple by the Nauvoo Brass Band. The dedicatory ceremonies
were performed by Worshipful Master Hyrum Smith, and Elder
Erastus Snow delivered an able Masonic address. The building
was considered the most subtantial and best finished Masonic
Temple in the Western States.

The day after the dedication of the Masonic Temple, the
annual conference of the Church convened. A unique feature of
the restored Church has been its plenary meetings, to which
friends and strangers as well as members have been welcome to
attend. The April gathering was to include the date on which
the Church was organized, April 6. Several days were designated
and used for instruction, the discussion of problems, filling vacancies in priesthood quorums, hearing reports, ordaining, etc. It
was a time of spiritual uplift, counseling, encouragement. The
ties of the Church were strengthened by the rededication of purpose, increased loyalty and devotion of its members. Conferences
provided opportunity for the people to get acquainted with
their leaders, to hear their voices and feel the spirit which
strengthened the bonds of love and fellowship. Over the years,
each such conference was anticipated with real interest and was
attended with zeal to overflowing. It was a source of testimony
to both members and investigators.

The Church symbolized the greatest fraternity under God on
the earth. And its conferences were like a family gathering of
kindred spirits, marked by much hand-shaking, embracing, visiting, renewing old acquaintances, meeting former missionary companions.

The approaching crisis resulting from the movement of opposite forces toward each other separated the sheep and the goats,
the righteous from the wicked and those of skepticism from those
of great faith. The appraisal of Hyrum Smith may again be
made because of the peculiar circumstances arising at this time.
He did not compromise with sin when found among the charity

cases of his household; he fearlessly vetoed the request of his daughter's hand in marriage by his enemy; he refuted unequivocably charges against him of immorality; his great faith in the erection of the temple and obtaining workmen and material for its early completion electrified the membership of the Church to action, and his fearlessness before traitors and the unscrupulous in the law profession exposing their sinister and wicked designs reveal the soul and character of the man second in command.

After the conference Hyrum's time was divided between his home, his official duties, and his farm east of town. He was a farmer at heart and enjoyed supervising the tasks of the farm and watching the varied landscape that accompanied the changing seasons. He and his family would often ride out to be by themselves where they could enjoy a quiet hour and temporarily forget the cares of the day. Hyrum seemed to draw strength from these quiet moments which filled his soul with the sheer joy of living.

CHAPTER XXXI

THE LAST GREAT CONFERENCE

A soft breeze wafting in from the southwest lent a tranquil spirit to the throngs assembling at the meeting place near the temple. Mother nature seemed to have prepared for the occasion by putting on her most becoming frock of green. The trees, the grass, the flowering plants and shrubs were resplendent; and the roads leading to Nauvoo had been well traveled as was evidenced by the line of horses, wagons, and carriages, in view a short distance away.

The fourteenth annual conference of the Church was to be a significant one, not because of the increased membership in attendance nor of the nature of the sermons nor of the work of sending the most able missionaries into the eastern states to proclaim Joseph Smith a candidate for President of the United States, but because this occasion was to be the last time two key men in this Dispensation of the Fulness of Times would stand before them in their official capacity at a general conference, men who had been instruments in the hands of Almighty God in laying the foundation for the kingdom of God here upon the earth. Hyrum and Joseph Smith were to be ruthlessly murdered before another six months had passed.

This great convocation of the faithful symbolized the successful growth and power of the new religious society. It was tangible evidence of the capable leadership God had provided for his Church.

The scene which greeted their eyes as they occupied their places on the temporary lumber rostrum pleased Joseph and Hyrum. All the seats before them were filled; many around the outer fringe of the crowd were standing. At 10:30 a.m. that morning (Friday, April 5, 1844), Elder Brigham Young called the meeting to order. Next to Hyrum and Joseph sat Sidney Rigdon and William Marks, and then Heber C. Kimball, Willard Richards, Wilford Woodruff, John Taylor and George A. Smith, followed by members of the high council and many elders.

The choir, a well-trained and skilfully conducted group, sang an opening hymn appropriate for the occasion. Then the Prophet Joseph arose and made a few remarks about devoting the time to instructing the Saints on the eternal principles of the gospel rather than on things too trivial to occupy the attention of so large a body. He told them that because of the attendance of so large a crowd and of the weakness of his lungs he would listen to the elders and make such comments and corrections as he saw fit. He said:

... Those who feel desirous of sowing the seeds of discord will be disappointed on this occasion. It is our purpose to build up and establish the principles of righteousness, and not to break down and destroy. The Great Jehovah has been ever with me, and the wisdom of God will direct me in the seventh hour. I feel in closer communion and better standing with God than ever I felt before in my life, and I am glad of this opportunity to appear in your midst. I thank God for the glorious day he has given us. In so large a congregation it is necessary that the greatest order and decorum be observed. I request this at your hands, and believe that you will all keep good order.

The invocation was offered by W. W. Phelps, after which the choir sang a second hymn. Elder Sidney Rigdon spoke of his recent ill health, saying that for five years he had been unable to take his proper place in the councils of the Church. He bore a powerful testimony of the divinity of the work. He also dwelt on the early history of the Church. John Taylor followed him to the pulpit and spoke of the importance of freedom and of the responsibility of national leaders to uphold the Constitution and support the rights of its citizens.

The proceedings continued, with only an intermission at noon, until 5:30 p.m., and resumed on schedule the next day, with Sidney Rigdon completing his discourse on church history. His sermon was one of the several spiritual and faith-promoting sermons of the conference.

The afternoon session of the second day of the conference was dismissed at 5:00 p.m., without ceremony, with the appearance of ominous looking clouds. Scarcely had the crowd dispersed when a heavy shower accompanied by wind, thunder, and lightning, struck the spot which had been so crowded short moments before.

On Sunday, April 7, the conference opened with the choir singing "Ye Slumbering Nations That Have Slept." After the opening prayer, the choir sang "The Spirit of God like a Fire Is Burning," and the Prophet admonished the police to be vigilant in keeping order.

It was apparent that with literally thousands assembled, out-of-doors, utmost order must prevail if the proceedings were to be heard. Every available spot was occupied, even to the lumber frame work at the rear of the rostrum. Seated along this elevated place at the rear where he could hear every word was Goudy E. Hogan, a boy of fourteen, with his friends. He later wrote of this occasion:

> I was sitting close behind the Prophet Joseph Smith so that I nearly touched his clothes. I had not been long in the church and was somewhat superstitious and took particular notice of his manner of dress and action. I remember that he was not a proud man. I also remember while one was preaching the Prophet spoke to the Elders that were speaking to stop for a minute. Joseph the Prophet arose from his seat and said in a loud voice owing to the large congregation that was assembled saying he wished that some of those young men on the outside of the congregation who were talking loud to the young ladies would not do so but wait and go to their homes and speak to them by the consent of their parents. Joseph later left his seat and went to the source.[1]

During noon intermission that day thirty-five were baptized in the Mississippi River.

At 2:00 p.m. Patriarch Hyrum Smith arose to say something about the temple.

> We want 200,000 shingles as we shall resume work on the temple immediately. All who have not paid their tithing, come on and do it. We

---

[1]*History of Goudy E. Hogan*, BYU, Provo, Utah.

want provisions, money, boards, planks, and anything that is good; we don't want any more old guns or watches. I thought some time ago I would get up a small subscription so that the sisters might do something. In consequence of some misunderstanding, it has not gone on as at first. It is a matter of my own; I do not ask it as a tithing. I give a privilege to any one to pay a cent a week, or fifty cents a year. I want it by next fall to buy nails and glass. It is difficult to get money. I know that a small subscription will bring more than a large one. The poor can help in this way. I take the responsibility upon myself and call again upon the sisters. I call again until I get about $1,000. It requires two thousand subscribers.

I have sent this subscription plan to England and the branches. I am not to be dictated to by any one except the Prophet and God. I want you to pay in your subscriptions to me and it shall always be boldly said by me, the sisters bought the glass in that house, and their names shall be written in the Book of the Law of the Lord. It is not a tax, but a free will offering to procure something which shall ever be a monument of your works. No member of the Relief Society got it up. I am the man that did it. They ought not to infringe upon it. I am not a member of the female Relief Society! I am one of the committee of the Lord's House.

I wish to accomplish something; I wish all the Saints to have an opportunity to do something. I want the poor with the purse of five dollars to have a chance. The widow's two mites were more in the eyes of the Lord than the purse of the rich; and the poor woman shall have a seat in the house of God. She who pays her two mites as well as the rich, because it is all she has. I wish to have a place in the house. I intend to stimulate the brethren. I want to get the roof in this season. I want to get the windows in the winter, so that we may be able to dedicate the House of the Lord by this time next year, if nothing more than one room. I will call upon the brethren to do something.

I cannot make a comparison between the House of God and anything now in existence. Great things are to grow out of that house. There is a great and mighty power to grow out of that house. There is an endowment. Knowledge is power. We want knowledge. We have frequently difficulties with persons who profess to be Latter-day Saints. When the sacrament will be administered in the Lord's House it will do away with a great deal of difficulty that is now in existence. If we can have a privilege and confess our faults unto God and one another every Sabbath day, it will do away with these. You sisters will have a seat in that house. I will stand on the top of that pulpit and proclaim to all what the sisters have done. When you offer up your sacraments every Sabbath you will feel well a whole week; you will get a great portion of the Spirit of God, enough to last you a week—and you will increase. We are now deprived of the privilege of giving the necessary instruction, hence we want a house.

All the money shall be laid out for what you design it. It shall not be paid for anything else. I am one of the committee. The committee tells me the quarry is blockaded; it is filled with rock. The stone cutters are wanting work. Come on with your teams as soon as conference is over. It is not necessary for me to tell who will come and do it. I will prophesy that you will do it. There is not one in the city but what will do right if he knows it, with only one or two exceptions, and they are not worth notice. God will take care of them, and if He doesn't the devil will. . . .

. . . If you hear of any one in high authority that he is rather inclined to apostasy, don't let prejudice arise, but pray for him. God may feel after him, and he may return. Never speak reproachfully or disrespectfully; he is in the hands of God. I am one of those peacemakers who take a stand above these little things. It has been intimated we should have investigations this conference. Do you think I would trouble this conference with it? If I have a difficulty with a man, I will go and settle it. Let them settle their difficulties. There is not a man who has had a difficulty who would trouble this congregation about it. We ask no favors, we can settle it ourselves. Don't think anything about persons who are on the eve of apostasy. God is able to take care of them. Let God judge; do your duty and let men alone.

Never undertake to destroy men because they do some evil thing. It is natural for a man to be led and not driven. Put down iniquity by good works. Many men speak without any contemplation; if they had given the matter a little contemplation it would not have been spoken. We ought to be careful of what we say and take the example of Jesus; cast over men the mantle of charity, and try to cover their faults. We are made to enlighten and not to darken one another; save men, not destroy them. Do unto others what you would have them do unto you. It is well enough to root out conspiracy. Do not fear, but if you are in the right track, having God to guide you, He will save you; for God will save you, if He has to destroy the wicked so as by fire.

I want to put down all false influence. If I thought I should be saved and any in the congregation be lost, I should not be happy. For this purpose Jesus effected a resurrection. Our Savior is competent to save all from death and hell. I can prove it out of the revelation. I would not serve a God that had not all wisdom and all power.

The reason I feel so good is because I have a big soul. There are men with small bodies who have got souls like Enoch. We have. We have gathered our big souls from the end of the earth. The Gospel picks the big souls out of all creation, and we will get the big souls out of all the nations, and we shall have the largest city in the world.

We will gather all the big souls out of every nation. As soon as the Gospel catches hold of noble souls, it brings them all right up to Zion.

There is a thing called guiding star. The Gospel is similar. We will have a people great enough to be saved.

Popery could not write what Enoch preached. He told the people that God took him up into a high mountain, showed him the distress of the people—the destruction of the world, and he said his heart swelled wide as eternity. But adherents of Popery could not receive anything as large as that, and every man-made society is just like them. Men's souls conform to the society in which they live, with very few exceptions, and when men come to live with the Mormons, their souls swell as if they were going to stride the Republic of America. I can believe that man can go from planet to planet—a man gets so high in the mansions above.

A certain good sister came to my house and she was troubled because she heard so many big things. She thought it weakened her faith. I told her she had too much faith. She believed too much. I will tell you how you may know whether the thing is true or not. When any one comes to you with a lie, you feel troubled. God will trouble you, and will not approbate you in such belief. You had better get some antidote to get rid of it. Humble yourself before God and ask Him for His Spirit and pray to Him to judge it for you. It is better not to have so much faith than to have so much as to believe all the lies.

Before this conference closes, I want to get all the Elders together. I shall make a proclamation. I want to take the line and ax and hew you, make you as straight as possible. I will make you as straight as a stretched line. Every Elder that goes from Nauvoo to preach the Gospel, if he preaches anything else, we will silence him through the public print. I want all the Elders to meet and to understand; and if they preach anything but the pure truth, we will call them home.

The conference session ended at 3:15 p.m. After a brief intermission, another meeting was called to order and President Joseph Smith delivered the King Follett funeral sermon before twenty thousand Saints.[2]

There seemed to be a spirit of urgency among the brethren to teach the Saints certain principles of the eternal gospel. The thousands present had been gathered from different church groups. They had been believers in the Bible, in Jesus Christ, and in many of the principles of the gospel. However, their interpretations of the gospel message varied greatly, and their previous

---

[2]Joseph Smith, *op. cit.*, vol. VI, pp. 302-317. The Prophet spoke three and a half hours. He dwelt on the personality of God and many important concepts.

indoctrination affected, to some degree at least, their regard for the principles laid down by the Prophet Joseph Smith.

Therefore, as Hyrum, Joseph, and the twelve faced this vast audience, they felt the great responsibility of teaching, instructing, and counseling these, the charter members of the Church, who would soon be faced with the necessity of making momentous decisions. Their faith would be tried in the fires of adversity, and they would be called upon to lay down their lives for the gospel's sake. Sensing, perhaps, what lay ahead, the leaders called many meetings with sermons of long duration. They talked themselves hoarse in their efforts to be heard by all at the open air sessions.

The Sunday afternoon sermon of Hyrum Smith revealed his anxiety to complete the temple and his Christian spirit toward all men. He valued the dignity of the human personality, even of those who disagreed with him and those who were harboring the seeds of apostasy in their hearts. He was a peacemaker who counseled forbearance when people were brought before the courts. For him no decision could be made until both sides of the question were fully reviewed.

The conference continued Monday. The Prophet limited his talk because of insufficient vocal power, but he mentioned briefly the scope of Zion which included North and South America, and stated that Stakes of Zion would be established even in such large cities as Boston and New York."

On the fifth day of the conference, Hyrum Smith spoke again:

> You are to vote for good men, and if you do not do this, it is a sin. Choose the good and refuse the evil. Men of false principles have preyed upon us like wolves upon helpless lambs. Damn the rod of tyranny; curse it. Let every man use his liberties according to the Constitution. Don't fear man or devil; electioneer with all people, male and female, and exhort them to do the thing that is right. We want a President of the U. S., not a party President, but a President of the whole people; for a party President disfranchises the opposing party. Have a President who will maintain every man in his rights.

I wish all of you to do all the good you can. We will try to convert the nations into one solid union. I despise the principle that divides the nation into party and faction. I want it to grow up like a green bay tree. Damn the system of splitting up the nation into opposite belligerent parties. Whatever are the rights of men guaranteed by the Constitution of these United States, let them have them. Then, if we were all in union, no one dare attempt to put a warlike foot on our soil. I don't like to see the rights of Americans trampled down. I am opposed to the policy of all such persons as would allow Great Britain or any other power to take from us Oregon, or any portion of our national territory, and damn all who attempt it. Lift up your voices like thunder. There is power and influence enough among us to put in a President. I don't wonder at the old Carthagenian lawyer being afraid of Joseph Smith being elected.[3]

At 10:40 a.m. a call was made for preaching volunteers to march out to the green. A great company numbering 244 moved out and returned at the right of the stand.

The conference was considered a success, as the words of the Prophet testify:

The weather has been beautiful for the conference, and they have been the greatest, best, and most glorious five consecutive days ever enjoyed by this generation. There was much good accomplished. Many spectators were present from Quincy, Alton, Warsaw, Fort Madison and other towns. The large number and good order spoke well for the morality of the city.[4]

And trouble within the church again became a reality. On April 18, within ten days after the general conference, the Twelve Apostles and high council met to hear charges against Robert D. Foster, Wilson and William Law. After careful deliberation on the part of the brethren, these three were excommunicated from the Church. They were later joined by others who hated Hyrum and Joseph, so that there were Foster's brother Charles, and also Chauncey and Francis Higbee, who met Joseph in front of his office and engaged him in an argument, drew a pistol and attempted to shoot the Prophet. Charles Foster then went to Warsaw and had several vile articles published against the Prophet.

---

[3]*Ibid.*, pp. 322-324.
[4]*Ibid.*, p. 326.

Regular council meetings were held by the brethren. Members of the twelve were preparing to go on missions while the well-known enemies from within continued their conspiracy. Those who were cut off decided that Joseph Smith was a fallen Prophet; therefore they would organize a church of their own. The group met at Wilson Law's place on Sunday, April 28, and appointed Wilson Law to take the place of Joseph Smith, with Austin Cowles and William Law to be his counselors. A committee composed of William and Wilson Law, Austin A. Cowles, John Scott, Sr., Francis M. Higbee, Robert D. Foster, and Robert Pierce were to visit different families in the city.[5]

About this time, William Smith, one of the twelve, was away with his family in the East doing missionary work. Having been a candidate to the Illinois State Legislature, he withdrew his candidacy in favor of his brother Hyrum Smith. The editor of the Nauvoo *Neighbor* wrote:

> We know of no person that would be more qualified to fill this station than General Hyrum Smith (his, William's brother). We are not informed whether the General will accept of the office or not. If he will we don't know of any gentleman in Hancock Co. who would be more competent. General Smith is a man of sterling integrity, deep penetration, and brilliant talents. He is well versed in politics and unchangeable as the everlasting hills. He is a man of probity and virtue, and an unwavering patriot.
>
> If General H. Smith will allow his name to be brought forth we go it for him; and we know from the confidence and respect that is entertained for him as a gentleman and patriot, he will be elected. What say you, General?

Hyrum Smith already had far greater responsibilities than those involved in becoming a state senator. Yet here was an opportunity for him to serve his state, and it was unfortunate that the legislature had so few men of General Smith's caliber. Yet the need for Hyrum to remain at the side of his brother Joseph was more imperative than ever. With William Law, Counselor in the First Presidency, excommunicated, and Sidney Rigdon, the other member of the Presidency, soon to go to Pittsburgh, Penn-

---

[5]*Ibid.*, p. 346-347.

sylvania, to hide his true feelings toward the Prophet, Hyrum was doubly needed as a loyal support on whom the Prophet could lean heavily for both consolation and advice.

The plot on the lives of Hyrum Smith and his brother Joseph was hatching and the forces of mobocracy, neither knowing nor respecting law and order, were closing in. There was little time remaining for Hyrum to accomplish what he had hoped to do.

Chapter XXXII

THE CRISIS

The spring of 1844 was unusual because of so much rain. The first week in May was marked by severe thunderstorms but each time the clouds parted the earth appeared renewed, a verdant landscape of grass, shrubs, and trees. The young fruit trees covered with blossoms seemed to be symbols of heaven-sent blessings and gave hope and cheer to the Saints. Although the good reports from the mission field, especially from England had heartened Hyrum Smith, and a successful conference had been held from April 6 to 9, and new emigrants were coming to Zion, May 1844 was to be a troublesome month for him. As a general in the Nauvoo Legion, it was necessary for him to sit at a court-martial for Major-General Wilson and Colonel R. D. Foster, who had spread slander against the Prophet Joseph by saying that he kept a gang about his house for the purpose of robbing and plundering, and that he got half the plunder. They had also said that General Joseph Smith tried to get Foster to go and kill Governor Boggs.[1]

It was very depressing to Hyrum to see two prominent men such as Wilson and Foster dropped from their high position. However, action had to be taken because these men were part of a conspiracy to destroy Hyrum and Joseph. The courtmartial was held on Thursday and Friday, May 9 and 10. On the tenth the apostates distributed among the people a Prospectus of the Nauvoo *Expositor* which they were going to begin publishing.

Sunday morning, May 12, the Prophet spoke at the meeting. A shower the night before had imparted a special freshness to the atmosphere for the occasion, and the Prophet's remarks were timely. He said, defending his prophetic calling: "False prophets always arise to oppose the true prophets and they will prophesy so very near the truth that they will deceive almost the very

---

[1]Joseph Smith, *op. cit.,* vol. VI, pp. 350-362.

chosen ones." Continuing, he explained the doctrine of the resurrection of the dead and the fulness of the ordinances for both the living and the dead. President Hyrum Smith and Elder Lyman Wight also addressed the Saints.

About this time Hyrum received an anonymous letter threatening his life. Supposedly from Joseph H. Jackson, the missive called upon him to make his peace with God, for he would soon have to die.[2]

The brethren were kept posted on the general conditions at Nauvoo. The threats of the enemy and the apostasy among those of the higher councils did not blind them to the grand objective of Zion and the work of the Lord. A hopeful and optimistic spirit pervaded the letters sent abroad to the missionaries, and through the medium of the *Times and Seasons,* the membership was encouraged.

On Wednesday, May 15, an article written by the Prophet appeared in the above periodical. In it the Saints abroad were told that Nauvoo continued to flourish: New homes were being built, the temple was rapidly progressing, and the Saints continued to flock together from all parts of the continent and Islands of the sea; three shiploads of Saints had arrived from England that spring; of these many had discovered that Joseph Smith, contrary to former opinion was a gentleman and scholar. . .open, generous, and brave.

Speaking of the attitude of his enemies toward himself Joseph said in the article: "A few heartless villains can always be found who are watching for his downfall or death. . . .One or two disaffected individuals have made an attempt to spread dissention, but it is like a tale that is nearly told and will soon be forgotten."

Perhaps Hyrum, Joseph, and others were overly optimistic about conditions in Nauvoo, and more attention should have been paid to thwarting the enemy in such things as their establishment of a rival press in the form of the Nauvoo *Expositor.* The city

---

[2]*Ibid.,* p. 367.

council should have refused them permission to operate in order to prevent the spreading of trouble.

At this time a long letter was received from Elder Orson Hyde, reporting on the progress of the Memorial to Congress about annexing Oregon as a place of refuge for the Saints.[3] John E. Page and Parley P. Pratt had worked with him. Major Semple, senior member of Congress from Illinois, had discouraged any possibility of Joseph Smith or other volunteers being given army status for such a move. Judge Douglas was in favor of the Mormon proposal. He said that he thought the time was ripe for the settlement of Oregon and California and that if he could command the force Mr. Smith could, he would resign his seat in Congress and would be on the march to the country in a month. Elder Hyde had obtained a map of Oregon made by Lieut. J. C. Fremont, who said the distance from Nauvoo to Umpqua and Klamet, Oregon, was seventeen hundred miles from Nauvoo, through Iowa, along the north fork of the Platte River to South Pass and on through the Rocky Mountains.

Elder Hyde attributed to two causes the indifference of Congress toward his proposal: the approaching election and the jealousy among lawmakers of the rising power of Joseph Smith and the Mormons. The temper of the present group in Congress was that if a cause might endanger their political aspirations, it should be left alone, whether right or wrong. Each man, regardless of principle, must protect his office.

Elder Hyde and Elder Pratt had drafted a bill which they had given to the judiciary committee of the Senate, asking for two million dollars for the relief of the Saints expelled from Missouri from 1836-39. By this means the elders hoped to provoke Congress into doing something for the Saints. But the hope was a vain one.

This message from Orson Hyde foreshadowed the trek of the Saints across Iowa, along the north fork of the Platte River to South Pass and on to Salt Lake Valley and the Great Basin,

---

[3]*Ibid.*, pp. 373-376.

which would be undertaken within three short years without government aid.

The culmination of the proposal that Joseph Smith be a candidate for the presidency of the United States came on Friday, May 17, when the state convention met in the assembly room at Nauvoo. Minutes of the meeting reveal that a move was made to draft resolutions, and delegates from the various states of the Union were received by vote. The chairman, the Hon. John S. Reid, addressed the assembly, outlining the early court cases of the Prophet Joseph. He emphasized the character and worthiness of the Prophet for such a high position.[4]

In the meantime, however, the apostates, William Law and Robert D. Foster, were at Carthage stirring up trouble. They had secured a warrant for the Prophet's arrest on a charge of adultery, and the Prophet had remained at home for several days to avoid being arrested and taken to Carthage.

On Thursday evening, May 23, Hyrum Smith came to the Prophet and cautioned him against speaking so freely against his enemies, that is, in such a way as to make his words actionable. Joseph, being highly incensed over the many lies told about him replied that six months would not roll over Hyrum's head before their enemies would swear twelve as palpable lies about Hyrum as they had about himself.[5]

On Saturday, May 25, Joseph was advised by Edward Hunter and William Marks, who as members of the grand jury had just returned from Carthage, that there were two indictments against him: one charging him with false swearing, on the testimony of Joseph H. Jackson and Robert D. Foster; and the other charging him with polygamy, on the testimony of William Law. Francis M. Higbee had sworn so vehemently that Joseph had received stolen property that his testimony was rejected.[6]

After a long talk with Hyrum, Dr. Richards, William Marks, and others, the Prophet decided not to avoid his accusers any longer. Considering his social station and the love of the Saints

---

[4]Ibid., pp. 392-397.
[5]Ibid., p. 403.
[6]Ibid., p. 405.

for him, it was especially difficult for him to be hiding and waiting for circumstances to develop in his favor. No doubt he had
received assurance from the whispering of the Spirit that he
should risk his life by facing his enemies. Hyrum's advice, and
that of others, was to submit to arrest and see the charges
through.

Hyrum Smith was present when the Prophet spoke from
the stand on Sunday, May 26, at 10:00 a.m.. He spoke against
the dissenters at Nauvoo and tried to explain how certain ones
had perjured themselves before the court. His remarks in this
talk were tempered in contrast to those of previous talks, for he
took Hyrum's advice to avoid speaking so freely against his
enemies.

In his remarks Joseph compared his life to that of Paul of
old, saying:

> I, like Paul, have been in perils, and oftener than anyone in this
> generation. As Paul boasted, I have suffered more than Paul did. I should
> be like a fish out of water if I were out of persecution. . . . The Lord has
> constituted me so curiously that I glory in persecution.

The next morning, Monday, May 27, Hyrum and Joseph
with twenty or more of the brethren on horseback left Nauvoo
at eight o'clock for Carthage. They had decided that it was best
to meet his enemies before the circuit court and have the indictments against him investigated.

The news of his going to Carthage preceded him. When
they arrived at the Hamilton Hotel at Carthage, Joseph H. Jackson, Francis M. and Chauncey L. Higbee were in the hotel.
Charles D. Foster had ridden out three or four miles to meet the
company. In his conversation with the Prophet going into
Carthage, he seemed calmer than he had been previously. Soon
after the party arrived in Cathage, Charles Foster took the
Prophet into a private room and in a friendly manner told him
that there was a conspiracy to take his life. He later told some
of the brethren, with tears in his eyes, that there were some persons very determined that Joseph should not leave Carthage

alive. Jackson was seen to load his pistols and was heard to swear that he would have satisfaction of Joseph and Hyrum.

Joseph's counsel was unable to get the plaintiff to produce the particular witness for the trial. Judge Thomas treated Joseph with utmost courtesy, and it was decided to defer the court proceedings until the next term. The sheriff told the Prophet that he could go home where the sheriff would call and take bail at his own convenience. On their return to Nauvoo the brethren were detained by a thunder shower, arriving home about 9:00 p.m.

By June 1, the name of Joseph Smith was becoming widely known as a candidate for the presidency of the United States. Word came of a straw vote cast aboard the *Osprey* (a river steamer) in which Joseph Smith was the favorite candidate by a vote of three to one. One Joel H. Walker volunteered by letter for the proposed western movement to be headed by the Prophet. Word was received at Nauvoo that the Democrats had dropped Van Buren and substituted James K. Polk of Tennessee as their candidate for President of the United States.

At a meeting held the first Saturday in June, Hyrum Smith spoke of the Fosters, Higbees, and Laws and of their past "loyalty" to the Prophet. He said that while Joseph was under arrest during the Missouri persecutions these apostates would have been ridden out on a rail, if he (Hyrum) had not stepped forward to prevent it, because of their oppressing the poor. He also recalled Joseph H. Jackson's coming to Nauvoo and asking him for the hand of his daughter in marriage and the threats which had followed his refusal to give his permission for the marriage.

Hyrum spoke further of conspirators and of the editor of the Warsaw *Signal*, and of the importance of suppressing that spirit which had driven the Saints from Missouri. He recalled a number of occasions when William Law had oppressed the poor and had failed to keep his word. He also mentioned the impropriety of Wilson Law in his association with a seventeen year old orphan girl, a recent immigrant from England.

Hyrum called for the Prospectus of the Nauvoo *Expositor* to be read. This paper, so said the Prospectus, was to be published by the apostate faction every Friday beginning June 7, 1844. The publishers pledged to issue 52 copies to each subscriber. Among other things the Prospectus claimed that because of their particular stations, they had knowledge of the many gross abuses exercised under the "Pretended" authorities of the charter of the city of Nauvoo and by the legislative authorities of said city and of the insupportable oppression of the ministerial powers in carrying out the unjust, illegal, and unconstitutional ordinances of the same. . . . It advocated the repeal of the Nauvoo Charter.

The first issue of the Nauvoo *Expositor* made its appearance, as promised, on Friday, June 7. Its slander was directed primarily against the leaders of the Church, particularly against Joseph Smith, the Prophet. In its scurrilous pages the apostates achieved their designs and now waited for the reaction.

On Sunday, June 9, Hyrum Smith spoke from the stand. The Prophet was not well; his voice had been impaired by much public speaking. At six o'clock in the evening there was a meeting at the Mansion House. Something must be done to meet the crisis. It was decided that the city council should meet the next day and take whatever action seemed necessary.

At ten o'clock the following morning the city council met to investigate the merits of the Nauvoo *Expositor,* and after about seven hours of deliberation declared the *Expositor* a public nuisance. Except for one vote by Councilor Warrington, a non-Mormon, the following resolution was accepted:

Resolved, by the city council of Nauvoo, that the printing-office from whence issues the Nauvoo *Expositor* which may be or exist in said establishment and papers to be removed without delay in such a manner as he shall direct. Signed, George W. Harris, President, protem. W. Richards, Recorder.

The order to the mayor was as follows:

To the Marshal of said city, Greetings.
You are here commanded to destroy the printing press from whence issue the Nauvoo *Expositor* and remove the type of said printing establishment in the street, and burn all the *Expositors* and libelous handbills found

in said establishment, and if resistance is offered to your execution of this order by the owners or others, demolish the house, and if anyone threatens you or the mayor or the officers of the city, arrest them who threaten you and fail not to execute this order without delay, make due return hereon. By order of City Council, Signed, Joseph Smith, Mayor.

The council adjourned at 6:30 p.m. and by 8:00 p.m. the new press of one issue, which was its first and last, was destroyed.

Joseph Smith, mayor, had given the orders to city marshal, John P. Greene, who was assisted by a squadron of the Nauvoo Legion under the direction of acting Major-General Jonathan Dunham. The establishment was forcibly entered, the press, printed paper, and fixtures carried into the street and burned. The posse then returned with the marshal and several hundred citizens to the front of the Mansion House where the mayor addressed them. He assured them of the propriety of the action and that not one hair of their heads should be hurt for it. He stated also that he cared not how many papers were published in the city if they printed the truth but said that he would never submit to having another libelous publication in the city.[7]

Marshal Greene's reply read:

The printing press and type is destroyed . . . according to order on this 10th day of June, 1844, about 8:00 p.m., J. P. Greene, C. M.

Another order was given as follows:

Headquarters, Nauvoo Legion, June 10th, 1844. To Jonathan Dunham, acting Major General of the Nauvoo Legion. You are hereby commanded to hold the Nauvoo Legion in readiness forthwith to execute the city ordinances and especially to remove the printing establishment of the "Nauvoo Expositor," and this is what you are required to do at sight, under the penalty of the laws, provided the Marshall shall require it and need your services. Signed, Joseph Smith, Lieut.-General, Nauvoo Legion.[8]

The brethren were aware that the owners of the new press— the Laws, Fosters, Higbees, and others—had organized a secret society to destroy Joseph and Hyrum Smith and drive the Mor-

_____
[7] *Ibid.*, pp. 429-434.
[8] *Ibid.*, pp. 447-448.

mons from the state. Therefore the council passed an ordinance concerning libels and false statements made for the purpose of exciting the public mind against the chartered privileges, peace, and good order, or slander of any portion of the inhabitants of said city, etc. Such disturbers of the peace should be fined, upon conviction before the mayor or municipal court, the sum of $500, or imprisoned six months, or both at the discretion of said mayor or court. Furthermore, there should be nothing in foregoing ordinances to interfere with the rights of any person to be tried by a jury or to have freedom of speech or liberty of the press, according to the most liberal meaning of the Constitution.

Minutes of the meetings of the city council recorded Friday and Saturday of that week reveal, among other things, how the council discussed the record and characters of the apostate group supporting the *Expositor,* which had appeared over the signatures of William Law, Wilson Law, Charles Ivans, Francis M. Higbee, Chauncey L. Higbee, Robert D. Foster, and Charles A. Foster as publishers.

Counselor Hyrum Smith was in favor of declaring the *Expositor* a nuisance. The best way to be rid of it was to smash the press and pi the type. He spoke of the Warsaw *Signal* and disapprobated its libelous course.

It was suggested that perhaps a stiff fine of three thousand dollars would deter the enemies' efforts in perpetuating the libelous sheet. But, what good would that do, reasoned Hyrum, referring to the mortgages on the property of the proprietors of the *Expositor.* There would be little chance of collecting damages for libels.

Thus the problem of the *Expositor* was met and action taken. The enemy paper evoked instant retaliation which, for the moment, thwarted their plans. Characteristically the Prophet had faced the issue forthrightly.

At 2:00 p.m., Hyrum Smith, with a large group at the courtroom, listened for about two hours to Joseph speak on passing events. The Prophet told the group that he was ready to fight if compelled by the mob to do so, for he would not be in bondage.

He asked those present if they would stand by him, and they all cried "Yes!" At the close of the speech, Hyrum accompanied the Prophet to his home.

David Harvey Redfield reported to Hyrum and Joseph that just prior to the destruction of the *Expositor*, Charles A. Foster, speaking of the new press said, ". . . If they lay their hands upon it or break it, they may date their downfall from that very hour, and in ten days there will not be a Mormon left in Nauvoo."[9]

The destruction of the *Expositor* was like the lighting of a fuse, so rapidly did the news spread. The enemy boldly predicted that great calamity awaited the Prophet and the citizens of Nauvoo.

At 10:00 a.m. Wednesday, June 12, the second day following the destruction of the *Expositor*, an officer arrested Joseph and Hyrum Smith with sixteen others of the city council, on a complaint made by owners of the press upon the oath of Francis M. Higbee. The writ ordered the defendants to be brought before Justice of the Peace Thomas Morrison, at Carthage, or some other Justice of the Peace, to answer the charges and be further dealt with according to law.

After the writ was read Joseph pointed out the clause, ". . . or some other Justice of the Peace," and informed the officer that they would be ready to go before Esquire Johnson or any other Justice of the peace at Nauvoo. To this the officer, David Bettisworth, swore he would be damned, but he would carry them to Carthage. He was asked if he intended to break the law, for he knew the privilege of the prisoners, and they should be permitted to exercise it. Joseph called on all present to witness his offer to go before the nearest Justice of the Peace; Hyrum did the same, and they also called upon those present to witness whether or not the officer broke the law.

The Prophet took out a writ of habeas corpus and signed a petition to the local court giving reasons for his actions. The writ for his arrest was made upon the charge of "riot." Since there was no riot in carrying out the order for the destruction of

---

[9]*Ibid.*, p. 451.

the press, the charge was not valid. In addition, the person who made the charge (Francis M. Higbee), because of his previous conduct and threats against the life of the Prophet and the city of Nauvoo, had shown malice, private pique, and corruption. Such a charge for the arrest of the city council was outright persecution against the Prophet and Hyrum and was nothing more than part of the conspiracy to throw the defendants into the hands of their enemies.

The petition of the Prophet was granted by the Municipal Court of Nauvoo, and at 5:00 p.m. the same day the defendants were acquitted of the charge and released.

On Thursday, June 13, some 300 citizens met at Carthage to organize and draw up resolutions to avenge the destruction of the *Expositor* at Nauvoo. The charges were very inflammatory. It was stated that the act of destruction was violent and carried out in a tumultuous manner. Specific charges were made against Hyrum Smith as follows:

And whereas Hyrum Smith did, in the presence of the City Council and the citizens of Nauvoo, offer a reward for the destruction of the printing press and materials of the *Warsaw Signal*, a newspaper also opposed to his interests.

And whereas the liberty of the press is one of the cardinal principles of our government, firmly guaranteed by the several constitutions of the states, as well as the United States;

And whereas, Hyrum Smith has within the last week publicly threatened the life of one of our valued citizens, Thomas C. Sharp, the editor of the *Signal*; . . .

Resolved, that the time in our opinion has arrived when the adherents should then be demanded at their hands; and, if not surrendered, a war of extermination should be waged to the entire destruction, if necessary, for our protection of his adherents. And we hereby recommend this resolution to the consideration of the several townships, to the Mass Convention to be held at Carthage, hereby pledging ourselves to aid to the utmost the complete consummation of the object in view, that we may be utterly relieved of the alarm, anxiety, and trouble to which we are now subjected. . . .[10]

---

[10]*Ibid.*, pp. 463-464.

The resolutions ended by advising the different precincts to hold themselves in readiness to obey the officer in possession of the writs whenever called upon, in summoning the posse, and were signed by John Knox, President, John Doty, Lewis F. Evans, Vice-Presidents, and W. Y. Head, Secretary.

To counteract the above proceedings the Prophet wrote a letter to Governor Ford stating briefly the details of the *Expositor* affair, cautioning him against believing lying reports in circulation by the enemy "that there had been a mob at Nauvoo, and blood and thunder, and swearing that two men were killed."

This communique was followed by one from John M. Bernhisel, confirming the accuracy of the Prophet's report and also containing Mr. Bernhisel's appraisal of the Prophet. John M. Bernhisel had been a boarder in General Smith's family for over nine months. He had found Joseph Smith to be a man of strong mental powers and possessed with much energy and decision of character, great penetration and a profound knowledge of human nature. He found Joseph to be a man of calm judgment, enlarged views, and eminently distinguished by his love of justice. Mr. Bernhisel said that he was kind and obliging, generous and benevolent, sociable and cheerful, and was possessed of a mind of a contemplative and reflective character. He stated further that Joseph was honest, frank, fearless, and independent, and as free from dissimulation as any man to be found.

Still speaking of the Prophet, he wrote:

> But it is in the gentle charities of domestic life, as the tender and affectionate husband and parent; the warm and sympathetic friend, that the prominent traits of his character are revealed, and his heart is felt to be keenly alive to the kindest and softest emotions of which human nature is susceptible; and I feel assured that his family and friends formed one of the greatest consolations to him when the vials of wrath were poured upon his head, while his footsteps were pursued by malice and envy, and reproach and slander were strewn in his path as well as numerous and cruel persecutions, and severe and protracted sufferings in chains and loathsome prisons, for worshipping God according to the dictates of his own conscience.

He is a true lover of his country and a bright and shining example of integrity and moral excellence in all the relations of life. As a religious teacher, as well as a man, he is greatly beloved by his people. It is almost superfluous to add that the numerous ridiculous and scandalous reports in circulation respecting him have not the least foundation in truth. . . .

Another letter to Governor Ford was written by J. R. Wakefield, M.D., a stranger in Nauvoo, a guest for several weeks at the Mansion House. Speaking of the *Expositor* he said,

. . . It was a nuisance of the worst character and the authorities acted perfectly proper in destroying it, and in accomplishing the act there was no noise, tumult or riot. Furthermore, having remained for a few weeks at General Smith's house, I think it my duty to state that I have seen nothing in his deportment but what is correct in all his domestic relations, being a kind husband and an affectionate father, and all his affairs, both domestic and official, have not only been free of censure, but praiseworthy and ought to be initiated by every one desirous of order and peace.[11]

The fourth such letter, dated the same day, June 14, was sent by Sidney Rigdon in the hands of Samuel James. For some time the postal service had failed to make delivery of important messages because of their being intercepted by the enemy. In his letter Sidney Rigdon appealed to Governor Ford as an intelligent man. The trouble in Nauvoo, he said, was fomented by a number of citizens in Nauvoo. These individuals had used the Warsaw *Signal* to communicate their difficulties to the world. He assured the governor that there had been no violence or riot in Nauvoo.[12]

At this time Sidney Rigdon was not a member of the city council or connected in any way with the municipality of Nauvoo; hence his name was not listed among those who were arrested. He was careful to point out his status in the trouble by writing: ". . . In consequence of the difficulties now existing in this county, difficulties in which I have no concern"; and, at the end of the letter, a smilar expression in these words: "I send this to your Excellency as confidential as I wish not to take any part in the affair or be known in it.

---

[11]*Ibid.*, p. 469.
[12]*Ibid.*, pp. 464-471.

However, Sidney Rigdon gave the governor some timely advice in these words:

> The citizens of this county who do not reside in Nauvoo and those of other counties have indeed no interest of a personal kind at stake in this matter. There are no persons disturbing them nor going to do so, and this great excitement does savor of something else to me than a regard for the laws. Why not let the parties, as in all other cases of the kind, settle their difficulties as the laws of the country in such cases have provided.
>
> Have the citizens of Nauvoo ever interfered with cases of difficulty existing in other parts of the county, held public meetings to inflame the public mind in favor of one party and prejudice it against the other party? Most assuredly they have not. Why then must the citizens of this place be scourged with such attempts?
>
> If the citizens of Hancock want the supremacy of the laws maintained, let these tumultous assemblies disperse and let the civil officers, if resisted, do as in other cases, call for aid instead of assembling in advance and then call for persons to be brought into their midst as prisoners amidst threats and insults.[13]

By Saturday reports were received at Nauvoo that Colonel Levi Williams had demanded the surrender of all arms belonging to the Mormons in the vicinity of Lima. Two brethren from Lima visited the Prophet and were told that when they gave up their arms they should give up their lives with them as dearly as possible.

Rumors reached Nauvoo that a company was training at Carthage and that several boxes of arms had arrived from Warsaw and Quincy. There was to be a meeting at Carthage the middle of the following week.

The primary concern of the brethren was no longer the national political scene but to assure themselves and the Saints protection against the threats of their enemies at home. The Governor was in a position to take action against the rising mob spirit, but would he do so? Should Hyrum, Joseph, and others go to Carthage for a trial on charges growing out of the *Expositor* affair? The events of the following week brought the answer.

---

[13]*Ibid.*, 467-471.

Chapter XXXIII

HYRUM SMITH'S DECISION

The reverberations of the destruction of the Nauvoo *Expositor* echoed from town to town, from village to village, getting louder and louder and extending even to Missouri. The caldron of hate against Joseph Smith and Hyrum bubbled over in violent demonstrations.

The problem at the moment was to neutralize the supercharged atmosphere and restore a semblance of peace and understanding. Judge Jesse B. Thomas came to Nauvoo and advised Joseph Smith to go to some Justice of the Peace and have an examination of the charges specified in the writ from Justice Morrison of Carthage. Judge Thomas said that an acquittal on these charges would allay all the excitement, answer the law, and cut off all legal pretext for a mob.

This suggestion was complied with. The Prophet and Hyrum, with others previously arrested, were again arrested on the same charges on a complaint made by W. G. Ware. At 2:00 p.m. Monday, June 17, a trial was held before Justice Wells, and after a close examination they were discharged. But this court action did little to alleviate the tension.

Thomas C. Wilson brought word that fifteen hundred Missourians would assemble at Warsaw and from there would go to Carthage. Here they would be met by a company of Quincy Greys. They then would round up all Latter-day Saints in the vicinity and give them the choice of either denying Joseph Smith or leaving their homes for Nauvoo. Then on Thursday next the military body would proceed to Nauvoo and demand Joseph and Hyrum Smith and the city council of said city, and if Joseph and Hyrum Smith and the city council were not turned over to that body it would blow up the city and exterminate all the inhabitants of said city.

Colonel Isaac Morley sent a letter to the Prophet asking what to do if the mob carried out their threats. He was told to retain his arms and use them against the enemy in defense of the Saints unless prudence dictated the retreat of his troops to Nauvoo. In the event that mob militia came upon Nauvoo, he was told to do all he could do to thwart them by coming before them or following in the rear and being ready to cooperate with the main body of the Legion.

Forty gentlemen from Madison, up the river, came to Nauvoo to inquire into the difficulties. The Prophet met them at the Masonic Hall and gave them the desired information they asked for. Dr. Richards, the city recorder, read to them the minutes of the Council declaring the Nauvoo *Expositor* a nuisance, and the gentlemen expressed themselves satisfied.

Following the interview, Joseph addressed several thousand of the brethren, advising them to make no disturbance. He suggested that they organize and send a delegation of two or three to all the surrounding towns and villages to explain the present trouble and show people that all was peace at Nauvoo and that there was no cause for any mobs.

On this same day, Sunday, June 16, the Prophet wrote the governor of Illinois, inviting him to come with his staff on a visit to Nauvoo and investigate the whole matter without delay. He also wrote a proclamation explaining that no law had been violated in the destruction of the *Expositor*, that the city of Nauvoo was infested with a set of blacklegs, counterfeiters, and debauchers, and that the proprietors of the *Expositor* were of that class. He explained that the peace and happiness of Nauvoo demanded the destruction of the *Expositor* press, the virtue of their wives, and daughters demanded it, and their consciences demanded it as conservators of public peace.[1]

By this time the anxiety of the brethren had grown to such an extent that they felt their only recourse was to recall the apostles and missionaries abroad and prepare to defend Nauvoo by force of arms.

---

[1]Joseph Smith, *op. cit.*, vol. VI, pp. 473-481.

On Monday, June 17, steps were taken to alert the police of Nauvoo and the legion to be in readiness in case of an attack. The Prophet, as Lieut. General of the Nauvoo Legion, ordered Col. A. P. Rockwood to call out his (Joseph's) guard and staff immediately to Joseph's headquarters. He also ordered the legion to parade the next day. He asked his clerk, Thomas Bullock to remain at the Masonic Hall to hear reports as they came in and make affidavits of the same.

A refutation of Hyrum Smith's purported threat against the editor of the Warsaw *Signal* in the form of a public announcement was published in the *Neighbor* as follows:

> To the Public: We, whose names are undersigned, having seen in the *Warsaw Signal,* containing the proceedings of a meeting held at Carthage on the 13th instant, many statements calculated to arouse the indignation and wrath of the people against the citizens of Nauvoo, do certify that Hyrum Smith did not make any threats, nor offer any reward against the *Signal* or its editor in the City Council. Signed—John Taylor, Aaron Johnson, William Boles, George P. Styles, W. W. Phelps, Alanson Ripley, Orson Spencer, John P. Greene, George W. Harris, Phinehas Richards, Thomas Smith, Edward Hunter, Moses F. Clark, Levi Richards, Addison Everett, and Philip B. Lewis. Dated, Nauvoo, June 17th, 1844.[2]

The Prophet's clerks made a careful recording of events as they occurred. No detail of news, reports, or action of the city council passed without its being recorded. The Prophet Joseph was aware of the great importance of written testimony of all activities, for such would be used as a basis to judge the participants.

The Nauvoo *Neighbor* published an editorial in its June 17 issue which read, in part:

> . . . So does the simple truth calm the feelings of the irritated, and so we proceed to give the proceedings of the City Council relating to the removal of the *Nauvoo Expositor* as a nuisance. We have been robbed, mobbed, and plundered with impunity some two or three times and as every heart is more apt to know its own sorrows, the people of Nauvoo had ample reason, when such characters as the proprietors and abettors

---

[2]*Ibid.*, p. 495.

of the *Nauvoo Expositor* proved to be before the City Council, to be alarmed for their safety.

The men who got up the press were constantly engaged in resisting the authority or threatening something. If they were fined an appeal was taken, but the slander went on and when the paper came, the course and plan to destroy the press was carried out. The destruction of the city charter and the ruin of the Saints was the all-commanding topic.

Our lives, our city, our charter, and our characters are just as sacred, just as dear, and just as good as other peoples, and while no friendly arm has been extended from the demolition of our press in Jackson County, Missouri, without law, to this present day the City Council with all the laws of nuisance from Blackstone down to the Springfield Charter, knowing that if they exceeded the law of the land, a higher court could regulate the proceedings, abated the *Nauvoo Expositor*. . . .

All persons otherwise, who, without recourse to justice, mercy, or humanity, come out with inflammatory publication, destructive resolutions, or more especially extermination, show a want of feeling, a want of respect and a want of religious toleration that honorable men will deprecate among Americans as they would the pestilence, famine, or horrors of war. It cannot be that the people are so lost to virtue as to coolly go to murdering men, women and children. No, candor and common sense forbid it![3]

The above editorial reflects the point of view of the citizens of Nauvoo toward the enemy. There had been no protest of the old citizens against the Jackson County, Missouri, mob when they destroyed the press in 1833. One may ask why then should such an outburst be made against the destruction of the *Expositor* press? The Nauvoo paper, in comparison, was justly destroyed.

The parading of the legion was held on schedule. Tuesday morning at nine o'clock. A declaration of martial law was made by the mayor, Joseph Smith. This meant that the officers of the Nauvoo Legion, the police, and all others would strictly see that no persons or property pass in or out of the city without due orders.

At 2:00 p.m. the legion was drawn up in front the Mansion House. The Prophet and Hyrum were in full uniform, and with others occupied the top frame of a building across from the Mansion House. The Prophet spoke for an hour and a half.

---

[3]*Ibid.*, p. 496.

This was a memorable occasion. The Prophet, Hyrum, and the loyal brethren and Saints were present to hear and ponder every word. Judge Phelps read the Warsaw *Signal* extra of the 17th, wherein all the "old citizens" were called to assist the mob in exterminating the leaders of the Saints and driving away the people.

The occasion with the setting was like a great stage. The cause that had brought the multitude together seemed to climax the careers of two mighty prophets and seers of modern time. Like the great leaders he was, Joseph Smith was revealed to his beloved people in this hour of crisis, dignfied, fearless, a great citizen of deep feeling. He was a man raised up by God to do a certain work, and he had not failed. Standing like a granite pillar before the traditional forces of evil, he rose to heights of eloquence and inspiration. Hyrum by his side, was but a little older prototype of his younger brother. He too bore the Godly stamp of nobility. This was their finest hour; they had fulfilled their mission, and this occasion was the last time they would appear before the Saints.

The Prophet's words to his people were in part:

It is thought by some that our enemies would be satisfied with my destruction, but I tell you as soon as they have shed my blood they will thirst for the blood of every man in whose heart dwells a single spark of the spirit of the fullness of the Gospel. The opposition of these men is moved by the spirit of the adversary of all righteousness. It is not only to destroy me, but every man and woman who dares believe the doctrines that God hath inspired me to teach this generation.

The Prophet declared the innocence of the Saints and pointed out the perfidy of the law enforcement agency in pursuing a course contrary to the constitution. "It is better," he said, "to die defending your liberties than to live in a state of oppression, cruelty, and anarchy." In a solemn voice he continued: "Come all ye lovers of liberty, break the oppressor's rod, loose the iron grasp of mobocracy and bring to condign punishment all those who trample under foot the glorious Constitution and the people's rights." (Drawing his sword and presenting it to heaven he said):

I call God and angels to witness that I have unsheathed my sword with a firm and unalterable determination that this people shall have their legal rights and be protected from mob violence or my blood shall be spilt upon the ground like water and my body consigned to the silent tomb. While I live, I will never tamely submit to the domination of cursed mobocracy. I would welcome death rather than submit to this oppression, agitation, annoyance, confusion, and alarm upon alarm, any longer. . . .[4]

Following the assembly the Prophet, with Hyrum and his staff, took command and riding in front of the legion, marched up Main Street, and returned to their former parade ground. The number on parade was very large, considering the number of elders who had been sent upon missions.

That afternoon and evening, nine messengers arrived with letters and affidavits to the Prophet. One report said that Governor Ford was not too cordial with the mob militia leaders when they called on him. They damned Governor Ford for being as bad as old Joe Smith. Apparently the governor had advised them against marching on Nauvoo.

On Wednesday, June 19, plans for complete mobilization of the legion arrived from Green Plains, and at one o'clock that day a company of volunteers arrived from Iowa. These too Joseph escorted to the parade grounds.

During the afternoon orders were given to General Dunham to have a picket-guard under Col. Markham posted on all roads leading out of the city. An inner guard under Major Jesse P. Harmon was posted in all the streets and alleys in the city and on the river bank. Orders were given to have all powder and lead in the city secured and to see that all arms were in use and that all unclaimed arms be put into the hands of those that could use them.

---

[4]Ibid., p. 499.

It was learned that there were two hundred armed men at Rocky Run precinct, two hundred at Warsaw, two hundred in Missouri, the whole receiving constant additions.

On the twentieth of June, Joseph Smith, with his staff and Major General Dunham, went to the prairie to view the ground and select a location to meet the mob so that the city would be protected. At 11:00 a.m. Joseph reviewed the legion facing the Mansion House and went to parade on the banks of the river. Later in the day an affidavit was received that arms were being sent by steamboat from St. Louis, Missouri, to Warsaw, Illinois, and that word had been sent to St. Louis that if Warsaw needed five hundred to send word by the Steamer *Boreas*, and the men would be sent.

The same day Joseph Smith sent a letter to John Tyler, President of the United States, asking for protection guaranteed by the Constitution in case of "insurrection and rebellion" and to save the innocent and oppressed from such horrid persecution.

The Ramus Company belonging to the Legion arrived at Nauvoo. Their captain, Almon W. Babbitt, had refused to comply with the orders to bring his company to Nauvoo, but Uncle John Smith had assured the men that they would go and return in safety. Whereupon the company put the command on Uriah H. Yoger who accompanied them to Nauvoo. Many who were poorly shod were supplied by the quartermaster.

The Prophet instructed Willard Richards to write a letter to General James Arlington Bennett of New York in answer to one he had received from him the preceding April. The letter apprised the general of the local situation and temper of the people from Illinois to Missouri, and asked him if he would bring volunteers to assist the Saints. He was told that if he failed to help in this crisis his liberties would be next to go and where would it all end?[5]

The threats and rumours flooded in upon Joseph and Hyrum. There seemed to be no one they could appeal to who would come

[5]*Ibid.*, pp. 508-518.

to their aid. There were few men who appraised the Prophet and the Saints in a favorable light.

If there were others ready to help, they failed to express themselves or to lift a hand to support justice, law, and order. It was becoming more apparent that the survival of this downtrodden, maligned, persecuted, and hated people would depend upon themselves and their God.

Conditions now had so far deteriorated that the Prophet himself wrote calling the twelve home. It is assumed that Hyrum's letter to the twelve and the missionaries abroad was never sent. Perhaps the uncertainty of the mails was the reason, for at this time the postal system to Nauvoo was so unreliable that no letters were received and none sent, because of the enemy's interference.

The danger of mob action against Nauvoo was very real. The Prophet called on Theodore Turley to prepare artillery. Brother Turley agreed and inquired if he should also repair the small arms that were out of order. The Prophet in confidence then told him that there would not be a gun fired on their part during the fuss.

Hyrum Smith, with others at the Mansion House that evening, deliberated carefully what he should do. Joseph, writing of the possible escape of Hyrum, expressed himself:

> I advised my brother Hyrum to take his family on the next steamboat and go to Cincinnati. Hyrum replied, "Joseph, I can't leave you." Whereupon I said to the company present, "I wish I could get Hyrum out of the way, so that he may live to avenge my blood, and I will stay with you to see it out."[6]

Friday, June 21, at 10:00 a.m. the Prophet reviewed the Nauvoo Legion, now on active duty and ready to repel any invasion. In the afternoon a letter was received by special messenger from Governor Ford, who had arrived at Carthage. He requested Joseph Smith to send representatives to Carthage to

---

[6]*Ibid.*, p. 520.

brief him on the Mormon version of the trouble in order for him to give an impartial judgment of the whole affair.

At 4:00 p.m. the city council met and appointed Dr. J. M. Bernhisel, Dr. Willard Richards, and Counselor John Taylor to go to Carthage. A number of affidavits were read. On Saturday, June 22, the Prophet sent a letter and affidavits to Governor Ford inviting him to come to Nauvoo and personally investigate the whole matter. He expressed their unwillingness to come to Carthage because of the great danger of their being murdered by the mob. The letter was taken by Lucien Woodworth who replaced Dr. Richards as a delegate to the governor.

In the afternoon the Prophet requested General Dunham to take the regiment of the 2nd cohort the next day and use entrenching tools and work several hours to improve their position in case of an attack.

Lyman H. Calkin, in a sworn statement, revealed that the death of Hyrum Smith was desired by one William Nesbit, on board the steamboat Ohio from St. Louis to Nauvoo. Calkin swore that Nesbit had said he would go to Nauvoo and with pistols kill Hyrum himself. When asked if he would not be afraid to kill Hyrum in cold blood, he replied, "No, I would not; I would do it in a moment if I could get an opportunity." The following day Mr. Calkin saw Nesbit in the crowd and cautioned Richard Brazier to keep an eye on him, for he had sworn to wash his hands in Joseph and Hyrum's blood.[7]

Rumors came in of the mob moving about on the road from Carthage to Nauvoo and of the shooting of travelers. The three delegates arrived at the governor's quarters in Carthage and found him surrounded by fifteen or twenty men, among whom, according to John Taylor, were some of the worst, vilest, and most unprincipled men in creation. There were the Laws, Higbees, Jackson, and others. The governor treated the delegates very rudely. The communications of the Prophet were read to the governor in the presence of these mobocrats who interrupted the reader at almost every line with, "That's

7Ibid., pp. 528-532.

a damned lie!" and "That's a G—d—d lie!" The governor made no attempt to quiet them. It would appear that Governor Ford was completely under the mob spirit and that he had ordered the entire mob into service. In the governor's letter to the Prophet he charged him with violations of law and order based on falsehoods.

The governor kept the delegates waiting five or six hours to write his reply. In it he accused the mayor and city council of violating the Constitution by ordering the destruction of the *Expositor.* The writ of habeas corpus was improperly resorted to before the court with the executive and judicial branches of government combined. Also, martial law had been placed in force at Nauvoo and persons imprisoned unlawfully. The governor cited a similar act in France which caused a king to lose his throne, and said no such act had ever been committed in any of the states of America or its territories—that no civilized country can tolerate such conduct, etc. He ended the letter by a threat to use military forces if necessary to bring any one guilty from Nauvoo. It had been rumored that the Mormons had committed depredations on cattle and property. Furthermore, he would see that anyone summoned to Carthage for trial or as witness would be guaranteed safety.

The same day the Prophet wrote a lengthy reply to Governor Ford to counteract the charges. He answered the governor explaining the reasons for their actions. They had pleaded a habeas corpus only as a last resort to save them from being thrown into the power of the mobocrats who were threatening them with death. The Nauvoo Charter gave them this right, the same as the Springfield Charter, so that if the act declaring the press a nuisance was unconstitutional, then they couldn't see why the charter itself was not unconstitutional.

Continuing, the Prophet explained that martial law had been declared only to protect their lives. No property was seized or person imprisoned for the violation of the peace. He did not believe in the "union of legislative and judician power," and they did not understand such to be the case in this instance.

He stated also that to come to Carthage for a second trial on the same issue and be put twice in jeopardy of life for the same offense was contrary to the Constitution. However, notwithstanding this, they would not hesitate to stand another trial according to the governor's wish were it not that they were confident that their lives would be in danger. Joseph continued:

We dare not come. Writs we are assured are issued against us in various parts of the country. For what? To drag us from place to place, (as was the case in Missouri) from court to court, across the creeks and prairies, till some bloodthirsty villain could find his opportunity to shoot us. We dare not come, though your Excellency promises protection. Yet, at times, you have expressed fears that you could not control the mob, in which case we are left to the mercy of the merciless. Sir, we dare not come, for our lives would be in danger, and we are guilty of no crime.

You say, "It will be against orders to be accompanied by others if we come to trial." This we have been obliged to act upon in Missouri, and when our witnesses were sent for by the court, (as your honor promised to do) they were thrust into prison and we left without witnesses. Sir, you must not blame us, for "a burnt child dreads the fire." Although your Excellency might be well disposed in the matter, the appearance of the mob forbids our coming. We dare not do it.

The Prophet continued by saying that the Saints had been advised by legal and highminded gentlemen from abroad to lay their grievances before the Federal Government. The appearance of things as they now stood was not only treasonable against the Saints, but also against the state of Missouri. The mass meetings of the county declared utter extermination of the Mormons, and the Legion was not called out until complaints were made to the Mayor; the citizens were afraid of their lives, etc.

The Prophet's final appeal was:

We shall leave the city forthwith to lay the facts before the General Government; . . . We implore your Excellency to cause our helpless women and children to be protected from mob violence and let not the blood of innocence cry to heaven against you. We again say, if anything wrong has been done on our part, and we know of nothing, we will make all things right if the Government will give us the opportunity. Disperse the mob and secure to us our Constitutional privileges that our lives may not be endangered when on trial.[8]

The position and course of the Prophet was inspired by past treatment before the courts, by the mistreatment of witnesses, and the foul imprisonments from one filthy prison to another without recourse to legal procedures to defend themselves. The pattern of the enemy was all too familiar.

On Saturday afternoon, June 22, the Prophet called Hyrum, Dr. Richards, John Taylor, and John M. Bernhisel to his home to discuss the advisability of going to Washington to lay the matter before President Tyler. Before a decision was made, however, they were interrupted by the visit of two gentlemen, one, a son of John C. Calhoun who was anxious to meet the Prophet. Shortly after the interruption the council meeting was resumed, but the project of laying the matter before President Tyler was abandoned. Joseph had received an inspiration to go west with the assurance that if he did all would be well.[9]

About 7:00 p.m. the Prophet requested Reynolds Cahoon and Alpheus Cutler to stand guard at the Mansion and not admit any strangers to the house. At sundown he asked O. P. Rockwell to go with him on a short journey and Rockwell replied that he would.

A decision had to be made immediately on what course to follow. Time was too short to appeal to the President of the United States. Soon after dusk, Joseph called Hyrum, Willard Richards, John Taylor, William W. Phelps, A. C. Hodge, John L. Butler, Alpheus Cutler, William Marks, and others to come to his home. The men retired to the upper room and according to Brother Hodge, the following conversation occurred:

"Brethren, here is a letter from the Governor which I wish to have read." After it was read through Joseph remarked, "There is no mercy, no mercy here." Hyrum said, "No, just

[8]*Ibid.*, pp. 533-541.
[9]*Life of John Taylor*, p. 125.

as sure as we fall into their hands we are dead men." Joseph answered, "Yes," and then asked, "What shall we do, Brother Hyrum?" Hyrum replied, "I don't know." All at once Joseph's countenance brightened up and he said, "The way is open. It is clear to my mind what to do. All they want is Hyrum and myself; then tell everybody to go about their business and not to collect in groups, but to scatter about. There is no doubt they will come here and search for us. Let them search; they will not harm you in person or property and not even a hair of your heads. We will cross the river tonight and go away to the West!" He made a move to go out of the house to cross the river. When out of the house he told Butler and Hodge to take the *Maid of Iowa* (in charge of Repsher) get it to the upper landing, and put his and Hyrum's families and effects upon her; then go down the Mississippi and up the Ohio River to Portsmouth where they should hear from them. He then took Hodge by the hand and said, "Now, Brother Hodge, let what will come, don't deny the faith and all will be well."[10]

The following was the last direct quotation of the Prophet:

I told Stephen Markham that if I and Hyrum were ever taken again we should be massacred, or I was not a Prophet of God. I want Hyrum to live to avenge my blood, but he is determined not to leave me.[11]

Hyrum and Joseph gathered their most trusted friends around them hoping for support in their last-minute decision. The leaders of this latter-day movement always sought advice. Their desire was ever to proceed with a spirit of unity based on

---

[10]Joseph Smith, *op. cit.*, vol. VI, pp. 545-546.

[11]*Ibid.*, p. 546. Here the direct quotations of Joseph end. Concerning the Prophet's desire to have Hyrum live and the purpose of it Mr. Edward Tullidge in his *Life of Joseph and the Prophet* gives a different version: "*I want Hyrum to live to lead the Church, but he is determined not to leave me.*" (Tullidge p. 491.) On what authority Mr. Tullidge makes the change is not known, but there is evidence in addition to this statement that the Prophet did desire to have Hyrum Smith succeed him in the Presidency of the Church, and even that he "ordained" him to take that place. At the October conference following the martyrdom of the brothers, President Brigham Young said: "*Did Joseph ordain any man to take his place? He did. Who was it? It was Hyrum. But Hyrum fell a martyr before Joseph did.*" (*Times and Seasons*, vol. V., p. 683).

the full confidence and support of the people. As leaders they felt they must have the love, respect, confidence, and support of the Saints.

Hyrum concurred in the Prophet's decision to go West, and in the other emergency measures to help resolve the crisis. There had been no division of opinion on major issues. The Patriarch had consented to the action taken against the *Expositor*, to the declaration of martial law in Nauvoo, to the calling home of the apostles and to the decision to resist going to Carthage for trial. And it certainly was not Hyrum's intention to foresake his brother now. The die had been cast. It was either life or death for both. There was no turning back and no compromise.

CHAPTER XXXIV

HYRUM SMITH AT CARTHAGE

By late June, 1844, the only way open to Hyrum and Joseph Smith to avoid massacre was to flee to the Rocky Mountains. The movement that had begun fourteen years before had no earthly sponsor. There had been no precedent established. There was no mother institution on which to lean during its formative period.

This vigorous new religion had tremendous powers of growth and rejuvenation. Whenever an attempt was made to stifle or suppress the movement by apostasy from within the ranks or by mob violence, it had modified its position and maneuvered in such a way as to keep growing. Each crisis had thus far been surmounted successfully and been followed by an upsurge in activity and growth. This "unorthodox" religion was a phenomenon no one could explain. Even the few who looked upon it with favor feared that sometime, somewhere, if it continued, it would bring trouble.

The Nauvoo Charter had made of Nauvoo a virtual state within a state, with courts, a military establishment, municipal government, educational institutions and church-controlled business in real estate. Already their capital city, Nauvoo, was outstripping other centers in population, commerce, manufacturing, religion, and social advancement. What at first appeared to be a harmless, suffering, outcast people, greatly wronged, now wore a coat of a different color. What the Mormons offered in the way of increased economic aid in paying indebtedness was soon replaced by a growing desire to get rid of this "menace" which they thought would overrun and absorb them.

Thus it was that the closing events in the life of Hyrum Smith were crowding in upon him in rapid succession. The establishment of the Church had resulted from a great revelation. Hyrum, as well as Joseph, had been designated prophet, seer, and revelator. He was a second witness to a divine plan, and the drama of his life was hastening to an inevitable climax. In this hour of crisis his role was accentuated by the decisions he was forced to make, but a pattern of comradeship had developed between him and Joseph. Here was a meeting of minds which swept aside the dread loneliness of choosing between alternatives in a crisis. The reaction of the Patriarch became a sounding board, so to speak, for the President of the Church and between the two a solution was always forthcoming regardless of the difficulty of the problem.

Thus, at the beginning of the fourth week in June, 1844, Hyrum Smith prepared to by-pass his enemies and go away with Joseph in order to preserve their lives and calm the fury of the gathering mobs. The Prophet's historians record the events of Saturday, June 22, 1844, as follows:

On this day, about 9 p.m., Hyrum Smith came out of the Mansion House and gave his hand to Reynolds Cahoon, at the same time saying, "A company of men are seeking to kill my brother Joseph and the Lord has warned him to flee to the Rocky Mountains to save his life. Good-by, brother Cahoon, we shall see you again." In a few minutes afterwards Joseph came from his family. His tears were flowing fast. He held a handkerchief to his face and followed after Brother Hyrum without uttering a word.[1]

---

[1]Mercy Rachel Thompson described Hyrum's farewell. . . . A few days after this he (Joseph) called at his brother Hyrum's to take leave of the family previous to their crossing the Mississippi River, intended to go west to the Rocky Mountains to seek out, if possible, a place of peace and safety for the Saints. His parting words to my sister Mary, as she wept at their going, were these: Sister Mary, don't feel bad, the Lord will take care of you, and He will deliver us, but I do not know how. The two brothers then started to cross the river, not knowing whether they would ever see their home again or not. But on account of the feelings expressed by some of the brethren, who should have been their truest friends, and by their urgent request, sent after them, the brothers returned to Nauvoo the following day. Watching from a chamber window I saw them being rowed in a skiff across the river until they landed, and walked up the river bank to Hyrum's house, where they entered, Joseph seating himself, while Hyrum made some changes in his clothing, when they went on to the Mansion. Although I did not know that the brothers had returned home to be taken as 'lambs to the slaughter', my feelings were indescribable, and the very air seemed burdened with sorrowful forebodings. The awful scene at Carthage followed in a few days, and here all men must draw the veil, for until all the truth concerning these good men, and this black deed of their murderous foes, can be told and understood the history of this time will not be written. But the day will come when God will speak, and the martyrs and their history will be made known." — Mercy R. Thompson — *The Instructor*, 27:400.

Between 9 and 10 p.m. Hyrum, Joseph, and Willard Richards while waiting on the bank of the river for a skiff, sent for William W. Phelps and instructed him to take their families to Cincinnati by the second steamboat, arriving at Nauvoo. When he arrived there he commenced petitioning the President of the United States and Congress for redress of grievances to see whether they would grant the Church liberty and equal rights. Joseph then said: "Go to our wives and tell them what we've concluded to do and learn their feelings on the subject; tell Emma you will be ready to start by the second steamboat, and she has sufficient money wherewith to pay the expenses. If you ascertain by tomorrow morning that there is anything wrong, come over the river to Montrose to the house of Captain John Killien, and there you will learn where we are.

About midnight, Hyrum, Joseph, and Dr. Richards called for Orrin P. Rockwell at his lodgings, and all went up the river bank until they found Aaron Johnson's boat which they got into and started about 2 a.m. to cross the Mississippi River. Rockwell rowed the skiff which was very leaky, so that it kept Hyrum and Joseph and the doctor busy bailing out the water with their boots and shoes to prevent it from sinking.

Sunday 23rd at daybreak, they arrived on the Iowa side of the river. They sent Orrin P. Rockwell back to Nauvoo with instructions to return the next night with horses for Hyrum and Joseph, and to pass them over the river in the night secretly, so that they might be ready to start for the Great Basin in the Rocky Mountains.

Hyrum, Joseph, and Dr. Richards walked up to Captain John Killien's house where they arrived at sunrise, but he being not at home, they went thence to Brother William Jordon's. About 9 a.m., Dr. Bernhisel came over the river to visit Joseph. Also Reynolds Cahoon who made some explanations respecting Governor Ford's letter.

Early in the morning a posse arrived in Nauvoo to arrest the Prophet, but as they did not find him, they started back to Carthage immediately, leaving one man by the name of Yates behind them who said to some of the brethren that Governor Ford designed that if Joseph and Hyrum were not given up, he would send his troops and guard the city until they were found if it took three years to do it.

At 1 p.m. Emma sent over Orrin P. Rockwell, requesting him to entreat Joseph to come back. Reynolds Cahoon accompanied him with a letter which Emma had written to the same affect, and she insisted that Cahoon should persuade Joseph to come back and give himself up. When they went over they found Hyrum, Joseph, and Willard in a room by themselves, having flour and other provisions on the floor ready for packing.

Reynolds Cahoon informed Joseph what the troops intended to do, and urged upon him to give himself up inasmuch as the governor had pledged his faith and the faith of the state to protect him while he underwent a legal and fair trial. Reynolds Cahoon, Lorenzo D. Wasson, and Hiram Kimball accused Joseph of cowardice for wishing to leave the people, adding that their property would be destroyed and they be left without house or home. Like the fable, when the wolves came, the shepherd ran from the flock, and left the sheep to be devoured. To which Joseph replied, "If my life is of no value to my friends, it is of none to myself."

Joseph said to Rockwell, "What shall I do?" Rockwell replied, "You are the oldest and ought to know best; as you make your bed, I will lie with you." Joseph then turned to Hyrum, "You are the oldest, what shall we do?" Hyrum said, "Let us go back and give ourselves up and see the thing out." After studying a few moments, Joseph said, "If you go back, I will go with you, but we shall be butchered." Hyrum said, "No, no; let us go back and put our trust in God and we shall not be harmed. The Lord is in it. If we have to die, we will be reconciled to our fate."

After a short pause, Joseph told Cahoon to request Captain Daniel C. Davis to have his boat ready at half-past five to cross them over the river.

Hyrum and Joseph wrote the following letter:

Banks of the River Mississippi
Sunday, June 23rd, 1844, 2 p.m.

His Excellency Governor Ford:

Sir, I wrote you a long communication at 12 last night, expressive of my views of your Excellency's communication of yesterday. I thought your letter rather severe, but one of my friends has just come to me with an explanation from the Captain of your posse which softened the subject matter of your communication and gives us greater assurance of protection, and that your Excellency has succeeded in bringing in subjection of the spirits which surround your Excellency to some extent. I declare again the only objection I ever had or ever made on trial by my country at any time was what I have made in my last letter—on account of assassins, and the reason I have to fear deathly consequences from their hands.

But from the explanation, I now offer to come to you at Carthage on the morrow, as early as shall be convenient for your posse to escort us into headquarters, provided we can have a fair trial, not be abused, nor have my witnesses abused, and have all things done in due form on my honor without the show of a great armed force to produce excitement in the minds of the timid.

We shall meet your posse, if this letter is satisfactory, (if not inform me) at or near the mound, at or about two o'clock tomorrow afternoon which will be as soon as we can get our witnesses and prepare for trial. We shall prepare to take our witnesses with us and not have to wait a subpoena or part at least, so as not to detain the proceedings although we may want time for counsel.

We remain most respectability, your Excellency's humble servants,

Signed—Joseph Smith
Hyrum Smith[2]

About 4:00 p.m. Hyrum, Joseph, the doctor, and others started back. While walking towards the river Joseph fell behind them with Orrin P. Rockwell. The others shouted for them to "Come on," to which Joseph replied, "It's no use to hurry, for we are going back to be slaughtered." He continually ex-

[2]*Op. cit.,* pp. 547-550.

pressed the wish that he could get the people once more together and talk to them that night. Rockwell said that if that was his wish he would get the people together, and Joseph could talk to them by starlight.

Joseph sent the letter of this date to Governor Ford in the hands of Col. Theodore Turley and Elder Jedediah M. Grant who carried it to Carthage, arriving about 9:00 p.m. They gave the letter to Governor Ford who at first agreed to send a posse to escort General Smith in safety to Carthage. Immediately afterward, however, a Mr. Skinner came in and made a very bitter speech to the governor in which Wilson Law and Joseph H. Jackson joined, telling him naught but lies, which caused Elder Grant to ask if messengers to the governor were to be insulted in that manner. The governor treated the brethren coldly and revoked his promise, refusing to send or allow an escort to go with Joseph and saying this was an honor not given to any other citizen. He would not allow the messengers to stay in Carthage through the night and wrote orders for Joseph and Hyrum to start at ten o'clock the following morning, without an escort, threatening that if General Smith did not come at that time, Nauvoo would be destroyed and all the men, women, and children that were in it. Brothers Grant and Turley began the return journey immediately but because of the weariness of their horses did not arrive in Nauvoo until 4:00 a.m. on the 24th. They went at once to General Smith to report to him the state of excitement in Carthage. But Joseph heeded no word of their warning, being now determined to go to Carthage and give himself up to the governor.[3]

As Hyrum, Joseph, and others neared the wharf on their return to Nauvoo, Hyrum's boy, Joseph Fielding, was playing on the bank of the river and saw the boat come in above a sandy spit which extended some distance out from the shore. As they came near, the six-year-old boy noticed the group of men leave the boat, and as they approached, the lad was happy

---

[3]*Ibid.*, pp. 551-552.

to see his father who took him by the hand and went with him to his home.

As they neared Hyrum's home, Joseph remained with his brother while the others parted with plans to meet the following morning. After greeting his wife and children, Hyrum freshened up and while shaving, heard Joseph say, "This boy of yours, Hyrum, is pale, too much milk in his diet." To which Hyrum replied, "He should have more solid food." Hyrum then accompanied Joseph to his home for last minute preparations for the journey to Carthage early the next morning.[4]

That night Joseph conversed with Captain Anderson who reported that the mob at Warsaw had stopped his boat and threatened to fire into her with his cannon. A letter was received from Ed. Johnson stating that it would be impossible for him to represent Joseph at the trial and recommending Mr. Adams in his place.

Joseph gave directions to obtain horses to carry them and his friends to Carthage. Although the governor had threatened to send his troops into the city, none had as yet appeared.

On Monday, June 25, Francis M. Higbee having sworn out a writ before Thomas Morrison, a justice of the peace at Carthage on the 11th instant, against Joseph Smith, Hyrum Smith, Samuel Bennet, John Taylor, William W. Phelps, John P. Greene, Stephen C. Perry, Dimick B. Huntington, Jonathan Dunham, Stephen Markham, William W. Edwards, Jonathan Holmes, Jesse P. Harmon, John Lytle, Joseph W. Coolidge, David Harvey Redfield, Orrin P. Rockwell, and Levi Richards for riot in destroying the Nauvoo *Expositor* press, the property of William and Wilson Law and others on the 10th instant, and Governor Ford, having sent word by the posse that those eighteen persons should be protected by the militia of the state, they, upon the assurance of that pledge, at half-past six in the morning, started for Carthage, with Willard Richards,

---

[4]Joseph F. Smith as he remembered it as told to his descendants.

Dan Jones, Henry G. Sherwood, Alfred Randall, James Davis, Cyrus H. Wheelock, A. C. Hodge, and several other brethren, together with James W. Woods as counsel, accompanying them.

That morning, as Hyrum prepared to leave his home to go to Carthage, his anxious family gathered around to bid him good-bye. His twelve-year-old John watched him take his watch and chain and hang it up and replace it with an older watch. The leave-taking was very difficult. John later wrote: "Father rode his large white horse, Sam."

As his father rode away, the lad remembered how Hyrum and Joseph had often ridden together on parade in full uniform at the head of the Nauvoo Legion, and how his Uncle Joseph rode old Joe Duncan, a chestnut sorrel pacing horse and Aunt Emma rode old Charley, a jet black trotting horse. He had heard his father and Joseph preach many times and had chased balls for Uncle Joseph which was a sort of recreation (playing ball) of which he, John, was very proud. The lad remembered Joseph preaching to the Indians on the lot across the road, southwest from the Mansion House. He also remembered his Uncle Joseph's last speech on the frame opposite the Mansion.[5]

The company paused when they got to the temple and looked with admiration first on that edifice and then on the city, and Joseph remarked, "This is the loveliest place and the best people under the heavens. Little do they know the trials that await them." As he passed out of the city, he called on Daniel H. Wells, Esq., who was unwell, and on parting from him said, "Squire Wells, I wish you to cherish my memory and not think me the worst man in the world either."

At ten minutes of ten they arrived at Albert G. Fellow's farm, four miles west of Carthage, where they met Captain Dunn with a company of about sixty mounted militia. On seeing them Joseph said, "Do not be alarmed, Brethren, for they cannot do more to you than the enemies of truth did to the ancient Saints; they can only kill the body." The company made a halt, then Hyrum, Joseph, and several others went into

---

[5]John Smith Document in his own handwriting owned by his descendants.

Fellow's house with Captain Dunn, who presented an order from Governor Ford for all the state arms in possession of the Nauvoo Legion, which Joseph immediately countersigned.

Henry G. Sherwood went up to Joseph and said, "Brother Joseph, shall I return to Nauvoo and regulate about getting the arms and get the receipts for them?" Joseph inquired if he were under arrest or expected to be arrested. Sherwood answered "No"; whereupon Joseph directed him to return ahead of the company, gather the arms, and do as well as he could in all things. Joseph then said to the company who were with him, "I am going like a lamb to the slaughter, but I am calm as a summer's morning. I have a conscience void of offense toward God and toward all men. If they take my life I shall die an innocent man and my blood shall cry from the ground for vengeance, and it shall be said of me 'He was murdered in cold blood!'" He then said to Father Sherwood, "Go, and God bless you." Sherwood then rode as swiftly as he could to Nauvoo.

This order for the delivery of the state arms was evidently designed to drive the citizens of Nauvoo to desperation so that in the heat of their indignation they might commit some overt act which the governor could construe as treason and thus provide the excuse for his mob militia to destroy the Mormons.

Captain Dunn requested the company to return to Nauvoo to assist in collecting the arms and pledged his word as a military man that Joseph and his friends should be protected even if it were at the expense of his own life, and his men responded to the pledge by three cheers. Captain Dunn, no doubt, feared that the order of the governor would excite the inhabitants of Nauvoo beyond endurance and therefore chose to depend on the well-known integrity of General Smith than to risk the chances of exciting the feelings of a much-abused people. At the same time Joseph sent a messenger to the governor with the following letter:

Four miles west of Carthage Mound,
Hancock County, Illinois
Monday, 10 o'clock

His Excellency Governor Ford:

Dear Sir.—On my way to Carthage to answer your request this morning, I here met Captain Dunn, who had here made known to me your orders to surrender the state arms in possession of the Nauvoo Legion, which command I shall comply with; and that the same may be done properly and without trouble to the state, I shall return with Captain Dunn to Nauvoo, see that the arms are put into his possession, and shall then return to headquarters in his company, when I shall most cheerfully submit to any requisition of the Governor of our state.

With all due respect to your Excellency, I remain your obedient servant.

Signed—Joseph Smith[6]

The Prophet then wrote ordering General Dunham to carry out the order of the commander-in-chief, Governor Ford, to collect the arms, and requesting that the state arms be taken to the Masonic Hall without delay.

Hyrum said to Abram C. Hodge, "You go on to Carthage and see what is going on and hear what is said on this matter."

Joseph and his company then returned with Captain Dunn, and arrived in Nauvoo at half-past two p.m.

When Hodge arrived at Carthage, he met with Rev. Mr. Dodge, who had some time previously been very kindly treated by Hyrum. He warned Hodge that as sure as Hyrum and Joseph came to Carthage, they would be killed. Hodge also saw Hamilton, the innkeeper, who, pointing to the Carthage Greys, said, "Hodge, there are the boys that will settle you Mormons." Hodge replied, "We can take as many men as there are there out of the Nauvoo Legion, and they would not be missed."

When the fact of the order for the state arms was known in Nauvoo, many of the brethren looked upon it as another

---

[6]Joseph Smith, op. cit., pp. 553-556.

preparation for a Missouri massacre; nevertheless, as Joseph requested that it should be complied with, they willingly gave up the arms.

About 6 p.m. when all the states' arms were collected, and the company was ready to start, Captain Dunn and Quartermaster-General Buckmaster made a short speech, expressing their gratitude at the peaceable conduct of the citizens of Nauvoo, and stated that while they thus conducted themselves they would protect them.

Governor Ford appeared to fear that the Nauvoo Legion, although disbanded, might avenge an outrage that might hereafter be committed on the persons of their leaders, and so thought he had better disarm them as he had previously disbanded them; yet the mob was suffered to retain their part of the states' arms, even when within a half-day's march of Nauvoo, and they in a threatening and hostile attitude, while the Nauvoo Legion had not evinced the least disposition whatever to use them, except to defend their city in case it should be attacked; and they had not set a foot outside the limits of the corporation.

Joseph rode down home twice to bid his family farewell. He appeared solemn and thoughtful and expressed himself to several individuals that he expected to be murdered. There appeared no alternative but that he must either give himself up, or the inhabitants of the city would be massacred by a lawless mob under sanction of the governor.

The company (about fifteen) then started again for Carthage, and when opposite the Masonic Hall, Joseph said, "Boys, if I don't come back, take care of yourselves; I am going like a lamb to the slaughter!" As he passed his farm he looked long upon it, and after they had passed it turned around several times to look again, at which some of the company made remarks. Joseph then said: "If some of you had got such a farm and knew you would not see it any more, you would want to take a good look at it for the last time!" When they got to the edge of the woods near Nauvoo, they met A. C.

Hodge returning from Carthage. He reported to Hyrum what he had heard in Carthage, told him what his feelings were and said, "Brother Hyrum, you are now clear, and if it was my duty to counsel you, I would say, do not go another foot, for they say they will kill you, if you go to Carthage," but as other persons gathered around, nothing further was said.[7]

About this time the Prophet received a letter from attorney H. T. Reid,[8] accepting the offer to defend the Prophet in court, and requesting certain papers and documents on the destruction of the Nauvoo *Expositor*. He particularly wanted to establish the fact that the press was not destroyed in a riotous or tumultuous manner.

About 9:00 p.m. the company arrived at Fellow's house four miles west of Carthage where they stopped about half an hour, and partook of such refreshments as they had brought with them. Captain Dunn and his company of mounted militia, returning with the states' arms from Nauvoo, joined them here, and escorted them into Carthage, where they arrived at five minutes before midnight and went to Hamilton's tavern. While they were passing the public square, many of the troops, especially the Carthage Greys, abused them in foul language which must have echoed in the ears of the governor and hundreds of others.

On hearing the commotion the governor put his head out of a window and called chidingly, "I know your great anxiety to see Mr. Smith, which is natural enough, but it is quite too late tonight for you to have the opportunity; but I assure you, gentlemen, you shall have the privilege tomorrow morning, as I will cause him to pass before the troops on the square, and I now wish you, with this assurance, quietly and peaceably to return to your quarters!" When this declaration was made, there was a faint "Hurrah for Tom Ford," and the boisterous crowd instantly obeyed his wish.

[7]*Ibid.*, pp. 557-558.
[8]Attorney H. T. Reid was not the same man who defended Joseph in the early history.

Tuesday morning, June 25, Hyrum and Joseph voluntarily surrendered themselves to the constable, Mr. Bettisworth, who held the writ against them. The governor had pledged his own faith, and the faith of the state of Illinois, that the Smiths and other persons should be protected from personal violence, and should have a fair and impartial trial, if they would surrender themselves to be dealt with according to law. This the governor did repeatedly affirm to legal counselors of the Smiths.

At 8:00 a.m. while in conversation with William G. Flood of Quincy, United States Receiver of Public Moneys, the Prophet was arrested by Constable David Bettisworth for treason against the state of Illinois.

Hyrum Smith was arrested at the same time, on the same writ, granted on the affidavit of Henry O. Norton:

WRIT OF ARREST FOR TREASON — HYRUM SMITH

State of Illinois
Hancock County

The people of the State of Illinois, to all Sheriffs, coroners, and constables, greetings:

Whereas complaint has been made before me, one of the justices of the peace, in and for the county of Hancock, upon the oath of one Henry O. Norton, that one Hyrum Smith, late of the county of Hancock and state of Illinois, did, on the 19th day of June, 1844, commit the crime of treason against the government and people of the state of Illinois aforesaid.

These are therefore to command you to take the body of the said Hyrum Smith if he be found in your county, or if he shall have fled that you pursue after the said Hyrum Smith into any county within this state, and take and safely keep the said Hyrum Smith, so that you have his body forthwith before me, to answer unto the said complaint, and be further dealt with according to law.

(Seal) Given under my hand and seal, this 24th day of June, 1844.

/s/ R. F. Smith, J. P.

At 8:30 a.m. Governor Ford called all the troops and ordered them to form a hollow square on the public ground near the courthouse; and when formed, he climbed atop an old table and addressed them, exciting the feelings of indignation against generals Joseph and Hyrum Smith which were already burning in their breasts and had been occasioned by the rumors and misrepresentations that were in circulation. The governor gave this assent and sanction to the rumors that had gathered them together, and stated that although they were dangerous men in the community, and guilty of all that they might have alleged against them, still they were in the hands of the law, which must have its course. He continued speaking twenty or thirty minutes.

At 9:15 a.m. the governor came in and invited Joseph to walk with him through the troops. Joseph asked for a few moments' private conversation with him but was refused. They then walked through the crowd with Brigadier General Miner R. Deming and Dr. Richards, to General Deming's quarters. The people appeared calm until a company of Carthage Greys flocked around the doors of General Deming in an uproarious manner, of which notice was sent to the governor. In the meantime the governor had ordered the McDonough troops to be drawn up in line so that Hyrum and Joseph must pass in front of them, the troops having requested that they might have a clear view of the Generals Smith. In a ten-minute conversation with the governor, Joseph again received that official's pledge that Joseph and his friends should be protected from violence.

From the general's quarters Hyrum and Joseph passed before the whole line of troops, Joseph being on the right of General Deming, and Hyrum on his left, with Elders Richards, Taylor, and Phelps following. Hyrum and Joseph were introduced by the governor as Generals Joseph and Hyrum Smith about twenty times along the line, the governor walking in front on the left. The Carthage Greys refused to receive them by those names, and some of the officers threw up their hats, drew their swords, and said they would introduce themselves to the damned Mormons in a different style. The governor mildly entreated them not to act so rudely, but their excitement increased. The governor, however, succeeded in pacifying them by making a speech, and promising them that they would have "full satisfaction." General Smith and party returned to their lodgings at five minutes past ten.

At ten thirty, news reached Joseph at the hotel that the Carthage Greys had revolted and were put under guard by General Deming. Joseph told all his friends to come into the two rooms they occupied in the hotel, but by ten-fifty quietness was apparently restored among the Carthage Greys.

At eleven-fifteen news arrived that the Warsaw troops were near Carthage, having come of their own accord. A Mr. Prentice, United States marshal for Illinois, called to see Joseph.

At twelve-forty-eight Joseph learned that the Laws, Higbees, Fosters, and others were going to Nauvoo to plunder. When the governor called at the door with some gentlemen, Joseph informed him of what he had heard and requested that he send a guard to protect the city of Nauvoo. . . .

At two-thirty, the governor sent word that he had ordered Captain Singleton with a company of men from McDonough county, to march to Nauvoo to co-operate with the police in keeping the peace and that he would call out the legion if necessary.

Joseph wrote to Emma.

Joseph also sent a message to Orrin P. Rockwell telling him not to come to Carthage, but to stay in Nauvoo, and not suffer himself to be delivered into the hands of his enemies, or to be taken a prisoner by any one.

Israel Barlow reported that he had heard read some resolutions of the Warsaw troops to the affect that they would return to Warsaw at 3:00 p.m.; then go to Golden's Point on Thursday, and thence to Nauvoo.[10]

Just prior to 4:00 p.m. several officers of the troops at Carthage and some others came to Hyrum and Joseph's room at the hotel to satisfy their curiosity to see the Prophet. He asked them if he looked like a desperate character. They answered

9Joseph Smith, op. cit., vol. VI, pp. 561-565.

"No, just the contrary" but remarked that they couldn't tell what was in his heart. Joseph replied that that was true, and that therefore, they were unable to judge him. But he assured them that he could see what was in their hearts. He said:

I can see your thirst for blood, and nothing but my blood will satisfy you. It is not for crime of any description that I and my brother are thus continually persecuted and harassed by our enemies, but there are other motives . . . and inasmuch as you and the people thirst for blood, I prophesy, in the name of the Lord, that you shall witness scenes of blood and sorrow to your entire satisfaction. Your souls shall be perfectly satiated with blood, and many of you who are now present shall have an opportunity to face the cannon's mouth from sources you think not of; and the people that desire this great evil upon me and my brethren, shall be filled with regret and sorrow because of the scenes of desolation and distress that await them. They shall seek for peace, and shall not be able to find it. Gentlemen, you will find what I have told you to be true.[10]

At twelve minutes before four o'clock word came from the apostate group in Carthage that *there was nothing against these men; the law could not reach them but powder and ball would,* and they should not go out of Carthage alive.

Hyrum and Joseph, and thirteen others, were taken before Robert F. Smith, a justice of the peace residing in Carthage, on the charge of riot in destroying the printing press of the Nauvoo *Expositor.*

Robert F. Smith was also commander, a captain of the Carthage Greys who had already been arrested for mutiny, and was thus a greater enemy than Thomas Morrison, the justice of the peace who first issued the writ. When the defendants had been taken before Esquire Wells of Nauvoo and acquitted, the prosecution had objected, saying the writ should be returned to the justice of the peace who had issued it. The governor made the same suggestion in a letter to the Prophet. But now, with the defendants in Carthage they could overrule their own former objections by taking the prisoners before another justice of the peace, one who was known to be an even greater enemy than Justice Morrison.

[10]*Ibid.,* p. 566.

Apparently sparring for time, the court, by motion of Chauncey L. Higbee, moved for an adjournment. To this move, H. T. Reid and James W. Wood on behalf of the defendants, objected strongly, but in order to have a recognition for crime committed and to prevent an increase of excitement, the defendants agreed to be bound over to the circuit court. To guarantee their appearance bail was asked in the amount of $7,500. The high sum indicated a plot to imprison them if the proper sureties could not be obtained.

The bail was pledged. Captain Smith did not call upon Hyrum and Joseph to answer charges of treason but disappeared without issuing any subpoenas for witnesses in behalf of the defendants. This seemed to be in keeping with the expression of the enemy the day before, that the law could not touch them, but that powder and ball could.

Dan Jones reported to Joseph that evening that he had overheard Wilson Law say that they would get another warrant for Joseph's arrest on the charge of treason because of what Wilson heard Joseph preach from Daniel, chapter 2 verse 44, saying that the kingdom referred to was already set up and that he (Joseph) was the king over it. Jones also heard Jackson say that he had eighteen accusations against Joseph and if one failed they would use another—they had had so much trouble in getting him to Carthage, that they would not let him get out alive.

About 7:30, Dr. Levi Richards and most of the brethren, after they had signed the bonds, left for Nauvoo, after which Hyrum and Joseph went into the governor's room for an interview. After a few minutes the governor left the room to order the captain of the guard to give the brethren some passes.

After supper, about 8:00 p.m., Constable Bettisworth came to Hyrum and Joseph's room and insisted that they should go to jail. Joseph demanded to see the mittimus (warrant of committal) which request was refused. Messrs. Reid and Wood, as counsel, insisted that the prisoners were entitled to be brought before a justice of the peace for examination before being sent to jail. The constable to their surprise, then exhibited the warrant signed by R. F. Smith, J. P.

The plot against Hyrum and Joseph was carried out carefully and skilfully. Lawyer Wood requested officer Bettisworth to wait until he could see the governor before taking the prisoners to jail. The officer said he would wait only five minutes. The governor when reached said that he could not interfere with the judicial functions of the courts and felt that the law should take its course.

As a former associate justice of the supreme court of the state, the governor knew the proceeding was illegal. When Captain Robert F. Smith, who was both a civil and a military officer, asked the governor what he should do in the face of such illegal procedure, the governor replied, "You have the Carthage Greys at your command!" Captain Smith, therefore, commanded his Greys to carry out his illegal mittimus as a magistrate, thereby practically blending the civil and military in the same person at the same time. The prisoners were thus forced into jail without an examination, after having already met the requirements of a bail for their liberty.

The governor must be held responsible for the illegal proceedings. As the chief magistrate of the state he was under oath to see that the laws were faithfully and properly executed and not, as in this instance, violated by his prompting one of his officers in a lawless course.

Elder John Taylor had gone immediately to the governor and informed him of the illegality under the law, and also reminded him of the disreputable character of those who had made the charge, and of the outrageous nature of the charges and the indignity suffered by men in their position. He stated that it was a vexatious persecution, and that they were not guilty of anything. The governor replied that it was an unpleasant affair, and looked hard, but that it was a matter beyond his control. John Taylor reminded him of his solemn promise to him and Dr. Bernhisel concerning their coming to Carthage without a guard or arms and reminded him that they had relied upon his faith and had placed themselves implicitly under his care, and had complied with all his requests, although extra-judicial.

The governor promised that he would detail a guard to see that they were protected. Elder Taylor later wrote his sentiment in these words,

> I expressed my dissatisfaction at the course taken, and told him if we were going to be subject to mob rule, and be dragged contrary to law into prison, at the instance of every infernal scoundrel whose oath could be bought for a dram of whiskey, his protection availed very little, and we had miscalculated his promises.
>
> Seeing there was no prospect of redress from the governor, I returned to the room and found Constable Bettisworth, very urgent to hurry Brothers Joseph and Hyrum to prison, while the brethren were remonstrating with him.
>
> At the same time a great rabble was gathered in the streets and around the door, and from the rowdyism manifested, I was afraid there was a design to murder the prisoners on the way to the jail.
>
> Without conferring with any person, my next feeling was to procure a guard, and seeing a man habited as a soldier in the room, I went to him and said, "I am afraid there is a design against the lives of Messrs. Smith; will you go immediately and bring your captain, and if not convenient, any other captain of a company, and I will pay you well for your trouble."
>
> He said he would, and departed forthwith, and soon returned with his captain, whose name I have forgotten [it was Captain Dunn] and introduced him to me.
>
> I told him of my fears, and requested him immediately to fetch his company. He departed forthwith, and arrived at the door with them, just at the time the constable was hurrying the brethren downstairs.
>
> A number of brethren went along, and one or two strangers, and all of us safely lodged in prison, remained there during the night.[11]

Attorney Wood met Captain Dunn with twenty men, they having come to guard the prisoners in jail. Mr. Wood accompanied Governor Ford to see justice of the peace (captain of the Greys) Robert F. Smith, who said his reason for issuing the warrant of committal was that the prisoners were not safe at the hotel. Mr. Wood then requested the governor to have a company of troops from some other county detailed to guard the jail.

---

[11]*Ibid.*, pp. 572-573.

Captain Dunn with his company, escorted Hyrum and Joseph Smith from their lodgings, together with Willard Richards, John Taylor, John P. Greene, Stephen Markham, Dan Jones, John S. Fullmer, Dr. Southwick, and Lorenzo D. Wasson, to the jail. Markham had a very large hickory cane, which he called "the rascal beater." Dan Jones had a smaller walking stick, and they walked on each side of Hyrum and Joseph, keeping off the drunken rabble, which several times broke through the ranks.

They were received by the jailer, Mr. George W. Stigall, and put into the criminal's cell; but he afterwards gave them the debtor's apartment, where the prisoners and their friends had amusing conversations on various subjects, which engaged them until late. Prayer was offered, which made Carthage prison into a gate of heaven for awhile. They finally lay down on the floor, where they all slept from about 11:30 p.m. until 6:00 a.m. of June 26.

Counselor H. T. Reid, in his published statement, writes as follows:

> The recital of the mittimus, so far as they relate to the prisoners, having been brought before the justice for trial, and it there appearing that the necessary witnesses of the prosecution were absent, are wholly untrue, unless the prisoners could have appeared before the justice without being present in person or by counsel; nor is there any law of Illinois which permits a justice to commit persons charged with crimes to jail without examination as to the probability of their guilt.[12]

Apparently, nothing could be done to obtain justice for them. The court machinery set up to give every citizen a fair and orderly trial had broken down. Hyrum and his brethren were like sheep among wolves, who awaited only an opportune moment to devour them. The few hours remaining were to be filled with events which mocked law and justice, but nothing could turn the tide. Only one scene remained to complete the tragic drama.

---

[12]*Ibid.*, pp. 571-574.

Chapter XXXV

THE BLOOD OF THE PROPHETS SEALS
THEIR TESTIMONY

The final chapter in the lives of two of God's noblemen awaited only its conclusion. The stage was set for the climactic scene. Evil men had planned well. That justice, liberty, and morality for which the founders of a great nation had given their lives was temporarily obscured by the machinations of cunning and wicked men. Although the destiny of this great land was to be a haven for the down-trodden, the persecuted, and maligned who might come to her shores, the elements of intolerance and hatred had not yet been erased. In Western Illinois and Missouri, in June 1844, the sober God-fearing element may have been in the majority, but their voice was weak and faltering when justice and liberty were being flouted by a pack of ravening wolves.

About six o'clock in the morning, Wednesday, June 26, 1844, the prisoners in Carthage Jail arose after a fitful night's rest strangely reminiscent of other nights spent under similar circumstances. About 7:30 a.m. they sat down with the jailer Stigall for breakfast. They then retired to the room upstairs, which had temporarily become the official headquarters of The Church of Jesus Christ of Latter-day Saints. The business at hand was to exhaust every possible legal means to secure justice.

Outside were a number of guards, very official looking, who demanded of people going and coming that they be identified with special passes. The prisoners were seeking a change of venue to Quincy, Adams County; therefore, several of the brethren were dispatched to the governor at the Hamilton Hotel, about a quarter of a mile away.

The prisoners felt their situation to be desperate. They were incarcerated illegally, and the mob hovered about the prison like vultures circling their prey.

Dr. Southwick was the first sent to the governor. Then, at 7:30, Markham, Wasson, and Jones took messages both to Governor Ford and to their lawyers. No reply was immediately received. Meanwhile, Mr. Stigall told them that the mob had been scheduled to attack Nauvoo the previous Wednesday but that of the 9,000 persons expected only 200 came. Runners had been sent to Missouri and all around the counties in Illinois.

Having received no reply from the governor by 8:10 a.m., Joseph sent a message by the jailer asking the governor for an interview concerning their unlawful imprisonment. The tension was somewhat relieved by the return of Markham and Jones with a message that the governor had been taken by surprise the night before and was afraid they would think he had forfeited his word about having an interview. Then at 8:45 the governor replied to their request for an interview by stating that he would come to the prison at his earliest leisure that day.

At 8:50 Lawyer Reid arrived and concluded to take a change of venue to Augusta, Hancock County, before Justice Greenleaf. A list was made of twenty witnesses they would need from Nauvoo. Finally, at 9:27, the governor, with Colonel Thomas Geddes, arrived at the jail. At the governor's request the Prophet outlined in a general way the details of the state of the country, the tumultuous, mobocratic movements of the enemy, and the precautionary measures taken by himself and the city council against the Nauvoo *Expositor.*

He stated that the Nauvoo Legion had been called out only to defend themselves against an attempted invasion by an infuriated mob, and that a record of all decisions, orders, and affidavits had been forwarded to the Governor. Joseph explained that the reason for their not yielding to the posse of officers who had returned to Carthage the Sunday before was that a decision of such grave import could not be made in a hurry.

John Taylor, who was present at this historic meeting, quoted Governor Ford as saying in part:

The press in the United States is looked upon as the great bulwark of the American freedom. There is a disposition on your part to suppress liberty of speech . . . you are represented to me as turbulent and defiant of the laws and institutions of your country.

Joseph then said:

Governor Ford, you, sir, as governor of this state, are aware of the prosecution and persecution that I have endured. You know well that our course has been peaceable and law-abiding, etc. . . . Was it the Mormons or our enemies who first commenced these difficulties? You know well it was not us; and when this turbulent, outrageous people commenced their insurrectionary movements, I made you acquainted with them, officially, and asked your advice, and have followed strictly your counsel in every particular. Who ordered out the Nauvoo Legion? I did, under your direction. For what purpose? To suppress these insurrectionary movements. It was at your instance, sir, that I issued this proclamation, etc.

The governor, in their conversation referred to the decision of the Nauvoo city council to take action on the press. That this was an act of making laws which should be confined to the legislature then executing such laws, was wrong, in his opinion, he said. "Concerning your being in jail," he continued, "I am sorry for that; I wish it had been otherwise. I hope you will soon be released, but I cannot interfere."

The Prophet made his defense, declaring the press a nuisance, and stating his willingness to have the courts determine the legality of what they did. Continuing he said:

I shall look to you for protection. I believe you are talking of going to Nauvoo; if you go, sir, I wish to go along. I refuse not to answer any law, but I do not consider myself safe here.

Governor Ford replied:

I am in hopes you will be acquitted, but if I go I will certainly take you along. I do not, however, apprehend dangers. I think you are perfectly safe either here or anywhere else. I cannot, however, interfere with the law. I am placed in peculiar circumstances and seem to be blamed by all parties.

Joseph then said,

> Governor Ford, I ask nothing but what is legal; I have a right to expect protection at least from you; for, independent of law, you have pledged your faith, and that of the state, for my protection, and I wish to go to Nauvoo.

And the governor answered,

> You shall have protection, General Smith. I did not make this promise without consulting my officers, who all pledged their honor to its fulfillment. I do not know that I shall go tomorrow to Nauvoo, but if I do, I will take you along.[1]

After a 45 minute interview the governor left, repeating his desire to take Joseph along, perhaps to insure his own safety.

The Prophet's clerk, Dr. Willard Richards, was busy making copies of orders to John P. Greene and General Jonathan Dunham. Joseph said he had felt a great deal of anxiety about his safety since he left Nauvoo, that he had never felt before. Dan Jones and Stephen Markham spent the morning whittling with their penknives on a warped door in order to have it close properly on the latch.

Patriarch Hyrum Smith and the others took turns preaching to the guards. Some were convinced of the innocence of the prisoners, and more than one was heard to say: "Let us go home, boys, for I will not fight any longer against these men."

Hyrum tried to encourage Joseph by asking him if he didn't think that the Lord, for the sake of his Church, would release him from prison. Joseph replied, "Could my brother Hyrum but be liberated, it would not matter so much about me."

The Prophet then thought about Sidney Rigdon, and said, "Poor Ridgdon, I am glad he is gone to Pittsburgh out of the way; were he to preside he would lead the Church to destruction in less than five years."[2]

---

[1]Joseph Smith, op. cit., vol. VI, pp. 575-585. Note: After the interview, Col. Thomas Geddes said Governor Ford told him that the Mormons would have to be driven out sometime, and he would not interfere until it was accomplished. See Thomas Gregg, History of Hancock County, page 372.
[2]Ibid., pp. 592-593.

As Willard Richards wrote, John Taylor amused him by singing. Joseph, much depressed, related a dream about William and Wilson Law, and one about trying to save a steamboat in a storm.

Lawyer Reid brought a message from General Miner R. Deming that the governor had asked him to provide the prisoners with what protection was necessary. All persons were to be excluded from the jail except those with passes.

Mr. Reid said that the counsel for the prosecution had asked that the prisoners be released to answer to the charges of treason, but this was impossible until they could be released by due course of law. He stated also that since the prisoners were admitted to prison on a false mittimus, without examination, the magistrate had no more jurisdiction in the case and that he would not agree to trial unless (Captain) Justice Smith would go to Nauvoo for examination, where witnesses could be had.

Reports of threats against Hyrum and Joseph continued to come in. In the dining hall of the hotel in the presence of the governor it was common to hear such remarks as, "The law is too short for these men, but they must not be suffered to go at large"; and, "If the law will not reach them, powder and ball must."

At half past two, Constable Bettisworth came with Alexander Simpson, bearing an order demanding the release of the prisoners, but the jailer couldn't find a law authorizing him to release them. When the jailer's action was reported to Justice Smith, he asked the governor what to do. Governor Ford replied, "We have plenty of troops; there are the Carthage Greys under your command; bring them out." When this report reached Joseph, he promptly sent Lorenzo D. Wasson to get his lawyers, Reid and Woods, whom he told of the threats in these words:

We are informed that Dr. Foster has said that they can do nothing with us, only by powder and ball, as we have done nothing against the law.[3]

---

[3]*Ibid.*, pp. 594-595.

At twenty minutes to four, the constable with a company of Carthage Greys under the command of Frank Warrell, marched to the jail, and by intimidation and threats, compelled the jailer to deliver Hyrum and Joseph into his hands. It was a critical moment, for the mob began to gather at the jail. Something must be done immediately.

Hyrum and Joseph surveyed the situation and putting on their hats walked boldly into the midst of a hollow square of the Carthage Greys, expecting to be massacred before they arrived at the courthouse. They politely locked arms with the worst mobocrat they could see, were followed by Dr. Richards, and escorted by a guard. Elders Taylor, Markham, and Fullmer followed, outside the hollow square, and accompanied them to the court house.

The trial commenced at 4:25 p.m. Joseph's clerk took minutes of the proceedings. Counsel for the prosecution were C. L. Higbee, O. C. Skinner, Thomas Sharp, Sylvester Emmons, and Thomas Morrison. It was finally decided to wait until witnesses could be brought from Nauvoo, and the court adjourned until twelve o'clock the next day. A second mittimus was issued for their return to jail.

At 5:30 p.m. Joseph and Hyrum were returned to jail and thrust into close confinement. John Smith came from Macedonia to see his nephews. On the way he was threatened by three mobbers who recognized him and snapped guns at him. When he arrived at the jail, guards refused to let him in. Joseph, seeing him through the window said to the guard, "Let the old gentleman come in; he is my uncle." The guards retorted that they did not care who the hell he was uncle to; he should not go in.

But when Joseph said, "You will not hinder so old and infirm a man from coming in. Come in, Uncle"; the guard searched him closely and let him into the jail, where he remained for about an hour. He asked Joseph if he should again get out of the hands of his enemies, and Joseph replied, "My brother Hyrum thinks I shall." He told Uncle John to tell Alman W. Babbitt to come and assist them on the morrow as an attorney for their trial. (At 8:15 that night when Patriarch John Smith met Lawyer Babbitt and delivered the message, Babbitt replied, "You are too late, I am already engaged on the other side."

Dr. Bernhisel brought a note from the governor to the jailer, which read, "I would advise the jailer to keep the Messrs. Smith in the room in which I found them this morning, unless a closer confinement should be clearly necessary to prevent an escape. Signed. . .Thomas Ford, Governor and Commander in Chief.

At 6:15 p.m. a letter dated June 26 was received from William Clayton in Nauvoo. In it Brother Clayton reported that Mr. Marsh, who lived down the river, and of whom Joseph had obtained corn, pork, etc, had offered to give bail to Joseph, if needed, for any amount. Also, Captain Singleton who had come as head of the police to Nauvoo had written the governor to call them home. In his letter he told the governor that there was no trouble in Nauvoo, but that there was plenty to settle at home. He said further that while the police were at Carthage they were treated as soldiers, but since they had come to Nauvoo they had been treated as gentlemen. He ended the letter by saying, "All is peace in Nauvoo. Many threats keep coming that the mob are determined to attack the city in your absence, but we have no fears."

The thoughts of the prisoners were on preparing for the trial the following day. Reynolds Cahoon was sent to Nauvoo to secure important papers, and a message was sent to Attorney Woods to get subpoenas for Samuel James, Edward Hunter, and Philip B. Lewis, with instructions to bring with them to the governor at Springfield the papers they carried, since the governor had not seen these papers. He had started for Carthage before they arrived at Springfield.

After supper Lawyers Woods and Reid called, with Elder John P. Greene, and said that the governor and military officers had held a meeting and decided that the governor and all the troops except one company of about fifty men would march to Nauvoo at eight o'clock the next morning, in order to gratify the troops, and would return the next day. The company of fifty men was to be selected by the governor from those of the troops whose fidelity he could most rely on to guard the prisoners, and was to be left at Carthage Jail; the trial was to be deferred until Saturday, June 29. After the meeting Justice (Captain) Robert F. Smith altered the return of the subpoenas until June 29, another action taken without consulting either the prisoners or their lawyers.

After Lawyers Woods and Reid and Elder Greene returned to the Hamilton's Hotel at 9 p.m., the prisoners had prayer, with John Taylor acting as mouth. Willard Richards, John Taylor, John S. Fullmer, Stephen Markham, and Dan Jones stayed with Hyrum and Joseph.

During the evening Patriarch Hyrum Smith read and commented upon extracts from the Book of Mormon, on the imprisonments and deliverance of the servants of God for the gospel's sake.[4] Joseph bore a powerful testimony to the guards of the divine authenticity of the Book of Mormon, of the restoration of the gospel, and of the ministering of angels, and said that the kingdom of God was again established upon the earth, for the sake of which he was then incarcerated in the prison and not because he had violated any law of God or man.

They retired to rest late. Hyrum and Joseph occupied the only bedstead in the room, while their friends lay side by side on mattresses on the floor. Dr. Richards sat up writing until the last candle guttered out, leaving him in the dark. The report of a gun fired close by caused Joseph to arise, leave the bed, and lay himself on the floor, with Dan Jones on his left, and John S. Fullmer on his right. Joseph stretched out his right arm and said to John S. Fullmer, "Lay your head on my arm for a pillow, Brother John"; and when all were quiet they conversed in low tones about the prospects of their deliverance. Joseph gave expression to his presentiment that he had to die, and said, "I would like to see my family again," and "I would to God that I could preach to the Saints in Nauvoo once more."

---
[4] Ether 12:36-38.

Fullmer tried to rally his spirits by saying he thought Joseph would often have that privilege, and Joseph thanked him for the remarks and the good feelings expressed to him.

Soon afterward, Dr. Richards retired to the bed which Joseph had left, and when all were apparently fast asleep, Joseph whispered to Dan Jones, "Are you afraid to die?" Dan said, "Has that time come, think you? Engaged in such a cause, I do not think that death would have many terrors." Joseph replied, "You will yet see Wales, and fulfil the mission appointed you before you die."[5]

The next morning the sun rose behind overhanging clouds to shine only dimly on a day of infamy which was to cast a dark shadow on the state of Illinois.

At 5:30 a.m. Joseph asked Dan Jones to go downstairs and inquire the reason for the disturbance during the night. Frank Warrell, officer of the guard and one of the Carthage Greys said to him in a bitter tone, "We have had too much trouble to bring Old Joe out here to let him escape alive, and unless you want to die with him you had better leave before sundown; and you are not a damned bit better for taking his part, and you'll see that I can prophesy better than Old Joe, for neither he nor his brother, nor anyone who will remain with them will see the sun set today."

Joseph directed Jones to report what he had heard to the governor. While on his way with the message, Jones listened to a speech made by the leader of an assembly of men: "Our troops will be discharged this morning in obedience to orders, and for a sham we will leave the town," he cried; "but when the governor and the McDonough troops have left for Nauvoo this afternoon, we will return and kill those men, if we have to tear the jail down."

He was applauded by three cheers from the crowd.

Captain Jones went to the governor and told him what he had heard in the night and the statements made by the officer of the guard and by the speaker whom he had heard on his way there. He earnestly solicited the governor's protection. His Ex-

[5]Joseph Smith, op. cit., vol. VI, pp. 594-601.

cellency replied, "You are unnecessarily alarmed for the safety of your friends, Sir; the people are not that cruel."

Irritated by such remarks, Jones urged the necessity of placing better men to guard them than professed assassins, and said, "The Messrs. Smith are American citizens, and have surrendered themselves to your Excellency upon your pledging your honor for their safety; they are also Master Masons, and as such I demand of your protection of their lives."

Governor Ford's face turned pale, and Jones remarked, "If you do not do this, I have but one more desire, and that is if you leave their lives in the hands of those men to be sacrificed. . ."

"What is that, sir?" the governor asked in a hurried tone.

"It is," said Jones, "that the Almighty will preserve my life to a proper time and place, that I may testify that you have been timely warned of their danger."

Jones returned to the prison, but the guard would not let him enter. He again returned to the hotel, and found Governor Ford standing in front of the McDonough troops, who were in line to escort him to Nauvoo.

The disbanded mob retired to the rear, shouting loudly that they were only going a short distance out of town, when they would return and kill Old Joe and Hyrum as soon as the governor was far enough out of town.

Jones called the attention of the governor to the threats then made, but the governor took no notice of them, although it was impossible for him to avoid hearing them.

Jones then requested the governor to give him passports for himself and friends to pass in and out of the prison, according to his promise made to the prisoners. The governor refused to give them passes, but told General Deming to give one to Dr. Willard Richards, Joseph Smith's private secretary.

While obtaining the pass for Dr. Richards Jones' life was threatened, and Chauncey L. Higbee said to him in the street, "We are determined to kill Joe and Hyrum and you had better go away to save yourself."

At 7:00 a.m. Hyrum, Joseph, Dr. Richards, Stephen Markham and John S. Fullmer ate breakfast together. Mr. Crane ate with them and wanted to know if the report were true that Joseph had fainted three times on Tuesday while being exhibited to the troops. He was assured of the falseness of the report.[6]

At 8:00 a.m., at Joseph's request, passes were given to C.H. Wheelock and John S. Fullmer, and at 8:20 Joseph wrote to his wife Emma, asking her to tell General Dunham to instruct the people to stay at home or go about their business and not to collect in groups. He said, however, that it was the duty of all men to protect their lives and the lives of their households, etc.

In a postscript he wrote:

> Dear Emma, I am very much resigned to my lot, knowing I am justified, and have done the best that could be done. Give my love to the children and all my friends. Mr. Brewer, and all who inquire after me; and as for treason, I know that I have not committed any, and they cannot prove anything of the kind, so you need not have any fears that anything can happen to us on that account. May God bless you all. Amen.

At 9:40 a.m. Messrs. Woods and Reid called to report the decision of the governor to countermand his previous orders of marching the whole army to Nauvoo. Later, Dr. Southwick who attended the meeting told Stephen Markham that the purpose of such a gathering was to take into consideration the best way to stop Joseph Smith's career, because his views on government were widely circulated and were taking hold like wildfire. Politicians feared that if he did not get into the presidential chair this election, he would be sure to the next time; and if Illinois and Missouri would join together and kill him, they would not be brought to justice for it.

Captain Dunn and his company were ordered to accompany the governor to Nauvoo. The Carthage Greys, who had but two days before been under arrest for insulting the commanding general and whose conduct had been more hostile to the prisoners than that of any other company, were selected by Governor Ford to guard the prisoners at the jail; other troops composed of

---

[6]*Ibid.*, pp. 602-604.

the mob whom the prisoner had found at Carthage, and had mustered into the service of the state with promises of "full satisfaction" and a march on Nauvoo, were disbanded and discharged in Carthage, although it was the duty of the governor to dismiss the troops into the hands of their several officers in order that they be marched home and there disbanded, not disbanded at a distance from home, and at a time and place when they were predisposed to acts of lawless violence, rapine and murder. And Governor Ford suffered two or three hundred men to remain encamped about eight miles off on the Warsaw road, apparently under the control of Colonel Levi Williams, a sworn enemy to Joseph, who had on many occasions threatened the destruction of Nauvoo and the Prophet's death.

Cyrus H. Wheelock states that prior to leaving Carthage he said to the governor, "Sir, you must be aware by this time that the prisoners have no fears in relation to any lawful demands made against them, but you have heard sufficient to justify you in the belief that their enemies would destroy them if they had them in their power; and now, sir, I am about to leave for Nauvoo, and I fear for those men; they are safe as regards the law, but they are not safe from the hands of traitors, and midnight assassins who thirst for their blood and have determined to spill it; and under these circumstances leave with a heavy heart."

Ford replied, "I was never in such a dilemma in my life; but your friends shall be protected, and have a fair trial by the law; in this *pledge* I am not alone; I have obtained the *pledge* of the whole of the army to sustain me."

After receiving these assurances, Wheelock prepared to visit the prison. The morning being a little rainy, favored his wearing an overcoat, in the side pocket of which he carried a six shooter. He passed the guard unmolested, and during his visit in the prison slipped the revolver into Joseph's pocket. Joseph examined it, and asked Wheelock if he had not better retain it for his own protection.

This was a providential circumstance, for most other persons had been thoroughly searched. Joseph then handed the single barrel pistol which had been given him by John S. Fullmer to his brother Hyrum, and said, "You may have use for this."

Hyrum observed, "I hate to use such things or to see them used."

"So do I," said Joseph, "but we may have to, to defend ourselves."

Hyrum then took the pistol.

Wheelock was entrusted with a verbal request to the commanders of the Legion to avoid all military display or any other movement calculated to produce excitement during the governor's visit. He was especially charged to use all the influence he possessed to have the brethren and friends of Joseph remain perfectly calm and quiet, inasmuch as they respected the feelings and well-being of the Prophet and Patriarch.

The prisoners also sent so many verbal messages to their families with Wheelock that Dr. Richards proposed writing them all down, fearing Wheelock might forget; but Hyrum fastened his eyes upon him and with a look of penetration said, "Brother Wheelock will remember all that we tell him, and he will never forget the occurrences of this day."[7]

Both Hyrum and Joseph bore a faithful testimony to the Latter-day work, and the coming forth of the Book of Mormon and prophesied of the triumph of the gospel over all the earth, exhorting the brethren present to faithfulness and persevering diligence in proclaiming the gospel, building up the temple, and performing all the duties connected with our holy religion.

At twenty minutes to ten, Joseph wrote a postscript to Emma as follows: "I just learned that the governor is about to disband his troops, all but a guard to protect us and the peace, and come himself to Nauvoo and deliver a speech to the people. This is right I suppose."

John P. Greene, Nauvoo city marshal, told Governor Ford that if he went to Nauvoo, leaving only the Carthage Greys to guard the jail, there was a conspiracy on foot to take the lives of

---

[7]*Ibid.*, pp. 604-609.

Joseph and Hyrum during his absence, to which the governor replied, "Marshal Greene, you are too enthusiastic."[8]

At 10:30 a.m. Governor Ford went to Nauvoo with that part of the troops who were most friendly to the prisoners. Despite his promise of the day before, the Governor made no offer to take Joseph Smith along. John S. Fullmer left the jail for Nauvoo to assist Wheelock in obtaining witnesses for the Saturday trial. James W. Woods, their principal lawyer also left for Nauvoo.

At 1:15 p.m. Hyrum and Joseph and Willard dined in their room; Taylor and Markham dined below. After dinner Dr. Richards was taken ill, and Joseph said, "Brother Markham, since you have a pass from the governor to go in and out of the jail, go and get the doctor something that he needs to settle his stomach," and Markham went out for medicine. When he had secured the remedies desired and was returning to the jail, a man by the name of Stewart called out, "Old man, you have got to leave town in five minutes!"

Markham replied, "I shall not do it." Then a company of Carthage Greys gathered around him, put him on his horse, and forced him out of town at the point of the bayonet.

At 3:15 p.m. the guard began threatening among themselves and telling what they would do when the excitement was over.

John Taylor liked to sing and used his voice to help dispel the gloom. He sang all fourteen verses of "A Poor Wayfaring Man of Grief" which seemed to meet the need of the moment. At Joseph's request he sang it again. Then Hyrum read extracts from Josephus.

The conspiracy had progressed as planned. Governor Ford was gone, and at the Carthage Jail the afternoon was waning. This Thursday, June 27, 1844, had been a day of overcast clouds and drizzling rain, even the weather seemed to accentuate the feeling of gloom.

The guard at the jail was changed at 4:00 p.m., only eight being stationed at the jail, while the Carthage Greys were camped a quarter of a mile away, on the public square.

---

[8]*Ibid.*, pp. 610-611.

At 4:15 p.m. Joseph commenced conversing with the guard about Joseph H. Jackson, William and Wilson Law, and others of his persecutors, and Hyrum and Dr. Richards continued conversing together until a quarter past five.

At 5:00 p.m. Jailer Stigall returned to the jail and said that Stephen Markham had been surrounded by a mob which had driven him out of Carthage, and that he had gone to Nauvoo.

Stigall suggested that they would be safer in the cell, and Joseph said, "After supper we will go in."

Mr. Stigall went out, and Joseph said to Dr. Richards, "If we go into the cell, will you go in with us?"

The doctor answered, "Brother Joseph, you did not ask me to come to Carthage—you did not ask me to come to jail with you —and do you think I would forsake you now? But I will tell you what I will do; if you are condemned to be hung for treason, I will be hung in your stead, and you will go free!"

Joseph said, "You cannot!"

The doctor replied, "I will."

Before the jailer came in, his boy brought in some water, and said that the guards wanted some wine. Joseph gave Dr. Richards two dollars to give the guard; but the guard said one was enough and would take no more.

The guard immediately sent for a bottle of wine, pipes, and two small papers of tobacco, and one of the guards brought them into the jail soon after the jailer went out. Dr. Richards uncorked the bottle, and presented a glass to Joseph, who tasted it as did also Brother Taylor and the doctor, and the bottle was then given to the guard, who turned to go out. When he was at the top of the stairs, someone below called him two or three times, and he went down.

Immediately there was a little rustling at the outer door of the jail, and a cry of surrender, instantly followed by a discharge of three or four firearms. The doctor glanced out the curtained window and saw about a hundred armed men with painted faces around the door.

The guards elevated their firelocks, and boisterously threatened the mob, discharging their firearms over their heads. The mob encircled the building. Then, some of them, rushing by the guard and up the flight of stairs, burst open the door and began the work of death. Others fired in through the open windows.

Hyrum, Joseph, and Elder Taylor all had their coats off. Joseph sprang to his coat for his six shooter, Hyrum for his single barrel, Taylor for Markham's large hickory cane, and Dr. Richards for Taylor's cane. All then plunged against the door. The balls whistled up the stairway and on the instant one came through the door. With their canes, the prisoners tried to knock aside the guns of the ruffians.

Hyrum was retreating in front of the door and had just snapped his pistol when a ball struck him on the left side of the nose, and he fell backward to the floor saying, "I am a dead man!" As he fell to the floor another ball from outside the building entered his left side and passed through his body with such force that it completely broke to pieces the watch he wore in his vest pocket, and, at the same instant, another ball from the door grazed his breast, and entered his head by the throat; subsequently a fourth ball entered his left leg.

A shower of lead was pouring into the room, much of which lodged in the ceiling just above Hyrum.

Continual discharges of musketry came into the room. Elder Taylor continued parrying the guns until they had got them about half their length into the room, when he found that resistance was vain and attempted to jump out of the window. A ball fired from within struck him in the left thigh, hitting the bone and passing through to within half an inch of the other side. He fell on the windowsill, and a ball fired from the outside struck the watch in his vest pocket, throwing him back into the room.

After he fell into the room he was hit by two more balls, one of them badly injuring his left wrist and the other entering at the side of the bone just below the left knee. He rolled under the bed, which was at the right of the window in the southeast corner of the room.

While he lay under the bed he was fired at several times from the stairway; one ball striking him on the left hip and tearing the flesh in such a manner that large quantities of blood were scattered upon the wall and floor.

When Hyrum fell, Joseph exclaimed, "Oh, dear brother Hyrum!" and opening the door a few inches discharged his six shooter down the stairway two or three balls missing fire.

Then, seeing that there was no safety in the room and no doubt thinking that it would save the lives of his brethren in the room if he got out, Joseph turned calmly from the door and sprang into the window where two balls pierced him from the door, and one entered his right breast from without. He fell forward into the hands of his murderers, exclaiming, "O Lord, my God!"

Dr. Richards' escape was miraculous; although he was a very large man and stood in a veritable shower of lead, he emerged unscathed, with the exception of a ball which grazed the lower tip of his left ear. His escape literally fulfilled a prophecy which Joseph had made to him over a year previously that the time would come when "the balls would fly around him like hail, and he would see his friends fall on the right and on the left, but that there should not be a hole in his garment!"[9]

Dr. Richards' description of that terrible hour follows:

... As his feet (the Prophet's) went out of the window my head went in, the balls whistling all around. He fell on his side a dead man.

At that instant the cry was raised, "He's leaped the window!" and the mob on the stairs and in the entry ran out.

I withdrew from the window, thinking it of no use to leap out on the hundred bayonets then around Joseph Smith's body.

Not satisfied with this I again reached my head out of the window and watched some seconds to see if there was any signs of life regardless of my own, determined to see the end of him I loved. Being fully satisfied that he was dead, with a hundred men near the body and more coming around the corner of the jail, and expecting a return to our room, I rushed towards the prison door, at the head of the stairs, and through the entry

---

[9]*Ibid.*, pp. 615-620.

from whence the firing had proceeded, to learn if the doors into the prison were open.

When near the entry, Mr. Taylor called out, "Take me!" I pressed my way until I found all doors unbarred, returning instantly, caught Mr. Taylor under my arm and rushed by the stairs into the dungeon, or inner prison, stretched him on the floor and covered him with a bed in such a manner as not likely to be perceived, expecting an immediate return of the mob.

I said to Mr. Taylor, "This is a hard case to lay you on the floor, but if your wounds are not fatal, I want you to live to tell the story." I expected to be shot the next moment, and stood before the door awaiting the onset.[10]

While Willard Richards and John Taylor were in the cell, a company of the mob again rushed up the stairs, but finding only Hyrum's body they turned and were again descending the stairs when there came a loud cry of "The Mormons are coming!" which caused the whole band of murderers to flee precipitately into the woods![11]

The time of the deadly assult was fixed by John Taylor's watch, which was struck by a ball from outside the window. The impact knocked him to the floor and smashed the time piece whose hands stopped at sixteen minutes twenty-six seconds past five o'clock.

Thus life ended for Hyrum Smith, the man who stood next to the founder of a dynamic religion, the man who had held the keys of authority jointly with his brother Joseph, the man in whom the Lord said "was no guile." His contribution to the establishment of the restored Church will stand as a monument throughout eternity. He was a peacemaker, a leader of men, a counselor, a patriarch to bless the Church. He had been a shield to Joseph, a fatherly adviser as well as a beloved brother.

Hyrum Smith could have saved his life, but he would not forsake his brother. What more can man do to show his love for a brother than to lay down his life for him? As they had been one in life so were they one in death, sealing with their blood their testimonies of a divine work.

---

[10]*Ibid.*, p. 621.
[11]*Idem.*

Chapter XXXVI

THE WIDOWS AND ORPHANS MOURN

When the roar of muskets had ceased and the fiends in human form with painted faces had fled into the woods of Carthage that evening of June 27, 1844, the two key men of the Dispensation of the Fulness of Times lay dead in a pool of their own blood. Two witnesses had been taken to bear testimony at the throne of God that they had done all they could to carry out the divine plan.

For the moment, the powers of perdition exulted, while the heavens wept in sympathy with the mourning Saints and the stricken widows and orphans. Some wept, for the Spirit whispered to them that evil was abroad and that some great calamity had befallen.[1]

The feeling of sorrow among the missionaries was soon understood, for the newspapers, with screaming headlines, announced the death of the Mormon leaders. And though justice and mercy were rudely insulted, a calloused world went on its way, happy in the thought that now the "Mormon menace" was at last destroyed and peace could reign undisturbed.

The life of Hyrum Smith had been one of crisis after crisis, beginning years before at Palmyra, New York. He had never known the joy of security. His place of abode had been sacrificed several times because of pressure from the enemy. He had been forced at the point of bayonets to leave his crying children and sick wife. Instant annihilation had several times hovered near, when it seemed certain that the jaws of hell would open to engulf both him and his family. And now the final blow had fallen.

When the acrid smell of gunsmoke had cleared away, and

---

[1]Parley P. Pratt and his brother, William, on a mission in the state of New York on the day of the martyrdom, had an experience similar to that of other missionaries. He wrote: ". . . My brother, let us keep silent and not open our mouths; let us observe an entire and solemn silence, for this is a dark day, and the hour of triumph for the powers of darkness. . . ."

the tumult and shouting of the murderers had ceased John Taylor and Willard Richards, two stalwart friends of the martyrs, were spared to tell the story. The original intention of the mob leaders had been to kill all four prisoners, but for some unknown reason, when the mob was apprised of Joseph and Hyrum's deaths, they fled, perhaps fearing reprisal from the Mormons.

Brother Richards, not knowing how soon the killers would return, crept to the east window, past Hyrum's body, and peering out saw the body of his beloved Prophet slumped down beside the well-curb. Joseph had been shot four times from outside the jail.

Soon some people, out of curiosity, entered the jail and came into the room. Among these was a doctor. Seeing Brother Taylor's wounds, the doctor proceeded to extract one of the musket slugs from his hand using a carpenter's compass and a penknife. Such crude instruments cutting and probing the flesh increased the pain almost unbearably. Brother Taylor later said:

> After sawing some time with a dull penknife, and prying and pulling with the compass, he ultimately succeeded in extracting the ball, which weighed about half an ounce. . . . He (the doctor) remarked afterward to a friend of mine that I had nerve like the devil to stand what I did in its extraction. I really thought I had need of nerves to stand such surgical butchery, and that, whatever my nerves may be, his practice was devilish.[2]

Brother Richards could give no immediate attention to John Taylor, for he was busy arranging the coroner's inquest and seeing to the removal of the bodies from Carthage to Nauvoo.

When the coroner's jury were gathered in the room around the body of Hyrum, the name of Francis Higbee was mentioned. Hearing this name Brother Taylor said, "Captain Smith, you are a justice of the peace; I have heard his [Francis Higbee's] name mentioned; I want to swear my life against him." When Higbee heard his name mentioned, he left the place.

---

[2]Joseph Smith, *op. cit.*, vol. VII, pp. 106-107.

Brother Taylor lay from a little after five that fateful evening until two o'clock the next morning, a total of nine hours before his wounds were dressed. Most of the people of Carthage had fled fearing an attack by the Mormons; hence there was little help available.

Willard Richards sent a message to Nauvoo which read:

> Carthage Jail, 8 o'clock 5 min p.m., June 27th, 1844. Joseph and Hyrum are dead. Taylor wounded not very badly. I am well. Our guard was forced by a band of Missourians from 100 to 200. The job was done in an instant, and the party fled from Nauvoo instantly. This is as I believe it. The citizens here are afraid of the "Mormons" attacking them; I promsed them no.
>
> Signed—Willard Richards
>
> NB—The citizens promise us protection; alarm guns have been fired.
>
> Signed—John Taylor.

John Taylor was more severely wounded than he admitted. He signed the message, taking great pains to write legibly, in order to convey to his wife that he was quite well so that she would not worry.

In the meantime the governor was making to the Saints in Nauvoo one of the most infamous and insulting speeches that ever fell from the lips of an executive. He spoke of the destruction of the *Expositor* press and of placing Nauvoo under martial law, and said that one cause of excitement was the Mormons' having so many firearms, which made the public afraid that they would be used against the government. Continuing, this official said:

> I know there is great prejudice against you on account of your peculiar religion, but you ought to be praying Saints, not military Saints. Depend upon it, a little more misbehavior from the citizens, and the torch, which is already lighted, will be applied, and the city may be reduced to ashes, and extermination would follow; and it gives me great pain to think that there is danger of so many innocent women and children being exterminated. If anything of a serious character should befall the lives or property of the persons who are persecuting your leaders, you will be held responsible.[3]

---

[3]Joseph Smith, *op. cit.*, vol. VI, p. 623.

The governor had been duly warned about an impending attack on the jail but felt that the promise made to him by his troops that they would protect the prisoners was a sufficient guarantee.

He had arrived at Nauvoo about four o'clock in the afternoon, and after making his speech and declining an invitation to stay overnight, he left for Carthage about 6:30 p.m. In marching up Main Street the escort performed a sword exercise, giving all the passes, guards, cuts, and thrusts and taking up the entire width of the street in an imposing show. This maneuvering was an obvious attempt to intimidate the people, for the governor had remarked in his speech that they need not expect to set themselves up against such "well disciplined troops." As they passed, the troops inspected the temple and broke off as a "souvenir" a horn from an ox replica.

When the governor and his party had proceeded about three miles from Nauvoo, they met two messengers (George D. Grant and David Bettisworth) hastening with the sad news to Nauvoo. The governor took them with him back to Grant's house, one and one-half miles east of Carthage, in order to prevent their delivering the news until he and the authorities had removed the county records and public documents, and until most of the inhabitants had left Carthage. Grant then took another horse and rode into Nauvoo that night with the news.[4]

At Hyrum's home on Water Street,[5] not far from the Mansion House, Mary, Hyrum's wife, was keeping vigil over a sick child. Martha Ann, three years old, had a severe case of measles accompanied by a congestion in her lungs, and she could not speak above a whisper. Her mother walked the floor much depressed in spirits. For relief she would occasionally read the Bible. Martha Ann pleaded vainly that she should come to bed. When George D. Grant knocked at the door and delivered the news, the widow stepped back and calmly exclaimed, "It cannot be possible, can it?" His answer was, "Yes, it is too true."

[4]*Ibid.*, vol. VI, pp. 623-624.
[5]See cut.

She fell back against the cupboard. Brother Grant helped her to a chair; and, as Martha Ann later wrote, "The news flew like wild-fire through the house, and the anguish and sorrow that was felt can be easier felt than described. But that will never be forgotten by those who were called to go through it."[6]

At midnight another message was sent from Carthage to Nauvoo, this one from Willard Richards, John Taylor and Samuel Smith, addressed to Emma Smith and Major-General Dunham of the Nauvoo Legion. The message said that the governor had just arrived and would take proper measures. The people were advised not to rush out of the city to Carthage, but rather to stay at home, and be prepared for an attack from Missouri mobbers. It affirmed that Joseph and Hyrum were dead, but that God reigned and said that the bodies would be removed as soon as possible.

Governor Ford added a note as follows: "Defend yourselves until protection can be furnished necessary." June 27 - 1844.

General Deming of the state militia enclosed a message to Orson Spencer which said: ". . .I was at my residence when the horrible crime was committed. It will be condemned by three-fourths of the citizens of the county. Be quiet or you will be attacked from Missouri."[7]

Samuel H. Smith, who lived at Plymouth, a few miles away from Nauvoo, on hearing of the imminent danger of Joseph and Hyrum had ridden his horse toward Nauvoo to warn his brothers of the grave danger they were in. At Bear Creek he met the mob stationed there to watch for movement of the Nauvoo Legion or any other group or person who might thwart their plans to kill the prisoners. They refused to let Samuel advance any farther toward Nauvoo.

---

[6]Mary Ann Smith Harris, *Message to My Posterity*, March 2, 1881, at Provo, Utah. The letter was opened the centennial year — April 6, 1930. Mary Ann remembered her mother's making a pair of pants for Hyrum and his walking back and forth. He was seldom cheerful and always looked anxious and sober. After his death her mother seldom smiled. If they could get her to laugh it was quite a feat. (Note: see Relics under bibliography for a description of Hyrum Smith's personal possessions.)
[7]Joseph Smith, *op. cit.*, vol. VI, pp. 624-625.

He then went to the home of a friend and obtained a fresh mount—one of the fastest in the country, and learning that his brothers were at Carthage, hastened toward the county seat; but every out-of-the-way trail he attempted to follow was guarded by the enemy. When he was recognized by one of the guards, they attempted to kill him, pursuing him over the prairie for two hours. As his assailants would come within shooting distance and raise their guns to fire he would wheel his fast mount and dash off in another direction, only to be confronted by other guards determined to kill him.

Finally he eluded them and rode his tired steed toward Carthage. On the outskirts of the village a man warned him not to advance farther, that he would be shot if he entered the town, but he eluded the man and a few moments later a hysterical Samuel reined in his tired horse at the Hamilton House.

"Rush inside and leave your horse for me," shouted Mr. Hamilton, recognizing Samuel. The courtyard was filled with excited men who were leaping the low fence and scattering from the village. Joseph and Hyrum had just been killed.

After the murderous mob had fled from the village, Samuel helped carry John Taylor to the hotel and dress his wounds. He also assisted in preparing the bodies of his brothers for the journey to Nauvoo. The next morning he and Mr. Hamilton, with an escort of eight soldiers left Carthage, bearing the remains of the martyrs to the grief-stricken "City of Joseph."

The physical and nervous exhaustion suffered the day of the martyrdom by the tender-hearted Samuel left him with a severe fever from which he never recovered. He died one month after the burial of his two brothers.[8]

The solemn procession which left Carthage at 8:00 a.m. had by 3:00 p.m. reached Mulholland Street, about a mile east of the temple in Nauvoo. Here it was met by a great assembly of the sorrowing citizens of Nauvoo, under the direction of the city Marshal.

---

[8]*The Prophet*, New York City, N. Y., quoted from E. Cecil McGavin, *Nauvoo the Beautiful*, pp. 186-187.

The city council, the lieut.-general's staff, Major General Jonathan Dunham and staff, the acting Brigadier-General— Hosea Stout—and staff, commanders and officers of the legion, and several thousands of citizens were there. And the most solemn lamentations that ever ascended unto the Lord of Hosts rose from their throats.

About eight or ten thousand persons were addressed by Dr. Willard Richards, William Phelps, Esquires Woods and Reid of Iowa, and Col. Stephen Markham. They told the people to go quietly home.

At seven o'clock Saturday morning, June 29, the bodies were put into their coffins which were covered with black velvet fastened with brass nails, and lined with white cambric. Over the face of each corpse was a lid fastened with brass hinges, in which was a square of glass to protect the face. Each coffin was placed in a rough pine box.

At 8:00 a.m. the room was thrown open so that the Saints could view the bodies of their martyred Prophet and Patriarch, and it is estimated that over ten thousand persons visited the remains that day. A perfect living stream of people entered at the west door of the Mansion House and left by the north door from 8:00 a.m. until 5:00 p.m., at which hour the family requested that the Mansion House be cleared so that they could take their farewell look at the remains.[9]

---

[9]The first to view the martyrs were of course the immediate families. The following description of the events in Nauvoo following the martyrdom is by a house guest, a Mr. Richmond from Palmyra, New York.

"When I entered the Mansion I found the wife of Joseph seated in a chair in the center of a small room, weeping and wailing bitterly, in a loud and unrestrained voice, her face covered with her hands. Rev. Mr. Greene came in **** approached Mrs. Smith and exclaimed: 'Oh, Sister Emma, God bless you!' ****The first words of the woman were 'Why, O God, am I thus afflicted? Why am I a widow and my children orphans? Thou knowest I have always trusted in thy law.' Mr. Greene rejoined to her that this affliction would be to her a crown of life. She answered quickly: 'My husband was my crown; for him and my children I have suffered the loss of all things; and why, O God, am I thus deserted, and my bosom torn with this ten-fold anguish?'

"I passed into the next room, and the aged mother of Joseph and Hyrum looked up to me with a gaze of wild despair, and clasping me with both hands she asked me why they had shot her dear children. . . .

"In another room the children of Joseph were huddled together, the eldest, an adopted daughter, I think, being about eighteen. Two young boys were lying on the

The coffins were then taken out of the boxes into the little bedroom in the northeast corner of the Mansion and there were sealed and the doors locked. Bags of sand were then placed in each end of the boxes, which were nailed up, and a mock funeral took place, the boxes being put into a hearse and driven to the graveyard by William D. Huntington, and there deposited in a grave with the usual ceremonies.

This was done to prevent the enemies of the martyred Prophet and Patriarch from getting possession of the bodies, as they had threatened to do. As the hearse passed the meeting ground accompanied by a few men, William W. Phelps was preaching the funeral sermon.

About midnight the coffins containing the bodies were taken from the Mansion by Dimick B. Huntington, Edward Hunter,

---

floor, and the other two were kneeling over them, mingling their grief in one wild scream of childish despair.

"At the home of Hyrum, a little way off, the scene was not less heart rending. His wife had gathered her family of four children into the sitting room, and the youngest about four years old sat on her lap. The poor and disabled that fed at the table of her husband, had come in and formed a group of about twenty about the room. They were all sobbing and weeping, each expressing his grief in his own peculiar way. Mrs. Smith seemed stupified with horror.

"While the scenes were being enacted in the city, the bodies were on the way from Carthage. To preserve peace and prepare the citizens to endure the ordeal with resignation, a general assembly was called at 10 o'clock A.M. . . .

"The officials formed around the bodies, the masses silently opening to give them way, and as the mournful procession moved on, the women broke out in lamentations at the sight of the two crude boxes in the wagon covered by an Indian blanket. The weeping was communicated to the crowd, and spread along the vast waves of humanity extending from the Temple to the residence of the Prophet. The groans and sobs and shrieks grew deeper and louder till the sound resembled the roar of a mighty tempest, or the slow, deep, roar of the distant tornado.

"When the bodies arrived at the mansion of Mrs. Emma Smith, the people numbering eight or ten thousand, mostly Mormons, and in close sympathy with the deceased, pressed about the house and the loud wails of the mourners outside, and of the family within, were truly terrible. . . .

"The bodies were carried into the dining room, and about a dozen resolute men who could stand the scent of blood were selected to lay them out. This occupied an hour or more, and they were then arranged near the west windows of the room, and their families were brought in to take a first look at the dead husbands, children and fathers. As the door opened the Prophet's wife entered with two attendants. She advanced a few steps towards the body of Hyrum, swooned and fell to the floor. Her friends raised her up and gave her water, but she fainted again, and was carried out insensible. . . .

"Six times she attempted to see the bodies, and six times she was removed in the arms of her two attendants. Hyrum's wife next entered the room with her four children, supported by no one, she having resolved to brave the scene with her poor orphans. She trembled at every step, and nearly fell, but reached her husband's body, kneeling down by him, clasped her arms around his head, turned his pale face upon

William D. Huntington, William Marks, Jonathan H. Holmes, Gilbert Goldsmith, Alpheus Cutler, Lorenzo D. Wasson, and Philip B. Lewis, preceded by James Emmett who was armed with his musket and acted as guard.

They carried the coffins through the garden, around by the pump, to the Nauvoo House, which was then built to the first joists of the basement, and buried them there.

Just as they finished interring the bodies and smoothing the ground as it was before, strewing chips of wood, stone, and other rubbish over all to make it appear the same as the rest of the ground around the graves, a heavy downpour of rain, accompanied by thunder and lightning, occurred, obliterating all traces that any tampering with the earth had been done in the vicinity.

---

her heaving bosom, and then a gushing, plaintive wail burst forth from her lips: 'Oh! Hyrum, Hyrum! Have they shot you, my dear Hyrum — are you dead, my dear Hyrum!' She drew him closer and closer to her bosom, kissed his pale lips and face, put her hands on his brow and brushed back his hair. Her grief seemed to consume her, and she lost all power of utterance.

"Her two daughters and two young children clung, some around her neck and some to her body, falling prostrate upon the corpse, and shrieking in the wildness of their wordless grief. In about ten minutes Mrs. Emma Smith, wife of the Prophet, came again into the room, between two attendants, in a half swooning state. She came toward the body of Hyrum, and knowing that the sensation of feeling a cold, dead body exerted a calming effect on the human nerves, I took her hand and laid it on Hyrum's brow and in a moment her strength returned. She murmured something in a low tone that I did not hear; her eyes opened, and she said to her friends: 'Now I can see him; I am strong now.' She walked alone to her husband's bed, kneeling down, clasped him around his face, and sank upon his body. Suddenly her grief found vent; and sighs and groans and words and lamentations filled the room. 'Joseph, Joseph,' she said, 'are you dead? Have the assassins shot you?' Her children four in number gathered around their weeping mother and the dead body of a murdered father, and grief that words cannot embody seemed to overwhelm the whole group. She continued to speak in low tones, but none of the words were audible save those which I have recorded. . . .

The multitude dispersed about dark, and the next day was set apart for the people to come and see the bodies, thousands passed in at one door and out at another, from morning till night they came and went, and in the house for the livelong day the lament was heard. . . . E. Cecil McGavin, *Nauvoo the Beautiful*, pp. 146-147.

Of this occasion Marietta Walker, described her feelings, ". . . Not a voice was raised, not a word spoken, as the unbroken line of men, women, and children, with bowed heads and tear-stained cheeks passed by . . . Tramp! tramp! tramp! the muffled sound ascended from the rooms below to those above, each one falling on the bereaved hearts of those mourners waiting there, like the sounds of the first clods upon the coffin lid . . . Will it never end? Will the people never have done coming?"

The Prophet's son Joseph later wrote: "I remember the gathering of the crowd at the Nauvoo Mansion, and recall Dr. Willard Richards on a platform erected in the frame house or building across the road from the Mansion on the south side of Water Street and the congregation of thousands who gathered to listen to him

The bodies remained in these graves in the cellar of the Nauvoo House until the fall, when they were removed by Dimick B. Huntington, William D. Huntington, Jonathan H. Holmes, and Gilbert Goldsmith, at Emma's request, to a place near the Mansion, where they were buried side by side and the bee house moved to cover the graves.

For security reasons, the above, taken from the historian's account, did not tell the exact location of the graves. The bodies were buried the second time across the street from the Nauvoo House near the Old Homestead (Joseph's former residence), under the dirt floor of the Spring House, a canopied cellar with a moist interior which provided refrigeration for food during the hot summer months. Soon afterward, the Spring House was torn down and the ground leveled. With the passing of time all knowledge of the correct location was lost. Rumors even circulated that the bodies were disinterred and taken west at the time of the exodus from Nauvoo. As years passed, tourist guides, when asked where the graves were located would point to a clump of lilacs in the yard, adjacent to the Homestead, as the approximate location. In 1926 the writer was a member of a conducted tour of Nauvoo and the guide pointed out the site of the flowering shrubs as the grave site. In 1928, the descendants explored near this location in an effort to learn the truth of the matter and uncovered the sacred tomb. Grave markers were then installed and the graves can be visited at the present time.[11]

Mary Fielding Smith, Hyrum's widow, in later years remembered the final burial of her husband, the Patriarch. Em-

---

and others detailing something of the tragedy and counseling quiet resignation." *Church History,* vol. VI, pp. 147-149.

Mother Lucy Smith expressed her feelings: ". . . I was swallowed up in the depth of my affliction; and though my soul was filled with horror past imagination, yet I was dumb, until I arose again to contemplate the spectacle before me. Oh! at that moment how my mind flew through every scene of sorrow and distress which we had passed, together, in which they had shown the innocence and sympathy which filled their guileless hearts. As I looked upon their peaceful smiling countenances, I seemed almost to hear them say — 'Mother, weep not for us, we have overcome the world by love; we carried to them the gospel, that their souls might be saved; they slew us for our testimony, and thus placed us beyond their power; their ascendancy is but for a moment, ours is an eternal triumph.'" Lucy Mack Smith.

[10]Emma Smith Bidamon was buried next to Joseph April 30, 1879. She had married Major Lewis Bidamon December 27, 1847.

ma had notified Mary of her intention to remove the bodies for reasons of greater security. The time for the removal was agreed upon, but for some unknown reason Emma changed the date. That night Mary went to bed with her children. About midnight she was impressed that there was something wrong. She got up and dressed, threw a shawl over her head and ran down to the spot where her husband was buried. She found the conspirators in the act of removing the bodies, and remained until she saw the removal of the bodies and knew exactly where they were placed in their new burial.[11]

The leaders were fully aware of the cloud of persecution which hung ominously over Nauvoo. The legion was patrolling the city to guard against any surprise attack by the enemy. There was great danger of having the graves dug up to obtain a reward of a thousand dollars that had been offered for Joseph Smith, dead or alive. Therefore, extra precaution must be taken to hide the bodies of the martyrs.

The burial of Hyrum and Joseph brings to a close the story of this biography, but the narrative would be incomplete without defining both Hyrum's role in establishing the Church and his place in history. His martyrdom with that of his brother gave the growing Church of Jesus Christ a mighty upward thrust. The events immediately following his death resulted in greater faith, loyalty, and devotion of the people to the principles of this new, yet old, gospel. The Church seemed suddenly to mature. The days of deep mourning had their counterpart in the great outpouring of the spirit of peace.

The membership of the Church had been subjected over the preceding years to a variety of new experiences, experiences alternating between exaltation and emotional depression. About a year prior to the martyrdom, Joseph and Hyrum rode triumphantly through streets lined with rejoicing people; Joseph had just been providentially snatched from the custody of police officers bent on taking him to Missouri. Now, a short year later,

---

[11]Susa Young Gates, *op. cit.*

the irony of life and death found the same multitude lining the streets, this time wrapped in the deep gloom of mourning.

Yet somehow that final, climactic scene caught them up in a surge of that heavenly spirit which welds the faithful into one great brotherhood. To them, the purposes of God Almighty had suddenly been revealed; the foundations of a mighty Church had been laid and what had been preached was profoundly true.

Although an era had come to a close, a new one was beginning, and the gold of God's crucible began to rise to the surface. The martyrs' lives became the scale on a barometer with the indicator at the highest point. Ideals and a standard of conduct had been established for the people and for generations yet to follow.

Hyrum Smith, during his last years, filled the role of Patriarch to the whole Church for which office he will be affectionately known among his people throughout eternity. He was ordained to this office by the same authority of the priesthood which ordained the patriarchs of old to the ancient office established to provide an evangelist to bless the people. From the very beginning, Adam, the Ancient of Days, blessed his posterity, and this office came down by lineage—Adam to Seth and Seth to Noah. In Genesis the line is given from Noah to his son Shem, on to Arphaxad, Salab, Eber, Peleg, Reu, Serug, Nahor, Terah, Abraham. (Genesis 11:10-26.) (Terah, the father of Abraham lost the office because of idolatry.) From Abraham to Isaac to Jacob; from Israel (Jacob) to Joseph, the oldest son of Rachel.

In this Dispensation of the Fulness of Times Joseph Smith, Sr., was ordained December 18, 1833; Hyrum Smith January 24, 1841; John Smith February 18, 1855; Hyrum G. Smith, May 9, 1912; Joseph F. Smith, October 8, 1942; and Eldred Gee Smith, April 10, 1947.

The office of Presiding Patriarch was held temporarily by others. For example, "Uncle" John Smith, the oldest living brother of the first Patriarch, held the office, as his right, until John, Hyrum's oldest son, came of age. William Smith was ordained May 24, 1845 but was not sustained by the vote of the

Church because of unworthiness.　He was excommunicated from the Church, October 19, 1845.

The Lord revealed to Joseph Smith that this birthright of the firstborn in Israel belonged to Joseph Smith, Sr., who became the first Patriarch in this dispensation.　This succession of authority from father to son is known as the "Law of Primogeniture."　The office of Patriarch was intimated in a revelation given through the Prophet to Hyrum in April, a few days after the organization of the church.　In this revelation the Lord said:

> Behold, I speak unto you, Hyrum, a few words; for thou also art under no condemnation, and thy heart is opened, and thy tongue loosed; and thy calling is . . . unto the church forever, and this because of thy family. (D&C 23:3.)

Hyrum and Joseph as brothers fulfilled the commandment of God to establish his Church and in so doing were favored with the gift of divine revelation; they endured persecution, mobbing and death.　They came out of the same mold, yet they were different in personality, in temperament, and in physical appearance.　Though they were God's anointed, they were yet human beings and exhibited the weaknesses and frailties common to mankind.　Frequently, in public and in private they acknowledged their faults and failings.　Their evident humility endeared the brothers to the Saints and generated a feeling of brotherhood and love.

As one remembers the early years of the Smith family, he realizes that it was Hyrum who assumed the responsibility of helping to support the family after the death of his older brother, Alvin.　He felt a deep sense of responsibility for his parents and his younger brothers and sisters and this affected his personality. He became serious minded and was not easily discouraged.　His role in the family placed him in the background where he was occupied with family management and duties, leaving the more aggressive Joseph to assume the more spectacular role of church leadership.

It is evident, from the many failures to establish themselves prior to the organization of the Church, that the Smiths were not endowed with the gift of money management or shrewdness in business affairs. Poverty, sickness, and failure dogged their footsteps from one place to another.

Throughout his life Hyrum reflected the family's kindheartedness toward the poverty-stricken. His hospitality knew no bounds. He would divide his substance with the poor even at the risk of starving his own family. Often he would take someone who was old and infirm into his home to be fed and cared for. His faith was that "the Lord would provide."

But his kind and trusting nature invited the unscrupulous to take advantage of him.

As a result of their expulsion from Missouri, the Smiths, like many others were stripped of all they had. Then, too, there were costs incident to lawsuits, and there was sickness in the family. When the state of Illinois passed the bankrupt law, Hyrum and his brother Joseph were forced by the unjustified lawsuits of their enemies to apply for and receive freedom from paying their debts. For this act which merely accentuated their ineptness in money matters, they were maligned by their enemies.

Hyrum, like Joseph, had little formal education. He had attended Hanover Academy for just one semester when an epidemic of fever forced him to quit and return home. His sermons and letters reveal a good mind educated by private observation and study. In his brief journal there is evidence of a need for much improvement in writing. But no doubt his carelessness in writing is an indication that he wrote for his personal use and not for publication.

Missionary work was of great interest to him. When calls came he would plan to leave at the earliest moment for an indefinite period of time. His missionary zeal was contagious and he enjoyed the spirit of his calling to a high degree. His companions often said: "Hyrum is a kind and delightful companion."

His dedicated attitude toward his work and his anxiety for its success gave him a ready insight into basic principles. His advice on numerous occasions to departing missionaries was evidence of his authority in this field. He seldom overlooked saying to these groups: "Preach the first principles and let the mysteries alone."

No one could accuse Hyrum of self-righteousness or exaggerated self-esteem. Nor did the power of office go to his head so that he attempted to exercise unjust dominion over his fellows. On the other hand, he did not shrink from assuming the role of a leader in initiating the building of the temple or in sitting on the stand officiating as a high officer in the Masonic Order, or in dressing up in clothes that were the fashion of the day, or in posing for a portrait. He walked and talked with dignity and self-control, and in his ornate officer's uniform upon his favorite mount occupied his place beside Joseph at the head of the Nauvoo Legion with poise and confidence. His unassuming bearing and sober mien carried great weight among the people.

Seldom did Hyrum become unnerved or act impulsively under pressure, even when taunted and maligned by the enemy; and this quality irritated a few. When a missionary was tried in Nauvoo for certain infractions of the missionary code while on a mission in the east, he was accused among other things of calling Hyrum "an old granny." Perhaps Hyrum seemed slow in making decisions, and sometimes he was absentminded, forgetting some details he had promised to attend to. Naturally, there were those among the Saints whose ideas clashed with Hyrum's, and there were those who envied him and secretly tried to belittle him and undermine his position.

Hyrum gave few parties at his home. Perhaps his house was always fully occupied with other essential matters or was not architecturally planned for festive occasions, or perhaps his helpmate was not socially inclined. But there was seldom a time that Hyrum and his wife missed a social or a party at the home of Joseph or his friends. And at Kirtland, Hyrum opened his

THE WIDOWS AND ORPHANS MOURN   437

home for the wedding of his old friend Newell Knight and had Joseph perform the ceremony, which was an endorsement on his part of sociability.

As a Counselor, Hyrum followed a policy of nonresistance. He was always one to recommend forbearance. The long period in the Missouri jail at Liberty might have been shortened had greater effort been made to escape.

Hyrum's wisdom seemed never to be doubted by Joseph. Joseph would write or say: "What shall we do, Hyrum?" And after Hyrum's reply, Joseph would say, "That is good enough." A report of the trial of an erring brother, said that "Hyrum pleaded for mercy, Joseph for justice. . . ."

It was Hyrum who suggested to Joseph that he record the controversial revelation on plural marriage, and who first read the revelation to the high council. It was Hyrum who refused to save himself by going with his family to Cincinnati when the crisis loomed which led to his death. It was Hyrum who advised that they recross the river and return to Nauvoo to give themselves up, live or die, rather than save themselves by fleeing to the Rocky Mountains. His advice to Joseph and others was generally accepted when decisions of far-reaching importance had to be made.

Hyrum was courageous and unflinching in the face of mob threats, and calm under pressure of evil rumors about the destruction of Nauvoo. He organized drives for workmen, funds and material with which to finish the temple. His faith was undeviating, although his wisdom under the conditions may have been somewhat faulty. A careful study of Church history and of the lives of Hyrum and Joseph reveals the great influence Hyrum exerted in shaping the course, movement, and the growth of the Church during the first fourteen years.

It may be said of him that he was a temple-builder. He initiated the construction of both the Kirtland and Nauvoo Temples. He acted as the chairman of both building committees. He accepted the idea of the penny fund, suggested by Mercy

Rachel Thompson, by which a sum of over $500 was raised to buy nails and glass for the temple.[12] His ability to organize, raise money, secure labor, and inspire support for the project was utilized at a critical time in the history of the Church. There are important blessings contingent on the completion of the temples, and the name of Hyrum Smith is one of the foremost among those who have taken a leading part in building temples and encouraging the work therein.

To know Hyrum Smith and his place in the esteem of God and of men, we must examine his ecclesiastical position and his part in bringing forth new revelation in the establishment of the Church.

Hyrum was one of the eight witnesses to the Book of Mormon, and a charter member of the Church. He was ordained an elder, a high priest, a Counselor in the First Presidency, and Associate President to his brother, Joseph Smith, taking the place of Oliver Cowdery. He was a member of the Nauvoo City Council and an officer in the Nauvoo Legion.

That his place in the love of the Lord is secure is evident in these words:

> And again, verily I say unto you, blessed is my servant Hyrum Smith; for I, the Lord, love him because of the integrity of his heart, and because he loveth that which is right before me, saith the Lord. (D&C 124:15.)

---

[12]In regard to the Temple Penny Fund, Mercy Thompson wrote: "At one time after seeking diligently to know from the Lord if there was anything I could do for the building up of the Kingdom of God, a most pleasant sensation came over me with the following words, 'Try to get the sisters to subscribe one cent per week for the purpose of buying glass and nails for the Temple.' I went immediately to Joseph and told him what seemed to be the whisperings of the Spirit of the still small voice to me. He told me to go ahead, and the Lord would help me. I then mentioned it to Brother Hyrum who was much pleased, and did all in his power to encourage and help by speaking to the sisters in private and public promising them they would receive their blessings in the Temple. All who subscribed the one cent per week should have their names recorded in the *Book of the Law of the Lord*. I was assisted by my sister Mary, and took down and kept a record of all the names, and notwithstanding the poverty of the people, we had, by the time the committee was ready for the glass and the nails in the treasury, about $500.00 which they gladly received just in time of need. Perhaps I should have mentioned while the mob was threatening to mob and massacre the inhabitants we hid up the box containing the money in a pile of brick Hyrum had intended for building had his life been spared.

The foregoing sentence brings to my mind a picture which beggars description: an affectionate husband, loving Father, a faithful friend, a warm hearted benefactor, being torn from wives, children, friends and dependants. The family at that

The devotion and faith of Hyrum Smith both to the Church and to Joseph during the New York, Kirtland, Ohio; and Illinois periods placed upon him still greater responsibility. The pathos and grandeur of Joseph and Hyrum's relationship is revealed in Joseph's often expressed love for his older brother. At Kirtland when trouble flared between Joseph and William, the soothing influence of Hyrum caused Joseph to exclaim:

And I pray in my heart that all my brethren were like unto my beloved brother Hyrum, who possesses the mildness of a lamb, and the integrity of a Job, and in short, the meekness and humility of Christ; and I love him with that love that is stronger than death, for I never had occasion to rebuke him nor he me.

In Nauvoo in 1842, when the heavy hand of oppression was on the Prophet, with some of his associates and friends turning against him, he turned for fellowship and friendly assurance to Hyrum and said of him:

There was Brother Hyrum who next took me by the hand—a natural brother. Thought I to myself, Brother Hyrum, what a faithful heart you have got! Oh, may the eternal Jehovah crown eternal blessings upon your head as a reward for the care you have had for my soul.

---

time numbering twenty (20), never to see their faces more and we never to see him but a mangled bleeding corpse. Perhaps my feelings can be better imagined than described." Mercy R. Thompson — *Letter to My Posterity.*

During the latter part of 1844 the penny fund served a very useful purpose. The Quorum of the Twelve, the trustees and members of the building committee needed a sum of money to save some church lands. After due deliberation President Young said, "My feelings are to draw the money lying in possession of Sisters Mary Smith, and Mercy R. Thompson and A. Cutler, which money has been donated by the sisters of the church, by paying one cent a week, for the purpose of purchasing the nails and glass for the Temple and which amounts to five or six hundred dollars already collected. It is considered wisdom to do this to save the church property from the hands of our enemies."

The order read:

To Mrs. Mary Smith and Mercy R. Thompson,

Dear Sisters:

We are under the necessity of raising a considerable sum of money for the use of the church within a few days. We have counseled together on the subject, and have considered it wisdom to call upon you for the money in your hands, donated by the sisters as penny subscriptions. You will therefore, please deliver the same to Bishop Whitney when he presents this order.

Done by order of the Quorum of the Twelve, for and in behalf of the Church of Jesus Christ of Latter-day Saints. Signed, Brigham Young, President of the Quorum of Twelve. *Church History,* vol. VII, p. 322.

Oh, how many the sorrows we have shared together, and again we find ourselves shackled with the unrelenting hand of oppression. Hyrum, thy name shall be written in the *Book of the Law of the Lord,* for those who come after thee to look upon that they may pattern after thy works.

The strength of Hyrum in the eyes of Joseph was expressed when the Prophet was constrained to bestow a special blessing upon him. In these words he said:

Blessed of the Lord is my brother Hyrum for the integrity of his heart. He shall be girt about with strength, and faithfulness shall be the strength of his loins. From generation to generation he shall be a shaft in the hands of his God to execute judgment upon his enemies. His children shall be many and his posterity numerous, and they will rise up and call him blessed. (*Church History* vol. I, p. 466.)

Among God's great Prophets and seers, none have stood together as associates with so nearly equal heavenly authority and power as did Hyrum and Joseph. It is quite likely that had Hyrum been spared martyrdom he would have been chosen and sustained as the Prophet's successor in the First Presidency of the church. This fact was so declared by President Brigham Young, when the question of succession was before the people in Nauvoo.

When Hyrum and his prophet brother were felled at Carthage by the assassins' bullets, they were consigned to the ages. The blood of these martyrs had become the seed of the Church. And as Paul the ancient apostle said, "For where a testament is, there must also of necessity be the death of the testator. For a testament is of force after men are dead: otherwise it is of no strength at all while the testator liveth." (Heb. 9:17-18.) The deaths of Hyrum and Joseph put the seal of divinity upon their work.

When they were approaching the hour of death the power of Prophecy overflowed when Joseph said,

I am going like a lamb to the slaughter; but I am calm as a summer's morning; I have a conscience void of offense towards God, and towards all men. *I shall die innocent, and it shall be said of me, he was murdered in cold blood.*

The same morning, after Hyrum had made ready to go—Shall it be said to the slaughter? Yes, for so it was—he read the following paragraph of Ether in the Book of Mormon, and turned down the leaf upon it:

And it came to pass that I prayed unto the Lord that he would give unto the Gentiles grace, that they might have charity.

And it came to pass that the Lord said unto me: If they have not charity it mattereth not unto thee, thou hast been faithful; wherefore, thy garments shall be made clean. And because thou hast seen thy weakness thou shalt be made strong, even unto sitting down in the place which I have prepared in the mansions of my Father.

And now I . . . bid farewell unto the Gentiles, yea, and also my brethren whom I love, until we shall meet before the judgment-seat of Christ, where all men shall know that my garments are not spotted with your blood. (Ether 12:36-38.)

Hyrum was bidding farewell to those he loved, and thus expressed his forgiveness to his enemy and the gentiles. His garments were clean from the blood of this generation, and his conscience was clear.

Hyrum's and Joseph's names are "classed among the martyrs of religion; and the reader in every nation will be reminded that the Book of Mormon, and this book of Doctrine and Covenants of the church, cost the best blood of the nineteenth century to bring them forth for the salvation of a ruined world; . . . They lived for glory; they died for glory; and glory is their eternal reward. From age to age shall their names go down to posterity as gems for the sanctified." (D & C, 35:4-6.)

And thus we bring to a close the life story of Hyrum Smith who was a leading actor in God's divine drama of the latter days. He fulfilled the role foreordained to him; he helped to consummate the decreed destiny of this land, choice above all other lands. And through revelation he helped to establish the kingdom of God in the latter-days, the kingdom destined to bring peace to a troubled world.

AN EPILOGUE

The family of Hyrum Smith, under the continuing threat of the mob to annihilate Nauvoo, decided to join the pioneers on their trek to the Rocky Mountains. After the first wagons going west had crossed the Mississippi River, February 6, 1846, the days and nights of those left behind were full of fear and evil forebodings. Their beloved city, without its charter, was unprotected except for a temporary organization which kept the lawless elements from completely overrunning the city.

Mary Fielding Smith waited for the most opportune time to move. She had to arrange for wagons, oxen, and food, and all the other necessities for so long a journey. But her drive and courage, together with the co-operation of her young family made it possible for her to start, finally, early in September. She had watched her neighbors and friends, and the Authorities of the Church pack up a few choice belongings, load them on hastily built wagons, and take affectionate leave of those who had to wait.

The city had begun to look deserted, with the old and infirm and a few of the more needy practically the only ones remaining. The river wharf had been busy for weeks with a never ending line of white-top covered wagons moving steadily over the river onto the undulating plains of Iowa. The number of those leaving ran into the thousands.

And now it was Mary's turn to leave. She would miss the friendship and society of her widowed kinswomen, Mother Lucy Mack Smith, bereft of five sons and her husband, Emma Smith, Levira Clark Smith and Agnes Coolbirth Smith, widows of Joseph, Samuel, and Don Carlos Smith, respectively. The sad farewell was described, years later by Martha Ann Smith, then five years old:

. . . We left our home, just as it was, all the furniture, in fact everything we owned. The fruit trees were loaded with rosy peaches and apples. We bid goodby to the loved home that reminded us of our beloved father everywhere we turned. We crossed the Mississippi River on a skiff in the dusk of the evening. We bid goodby to our dear old grandmother, Lucy Mack Smith. I can never forget the bitter tears she shed when she bid us goodby for the last time. She knew it would be the last time she would see her son's family again in this life. We did not realize this so much at the time as we have since. . . . I went with my mother every day for three weeks while she worked in the Nauvoo Temple. What joy that was to me. My mother to this very day is perfect in my mind's eye. God bless her memory.[1]

The grandmother, Lucy Mack Smith, was living at the Mansion House with Emma Smith when Mary Fielding Smith came by to bid them farewell. She had grown feeble and stood in the doorway supported by a cane in each hand as the last good-byes were said.

The evening of September 8, 1846, Hyrum's family camped on the Iowa side of the Father of Waters.[2] They remained here several days, until they heard the cannonading of Nauvoo which began about September 12, lasting four days.[3] Then they moved on a few miles.

The story of the family's trek to Winter Quarters and later of their crossing the plains was one of hardship and privation, and also one of faith, courage, and heroism. They remained at Winter Quarters until June, 1848, and after about six weeks arrived in Salt Lake Valley on September 23rd.[4]

---

[1]Martha Smith Harris, op. cit.
[2]The family of six children included Lovina, 19; John, 14; Jerusha, 10; Sarah, 9; Joseph Fielding, 8; and Martha Ann, 5 years old. Others in the group were Mercy Rachel Thompson, her daughter, May Jane, Hannah Grinnels, George Mills, and Elder James Lawson.
[3]Joseph Fielding, description of crossing the Mississippi River. ". . . We moved to Hyrum's farm—he said Mary and family left just prior to the mob entering Nauvoo. . . . They marched into Nauvoo; my two sisters Smith and Thompson and myself with our families had just got over the River Mississippi with all our goods except two boat loads before they came in contact with the citizens. They came and camped on the farm (Hyrum's) that I had just left.

"The sisters had barely time after returning home from the temple where they had been working to commence preparation for the journey west. . . . Mary and the children, driven by the mob, barely escaped from the city of Nauvoo before its destruction. The mother had succeeded in getting provisions, bedding, wagons, ox-teams, her husband's big white horse, and a few other necessities, loaded on a flat boat and taken across the Mississippi River to Montrose, Iowa. The children were taken across in a skiff and they and their mother spent the night in their camp on the banks of the river listening to the bombardment of the city of Nauvoo. It was September 9, 1846 when they crossed."—Richard P. Harris, "Martha Ann Smith Harris"—*The Relief Society Magazine*, vol. XI, p. 12.
[4]Susa Young Gates, op. cit.

Mary Smith settled in Mill Creek, south of Salt Lake City, where with the help of her boys she expected to engage in farming. She had a small cabin built in which to do the cooking, but she and most of her family lived in the wagons during the winter of 1848. How they survived through the winter they hardly knew. They were thinly clad and in such flimsy shelter suffered intensely from the cold.

Within two years, however, with the help of her sons and daughters she had secured some valuable property. John by then was sixteen years old and able to give help a great deal. When others were unemployed and receiving church aid, Mary Smith and her family were making their own way. She was blessed with tireless energy and was the soul of thrift and industry.

Honest with all her fellow men, she was equally as honest with God as was evidenced by her payment of tithes.[5]

But the continued toil and hardship of this frontier life were too much for her frail body, and she broke under the intense strain. On December 11, 1852, after two months of illness she died in the home of Heber C. Kimball; and it was written of her: "Mary Fielding Smith was a Saint, if ever one lived on this troubled earth. She was a heroine in her own right, by reason of her greatness of spirit and soul. She was beautiful to look upon. When she and her equally handsome sister, Mercy, came to Kirtland in 1837, trim, straight, dark-haired and dark eyed, with delicately blooming cheeks and finely molded, graceful figures, clad in dainty silks of modern grace, they were the observed of all observers. Their refined and stately ways made them a shining mark in Kirtland Society. Wherever they went they were spoken of as those 'lovely English girls.' Refinement, strength, courage, integrity, modesty and infinite sweetness and tenderness—these were the prevailing characteristics of the Fielding sisters."[6]

*   *   *

The posterity of Hyrum Smith have been continuously identified with the growth of the Church ever since the Nauvoo

[5]Joseph Fielding Smith, op. cit., pp. 155-158.
[6]Idem.

period. His children, grandchildren, and their children have helped to pioneer the valleys of the mountains, to establish cities and towns, and to build roads, irrigation canals, and industry. Hyrum's descendants are identified with agriculture, commerce, and the professions.

Ecclesiastically, they have been active in the priesthood. Their role has been one of leadership in the Church, of helping to organize branches, missions, wards, stakes, and to build temples. Many have inherited the missionary spirit of their grandsire and have carried the gospel message to people at home and abroad.[7]

Surely the blessings of posterity pronounced on the head of Hyrum Smith have been and are now being fulfilled. The six children who survived him followed the example of their illustrious father by marrying and rearing fine families.

The memory of Hyrum Smith has been perpetuated in this posterity and in bronze and granite and literature as well. In the Salt Lake City cemetery, at the site of the family burial plot, rises a thirty-two-foot (Vermont granite) shaft, engraved on the four sides of its base with an account of Hyrum's place and election in helping to establish the Church.[8] On Temple Square, cast in bronze, is a life-size statue of Hyrum with an appropriate inscription.

The work of Hyrum Smith has not ended. He left a rich legacy to the Church of integrity, faith, love and devotion, and set an example of intense interest in missionary and temple work. His life was the life of a creator, and his work has left the stamp of his memory forever within the church.

---

[7]Joseph F. Smith was identified with the Church as a missionary, Counselor in the First Presidency, and President of the Church. His sons Hyrum M. Smith and Joseph Fielding Smith were apostles, and David A. Smith, a counselor to the Presiding Bishopric of the church. His oldest son John Smith was ordained presiding Patriarch at twenty-two years of age.

[8]The unveiling of Hyrum Smith's thirty-two-foot monument, a polished shaft of Vermont granite, occurred on Thursday, June 27, 1918.

Note — On February 9, 1922, the birthday of Hyrum Smith was commemorated by a Salt Lake Temple session, which 311 attended. President Heber J. Grant and five apostles were present.

BIBLIOGRAPHY

PRIMARY SOURCES

Unpublished Material
Adams, William, *Autobiography of*, 1822-1844.
Allen, Joseph, *Autobiography of*, 1840-1844.
Andrus, Milo, *Autobiography of*, 1779, 1875.
Bailey, Raymond, *Emma Smith*, (Master's Thesis) BYU 1952.
Black, Joseph Smith, *Diary* 1836-1910.
Burns, Enoch, *Biography of*, 1833-1844.
Bushman, John, *Life and Labors of*, pp. 368-369, 1843.
Carter, Jared, *Private Journal*, Historian's Office, Salt Lake.
Clark, Joshua R., *Diaries and Records of*,
Clark, Mary Louisa Woolley, *Diaries and Records of Joshua R. Clark*.
Cox, Edwin Charles, *Record Book of*,
Diary, Author Unknown, 1835.
Duncan, Chapman, *Biography of*, 1812-1900.
Fielding, Joseph, *Correspondence, Journal*, 1839, 1846.
Earl, Sylvester H., *Diary*, 1838-1854.
Gardner, Martha Tuttle, *A Sketch of*,
Griffen, Charles E., *History of*,
Griffin, C. E., *Letter* April 14, 1878. Husband of Sarah Smith Griffin to Martha Ann Smith Harris.
Griffin, Sarah Smith, *Letter* to Martha Ann Smith Harris, from Coalville, Utah, April 12, 1871
Haight, Isaac Chauncey, *Biography, Sketch and Diary*, 1813-1862.
Harris, Martha Ann Smith, *Centennial Letter* written March 22, 1881, Provo, Utah, opened April 6, 1930
Harmon, Appleton Milo, *Early History and Journal*, 1843-1844.
Hogan, Goudy, *History of*, 1844.
Holbrook, Joseph, *Life of*, 1806-1871.
Huntington, Oliver B., *Diary*, 1838-1844, Pt. I.
Huntington, William, *Diary*.
Johnson, Joel Hills, *Diary*, 1802-1882.
Jones, William Ell's, *Journal*, 1861-1896.
Journal History, Historian's Office, Salt Lake City, Utah, 1830-1846.
Journal of History, Vol. XVII.
Kartchner, William Decator, *Diary*, 1839-1844.
Lyman, Eliza Maria Partridge (Smith), *Diary*, 1820-1885.
McBride, James, *An Autobiography of*, 1838.
Morris, George, *Autobiography of*, 1844.

Murdock, John, *Journal*, Historian's Office, Salt Lake City, Utah.

Pace, James, *Diary and Biography of*, 1842-1844, BYU, Provo, Utah.

Philips, Edward, *Biographical Sketch*.

Phillips, Sylvia, *Biographical Sketch of Edward Phillips* in 1888 from dictation.

Porter, Mary R., Jerusha Barden Smith, *Genealogy*.

Pulsipher, John, *Diary* Vol. 1.

Rogers, Samuel H., *Journal of*, 1837.

Smith, Bathsheba Bigler, *Diary*.

Smith, George A., *Journal*.

Smith, George A., *Memoirs of*, Salt Lake City, Utah, 1833-1834-1835-1836-1837-1842.

Smith, Hyrum, *Diary*, size 3" x 4" x 1/4"—Entries, 1831-1832, 1833-1835. Home-made with lined paper folded and sewed along the crease with flax thread. The black oil-cloth back contains yellow and red painted flowers.

Smith, Hyrum, *Account Book* Entries March 30, 1835 to January 1844. Size 6.5" x 7.75" x 1/5". Paste-board back—pages yellow with age. Written black and purple ink, also in lead pencil. On the inside of back cover appears "H. Smith" longhand. Some of the accounts read: "salt ½ bu., full to one bushel corn—two blessings, etc.

Smith, Hyrum, *Patriarchal Blessing*—date March 6, 1843. Nauvoo, Illinois, to Elias Harmer—unlined paper—7½" x 12¼"—Napthalai Lineage.

Smith, John (son of Hyrum Smith), *Document*, size 7½ x 11½, longhand—black ink—large writing.

Smith, John, (Uncle), *Diary*, 1839-1852.

Smith, John William, *Diary*, 1826-1905.

Smith, Lucy M., *Historical Narrative*, wife of George A. Smith.

Stout, Hosea, *Diary* Vols. 1-2, 1835-1846.

Thompson, Mercy Rachel, *Letter to My Posterity* written December 20, 1880, Salt Lake City, Utah. Opened April 6, 1930.

Walker, H. S. Sr., *Letter*. Son of Lovina Smith Walker—to Martha Ann Smith Harris, April 29, 1920.

Williams, Henrietta E. C. and Burns, Enoch, *Diary*, 1833.

Wilson, Mary Julia Johnson, *Ancestral Sketch and Memories of*, 1776-1877.

Wilford Woodruff, *Journal*, 1840-1841-1842-1843-1844—Historian's Office, Salt Lake City, Utah.

Published Material

Berrett, William E., and Burton, Alma, *Readings in LDS Church History*, Vol. 1, Deseret Book Company, Salt Lake City, Utah.

Bible.
Book of Mormon.
Doctrine and Covenants.
Jensen, Andrew, *Historical Record* Vols. II, V, VI, VII, VIII.
Jensen, Andrew, *LDS Biographical Encyclopedia,* Salt Lake City, Utah, 1889.
Johnson, Carrie Polk, *History of Clinton and Caldwell Counties, Missouri,* Historical Publishing Co., 1923, Topeka-Indianapolis, Pt. II History of Caldwell County.
McClumphy, W. H. S., *History of Caldwell County,* Historical Publishing Co., 1923—Topeka, Indianapolis.
Pearl of Great Price.
Smith, Herman C., Smith, Frederick M., and Ass't Historian, *Journal of History* (Reorganized), Lamoni, Iowa.
Smith, Joseph, *History of the Church* (Documentary), Vols. 1-7.
Thompson, Anna May, B. S., *Mormons in Missouri,* Thesis, University of Colorado, Dept. of History, 1932, pp. 1-82.
Wood, Wilford, *Joseph Smith Begins His Work,* copyright, Wilford C. Wood. Deseret News Press, Salt Lake City, Utah, 1958.

SECONDARY SOURCES

Anderson, Mary, Audentia Smith, *Ancestry and Posterity of Joseph Smith and Emma Hale,* Independence, Missouri, 1929.
Berrett, William E., *The Restored Church,* LDS Dept. of Education, Salt Lake City, Utah, 1944.
Bean, Willard A. D. C., *History of Palmyra and the Beginning of Mormonism.*
Bennett, John C., *History of the Latter-day Saints or An Expose of Joe Smith and Mormonism,* Boston, Washington, D. C., New York, Cincinnati, 1842.
Bennion, Lowell L., *Religion of the Latter-day Saints,* LDS Dept. of Education, Salt Lake City, Utah, 1948.
Brodie, Fawn M., *Joseph Smith, No Man Knows My History,* Knoff Publishers, New York, 1944.
Burton, Alma P., *Mormon Trail From Vermont to Utah,* Deseret Book Co., Salt Lake City, Utah, 1953.
Cannon, George Q., *The Life of Joseph Smith,* Salt Lake City, Utah. The Juvenile Instructor Office, 1888.
Cannon, George Q., *The Life of Joseph Smith,* Salt Lake City, Utah, 1907.
Chase, Daryl, *Christianity through the Centuries,* LDS Dept. of Education, Salt Lake City, Utah, 1948.

Cross, Whitney R., *The Burned-Over District*, Cornell University Press, Ithaca, New York, 1950

Cowley, Mathias F., *The Blood of the Prophets*, Salt Lake City, Utah, Biographical Sketches—selected from his work entitled Prophets and Patriarchs, Chattanooga, Tenn., by Ben E. Rich, Jan., 1902.

Cowley, Mathias F., *Wilford Woodruff*, Salt Lake City, Utah, 1909.

Cowley, Mathias, *Wilford Woodruff, History of Life and Labors*, Salt Lake City, Utah, 1892.

Davis, Inez Smith, *The Story of the Church*, Herald House, Independence, Missouri.

Durham, Homer, *Joseph Smith, Prophet Statesman*, Salt Lake City, Utah, 1944.

Evans, John Henry, *Joseph Smith, The American Prophet*, Macmillan Company, N. Y., 1933.

Gates, Susa Young, *Lydia Knight's History*, Juvenile Instructor Office, Salt Lake City, Utah, 1883.

Johnson, Benjamin Franklin, *My Life's Review*, Zion's Printing and Publishing Co., Independence, Missouri, 1947.

Johnson, Carrie Polk, *History of Clinton and Caldwell Counties*, Historical Publishing Company, Topeka, Indianapolis, 1923.

Kirkham, Francis W., *A New Witness of Christ in America*, Independence, Jackson County, Missouri, 1942.

Little, Malcolm Jr., *A Biographical Sketch of the Life of James A. Little*, BYU, Provo, Utah.

Littlefield, Lyman D., *The Martyrs*, Juvenile Instructor Office, Vol. 10, Salt Lake City, Utah, 1882.

McGavin, E. Cecil, *Nauvoo the Beautiful*, Stevens and Wallis, Inc., Salt Lake City, Utah, 1946.

Nibley, Preston, *Joseph Smith The Prophet*, Deseret Book Co., Salt Lake City, Utah, 1944.

Piercy, Frederick, *Route from Liverpool to Great Salt Lake Valley*, Illustrated—Edited by James Lindford, Liverpool—Pub. by Franklin D. Richards, 36 Islington, London, 1885.

Roberts, Brigham H., *Comprehensive History of the Church of Jesus Christ of Latter-day Saints*, Salt Lake City, Utah, 1921.

Roberts, B. H., *The Life of John Taylor*, Salt Lake City, Utah, 1892.

Scraps of Biography—Tenth Book of the Faith Promoting Series, Juvenile Instructor Office, Salt Lake City, Utah, 1883.

Smith, Joseph III and Smith, Herman C., *History of the Reorganized Church*, Vols. 1—4, Herald House, Independence, Missouri.

Smith, Lucy Mack, *History of Joseph Smith*, Salt Lake City, Utah, 1945 —Ed. Preston Nibley, also edited by George A. Smith and Elias Smith, 1902.

Smith, Joseph Fielding, *Life of Joseph F. Smith,* Deseret News Press, Salt Lake City, Utah, 1938.

Smith, Lucy Mack, *History of Joseph Smith the Prophet,* (Reorganized Church), Independence, Missouri, 1880.

Smith, Lucy Mack, *Joseph Smith the Prophet,* Independence, Missouri, 1880.

Smith, Heman C., *Missouri Historical Review,* Vol. 4.

Stout, Wayne, *Hosea Stout, Utah's Pioneer Statesman.*

Tucker, Pomeroy, *Origin, Rise and Progress of Mormonism,* Palmyra, New York, D. Appleton and Company, 1867, N. Y.

Whitney, Orson F., *Life of Heber C. Kimball,* Salt Lake City, Utah, 1888.

PERIODICALS

Albright, R. Wilson, Editor, *Lee County Democrat,* Vol. 1, Fort Madison, Iowa Territory, (Clippings), 1842.

Albright, R. Wilson, Editor, *Lee County Democrat,* 1842-1846.

Bailhoche, John, Proprietor, *Alton Telegraph and Democratic Review,* Vol. 10, No. 28, Alton, Illinois.

Bartlett and Sullivan, Editors, Quincy *Whig,* Quincy, Illinois, 1838.

Bassett, J. M. and Terry E., Editor, Quincy *Argus,* Quincy, Illinois, April 25, 1840, July 24, 1841

Bennett, F. Archibald, *The Improvement Era,* Vol. 58, 59, Salt Lake City, Utah.

Chambers, Harris and Knapp, Editors, *Missouri Republican Daily,* St. Louis, Missouri, 1839.

Clark, James, Editor, *International Gazette,* Vol. 2, Burlington, Iowa Terr.

Clark, James, Editor, *Iowa Territory Gazette,* Burlington, Iowa Territory, August 25, 1838, May 26, 1849.

Corrill, John, *Far West Record,* Historian's Office, Salt Lake City, Utah, September 2, 1831.

Deseret News, "Hyrum Gibbs Smith, Presiding Patriarch—Life Sketch—Death." February 4, 1932.

Edwards, Broadwell, Editors, Burlington *Hawkeye,* Burlington, Iowa, 1843-1848.

Edwards, James G., Editor, *The Iowa Patriot,* Vols. I-II, Burlington, Iowa Territory, 1839.

Elders Journal, Kirtland, Ohio, Discontinued December 1873.

Emmons, Sylvester, Editor, Nauvoo *Expositor,* Nauvoo, Illinois (one issue), June 7, 1844.

Gates, Susa Young, *The Relief Society Magazine,* Vol. 3, No. 3, Salt Lake City, Utah.

Gilbert, E. S., Editor, *The Evening and Morning Star*. A reprint—Historical Library, St. Louis, Missouri, 1832-1833.

Gregg, T., Editor, *Iowa Morning Star*, Keokuk, Iowa Territory, April 2, 1845—May 1, 1845—May 1, 1845.

Gregg, Thomas, Editor, Warsaw *Message* (Incomplete File). Warsaw, Illinois, 1843-1844.

Gunn, Calvin, Editor, *Jeffersonian Republican*, Jefferson, Missouri, Vol. 12.

Houghton and Breath, Editors, *North Western Gazette and Galena Advertizer*, 1839

Houghton, H. H. and Thomas, W. C. E., Editors, *North Western Gazette and Galena Advertizer*, Galena, Illinois, 1838-1848.

Messenger and Advocate, Kirtland Edition, Historian's Office, Salt Lake City, Utah.

McKenney, John H., Editor, *Iowa Territorial Gazette and Advertizer*, Vol. 4, Burlington, Iowa, Iowa Territory.

Niles, H., Editor, *Niles Register*, Baltimore, Maryland, 1831, 1833, 1834.

Ogden, J. W., and R. B. Publishers, The Keokuk *Register*, Keokuk, Iowa Territory, May 26, 1849, March 15, 1849.

Pettet, John H., Editor, Quincy *Herald*, (Incomplete file), Quincy, Illinois, Oct., 1841-Dec., 1842.

Ricks, Artel, *The Improvement Era*, "Hyrum's Prophecy." Salt Lake City, Utah, May, 1956.

Sharp, Thomas C., Editor, Warsaw *Signal*, (Incomplete File), Warsaw, Illinois, 1844-1848.

Smith, Joseph Fielding, *The Improvement Era*, Vol. 59, No. 11. "Patriarchal Priesthood," Salt Lake City, Utah.

St. Louis *Evening Gazette*, St. Louis, Missouri, 1838.

Tenney, J. A., and H. W., Editors, Galena *Jeffersonian*, Galena, Illinois, Semi-weekly, Nov. 1845-Oct. 1846.

Tibbett, H. A., *Bedfordshire Magazine*, Vol. 5, No. 36. "Bedfordshire Biographies XXII, Westward Across the Atlantic," Mary Fielding, spring 1856.

Turner, J. D., Editor, Illinois *Statesman*, Jacksonville, Illinois, July 1843-March 1844.

Walters and Weber, Publishers, *Illinois State Register*, Springfield, Illinois, 1838-1848.

Watson, Thomas and Son, Editors, *Missouri Argus*, St. Louis, Missouri, 1839.

Widtsoe, Osborne T. P., *The Utah Genealogical and Historical Magazine*, Vol. 2.

Wilson, Albright, Editors, *Fort Madison Courier*, Fort Madison, Iowa, 1841.

INTERVIEWS

Dale, Thomas, Kirtland, Ohio, elderly resident.

Heaps, Sarah Edith, great-granddaughter of Hyrum Smith and Jerusha Barden (Sarah Smith line).

McFarland, Dora, Kirtland, Ohio, former owner of Hyrum Smith's home.

Passey, Sarah, granddaughter of Hyrum Smith and Mary Fielding (Martha Ann line).

Pratt, Zina Furner Dennis, granddaughter of Hyrum Smith and Mary Fielding (Martha Ann line).

Smith, Eldred G. Smith, Presiding Patriarch, great-great-grandson (John Smith line).

Smith, Ralph G., great-grandson of Hyrum Smith and Jerusha Barden (John Smith line).

Startup, Artie, granddaughter of Hyrum Smith and Mary Fielding (Martha Ann line).

RELICS

Bible, Hebrew, cover torn off—size 5.6″ x 8.5″ x 2.5″.

Brush, shaving, worn, leather band holding bristles cracked—The four-inch brush shows much wear.

Cane, wood with ivory nob—an inlaid silver colored metal shaft from the nob-hand grip. Engraved in the metal are the initials "H. S." A six-inch round tapered stainless steel tip fitted into well preserved wood.

Chest, wooden—the first such repository for the gold plates. The name "Alvin" is carved in the wood at the right of the metal lock set in wood an inch in width. Size—16¼″ x 14½″ x 6¼″ inside measurement. A sloping, inch thick wooden lid attached by two metal hinges to a 4″ width strip across top. A keyhole is located where the lock is. The chest contained also the breastplate and the Urim and Thummim.

Clothes, worn while martyred—*trousers* homespun cotton serge—brown tinged—two large pockets in front—high waist line at back. Bullet holes on right side under belt, and also in right leg above knee.

Vest—cotton, light brown, sleeveless—six buttons low cut front vent —two pockets on both sides. On the back appears a hole where a ball pierced his body and broke his watch.

Drawers—white cotton, home spun—bullet holes conform to those found in trousers.

Shirt—White cotton, closed front except for a twelve-inch opening from the neck. Worn prior to the martyrdom.

Dagger, Masonic ten inch, stainless steel—wooden handle—Masonic symbols on blade.

Emblematic parchments—Masonic—three, original hand painted on heavy bodied paper—on border appears initials "I. H. S."

Footstool, of mother Lucy Mack Smith. Used when side-portrait was painted. It has a circular top—dished—twelve inches in diameter, wood 1½" thick, oak stained 6.5" high, four legs, slightly slanted outward, connected with wooden rounds. Very sturdy and well preserved.

Gun, muzzle-loading rifle, 45mm size with deep engraved rifles visible at the muzzle opening. A wooden ramrod is attached to the underside of the barrel. The shoulder groove on the wooden stock is plated by a silver colored metal. The octogon steel barrel is thick and heavy.

Mortar and Pestle—Blac cast iron bowl six inches high—four inches in diameter—hardwood oval-ended pestle.

Pin, Mason—gold—One inch square—clover-leaf pattern—pin missing— worn on lapel of coat while at Carthage.

Pouch, Masonic cotton fabric 4" x 4" with draw string attached.

Sunglasses, green lenses, with blue side shades fit in silver rims and ear braces. Are collapsible for carrying in a case. The case is made of compressed paper with opening at the end covered by a lid connected by a metal hinge. Well preserved.

Sword, Dress—Nauvoo Legion. Ornate hilt of polished brass—straight pointed stainless steel blade, forty-two inches in length—a leather strap attached. The scabbard is of polished brass, well-preserved.

Watch, silver case—key winder—sold in Sheffield, England in 1839—made in Chester, England, a suburb of Liverpool—maker, Robert Roskell —serial No. 29737. Pat. No. 2273—a blue jewel is visible. Ring on stem intact. Was left at home at time of martyrdom.

Watch—silver case—Roman numerals. Inscribed on works "London Assay Office—movement chain and fusee wound with verge escape. Lion Password (33) London, year 1830." Face shattered. One fourth of the face has original enamel. Inner works are jammed. The watch ring is intact.

INDEX

Joseph and Hyrum leave for Rocky Mountains, 385-386; return to, to face trial, 387ff; see Carthage Jail
Carthage Greys, 393, 395ff, 408ff
Carthage Jail, 10; Hyrum and Joseph committed to, 402ff
Cass, Lewis, 322, 331
Catechisms, visions and revelation done away with, erroneously stated by, 149
Cavalry, 175
Celestial marriage—see Plural marriage
Chandler, Michael, Egyptian mummies brought to Joseph Smith by, 150
Charity, cast over men the mantle of, 350
Chastity, 273
Chest, used for gold plates and Urim and Thummim, 39, 452
China, Joseph Sr.'s transaction to sell ginseng root in, 7
Chippewa Indians, 341
Cholera, in Zion's Camp, 135, 136, 137; crown of glory promised to those who died of, 143
Christian persecutions, ix
Church of Jesus Christ of Latter-day Saints, The, organized, xiv, 61ff, 344; revolutionary doctrines of, 64; like one established by Jesus Christ, 65; a missionary, 65; doctrines of, were satisfying to investigators, 101; put to test by persecution, 118; Satan's fight against, 118; Lord said his church in the last day would be called, 172-173; growth of, 247ff; members of, uphold the law of the land, 264; God is author of, 292; president of, 310; rededication of purpose increased strength of, 344; established by revelation, 384; in Carthage Jail, 404
City council of Nauvoo, 249ff
Civil law, six persons needed to initiate religious organization, demanded by, 61
Clark, General John B., 178, 184, 194, 219
Clark, Joshua R., 304
Clay County Jail, description of, 200
Clay, Henry, 322, 331, 341
Clayton, William, 293ff; letter to Carthage about bail for Joseph, 410
Clergymen, Smith family doomed to hell by, 27
Coffee, 275
Cole, Squire, 55, 58
Collection plates, absence of, in LDS Church, 65
Colonial period, vii
Columbus, vii
Commerce, Illinois, 221; Saints purchased land at, 223; malaria epidemic at, 225-226; changing of name to Nauvoo, 232

Comstock, Captain Nehemiah, 185
Conference, first of church held, 65; the last great, 346ff; Hyrum's sermon at, 348ff
Congress, 229, 271, 321ff, 343, 358
Conspiracy, among brethren, 342ff, 353ff
Constitution for the organization and government of the Camp, 168
Constitution of the United States, Saints were American citizens under the, and deserved protection, 127-128, 181, 268, 322ff, 375ff, 381; Joseph said the, was written for love of God and good will to man, 218; leaders of church vowed to support, 250, 296, 347, 352
Contention, revival confusion caused, 19
Continental Army, 4
Conversion, of Samuel Smith, 47; John P. Greene, 66; Heber C. Kimball, 107
Converts, 64, 100; diversified philosophies of, 151; in Ohio, 85ff; in Missouri, 87ff, 168ff; in Illinois, 225ff
Coolbirth, Agnes, wife of Don Carlos Smith, 254
Cooper, Lovisa, 88
Cooper's trade, Hyrum and Joseph learned, 14
Copley, Leman, 87
Cornerstone, Kirtland Temple, 113; see Nauvoo Temple
Corrill, John, 88ff, 114, 127, 212
Court proceedings, false against Hyrum Smith and other Mormons, 188ff; against Hyrum and Joseph at Carthage, 399-401
Courtmartial, of Major-General Wilson and Colonel R. D. Foster, 356
Covey, William, 202
Cowdery, Lyman, 46, 50
Cowdery, Oliver, transgression, lost his place by, xivff; Joseph Smith Sr. told Joseph Smith story to, 46; served as scribe in translation, 46ff; plates at hands of Angel Moroni seen by, 52; chosen as witness, 52; ordained elder by Joseph Smith and then ordained Joseph, 62; served as missionary, 77; called to instruct Lamanites, 76, 91; Patriarchal blessings given by, 119 footnote, held keys of priesthood, 119; Kirtland Temple appearance of the Lord, Moses, Elias, Elijah to, 156; cited before high council, 173
Creation, man is God's greatest, 63
Creator, purpose of, in America being hidden for centuries, vii; Smith family believed in an all-wise, 18; Nauvoo believed planned for by, 237

Jews, a call to preach among gentiles and, 144; dedication of Palestine for return of, 232, 234, 253

John, 48

John the Baptist, keys of Aaronic Priesthood conferred by, 47, 48

Johnson, Joel Hills, 236

Johnson, Lyman E., 158, 163

Johnson, Richard M., 322

Johnson, Seth, Justice of the peace married Lucy Mack and Joseph Smith, Sr., 4

Jones, Dan, 403ff

Journal, of Hyrum Smith, 95ff, 103ff, 110ff

Judas, in General Smith's cabinet, 328

Judgment, eternal, Hyrum Smith address on, 236

Judicial authorities, intimidation of, 209

Justice, machinery of, broken down, 209, 377, 403; for Mormons, appeal merited, 227ff, 285ff, 288-289, 321ff; Nauvoo Legion to enforce, 323ff; lack of, toward Saints, 325; tyranny versus, 330

— K —

Kaw Township, Missouri, 87

Kentucky, Ohio, 38

Keokuk, Indian chief, visits Nauvoo, 255

Keys, of authority and presidency, xivff, 64; counselors to prophet to share and hold equally the, 115; of priesthood restored, 156, 272, 292

Killien, Captain John, 386

Kimball, Heber C., conversion of, 107; Hyrum, while in Liberty Jail, trusted in, to aid Saints, 193, 198; letter to, from Joseph that he would help manage affairs of Church while Joseph and others imprisoned, 200; visited Joseph and Hyrum in jail, 202; arrived in Nauvoo, 253-254, 270, 292; 321, 347, 387; Mary Fielding Smith died in home of, 444

Kimball, Hiram, 275

Kingdom of God, except a man be born of water and Spirit, he cannot enter, 48; Joseph Smith asked brethren to accept him and Oliver Cowdery as teachers in the, 62; establishment of, 230-231, 247, 273, 346; Joseph testified of establishment of, to guards in Carthage Jail, 411

Kirtland Safety Society, 159, 161

Kirtland Temple, x; Joseph Smith revelation to build, 111ff; rebuke from the Lord concerning, 112; site of, 112; architectural plans of, 112; laying foundation of, 116; citizens resent work on, and threaten, 119ff; building of intensified, 121, 138, 146; tangible evidence of loyalty of Saints, 149; final inspection of, 153; dedication of, 155ff; spiritual manifestations in, 155; used for school, 160-161; bidding farewell to, 169; defiled, 261

Kiskukosh, Indian chief visits in Nauvoo, 255

Knight, Joseph, 34, 51, 67

Knight, Newel, 76; Satan cast out by a healing of, 76; called as missionary, 77; migration to Missouri led by, 87ff; marriage of, 147-148; in Commerce, 225

— L —

Lamanites, Oliver Cowdery instructed through revelation to go on mission to, 76, 91; a remnant of the House of Israel, 76; Parley P. Pratt's failure in taking gospel to, 85; part of God's chosen people, 218, 299; see Indians

Lambs, Hyrum possesses mildness of, x; Joseph and Hyrum taken as, to the slaughter, 385, 388, 392, 394

Land speculation, 159

Law of primogeniture, 439

Law, William, appointed counselor, 248-249; to sell stock for Nauvoo House, 251; dissatisfaction of, 270; met with Prophet, 280, 292; administered to Prophet Joseph Smith, 305; name deleted from official letters, 310; case of, 328ff, 330; conspiracy of, 342, 353ff, 378

Law, Wilson, general, 282, 285, 295, 325; conspiracy of, 342, 353ff, 378, 389

Laws of the kingdom, 80

Laws of the land, Saints uphold, 264, 267-269

Leadership, success of new Church depended on, 64

Lebanon, New Hampshire, 9, 11

Legislature, Missouri, passed resolution to investigate Mormon War, 196

Liberty Jail, x; Hyrum and Joseph confined at, for six months, 190ff; escape from, 208ff, 247

Light, Joseph Smith surrounded by, 23, 28ff

Liquor, 275

Little Blue River, 91

Little Fishing River, 131

Lord of hosts, 244

Lot, 323

Love, Smith family had for each other, 31

Lucas, General, 185, 194, 195; as Governor received letter concerning Saints settling in Nauvoo, 222

Luther, Martin, 317

Lyman, Amasa, 309

— M —

Mack, Alvira, 88
Mack, Daniel, 12
Mack, Lydia Gates, mother of Lucy, 5, 12-13
Mack, Solomon, 8; Revolutionary War soldier, 8; family of, see footnote, 8
Mack, Stephen, General, brother of Lucy, 1, 88
Maid of Iowa, 298, 382
Major's store, Joseph, Sr. met Lucy Mack at, 4
Malachi, 29, 272
Malarial fever, at Commerce, 225ff
Manchester Township, Ontario County, 15
Mansion House, The, 263; party at, 310ff; Christmas holiday festivities at, 326, 329; meeting on crisis, at, 362, 376ff; Joseph Smith's last speech at, 391; viewing of martyrs at, 428
Manuscript, 116 pages of translated, lost by Martin Harris, 42ff; Book of Mormon, taken to printer, 53ff
Markham, Stephen, 293, 302, 375, 382, 403ff
Marks, William, 346, 359
Marriage, patriarchal, 273
Marsh, Thomas B., 162; named to assist in heading the Church, 173; apostate, 184, 191
Martial law, 373ff, 383
Martyrdom, xv; Joseph Smith prophesied many would suffer, for the sake of religion of Jesus Christ, 86; of Joseph and Hyrum, 404ff; see Smith, Joseph Jr., and Smith, Hyrum
Masonic dagger, 453
Masonic fraternity, 269, 294, 344
Masonic Grandmaster Jonas, visit to Nauvoo, 267; article of, 267-269
Masonic Hall, 371ff, 393-394
Masonic Order, 436
Masonic Temple, 343-344
Mason, unit of Ancient York, 278ff, 294
Massacre, see Haun's Mill
McDonough Troops, 412, 413
McLellin, William, 163, 173; excommunicated, 173
Medes, 311
Melancthon, 317
Melchizedek, Priesthood, xv; elders ordained to, 87, 171, 274, 305
Memorial, city of Nauvoo drew up a lengthy, to Congress, 325ff, 358
Menomanee Indians, 340
Mercy, Joseph Smith sought, for loss of 116 pages of manuscript, 44
Meridian of Time, ministry during, 142

Messiah, see Jesus Christ
Methodists, 5, 13, 18, 20; minister of, turned against Joseph, 25; opposed Book of Mormon, 56; minister of, challenged principle of baptism by immersion, 89; former ministers of, 102; a minister of, member of mobocrats, 181
Mexico, annexing of, 332, 339
Michael, the Prince, Adam was, 180
Migration, westward, 335ff; people prepared for, 85; to Ohio, 85ff; to Missouri, 87ff, 168ff; to Nauvoo, 213ff, 266ff
Militia men, 122; see Volunteers
Mill Creek, Mary Fielding Smith settled at, 444
Millennial Star, 329
Ministering spirits, 257
Missionaries, bring restored gospel to world, xvii; called for foreign missions, 224; called to Palestine, 232, 234; called to Nauvoo for anointings, etc., 270; more called from Nauvoo, 282; plan to recall to defend Nauvoo, 371ff
Missionary, Samuel Smith was church's first, 66
Missionary church, LDS is a, 65
Missionary work, spirit of, 66; names of those first called to, 77-78; intensification of the, 100
Mississippi River, x; see Nauvoo
Missouri, a land consecrated to remnants of Jacob, 87; revelation to preach gospel in, 87; migration to, 87ff; editors of, did not tell truth of Mormon War, 197; driving of defenseless people from, 177ff, 198; pressure of the enemy from, 283ff; honorable men desired to wipe out stain that rested on, 321ff, 333
Missouri Argus, 212
Missouri Republican, 197, 212
Missouri River, 179
Mob Militia, 371ff, 392ff, 396ff
Mobocracy, broke out in Missouri, 116; in Illinois, 355ff, 370ff, 405; see Mobs, Mob Militia
Mobs, plan of, for destruction of church in Jackson County, 116ff; Prophet Joseph and Lyman Wight brought to court on false accusations of, 325ff, 370ff, 384ff, 390, 392; hovered about Carthage Jail, 404ff; attack of, at Carthage Jail, 418ff; plan of, to annihilate Nauvoo, 442
Mock funeral, for Joseph and Hyrum, 429
Molestation, constant, to secure gold plates, 41; of mobs to rid country of Saints, 181
Monmouth, trial at, 253
Moredock, Esquire, 11